BARRON'S

D0471675

Strategies and Practice

for the HSPT®

Sandra Smith Martin, M.B.A., M.S.Ed.

BARRON'S

Dedication

This work is dedicated to my three children, Charles, Elizabeth, and Kaylee, and to my mother Kathleen. It is their love and belief in me that helps me to realize my potential in all that I do. I am forever blessed and grateful.

Acknowledgments

Thank you to the hundreds of students who I have worked with over the years. I'm humbled to be able to help you reach your goals. I'd like to offer a special thank you to Annie Bernberg at Barron's for her expert advice, support, and guidance throughout the process of writing this book.

About the Author

Sandra Smith Martin is a mathematics teacher and director of the Test Prep Center at St. John's Preparatory School in Danvers, MA. For fifteen years, she has developed curriculum for faculty and has worked with students to raise test scores and gain admission to high schools and colleges. Sandra has a B.A. from Regis College, an M.B.A. from Salem State University, and an M.S.Ed. in Mathematics from Kaplan University. You can connect with Sandra at *www.testsmart.org*.

Published by Kaplan, Inc., d/b/a Barron's Educational Series
750 Third Avenue
New York, NY 10017
www.barronseduc.com

ISBN: 978-1-4380-1094-6
Library of Congress Control Number: 2017957371

9 8 7 6 5 4

Kaplan, Inc., d/b/a Barron's Educational Series print books are available at special quantity discounts to use for sales promotions, employee premiums, or educational purposes. For more information or to purchase books, please call the Simon & Schuster special sales department at 866-506-1949.

Contents

APPENDICES

PRACTICE TESTS

Introduction

C ongratulations on purchasing the best book on the shelves today for HSPT preparation. Whether you are browsing in the bookstore or have just purchased this book and want to learn more about it, read below to see what distinguishes this book from the other choices you have.

HSPT Only

This book, unlike others currently on the market, is dedicated solely to the HSPT. This is the most comprehensive HSPT book available today. Each chapter includes test-specific content, practice questions, and detailed explanations to help you prepare specifically for the HSPT. If there is a concept or topic that is not in this book, it is not on the HSPT. Likewise, if it is on the HSPT, it is in this book. Other books attempt to teach all middle school concepts for both verbal and non-verbal topics, but this is not middle school. You just want to increase your score on the HSPT, so this is the book to help you do that.

Detailed Explanations

After each practice set of questions, subtest, or full-length practice test, you will find not only the answers but detailed explanations for each. You should take the time to read the explanations for any questions that you answered incorrectly as well as for those that may have taken you too long. You will find time-saving tips in the explanations as well as detailed step-by-step descriptions for math questions.

Vocabulary

Chapter 3 is dedicated to vocabulary. While there is not a subtest on the HSPT specifically for vocabulary, it remains one of the most important means of improving your score on the verbal sections of this test. You will learn ways to improve your overall vocabulary here with specific strategies, including a set of practice questions for each technique. You will also find a comprehensive list that includes grade appropriate words that you are likely to see on your HSPT.

Full-Length Tests and Additional Subtests in Each Chapter

This book includes two full-length practice tests that will allow students to become familiar with the test format, content, and timing. Each test is formatted to match the current HSPT in both content and appearance.

Scoring Rubrics

After each practice subtest and HSPT test, there is a scoring rubric that will help you identify areas of strength and areas that need improvement. This will give you direction of where to focus your efforts. This will also help you track your overall progress.

Wrap It Up with Practice

At the end of each chapter, you will find a summary of important test-taking tips specific to the subtest. You will also find a full-length practice subtest at the end of the five subtest-specific chapters. This is your chance to immediately practice the content and strategies that you have learned in those chapters. Each subtest is representative of the most current HSPT.

Additional Resources

Although this book covers everything you need to know for the HSPT, there are many other places where you can find additional practice and review. Throughout this book, you will find suggested activities, like keeping a vocabulary journal and math notebook, as well as helpful online resources and apps for extra review. These additional resources will help with reading comprehension, vocabulary, and math facts. You can also visit the STS website for the most up-to-date information about the HSPT.

Scholastic Testing Service Inc.
480 Meyer Road
Bensenville, IL 60106
800-642-6787
sts@ststesting.com

In addition, make sure to visit the author's website for PowerPoint presentations and even more practice materials for the HSPT:

www.testsmart.org

About the HSPT

1

The HSPT, High School Placement Test, is a standardized test generated by the Scholastic Testing Service Inc., and administered by high schools across the country. Over 100,000 students take this exam each year as part of their application and admission process for private and independent high schools. High schools use the results of the exam to help make decisions regarding admission, merit scholarships, and placement for 9th grade math and English classes.

The HSPT is designed to measure basic and cognitive skills using five subtests: Verbal Skills, Quantitative Skills, Reading, Mathematics, and Language. It is strictly a multiple choice test with no essay component and no open-response questions. Students must answer 298 questions in approximately two and a half hours.

TEST INFORMATION FOR STUDENTS

You have taken a big step towards your success by reading this book. Many students do not prepare for the HSPT, so you are already ahead of the game and on the road to achieving a high score. The HSPT test is scored as a percentile, which means that your score is compared to the scores of other students. Students taking the HSPT have most likely learned similar material in their middle school classes, so in that regard you are all in the same boat. However, knowing the material is not the only component to scoring well. You must also be familiar with the test format and learn strategies to help you finish the test in the time allowed. You will learn about each of these as you read this book. For now, here is a list of questions that are frequently asked by students.

Where can I take the HSPT?

HSPT testing dates are determined by individual schools but are typically offered in the fall. The HSPT is often administered by the high school where you are applying. If it is not offered there, you should check with the admissions office to determine the nearest location. You will have to register at the place where the test is being administered and not with the Scholastic Testing Service. There is a fee for taking the test, which is set by the school where the test is administered.

When should I take it, and can I take the HSPT more than once?

Typically, students take the HSPT in the fall of 8th grade. The test is usually offered for two or three different dates. Most students take the HSPT the first time it is offered; however, it is in your best interest to take the test on the later date if given the choice. You will have an additional month or more to study as well as additional classroom time at your middle school. The material that you are learning in school is most likely similar to the content of the HSPT, so the more you learn, the better prepared you will be for the test. Most high schools allow you to take the HSPT only once.

I have an education plan that allows me to have extra time in school on tests. Will I also have extra time on the HSPT?

You must contact the high school where you will be taking the HSPT and ask what you must submit to qualify for additional time. Most schools will ask that you provide your education plan well in advance of the test day. They will inform you if you qualify for additional time. Some students, depending on their individual education plan, may receive up to 50 percent additional time on each subtest. If you do qualify for additional time, it is important that on test day your proctor is aware of this. You don't want to end up in the wrong room and possibly miss out on your added time. You should be in a room with other students who receive additional time.

What if I need special accommodations?

In advance of the test day, make sure that your parents notify the school about your needs. The school will likely have the accommodations you require, but to be certain, call in advance. They will want to assist you in any way, but they can only do so if aware of your needs. The HSPT is available in large print for students with impaired vision and is also available electronically for students who cannot write. If you have an injury or a special need, then you should contact the school well in advance of your HSPT test date.

How soon after the test will I get my results?

This is up to the school where you take the HSPT. Some schools send the results about a month after the test day, while others send the scores once the admission decision letters are sent. You'll have to check with the school where you will be taking the HSPT.

How should I prepare for the HSPT?

This is a big question and needs its own chapter. For information about how to use this book and how to prepare, as well as a timeline to follow, please read Chapter 2 "Preparing for the HSPT."

For an up-to-date list of FAQ's, feel free to visit the author's website:

www.testsmart.org

IMPORTANT INFORMATION FOR PARENTS

Navigating the high school admissions process can be a daunting task. Most private and independent high schools have a very clear application process described on their school website and in their printed materials distributed at open houses. This is the best way to get started. By now you may have had a chance to attend some open houses with your child and have narrowed your choices to a couple of schools. The next step is to contact the school, or schools, to learn about their admissions process.

Applications are somewhat different from school to school but share some key components. Each school will require transcripts, letters of recommendation, and results from a standardized test. Here is where schools can differ widely; most independent schools accept scores from either the SSAT (Secondary School Admission Test) or the ISEE (Independent School Entrance Exam). Catholic schools that utilize the HSPT often accept scores from the SSAT or ISEE as well.

My child is applying to both Catholic and Independent schools. She has a choice of different exams at each school. Will she have to take two different tests?

Very often the situation will be that the independent school will accept the SSAT or the ISEE but NOT the HSPT. The Catholic school is likely to accept scores from the HSPT or the SSAT. Because the HSPT and the SSAT are very different exams, your child should take both exams as they may score higher on one than the other. If applying to both Catholic and independent schools, your child will likely have to take the ISEE or the SSAT for the independent school and then have the option of sending those scores to the Catholic school. You *may* choose to have your child take the HSPT for the Catholic school. The HSPT test is much less expensive than other tests, so if this is a format that works better for your child, then it's recommended that he or she take it in addition to the independent high school test.

If my child is applying to Catholic schools only, but has the option of taking the SSAT or the HSPT, which one should she take?

This is an easy one—the HSPT. It's not that the HSPT is an easier test, but it is more predictable, which makes the preparation easier. More students nationwide take the SSAT and the SSAT board is constantly making changes and updates to the test. Just a few years ago, the SSAT underwent major changes in content, making the test more difficult. This should not affect the percentile scores, but it does make for a more challenging preparation. The HSPT, however, has remained stable in format, content, and level of difficulty.

Schools look at the percentiles rather than the raw scores, and mathematically speaking, it's easier to score in the top ten percentile if you are competing with 100 students than 1,000. This is particularly important if scholarships are involved. Some schools offer academic scholarships based, in part, on results of admission test percentiles. If your child performs in the top 1% or 2%, he or she may be eligible to receive a full scholarship. Since fewer students take the HSPT and also because it is a more predictable test, it will be easier to score in the top 1% on the HSPT than on the SSAT.

How can I help prepare my child for the HSPT?

There is information for parents and students in Chapter 2 regarding HSPT preparation. The most important role you will play in this process is one of a coach, providing support and encouragement. Read Chapter 2, and then encourage your child to come up with a customized preparation plan.

For an up-to-date list of FAQs, you can visit:

www.testsmart.org

TEST FORMAT AND QUESTIONS

The HSPT is made up of five subtests as shown below. The test consists of 298 questions. Each subtest is timed separately but the questions are numbered consecutively throughout the test. In the table below you can see the individual subtests as well as the timing and number of questions for each.

Subtest	Timing	Number of Questions
Verbal Skills	18 minutes	60
Quantitative Skills	30 minutes	52
Reading	25 minutes	62
Mathematics	45 minutes	64
Language	25 minutes	60
Total	2 hours 23 minutes	298

Verbal Skills

Verbal Skills is the first of the five subtests of the HSPT. It is made up of five different question types: synonyms, antonyms, analogies, verbal classifications, and verbal logic. You can learn more about the Verbal Skills subtest in Chapter 4. This subtest attempts to measure your ability to perform reasoning tasks that involve vocabulary words. How well you do in this subtest is considered a predictor for how well you may perform in school in reading, language, and social studies. The Verbal Skills, together with Quantitative Skills, make up the Total Cognitive Skills (TCS) portion of the HSPT overall score.

Your vocabulary will be tested with a variety of **synonym** questions where you will be asked to find the word that is most similar in meaning to the word prompt.

Synonym

Inevitable most nearly means

(a) trivial.
(b) important.
(c) replace.
(d) unavoidable.

The directions for synonym questions are part of the question. *Inevitable* means to be *unavoidable*, so the correct answer is choice (d) *unavoidable*.

The Verbal Skills subtest will also assess your knowledge of vocabulary by asking you to find opposites, known as **antonyms**. These can be tricky because you must remember that you are looking for the opposite meaning, resisting the temptation to choose a word that is actually a synonym.

Antonym

Nomadic means the *opposite* of

(a) wandering.
(b) searching.
(c) idle.
(d) counting.

The word *nomadic* means to move from place to place. The word that means the opposite is answer choice (c) *idle*.

Analogies, while also testing your knowledge of vocabulary words, will assess your ability to determine relationships that exist between sets of words. In the HSPT, the analogy questions will each have the same format and will have one-word answer choices.

Analogy

Music is to ear as art is to

(a) canvas.
(b) eye.
(c) brush.
(d) sound.

STRATEGIES

You'll find more details and strategies for each of the questions in the following chapters:

4. Verbal Skills
5. Quantitative Skills
6. Reading
7. Mathematics
8. Language

Music is appreciated by the ear in the same way that art is appreciated with the eye. The correct answer is choice (b) *eye*.

Verbal classification questions assess your vocabulary as well as your ability to see relationships that exist among three of the four answer choices. Verbal classification questions will provide you with four answer choices, three of which will have something in common. Either three words are similar and the fourth is unrelated, or three words will be components of the fourth word.

Verbal Classification

Which word does *not* belong with the others?

(a) sing
(b) dance
(c) talk
(d) laugh

Sing, talk, and laugh are all things that a person does with their mouth or their voice. Dance is the only action that does not require the mouth, so the correct answer is choice (b) *dance*.

The last type of question in the Verbal Skills subtest is the **verbal logic** question. Here you will be given three sentences followed by a set of instructions. The first two sentences will be true. You will be asked to determine if the third sentence is true, false, or uncertain.

Verbal Logic

Chapter 1 has more words than Chapter 2. Chapter 3 has more words than Chapter 1. Chapter 2 has more words than Chapter 3. If the first two statements are true, the third is

(a) true.
(b) false.
(c) uncertain.

Because Chapter 3 has the most words (more than Chapter 1, which has more words than Chapter 2) the third sentence must be (b) *false*.

Quantitative Skills

The Quantitative Skills subtest is one of the two non-verbal subtests. This subtest is made up of three specific types of questions: sequences, comparisons, and computations. In Chapter 5, you will learn about each of these questions in detail, as well as the strategies to help you solve them. The Quantitative Skills subtest will assess your ability to perform reasoning problems that involve numbers rather than words. Your ability to do well in this skill area is considered to be a predictor of your academic performance in mathematics and science. The Quantitative Skills, together with Verbal Skills, make up the Total Cognitive Skills (TCS) portion of the HSPT overall score.

In **sequence** questions you will be given a list of numbers or letters and asked to determine what the next number or letter should be.

Sequence

In the sequence: 61, 68, 75, 82, . . . , what number should come next?

(a) 85   (b) 92   (c) 89   (d) 95

You must first figure out the pattern used to generate the sequence. In this case, each number is 7 more than the number before it. Therefore, the next number will be $82 + 7 = 89$ for a correct answer choice of (c) 89.

The **comparison** questions, like the sequence questions, are in two parts. You must first simplify the three expressions given, (A), (B), and (C), then read each of the answer choices to determine which is the correct comparison of the expressions. In some cases, you will compare pictures or graphs rather than mathematical expressions.

Comparison

Examine (A), (B), and (C) and find the *best* answer.

(A) $(2 \times 6) \div 3$
(B) $(2 \times 3) \div 6$
(C) $2 \times (6 \div 3)$

(a) (A) is equal to (C).
(b) (C) is greater than (A).
(c) (B) is greater than (A).
(d) (C) is equal to (B).

The three expressions can be simplified. (A) $(2 \times 6) \div 3 = 4$, (B) $(2 \times 3) \div 6 = 1$, and (C) $2 \times (6 \div 3) = 4$. The correct answer is choice (a).

The last type of question in the Quantitative Skills subtest is the **computation** question. In this question, you will be asked to perform calculations involving addition, subtraction, multiplication, and division in a multistep question.

Computation

What number subtracted from 97 leaves 3 less than $\frac{1}{4}$ of 80?

(a) 7   (b) 84   (c) 80   (d) 23

This is represented by the equation $97 - x = \left(\frac{1}{4} \times 80\right) - 3$. The correct answer is choice (c) 80.

Reading

The Reading subtest is made up of two parts; the first is reading comprehension and the second vocabulary. The Reading subtest will measure your ability to understand and remember important information, main ideas, and vocabulary in the context of a reading passage. How well you do on this subtest is thought to be an indicator of your overall success in school. The Reading, Mathematics, and Language subtests of the HSPT together make up your Total Basic Skills (TBS) score of the HSPT.

In the reading comprehension part of this subtest, students will be presented with four reading passages, each followed by ten questions. The questions will be either specific or general in nature. The specific questions will assess your ability to recall details, determine cause and effect, understand vocabulary in context, compare and contrast information, and recognize fact from fiction. The general questions will assess your ability to grasp the main idea, determine appropriate titles, and make predictions. Following the four reading passages and accompanying questions, there will be 22 vocabulary questions, where students are asked to identify one-word definitions. Here are some examples of the format for questions in the reading subtest.

Passage

Verbal Skills is the first of the five subtests of the HSPT. It is made up of 5 different questions types: synonyms, antonyms, analogies, verbal classifications, and verbal logic. You can learn more about the Verbal Skills subtest in Chapter 4. The Verbal Skills subtest attempts to measure your ability to perform reasoning tasks that <u>involve</u> vocabulary words. How well you do in this subtest is thought to be a predictor for how well you may perform in areas of reading, language, and social studies.

Words in Context

The word <u>involve</u>, as underlined and used in the passage, most nearly means

(a) interesting.
(b) include.
(c) shorten.
(d) rotate.

The correct answer is choice (b) *include.*

General

The best title for this passage would be

(a) "Everything You Need to Know about the HSPT."
(b) "Differences between Verbal Skills and Reading."
(c) "About the Verbal Skills Subtest."
(d) "What is the HSPT?"

The correct answer is choice (c) "About the Verbal Skills Subtest."

Specific

Which question type is not in the Verbal Skills subtest?

(a) synonyms
(b) antonyms
(c) analogies
(d) sequences

The correct answer choice is choice (d) sequences.

At the end of the Reading subtest there are 22 **vocabulary** questions. Unlike the synonyms in the Verbal Skills subtest, these will have some context.

Vocabulary

An elite pilot

(a) novice
(b) the best
(c) old
(d) large

The correct answer is choice (b) the best. You can see there is little context given, at most a word or two, but the context provides helpful clues for vocabulary words that may be unfamiliar to you.

Mathematics

Mathematics is the fourth and longest subtest of the HSPT. This subtest will assess your ability to perform mathematical operations and to apply mathematical skills to reasoning and problem-solving. The Mathematics score is part of the Total Basic Skills score (TBS) for the HSPT.

NOTE

The Mathematics subtest has a mix of various mathematical concepts and question formats. For a complete list, refer to Chapter 7.

Percent

In Kansas City, sales tax is 6% of the purchase. If Kelan buys a toy for $30.00 how much will he pay in sales tax?

(a) $1.80   (b) $0.44   (c) $18.00   (d) $1.44

The correct answer is (a) $1.80 because $0.06 \times \$30.00 = \$1.80$.

Probability

A jar holds 30 green marbles, 30 yellow marbles, and 10 blue marbles. If you choose a marble at random, what is the probability of choosing a green marble?

(a) $\frac{1}{7}$ (b) $\frac{3}{4}$ (c) $\frac{3}{10}$ (d) $\frac{3}{7}$

The correct answer is choice (d) $\frac{3}{7}$.

$$\begin{array}{r} 30 \\ +30 \\ \hline 60 \\ +10 \\ \hline 70 \end{array} \qquad 30/70 = 3/7$$

Language

The last subtest of the HSPT is the Language subtest. This is comprised of three different parts, each with its own set of directions. This subtest will measure your knowledge of punctuation, usage, capitalization, spelling, and composition. The Language subtest is part of your Total Basic Skills (TBS) score of the HSPT.

The directions for the Language subtest will be printed at the beginning of each section. They will be slightly different for each but will generally ask you to find errors in one of the answer choices. If you find a mistake, select the letter in front of that sentence as your answer. Some questions will give you the option of choosing *No mistakes*.

Capitalization, Usage, and Punctuation

Look for errors in capitalization, usage, or punctuation only.

(a) My aunt's business are very successful.
(b) The principal is well liked.
(c) Charles, please feed the dogs.
(d) Kaylee is the very best tennis player.

The correct answer is choice (a). Because *business* is singular, the verb should be *is* and not *are*.

Spelling

Look for errors in spelling only.

(a) His neice is Alice.
(b) The comment is not relevant.
(c) The occurrence of the flu is on the rise.
(d) No mistakes.

The correct answer is choice (a). *Neice* should spelled *niece*.

Composition

Choose the correct word or words to join the thoughts together.

I studied very long for my test, _____, I didn't pass it.

(a) however
(b) consequently
(c) so
(d) because

The correct answer is choice (a) *however*.

This was just a glimpse of the various questions that you will see on the HSPT. Read each chapter to learn more about the content that will be tested in each type of question and to learn valuable strategies to help you complete each subtest accurately and efficiently.

TEST SCORING AND REPORTS

The HSPT score report will be sent to you by the school that administered the test. The report will have more information than you may want, but there will be two scores that both you and your school will be most interested in. The first is your overall percentile score, and the second is the specific category percentiles. You may choose to read this section after you receive your scores. The following information will help you better understand the information that will be provided in your report.

There is no pass or fail grade for the HSPT. High schools are usually interested in the local or national percentile scores. Percentile scores allow the high school to compare your scores to those of other students who took the HSPT during that year. Schools may have a minimum acceptance, but this is usually not information the admissions office is willing to share. You can contact the schools to which you are applying to inquire about the average HSPT scores for accepted students.

Paper or Electronic Scoring

The HSPT can be taken in one of two ways. With the more conventional method, students use a test booklet and fill out answers on a bubble sheet. The bubble sheet is then collected and scanned by a computer. Some high schools administer the test using an e-scoring method. In this case, students receive a test booklet but submit all answers directly to the Scholastic Testing Service using a computer or tablet. The test is then scored immediately. Schools may use the e-scoring method with all students or on an individual basis. You can check with the school where you will be taking the test to see which method they use. The majority of high schools use the former and more traditional method.

Not All Standardized Tests Are Scored the Same

College entrance exams, such as the SAT, are all scored identically. If you take the SAT at a high school in California and apply to a local college there or take the SAT in South Dakota and apply to Harvard, your exams are graded the same way. Your scores are compared to all of the students nationwide who took the exam. The HSPT is quite different. High schools can test students independently or collectively. In either case, it is the high school and not the Scholastic Testing Service that determines the score distribution system. Scores may be compared to students in one school only, to a collection of schools, or nationwide as determined by the high school. It is also the high school's responsibility to distribute scores to families of students taking the exam at their school.

What if you are applying to more than one high school?

If you are testing at a school that is part of a collective, then you may decide to have your scores sent to other schools that are part of that collective. You can check with the high school where you are applying for more information about scoring and the timing of receiving your score report. If you decide after you have taken the test that you would like to have your scores sent to an additional school, you should contact the school where you took the exam to make the request and not the Scholastic Testing Service.

What if you don't receive your score?

If you do not receive your scores when you expected them, then you should contact the high school where the HSPT was administered. Because the school determines the score distribution system, the Scholastic Testing Service cannot send the scores directly to you.

What kind of information will be in the score report?

When you receive your HSPT score report, you will see many different numbers that in some way are used to compare you to the other students in your grade who also took the test, either at your school or as part of a collective of schools. Your report will contain your Raw Score, Grade Equivalence Scores (GE), National Percentile (NCTL), Cognitive Skills Quotient (CSQ), and other specific test results.

> ### KEEP SOME PERSPECTIVE
> The list of what this test is trying to measure is exhausting, and it is being done in just 298 questions. Of course, this is just a small snapshot of your academic potential, so take it for what it is, just one piece of the overall picture that is you. The schools that you are applying to know this as well.

Raw Scores

The raw score is the easiest score to understand. It is simply the number of questions that you answer correctly divided by the total of 298 questions. The Raw Score is then converted into a Standard Score. If you also took an Optional Test for the HSPT, you will receive a Raw Score for that test, separate from the traditional HSPT score report.

Grade Equivalent, GE

You will receive a GE for each of the basic skills: Reading, Mathematics, and Language. Each subtest, as well as the overall HSPT, will have a Grade Equivalent score. This is perhaps the most widely misunderstood grade in a score report. This score compares your performance to that predicted of students in other grades. Your score represents a grade level. A score of 10.6 does not mean 10 and 6 tenths of a grade. It is not a decimal but rather a notation meaning 10th grade and 6 months. A score of 6.3 represents three months into 6th grade. Of course you want this, and all of your scores, to be high, but just what does it mean? If you score an 11 does that mean that the high school that accepts you should send you straight to 11th grade? Of course not; you were never tested on 11th grade material. A score of 11.0 simply means that your score was very high, in fact, so high that if an 11th grader took the same HSPT, it is predicted they would score about the same as you.

The National Percentile, NCTL Percentile

A percentile is a score that lets you know the percent of students in the sample that you outperformed. If you scored in the 50th percentile that means that half, 50 percent, of the students in the sample scored higher than you, while half of the students scored lower. The National Percentile compares your scores to other students throughout the country. If you take the HSPT at a school that tests independently, or as part of a collective of schools, you may receive a Local Percentile, where your score is compared only to other students who took the HSPT at your school or in that collective.

Cognitive Skills Quotient, CSQ

The Cognitive Skills Quotient is a measure of a student's learning potential. The CSQ is just one number representing your overall score based on the five subtests of the HSPT. The term cognitive means having to do with knowledge or functioning. The CSQ is similar to an Intelligence Quotient (IQ) test in that it is meant to be a predictive indicator of a student's academic performance. The average CSQ is 100 and scores typically range from 55 to 145. The middle 50% of students taking the HSPT typically score between 90 and 109. Scores of 110 and above represent the top 25% while scores below 90 represent the lower 25%.

WHAT ARE THE OPTIONAL HSPT TESTS?

The Scholastic Testing Service also offers optional tests for the HSPT. You should contact your high school to determine if one or more of these tests will be required. There are three available optional tests: Mechanical Aptitude, Catholic Religion, and Science. These tests are used primarily for placement purposes. For more information on the optional tests, you should contact the high school to which you are applying.

Now that you have a better understanding of just what the HSPT is and how it is used, you can get started on your preparation. The next chapter will help you to determine an appropriate plan based on the amount of time you have. You have already made a commitment to your success in the high school application process and now must focus on seeing the plan through.

Preparing for the HSPT

2

Congratulations on taking an important step in preparing for the HSPT. This book is written specifically for the HSPT. Unlike other books, this focuses on only what you need to know and nothing else. There are plenty of math and English concepts that you learn at school that you don't have to know to be successful in taking the HSPT. If you don't need to know it for the HSPT, then you won't see it in this book. Successful performance on the HSPT can be the gateway to a successful high school education. By reading this book, you are already on your way to improving your score.

HOW TO USE THIS BOOK

The way you use this book will depend on how much time you have before your HSPT test day. Ideally you will want to begin studying approximately six months prior to your test date. Most schools administer the HSPT in the fall, so you should begin your preparation in the spring of 7th grade. This will give you the opportunity to ask your teachers for help on difficult topics, while also allowing you the leisure of studying over a longer period of time. Below are some tips for you to keep in mind when preparing for the HSPT.

Pace Yourself

Don't tackle everything at once. Spread your preparation over a three- to six-month period if possible. Limit your study sessions to a maximum of two hours, unless you are taking a practice test. Consistency is the key. You will be better prepared if you practice a little every week, rather than every day for one week and then not again for three weeks.

Know It? Skip It

If there is a section in the book that is very easy for you, don't waste your time reading it in detail. However, do not skip the sets of practice questions. It may be that you don't know the material as well as you thought. If you do very well on the practice questions, then you will have a nice confidence boost.

Make a Study Plan

Continue reading this chapter to learn how to put together a study plan that will work for you. Use the table on page 24 to track your practice results. Once you make a plan, have a parent or teacher look it over to make sure you have set realistic goals. The study plan should be something that boosts your confidence over time. Setting unrealistic goals will only make you feel discouraged with your results.

Gauge Your Progress

Because the HSPT is graded using percentiles, it is impossible for you to calculate your results. All you will be able to do is determine your raw score, the percent of questions you answered correctly. You should see this score increase with each additional practice.

Full-length Practice Tests

The first thing you should do is take HSPT Practice Test 1. This will give you an initial idea as to the format and content of the test. By doing this, you will be able to see improvements as you progress through reading this book. Always time your practice subtests and practice tests, so you will know how you are doing on timing as well as content. Use the grading rubric to see how well you do on individual question types. Do not discard your test when you are done. As you read each chapter on the individual subtests, refer back to your HSPT Practice Test 1 to see if you now understand the questions that you answered incorrectly. After you have completed reading the material in the book, take the HSPT Practice Test 2 and measure your improvement.

GETTING TO KNOW YOURSELF

No one is ever going to know you better than you know yourself. Your parents may help you prepare for the HSPT or perhaps you will take an HSPT class and an instructor will guide you. But only you will know what type of problem you excel at answering, what type of questions scare you, and what strategies work best for you. Others can certainly teach you both content and strategies, but it is up to you to learn and to apply what you have been taught.

Make Mistakes Now

Now is the time to make mistakes, and more importantly, the time to learn from those mistakes. For each question that you get wrong, you must analyze the reason. Was it a careless mistake? If so, is it one you have made before? What can you do to avoid making that mistake again? You have to get to know yourself and understand the mistakes that you are prone to make. Once you've identified this, you can ask your teacher for help in avoiding common mistakes. The more mistakes you make now (and fix now), the fewer you will make on test day.

Review

When you complete a set of practice questions, a subtest, or a complete practice test, it is critical that you go back and review your results. Only in doing this will you get to know yourself. If you don't review what you have done, you are unlikely to truly learn from it. If you finish your practice with 80 percent correct instead of the 60 percent that you scored correctly on the first set, celebrate, but then go back and review the other 20 percent you answered incorrectly and review the questions you got right but found to be difficult or time consuming.

Do What Works for You

If you learn a strategy you're not sure is helpful to you, try it before deciding not to use it. For example, you may find that labeling paragraphs in the reading subtest just wastes time for you; for this reason, try a strategy before you decide whether to use it.

Make a Schedule

You know yourself, so don't make a schedule that you won't keep. Come up with a plan that you think you can do and then ask a parent, sibling, or friend to help you to stay on track.

TOP TIPS TO RAISE YOUR SCORE

Throughout this book, you will learn many strategies specific to the question types you will be answering. Below is a list of things you should be doing throughout your preparation and on test day to boost your score.

1. Know the Test

For the HSPT you should become familiar with the format and question types prior to test day. This will reduce the time it takes you to finish each subtest and greatly improve your confidence. You don't want to be surprised on test day. The more familiar you are with your test format and content, the better prepared you will be. This translates to a higher score.

2. Don't Read the Directions

Become familiar with the directions for each subtest while you study. When you take the actual HSPT, you should already know the directions, so you can just skim over them. Each subtest begins with sample questions. These are there for students who are unfamiliar with the test. The proctor will read these aloud to you before beginning the timed part of your test. You'll know this test inside out on test day, so don't waste precious time reading sample questions.

3. Never Leave a Question Blank

Whether you answer a question incorrectly or leave it blank, you will lose one point. If you make a guess, chances are you will guess correctly one out of four times. Come up with a guessing strategy before test day. If you really are making a blind guess, don't waste precious time in figuring out which answer to choose. Decide ahead of time to always choose the same answer. Statistically speaking it won't matter, but it will save you time.

4. Expand Your Vocabulary and Read

Read Chapter 3 and learn as many of the vocabulary words as you can. The more you read, the better you will perform on the HSPT. Read as much as you can, whatever you can, between now and test day. Pick up the newspaper, read a poem or short story, peruse short articles, and get comfortable with various writing formats. This will improve both your reading speed and comprehension.

5. Eliminate Wrong Answers

Each question has only four answer choices. Even if you don't know the correct answer, try to eliminate at least one of the choices before you guess.

TIP

The proctor is there to help, so when she asks if you have any questions, ask her to let you know when there is just one or two minutes left in the test. This will give you just enough time to answer a couple of easy questions or to fill in blank bubbles.

6. Plug in Answer Choices for the Mathematics Subtest

If the correct method to answer the question is not immediately obvious to you, check to see if plugging in each of the answer choices to the question will help you to find the correct answer. This is particularly useful when solving for variables. When plugging in answers, always choose a value that is neither the highest nor the lowest option. If your result is too high, choose a lower number, and if your result is too low, choose a higher answer choice. This will reduce your time by eliminating at least one answer if not two.

7. Easy Does It

There are plenty of easy questions on the HSPT, so don't waste time getting stuck on difficult questions and miss out on the easy questions that may follow. Each question, easy or difficult, is worth only one point. Never spend too much time on one question. Practice will help you get comfortable with the allowed time for each subtest.

8. *Touch—Touch—Bubble*

The bubble sheet is not at all forgiving when it comes to mistakes. Testing can be stressful, so if you are not careful, you may find yourself bubbling in an answer in the wrong place or maybe even answering two questions in the same bubble row. Get in the habit of always touching your pencil to the question number on your test, then the same number on the bubble sheet and then bubble in your answer. Bubble each answer as you go, and do not wait until the end of each section or page.

9. Mark the Questions

Mark questions as you go. Do *not* mark the questions that you are certain you got correct. You will not have to revisit these questions when you have extra time. *Circle* the question number for those that you could solve if you had a little extra time. Put an *X* over the question number of any questions that you simply don't understand or feel like you cannot do even if you had more time. These questions you will do last and only after you've completed the question numbers that you circled. When practicing, you should also circle question numbers where you guessed the answers. When you review your subtest, make sure to better understand these questions.

As you answer questions throughout this and all subtests, remember to circle your answer choice in your test booklet. This will take very little time and may save you valuable time if you come back to check your work. Cross out answers you know are incorrect. When you come back later to check your work, you won't waste time on answers you've already ruled out.

10. Halfway Through

About halfway through the subtest, the proctor should announce that half of the time has passed. The proctor will also let you know what question you should be on if you are working at the correct pace. When you hear this, check to see which number question you are on. If you are not halfway through don't panic, but try to pick up the pace. If you still feel like you won't finish, take a guess on the difficult questions, and do your best to answer the easy questions.

11. The Finish Line

At the bottom of each page you will see in bold the words **"Go to the next page,"** and at the end of the subtest, you will see the word **STOP** in bold capital letters. Never stop until you see the word **STOP,** even if you see blank space at the bottom of the page.

12. Wasted Time

If you finish a section early, NEVER waste this precious time doodling, daydreaming, or staring at the wall. You're working hard now to learn ways to save time and you must use that time wisely. The first thing to do with extra time is to go back and finish the question numbers that you circled along the way. If time allows, you can take another look at the question numbers that you put an X through. Maybe something will come to mind that you missed the first time. If you still have extra time, go back and check every answer. As you check your work, remember that there was a reason why you chose the answer you did, even if you guessed, so do NOT change an answer unless you know it is wrong.

TEST ANXIETY AND STRESS

Everyone feels anxious at some point, especially when preparing for a big event, such as taking a standardized test. It is completely normal but something that you must pay attention to. Read the tips below to help reduce additional stress you may have, while also learning ways to reduce anxiety before and during your test.

EXERCISE: This will reduce your overall anxiety, even if you just take a short walk each day.

SLEEP: Try to get a good sleep each night. This will give your body and mind a chance to relax, feel rested and rejuvenate. Anxiety from the day before is less likely to creep into the next day after a good rest.

TALK IT OUT: Talk to your parents when you are feeling anxious. It's important for them to know how you are feeling so they can help. They may unknowingly be contributing to your anxiety, and you are the only one who can let them know.

WRITE IT DOWN: Have a clear goal and do your best to stick to it. This will give you a feeling of accomplishment throughout your preparation, reducing anxiety.

POSITIVE THOUGHTS: Rather than telling yourself "I'm going to do lousy on this test," instead try telling yourself "I can do this—I'm working toward my goals." Our brain tends to pay more attention to negative thoughts—it's instinctive. Between now and test day, train your brain to listen to your positive thoughts instead.

KNOW THE TEST: Become familiar with each section of the test and each set of directions. On test day you won't have any surprises. If you do the practice at the end of each chapter, you will be familiar with every question type that you will see on test day.

DON'T IGNORE THE EASY STUFF: If there is material that you already know well, then skip it; however, always try the practice questions. Knowing that there are parts of the test that you already understand well will boost your confidence. It may, however, be possible that the questions are not as easy as you originally thought.

REVIEW: Take a few minutes at the start of each study session to review past material. This will help you retain the information while boosting your confidence.

On Test Day

When you feel nervous on test day, try to focus on your accomplishments. Do your best to use your powers of positive thinking. Here are some tips to help you to feel calm on test day.

ARRIVE EARLY: Get to the test location early to allow yourself time to get settled. This will also eliminate that rushed feeling.

MUSIC: On the way to your test location, play a song that will get you feeling confident and relaxed—a favorite tune that makes you feel energized.

MOVE: Never miss an opportunity to get up and move around during the breaks. Try to get a good stretch in between each subtest.

BREATHE: Two or three long deep breaths will lower your blood pressure, making you feel more calm.

THREE IN A ROW: It is a myth that you should be nervous if you have three of the same answer choices in a row. The answers are random, and you are just as likely to have correct answers (a), (b), (c), as you are (c), (c), (c). Choose the best answer and don't look for trends in your bubble sheet.

DON'T PRESSURE YOURSELF: You should try to read each question but don't convince yourself that you have to answer every question correctly to have a great score. Try to at least skim each question so you can find the easy ones. Remember to guess on any question that you cannot answer.

REWARD YOURSELF: Have a reward planned for yourself for all of your hard work. When you feel stressed during the test, think of the reward you will have in just a few hours.

PLANNING FOR TEST DAY

Let's assume that, like most high school applicants, you will be taking the HSPT in the fall of 8th grade. You most likely fall into one of three categories:

- **PROCRASTINATOR:** You have put off preparing or have made a last-minute decision to apply to a secondary school. Now you have realized that you have to take the HSPT in just two to three weeks, maybe even just one week!
- **PRODUCER:** You don't want to plan too far ahead but will produce a great effort when you are ready. You have between one and three months to prepare.
- **PLANNER:** You like to plan ahead so you don't feel rushed. You have between three and six months to prepare.

Don't worry, whichever of the three P's you are, there is a schedule to help you to prepare. Let's start first with the Procrastinators, since there's no time to waste.

PROCRASTINATORS: TEST DATE IN 1–3 WEEKS

Goals:

- Do as much practice as possible before test day.
- Read the "Wrap It Up with Practice" sections in Chapters 4–8. This will provide you with a review of important strategies.

- Read this chapter completely to learn valuable tips on preparing for and taking the HSPT.
- Review Chapter 1, "About the HSPT," to become familiar with the test format.

You already know that you will not have enough time to read this entire book before test day, and that's okay. What you must do instead is complete as much practice as possible in the time that you have. Begin by taking a practice test. You can find Practice Test 1, along with the instructions, at the back of this book. After you grade the test, you will have a better idea of which topics you must focus on. After you review the test results, fill in the dates in the planner that follows this section.

PRODUCERS: TEST DATE IN 1–3 MONTHS

Goals:

- Complete two full-length practice tests.
- Build your vocabulary between now and test day.
- Skim each chapter focusing on concepts that need improvement.
- Complete the practice subtest at the end of each chapter.
- Read this chapter completely to learn valuable tips on preparing for and taking the HSPT.

You may not have time to read this entire book but that's okay—you have plenty of time to touch on the major points in each chapter. Begin your preparation by taking a practice test. You can find Practice Test 1, along with the instructions, at the back of this book. After you grade the test, you will have a better idea of which topics you must work on the most. After you review the test results, fill in the dates in the planner that follows this section.

PLANNERS: TEST DATE IN 6 MONTHS–1 YEAR

Goals:

- Complete two full-length practice tests.
- Set vocabulary goals for each month. Start a vocabulary journal for new words.
- Read each chapter in order. Feel free to skip information that is intended for your parents or information about interpreting your final scores.
- Keep a notebook for your work in the Quantitative Skills and Mathematics sections. Write down problems from the book that you find difficult and ask your teacher for help.
- Complete the practice subtest at the end of each chapter.
- Read this chapter completely to learn valuable tips on preparing for and taking the HSPT.

Congratulations for planning far in advance. This will reduce your stress level as well as provide you with ample time to study, practice, and review. You have the luxury of reading this book in the order in which it was intended. In addition, you should still have extra time when you complete this book to go back and review any areas that continue to be difficult for you.

Begin your preparation by taking a practice test. You can find Practice Test 1, along with the instructions, at the back of this book. After you grade the test, you will have a better idea of which topics you must work on the most. After you review the test results, fill in the dates in the planner that follows this section.

Creating Your Study Plan

Now that you know your goals and have determined what must be done before test day, follow these instructions for finalizing your study plan.

1. First, identify the column that best describes you and the amount of time you have between now and your test date. There you will enter dates or time frames for completing that module. If you are in the 1–3 week column, identify which chapters you feel need the most work and do these first.

2. Next, beginning with 1, put a number next to each module indicating the order in which you wish to complete it. If you have 6 months to 1 year to study, then you should complete the modules in order, beginning with module 1, "Chapter 1: About the HSPT," and ending with module 14, "Review Chapter 2 for tips 1 week before the test."

3. In the columns to the right of the description, write a date indicating when you plan to complete that module. Some of these chapters will take longer than others. Prior to setting your goal dates, browse through each chapter to get an idea of the length.

4. Last, as you complete each module, place a check mark or a fun sticker to the right indicating that you met your goal. Remember to record your scores on the progress chart at the end of this chapter.

Module Number	Description of Work	Time Remaining Before Test Day			Complete
		1–3 weeks Procrastinator Date	1–3 months Producer Date	3–6 months Planner Date	
	Chapter 1: About the HSPT				
	Chapter 2: Preparing for the HSPT				
	Practice Test 1				
	Score and Review Practice Test 1				
	Chapter 3: Vocabulary				
	Chapter 4: Verbal Skills				
	Chapter 5: Quantitative Skills				
	Chapter 6: Reading				
	Chapter 7: Mathematics				
	Chapter 8: Language				
	Practice Test 2				
	Score and Review Practice Test 2				
	Go back to individual chapters to review				
	Review Chapter 2 for tips 1 week before the test				

HOW TO GET THE MOST OUT OF YOUR STUDY TIME

When you sit down to study, set aside an amount of time and have a goal. For example, you may work on Friday afternoon from 3:00–4:30 P.M. and begin with the goal of learning ten new vocabulary words, reading part of the Verbal Skills Chapter, and completing at least one practice set of questions.

- Before you start each session, set a *realistic* goal of what you want to accomplish in your time, so you won't be overwhelmed.
- Begin each study session with a vocabulary review.
- Don't study for more than an hour or two each time. If you study longer, it is likely that you won't retain all that you have learned.
- Frequently review the material you have already learned. This will build confidence as you progress through the material as well as help you to retain what you have learned.

> ## A NOTE ABOUT PENCILS
> Use only #2 pencils and do *not* use mechanical pencils. You want to have a dull point on your pencil to reduce the time it takes you to fill in your bubbles. After you sharpen your pencils, scribble a bit to make the tip nice and dull, saving you valuable time as you fill in the 298 bubbles.

- It's your book, so make notes in it, check off pages you have completed, and circle areas you felt were difficult.
- Ask a parent, sibling, friend, or teacher to help you with the things that you circle.
- Use a highlighter to emphasize things you found particularly helpful and review your highlighted items when you complete each chapter.
- Read the explanations, even if you answered the question correctly. You may find that there is an easier or faster way to answer a question.
- When taking timed tests or subtests, use a timer or watch to keep track of time. It is important that you know if you are working at the correct pace. After you've finished the timed practice, feel free to go back and work through difficult or unfinished questions, but only after you've timed yourself.
- Always use bubble sheets when practicing. You will be less likely to make bubbling mistakes on test day if you are comfortable with the format and technique. Feel free to make copies of the bubble sheets from HSPT Practice Test 1 starting on page 303 for extra practice.
- You cannot gauge your progress based on your actual score because the HSPT is scored as a percentile, which you cannot know until test day. You can only track the percent that you score correctly—your raw score—and then look for improvement as you become more familiar with the test format and content. Remember that even when you answer a question incorrectly you are still learning—more so when you review your mistakes.

Track Your Progress

As you progress through the book, use the chart on the following page to record your raw score for each practice section. You will find a scoring guide after each test and subtest. When you calculate your raw score, record it in the following chart. As you complete the practice questions in each chapter, your confidence will increase by seeing your improvement over time. In the column to the far right, record your highest score for each practice set of questions. You should also record your overall score for each subtest.

Track Your Progress

Subtest	HSPT Practice Test 1	Chapter Subtest	HSPT Practice Test 2	Best Score
Verbal Skill Subtest Score (Overall Score)				
Verbal Logic				
Analogy				
Verbal Classification				
Antonym				
Synonym				
Quantitative Skills Subtest Score (Overall Score)				
Sequence				
Geometric Comparison				
Non-geometric Comparison				
Computation				
Reading Subtest Score (Overall Score)				
General				
Specific				
Vocabulary				
Mathematics Subtest Score (Overall Score)				
Basics and Conversions				
Geometry, Logic, and Word Problems				
Fractions, Decimals, Percents, and Ratios				
Exponents, Radicals, and Algebra				
Statistics and Probability				
Language Subtest Score (Overall Score)				
Capitalization, Punctuation, and Usage				
Spelling				
Composition				

TEST WEEK AND TEST DAY

As your test day approaches, you should feel good about the work that you've completed. Hopefully by now you have completed all of the study material from your study plan and have taken at least one full-length practice test. This is the most important thing you can do to prepare. In taking the practice test, you became familiar with the format of the test, learned the subtest directions, discovered your strengths, and worked on content that needed improvement. You should feel good about all you have done. Use the week before test day to do the following:

- One or two weeks before test day, complete another practice HSPT and review your results.
- Spend a few minutes each day to look through your vocabulary journal to refresh your memory of the new words you learned throughout your preparation.
- Reread the "Wrap It Up with Practice" sections at the end of Chapters 4–8.
- Reread the general strategies found in this chapter.
- Review any pages in this book that you feel need additional attention.
- A day or two before the test, read the following section, "The Day Before Test Day."

> ## PACKING LIST FOR TEST DAY
>
> ☐ #2 pencils   ☐ large eraser
> ☐ water bottle   ☐ sweater
> ☐ registration card   ☐ sugary snack
> ☐ eyeglasses if needed   ☐ watch

The Day Before Test Day

- Go to bed at a reasonable hour. Keep your normal routine. If you typically go to bed at 9 P.M. don't try to fall asleep at 7 P.M. You most likely will lay awake and get anxious. Keep your normal schedule.
- Don't study the night before. Use this time to relax. Certainly, if you want to practice with some vocabulary flash cards or look over your notes this is fine, but lots of studying will only make you feel stressed.
- Stay off of all electronics at least one hour before bedtime. This will help to ensure you have a restful sleep.
- Sharpen your #2 pencils (at least 3) so you won't have to sharpen them during the test. Remember to make them a little dull after you sharpen them to help you fill the bubbles quickly. Pack a good clean eraser.
- Pack a snack or two for the breaks. It is important to keep your energy up when taking a long test. Choose a snack that has some sugar to boost your energy, such as a granola bar. Pack a water bottle in case you get thirsty during the test. You are typically allowed to have a water bottle at all times during the test.
- Pack up everything that you will need for test day and leave it where you will remember it in the morning. This should include your registration card that you received confirming your test date.
- Know how to get to your test location, so you don't have to worry about getting lost the day of the test.

Test Day

- Get up early so you will not be rushed.
- Have a good breakfast—something your parents think is good (not donuts and soda). Don't eat a lot of sugar for breakfast. Avoid pancakes, muffins, and sugary cereals. These will provide energy for only a short time, leaving you feeling tired halfway through the test. Add some protein such as eggs or yogurt. This will slow down the digestion of sugars making your energy last longer.
- Dress comfortably and bring a sweater in case your test room is cold.
- If the proctor lets you choose your desk, sit where you can see the clock in the room. Remember, timing is everything in this test. Resist the urge to sit near a friend; this will be a distraction.
- If you get nervous, take three slow deep breaths, and you'll feel better.
- NEVER waste time during the test. If you finish a section early, go back and check the difficult problems. If you've already done that, then go back and redo the easy problems too. Don't put your head down and wait until time is called. You worked too hard for this to waste time.
- Don't miss an opportunity to stretch. If you are given a break, use it. Get up, move around, get a drink, and definitely stretch.
- If you worry that you did poorly on a section, don't let that feeling affect the next session. Start fresh and confident with each subtest.
- Don't rush. This may cause you to make careless errors. Work at a consistent pace and don't spend too long on one question.
- When you finish the test, feel good about your accomplishment—you deserve it!
- Your life will NOT be ruined forever if you do not do as well as you hoped. Your family and friends will still love you, you will still go to high school, and you will still get into a great college! This is just one piece of a much bigger picture.

TIP

When stretching at each break, reach your hands as if the perfect test score would be yours if only you could touch the ceiling. When you are as tall as you can be, lean to both sides to stretch even more, then relax!

ADDITIONAL RESOURCES FOR HSPT PREPARATION

For more preparation beyond this book, you can visit the author's website:

www.testsmart.org

There you will find additional practice materials, as well as presentations for the following HSPT subject areas: Verbal Skills, Quantitative Skills, Reading, Mathematics, and Language.

Vocabulary

3

While there's not a "Vocabulary" subtest on the HSPT, you can be certain that each of the five subtests will require a wide knowledge of vocabulary words. Definitions that are specific to the Quantitative Skills and Mathematics subtests will be discussed in the respective chapters. However, because the Verbal Skills, Language, and Reading subtests all require a similar foundation of good vocabulary, this chapter is designed to provide the skills you will need to expand your overall vocabulary.

AN IMPORTANT WORD ON VOCABULARY

Vocabulary is everywhere on standardized tests and especially on the HSPT. On the HSPT, the Vocabulary section is part of the Reading subtest and consists of 22 questions. In addition to the Vocabulary section, there are at least 40 vocabulary questions in the Verbal Skills subtest and another 10 or so in the Reading Comprehension subtest. Not only will you see vocabulary in the question prompts but in the answer choices as well. To summarize, vocabulary is VERY, VERY important, so you should start working on it today and continue throughout your high school years. Chances are the HSPT will not be your last standardized test.

Expanding your vocabulary will improve your score on the HSPT. It's difficult to predict exactly which vocabulary words you will see on your test, so it's best to continue adding new words to your vocabulary each day. If you're preparing early for the HSPT, you have some time to learn new words. If you are taking the test soon, you have limited time and should focus on the vocabulary words in this chapter.

EXPANDING YOUR VOCABULARY

Reading

Whether you tolerate reading or love it, you should try to expand your interests to include articles on the Internet, exclusives in magazines, or current events in newspapers. You can read anything and everything including, literature, history, online news, scientific studies, science fiction, fantasy, comic books, chapter books, music magazines, etc. Try to read a variety of genres and materials, so you are exposed to a wide range of vocabulary. Anytime you come across a word that you don't know, you should write it down.

Vocabulary Journal

Keep a journal of vocabulary words. Each time you read or hear a new word, write it down. When you have a chance, ask someone what it means or look it up. You may prefer to have a stack of flashcards instead of a journal. You should also write a sentence with each word. For the purpose of the HSPT, this is more important than the actual definition. Hearing or seeing the word in context will help you identify its synonyms or antonyms. You do not have to know the full definition.

Conversation

Use new vocabulary words in your everyday conversation. If you use a new word when talking to friends or family, you are more likely to remember it. You'll remember the situation in which you used the word, which will help you remember its meaning. Likewise, when you hear an unfamiliar word, don't be embarrassed to ask what it means. You can greatly improve your vocabulary with this everyday strategy.

Images

You are more likely to remember a new vocabulary word if you can picture it. This is easier than ever to do in today's electronic age. The next time you are on a computer or tablet consider the vocabulary word *confident*. To be confident is to be self-assured, certain of yourself. If you conduct an Internet search for the word confident you will first find that the definition will pop up along with synonyms and antonyms. If you select the "image" option, you will find images showing people in confident poses or perhaps raising their hands over their heads in victory. You'll be much more likely to remember the meaning of the word now that you can visualize it. Chances are you already knew what confident meant so now try *belligerent* and see what you can find. More than likely, once you look up images for *belligerent* you will quickly learn and remember that it means to be hostile. Here are some examples of what turned up when searching belligerent and confident. Can you tell which is which?

Apps

If you have a mobile phone, you can download apps that will quiz you on new vocabulary words every day. There are many of these apps out there, and most of them are free.

Recruit Your Family

Get your family involved. Each week make a list of words that you would like to learn. Leave this list where your parents and siblings can see it. Ask them to use those words during their daily conversations. This will help you remember the context of the word, and it's a fun way to get your family to help.

Other Tests

Don't hesitate to look at other tests in books or on the Internet, to find new word lists. Other tests include the Upper Level SSAT, COOP, Upper Level ISEE, and TACHS. These tests all have vocabulary designed for students currently in the 8th grade. Make sure you don't over challenge yourself with word lists meant for older students.

Don't Memorize the Definitions

When preparing for a standardized test, you are going for breadth not depth, quantity not quality. In other words, you want to expand your vocabulary by adding as many new words as possible. Your goal is not to have a thorough understanding of a limited number of words but rather to recognize a large number of words well enough to match them with their synonyms or antonyms.

Internet

If you have a computer or a tablet, you should create an electronic bookmark or a tab for a dictionary website. Find one that has definitions, synonyms, and antonyms such as *thesaurus.com*. Ideally, you want just one-word definitions, so having the thesaurus will help you to find the one word that you'll remember best. Games are another way to improve your vocabulary online. Search the Internet, and you will find many games and quizzes that are ideal for HSPT vocabulary, and many are free! Freerice.com is a website that donates rice to famine-stricken people for every vocabulary word you answer correctly. Now you have even more reasons to feel good about expanding your vocabulary. Check out these websites and look for new sites on your own.

thesaurus.com   *quizlet.com*   *freerice.com*
wordcentral.com   *vocabulary.com*   *membean.com*

Word Roots, Prefixes, and Suffixes

Understanding the more common roots of words will help you figure out the meaning of new words. *Membean.com* is a great website for looking up words that have a particular root. Here you can click on the root and see a tree filled with words that have that root in common. This is a great visual way to reinforce your knowledge of word parts.

TIP

Visual Vocab is an app that uses images to help you remember definitions. Other good apps include: Vocabulary HD, Word of the Day, and English Vocabulary Builder.

Learn Another Language

If you are learning another language in school or if you grew up speaking more than one language at home, then you already have an advantage. Sometimes words in another language look similar to English words. *Première* (French) or *primera* (Spanish) both mean *the first*, and in English *premiere* means a first performance.

CATEGORIZING: POSITIVE, NEGATIVE, OR NEUTRAL

Many words can be put into broad categories such as positive, negative, or neutral. For example, beneficial is a positive word, while annoying is considered a negative word. Words such as mediocre or conventional are neither positive nor negative. Sometimes, if you can identify a word as positive, negative, or neutral, you can match it to a word that is similar in meaning.

On the HSPT, you will not be asked to define a word or even to match a word with its definition. You will only have to find the word that is closest in meaning to the given vocabulary word. If you can remember only that the word has a positive or a negative meaning, this may help determine the correct answer. Perhaps you remember the setting in which you heard the word used, or the way you felt, or who said it. Anything you can remember may be the little bit that helps you answer the question correctly.

Take a few minutes and put a plus symbol (+) next to words you think are positive in meaning and a minus sign (–) next to those words you believe are negative (remember these are very general categories only—a word doesn't have to be really bad to be put in the negative category or overly good to be in the positive category). For words that are neutral, do not make any mark. When you are done, turn to the answers at the end of the chapter to see how you did. Add any unfamiliar words to your vocabulary journal.

1.	___	abdicate	16.	___	benign	31.	___	discrete
2.	___	abnormal	17.	___	benevolent	32.	___	dubious
3.	___	adept	18.	___	bolster	33.	___	embellish
4.	___	adorn	19.	___	candid	34.	___	enigma
5.	___	adverse	20.	___	congenial	35.	___	elite
6.	___	affront	21.	___	concise	36.	___	essential
7.	___	aggravate	22.	___	conspicuous	37.	___	exhibit
8.	___	alleviate	23.	___	contaminate	38.	___	fallacy
9.	___	altruistic	24.	___	contrive	39.	___	feeble
10.	___	animosity	25.	___	contrite	40.	___	feign
11.	___	arduous	26.	___	conventional	41.	___	forfeit
12.	___	astute	27.	___	debilitating	42.	___	futile
13.	___	authentic	28.	___	defer	43.	___	gullible
14.	___	banal	29.	___	delicate	44.	___	hamper
15.	___	belligerent	30.	___	diligent	45.	___	hapless

46. ___ hindrance	59. ___ mundane	72. ___ superficial
47. ___ impede	60. ___ nimble	73. ___ taciturn
48. ___ indispensable	61. ___ nomad	74. ___ tempest
49. ___ induct	62. ___ opaque	75. ___ tenacious
50. ___ irate	63. ___ petite	76. ___ tirade
51. ___ jubilant	64. ___ pilot	77. ___ tremble
52. ___ listlessness	65. ___ prohibit	78. ___ tyrant
53. ___ lucid	66. ___ pungent	79. ___ unique
54. ___ mar	67. ___ reprimand	80. ___ unkempt
55. ___ meager	68. ___ ratify	81. ___ verbose
56. ___ mediocrity	69. ___ rickety	82. ___ vigilant
57. ___ merit	70. ___ sever	83. ___ zeal
58. ___ morose	71. ___ severe	84. ___ zealot

(Answers are on page 47.)

COMMON WORD CATEGORIES

These words can also be put into more specific categories to help you better remember them. You can group words together that have to do with feelings, speech, actions, or behavior. Let's see how we can regroup the words into categories that are more specific than positive, negative, or neutral.

TIP

Keep a log in your journal to show your progress. It is easy to come up with a plan and also easy to forget it. Set up a chart showing how many new words you have learned each day, week, or month. Feel free to reward yourself after you reach a milestone.

Actions

abdicate: to give up power
advocate: support
agitate: to mix up
aggravate: to make worse
alter: to change
assist: to help
avert: to avoid
contrive: to concoct
desecrate: to destroy
embellish: to decorate
perturb: to annoy
placate: to calm
prohibit: to forbid
reimburse: to give back
sever: to cut off

Feelings

abhor: to hate
altruistic: unselfish
animosity: hostility
compassion: sympathetic
contrite: sorry
disdain: hate or indifference
grave: serious
morose: gloomy
jubilant: showing joy
zeal: eager desire

Behavior

abrasive: irritating
accountable: responsible
adept: skillful
candid: frank, open
congenial: kind, polite

Speech

banter: teasing
candid: frank, open
diction: speech
oration: sermon
reticent: quiet
taciturn: quiet
tirade: outburst
verbose: wordy

See if you can think of other categories to help you remember words and add these to your vocabulary journal.

In order to improve your vocabulary, you must continue to build it by adding a few new words every day, writing those words in your journal and using them in your everyday conversations.

ROOTS, PREFIXES, AND SUFFIXES

On the HSPT there will be many vocabulary words that you already know. That's the good news! The bad news, of course, is that there will also be words that you don't know. There will be some that you recognize but cannot define and others that you have never seen before. Understanding roots, prefixes, and suffixes can help you to decipher the meaning of unfamiliar words. There are pages and pages of roots, prefixes, and suffixes; however, you are only concerned with the few that may help you on the HSPT. For that reason, this section has an abbreviated list of the more common word parts that you should be familiar with. The roots, prefixes, and suffixes below are in alphabetical order. Each is followed by a brief description of its meaning, as well as an example of the word part in a vocabulary word. As you add new words to your vocabulary journal, underline word parts that will help you remember the meaning of the word. Take some time to review the list below. You most likely have seen most of these word parts before, but if you take the time to read the definitions and look at the examples, you will be more likely to put them to good use on the HSPT. Don't feel like you have to learn them all today, but instead try to learn a handful each time you study.

A

a, an	on	**afoot:** on foot
an	without	**anaerobic:** without or not requiring air
ab,	away from	**abdicate:** take away power
am	love	**amiable:** likeable
amb	to walk	**ambulatory:** able to walk
anim	life	**animate:** to bring to life
anti	against or opposite	**antidote:** cure against poison
aqua	water	**aquatic:** relating to water
auto	self	**autograph:** signature for yourself

B

bell	war	**belligerent:** argumentative
bene	good	**benefit:** advantage
bi	two	**bicycle:** having two wheels
bibli	book	**bibliophile:** book lover
bio	living	**biology:** study of living things

C

carn	flesh	**carnivore:** flesh eater
chrom	color	**chromatic:** having color
–cide	act of killing	**homicide:** act of killing a person
circum	around	**circumvent:** to go around
cred	believe	**incredible:** unbelievable
co	with	**cooperate:** work with someone
com	together	**community:** a group of people
con	with	**concur:** to agree with

D

dent	tooth	**dentist:** tooth doctor
derm	skin	**dermatologist:** a skin doctor
di	apart, two	**digress:** to go away, stray
dic	speak	**diction:** speech
dis	apart	**disconnect:** break a connection

E–G

ego	self	**egotistical:** loving oneself
equi	equal	**equator:** ring around the center
ex	out	**exclude:** to keep out
extra	outside	**extraterrestrial:** one from outside Earth
fore	in front of	**forebode:** to warn in advance
gen	birth	**generate:** to create

H–L

hetero	different	**heterogeneous:** made up of different materials
homo	same	**homogenous:** made up of the same materials
hypo	under	**hypotensive:** having low blood pressure
hyper	over	**hypertensive:** having high blood pressure
in	into	**inter:** to put into the ground
inter	between	**international:** between countries
intra	within	**intravenous:** within the veins
ject	throw	**eject:** to throw out
–less	without	**speechless:** not able to speak
lumin	light	**luminary:** an object that gives off light

M–O

magna	big	**magnify:** to make big
mal	bad	**malnourished:** poorly nourished, starved
mar	sea	**mariner:** one whose profession is on the sea
max	greatest	**maximum:** the most
micro	very small	**microscope:** used to look at very small things
mid	middle	**midterm:** exam in the middle of the term
mis	wrong	**misinterpret:** to interpret incorrectly
mort	death	**immortal:** not dying, living forever
multi	many	**multimedia:** includes multiple types of media
nom	name	**nominate:** to name someone to a position
nov	new	**novice:** someone who is new to something
numer	number	**numerous:** a large number
oct	eight	**octagon:** an eight-sided polygon
omni	all	**omnipotent:** all powerful

P–R

pan	everywhere	**panoramic:** all around
path	feeling	**apathetic:** having no feeling
phil	love of	**Anglophile:** one who admires England/English things
phobia	fear	**arachnophobia:** fear of spiders
post	after	**postdate:** put a later date
pre	before	**premonition:** forewarning
pro	support	**prognosis:** prediction of an event
re	again	**rewind:** to wind again, back up

S–T

scend	climb	**ascend:** to go up
semi	half	**semicircle:** a half circle
spec	look	**spectator:** one who watches
sub	under	**submarine:** underwater boat
super	over	**superficial:** on the surface
tact	touch	**tactile:** relating to touch
terra	earth	**territory:** area of land
tract	pull	**attract:** to pull together
trans	across	**transcontinental:** across the continent

U–Z

un	not	**unnatural:** not natural
uni	one	**unicycle:** one wheel
viv	live	**revive:** to bring to life
vis	see	**vision:** the ability to see
zo	animal	**zoology:** the study of animals

VOCABULARY WORD LIST AND DEFINITIONS

How Many Words Should You Know

You can't know every vocabulary word so don't put too much pressure on yourself. You just have to know more than the other students who are taking the HSPT! The following is a list of words that you may see on the HSPT. Of course they will not all be there, but this list contains many of the possibilities. You will have to know between 50 and 100 words to ace the HSPT, but you have no way of knowing which words, so you should learn as many as you can. A strong vocabulary is critical, vital, beneficial, essential (you get the idea) to your success on the HSPT.

How to Learn New Vocabulary Words

It is worth restating that you should not memorize the definitions of every word, but rather learn the word's synonyms and antonyms. Quantity not quality is your slogan for vocabulary. If you follow the simple steps below, it is likely that you will remember new words, and their meanings, for a very long time. When learning new vocabulary words:

- Write the word in a vocabulary journal.
- Look up a brief definition or synonym, or just ask someone.
- Write the definition on a flash card.
- Use the word in conversation some time that day or the next.
- Review your word list often so you don't forget new words.

Did you know if you speak a new word, you are 3 times more likely to remember it? Write it down, along with the definition, and you are 5 times more likely to remember it.

Let's Get Started

Take some time to review the following list and place a check mark, ✔, next to each word whose definition you know. This means that you can use the word in a sentence as well as identify synonyms and antonyms of that word. Each time you sit down to study for the HSPT, you should begin on this page (put a bookmark or sticky note here so you can quickly find your word list) by checking off any new words you have learned. In addition, you should randomly choose a few more words from the list to learn. Ask your parents to look your list over as well, so they can see the words you have to learn. They can help by using these words in everyday conversation with you.

A

__ **abbreviate** (*v.*) to shorten

__ **abdicate** (*v.*) to give up power

__ **abhor** (*v.*) despise

__ **abnormal** (*adj.*) not normal, average

__ **abode** (*n.*) residence

__ **abrasive** (*adj.*) irritating

__ **abrupt** (*adj.*) blunt

__ **absolution** (*n.*) forgiveness

__ **absolve** (*v.*) to free from guilt

__ **abstain** (*v.*) to hold back

__ **abundant** (*adj.*) plentiful

__ **accelerate** (*v.*) advance

__ **acclaim** (*v.*) to praise

__ **accommodate** (*v.*) to make room

__ **accountable** (*adj.*) responsible for

__ **accumulate** (*v.*) to collect

__ **accuse** (*v.*) to blame

__ **acrid** (*adj.*) bitter

__ **adamant** (*adj.*) determined

__ **adaptable** (*adj.*) able to change

__ **adept** (*adj.*) skillful

__ **adhere** (*v.*) to attach, to stick

__ **adjacent** (*adj.*) next to

__ **admonish** (*v.*) to warn

__ **adorn** (*v.*) to decorate

__ **adversary** (*n.*) opponent

__ **adverse** (*adj.*) opposing

__ **advocate** (*v.*) to support

__ **aesthetic** (*adj.*) about beauty

__ **affluent** (*adj.*) wealthy

__ **affront** (*n.*) deliberate act

__ **aggravate** (*v.*) to make worse

__ **aggressive** (*adj.*) forceful

__ **agitate** (*v.*) to shake, disturb

__ **ailment** (*n.*) mild illness

__ **ajar** (*adj.*) slightly open

__ **alleviate** (*v.*) to lessen

__ **allot** (*v.*) to allocate, to give out

__ **allocate** (*v.*) to give out

__ **aloof** (*adj.*) indifferent

__ **alter** (*v.*) change

__ **altercation** (*n.*) disagreement

__ **altruistic** (*adj.*) unselfish

__ **amass** (*v.*) to gather, to accumulate

__ **ambiguous** (*adj.*) unclear

__ **ambivalent** (*adj.*) uncertain

__ **amiable** (*adj.*) friendly

__ **amicable** (*adj.*) civil, cordial

__ **amiss** (*adj.*) wrong

__ **ample** (*adj.*) plenty, enough

__ **amplify** (*v.*) to increase

__ **analyze** (*v.*) to examine

__ **anecdote** (*n.*) story

__ **animate** (*v.*) to make alive

__ **animosity** (*n.*) hostility

__ **antagonize** (*v.*) to provoke

__ **anticipate** (*v.*) foresee

__ **antidote** (*n.*) a cure for poison

__ **apathy** (*n.*) indifference

__ **apex** (*n.*) peak

__ **appalling** (*adj.*) shocking

__ **apprehensive** (*adj.*) cautious

__ **arbitrary** (*adj.*) based on a whim

__ **archaic** (*adj.*) very old

__ **arduous** (*adj.*) difficult

__ **arid** (*adj.*) dry

__ **arrogant** (*adj.*) pompous, cocky

__ **asperity** (*n.*) harshness of tone

__ **aspire** (*v.*) to strive

__ **assent** (*v.*) to agree

__ **assist** (*v.*) to help

__ **astute** (*adj.*) sharp

__ **atone** (*v.*) to make amends

__ **atrocious** (*adj.*) awful

__ **atypical** (*adj.*) unusual

__ **audible** (*adj.*) able to be heard

__ **augment** (*v.*) to make greater

__ **authentic** (*adj.*) real

__ **avert** (*v.*) to avoid

___ **averse** (*adj.*) opposed to

___ **avid** (*adj.*) eager

B

___ **baffle** (*v.*) to confuse

___ **banal** (*adj.*) boring

___ **banter** (*n.*) teasing

___ **barter** (*v.*) to bargain or to negotiate

___ **belated** (*adj.*) after the event

___ **belligerent** (*adj.*) warlike

___ **belittle** (*v.*) to put down

___ **benefit** (*v.*) to gain an advantage

___ **benign** (*adj.*) favorable

___ **benevolent** (*adj.*) charitable

___ **berate** (*v.*) to scold

___ **biased** (*adj.*) partial

___ **bizarre** (*adj.*) odd

___ **blatant** (*adj.*) obvious

___ **bleak** (*adj.*) barren

___ **blithe** (*adj.*) happy

___ **boisterous** (*adj.*) noisy, rowdy

___ **bolster** (*v.*) to support

___ **brash** (*adj.*) bold

___ **brazen** (*adj.*) bold

___ **brisk** (*adj.*) fast, active

___ **broach** (*v.*) to bring up

___ **buttress** (*v.*) to reinforce

C

___ **callous** (*adj.*) careless

___ **candid** (*adj.*) frank, open

___ **cantankerous** (*adj.*) grouchy

___ **captivate** (*v.*) to enchant

___ **caustic** (*adj.*) corrosive

___ **censure** (*v.*) to criticize harshly

___ **ceremonious** (*adj.*) formal

___ **champion** (*v.*) to defend or support

___ **chastise** (*v.*) to scold

___ **choleric** (*adj.*) irritable

___ **circumvent** (*v.*) to go around

___ **clamor** (*v.*) to make commotion

___ **clandestine** (*adj.*) secretive

___ **clemency** (*n.*) mercy

___ **coarse** (*adj.*) rough

___ **cohesive** (*adj.*) sticking together

___ **collaborate** (*v.*) to work together

___ **commend** (*v.*) to praise

___ **compassion** (*n.*) sympathy

___ **competent** (*adj.*) able

___ **complacent** (*adj.*) at ease, happy

___ **comprehensive** (*adj.*) all-inclusive

___ **compromise** (*v.*) to give and take

___ **conceal** (*n.*) hide

___ **concede** (*v.*) admit

___ **conceited** (*adj.*) overly proud

___ **concise** (*adj.*) to the point

___ **conclude** (*v.*) to end

___ **concord** (*n.*) agreement

___ **concur** (*v.*) to agree

___ **condescend** (*v.*) to stoop or humble

___ **condescending** (*adj.*) snobby

___ **condone** (*v.*) to allow

___ **confiscate** (*v.*) to take away

___ **conflagration** (*n.*) a destructive fire

___ **congenial** (*adj.*) pleasing, friendly

___ **consequently** (*adj.*) as a result

___ **consolidate** (*v.*) to combine

___ **conspicuous** (*adj.*) obvious

___ **conspiracy** (*n.*) scheme

___ **construct** (*v.*) to build

___ **contagious** (*adj.*) communicable

___ **contaminate** (*v.*) to make impure

___ **contemporary** (*adj.*) modern

___ **content** (*adj.*) satisfied

___ **contort** (*v.*) to twist or bend

___ **contradict** (*v.*) to speak against

___ **contrite** (*adj.*) sorry

___ **contrive** (*v.*) to devise

___ **conundrum** (*n.*) a riddle

___ **conventional** (*adj.*) traditional

___ **corrupt** (*adj.*) dishonest

___ **counterfeit** (*adj.*) fake

___ **courteous** (*adj.*) mannerly

___ **critical** (*adj.*) fault-finding

___ **credible** (*adj.*) believable

___ **crucial** (*n.*) necessary

___ **culprit** (*n.*) one at fault
___ **culture** (*n.*) breeding, art
___ **cumulative** (*adj.*) successive adding
___ **cynical** (*adj.*) doubtful

D

___ **debilitating** (*adj.*) weakening
___ **debunk** (*v.*) to expose falseness
___ **decipher** (*v.*) to figure out
___ **declare** (*v.*) to announce
___ **decree** (*v.*) to command
___ **defer** (*v.*) to put off
___ **deficient** (adj.) lacking
___ **defile** (*v.*) violate, corrupt
___ **delay** (*v.*) suspension, put off
___ **delegate** (*v.*) to assign
___ **delicate** (*adj.*) fragile
___ **delinquent** (*adj.*) overdue
___ **deplete** (*v.*) to consume or use up
___ **deplorable** (*adj.*) shameful
___ **derelict** (*adj.*) irresponsible
___ **desecrate** (*v.*) to violate
___ **desist** (*v.*) to stop
___ **destitute** (*adj.*) very poor
___ **deter** (*v.*) to hinder
___ **detrimental** (*adj.*) harmful
___ **deviate** (*v.*) to stray from
___ **devious** (*adj.*) tricky, sneaky
___ **dexterity** (*n.*) aptitude
___ **diction** (*n.*) speech
___ **dilapidated** (*adj.*) falling apart
___ **diligent** (*adj.*) persevering
___ **diminish** (*v.*) to decrease
___ **disadvantage** (*n.*) a hurt or loss
___ **discern** (*v.*) to discover
___ **disclose** (*v.*) to reveal
___ **discredit** (*v.*) to cause disbelief
___ **discrete** (*adj.*) separate or distinct
___ **discriminate** (*v.*) to show prejudice
___ **disdain** (*n.*) hate or indifference
___ **disheveled** (*adj.*) messy
___ **dismal** (*adj.*) dreary
___ **dismantle** (*v.*) to take apart

___ **disparage** (*v.*) to belittle
___ **dispute** (*v.*) to argue
___ **disregard** (*v.*) to ignore
___ **distinct** (*adj.*) separate
___ **distort** (*v.*) to alter
___ **distraught** (*adj.*) upset
___ **diverse** (*adj.*) different
___ **divulge** (*v.*) to reveal
___ **docile** (*adj.*) tame
___ **dormant** (*adj.*) inactive
___ **dubious** (*adj.*) doubtful
___ **durable** (*adj.*) sturdy, strong
___ **duress** (*n.*) threat, hardship

E

___ **eccentric** (*adj.*) unusual
___ **ecstatic** (*adj.*) very happy
___ **edible** (*adj.*) meant to be eaten
___ **elated** (*adj.*) excited, happy
___ **elite** (*adj.*) the best
___ **eloquent** (*adj.*) skillful with words
___ **elusive** (*adj.*) hard to grab
___ **embark** (*v.*) to begin a journey
___ **embellish** (*v.*) to decorate, beautify
___ **emancipate** (*v.*) to free
___ **encroach** (*v.*) to trespass
___ **endanger** (*v.*) to threaten
___ **endorse** (*v.*) to advocate, to support
___ **endure** (*v.*) to get through
___ **enhance** (*v.*) to improve
___ **enigma** (*n.*) a puzzle
___ **enumerate** (*v.*) to name individually
___ **enthrall** (*v.*) to enchant
___ **ensure** (*v.*) to guarantee
___ **envious** (*adj.*) jealous
___ **epitome** (*n.*) perfect example
___ **eradicate** (*v.*) to eliminate
___ **erratic** (*adj.*) unpredictable
___ **essential** (*adj.*) necessary
___ **ethical** (*adj.*) moral
___ **eulogy** (*n.*) speech of praise
___ **excerpt** (*n.*) part of the whole
___ **exempt** (*adj.*) not required to

__ **exhibit** (*v.*) to display

__ **exorbitant** (*adj.*) excessive

__ **exonerate** (*v.*) to free of blame

__ **expedient** (*adj.*) advantageous

__ **expedite** (*v.*) to speed up

F

__ **fabricate** (*v.*) to dream up, to contrive

__ **fallacy** (*n.*) false belief

__ **feasible** (*adj.*) possible

__ **feeble** (*adj.*) weak

__ **feign** (*v.*) to pretend

__ **flagrant** (*adj.*) blatant

__ **flair** (*n.*) ability

__ **flaunt** (*v.*) to show off

__ **flexible** (*adj.*) easily changed

__ **florid** (*adj.*) elaborate

__ **fluctuate** (*v.*) to vary

__ **forfeit** (*v.*) to give up

__ **formidable** (*adj.*) awesome

__ **frenetic** (*adj.*) energetic

__ **frivolous** (*adj.*) trivial

__ **frugal** (*adj.*) thrifty

__ **fugitive** (*n.*) someone escaping

__ **fundamental** (*adj.*) basic

__ **futile** (*adj.*) ineffective

G

__ **garrulous** (*adj.*) chatty

__ **gaunt** (*adj.*) thin, bleak

__ **generate** (*v.*) to make

__ **generous** (*adj.*) giving

__ **gingerly** (*adv.*) cautious

__ **grandiose** (*adj.*) extravagant

__ **gratify** (*v.*) to satisfy

__ **grave** (*adj.*) serious

__ **grueling** (*adj.*) exhausting

__ **gullible** (*adj.*) easily deceived

H

__ **hamper** (*v.*) to hinder or slow

__ **hapless** (*adj.*) unlucky

__ **harbor** (*v.*) to protect

__ **harmonious** (*adj.*) agreeable

__ **hasten** (*v.*) to speed up

__ **haughty** (*adj.*) arrogant

__ **hinder** (*v.*) to get in the way of

__ **hindrance** (*n.*) something in the way

__ **humble** (*adj.*) modest

__ **hybrid** (*n.*) mixture

__ **hypothesis** (*n.*) formulation

I

__ **illiterate** (*adj.*) unable to read

__ **illustrious** (*adj.*) celebrated

__ **immaculate** (*adj.*) clean, spotless

__ **imminent** (*adj.*) about to happen

__ **immune** (*adj.*) unaffected

__ **impair** (*v.*) to damage

__ **impartial** (*adj.*) unprejudiced

__ **impeccable** (*adj.*) flawless

__ **impede** (*v.*) to obstruct

__ **impediment** (*n.*) a hindrance

__ **imperative** (*adj.*) important

__ **impulsive** (*adj.*) without thought

__ **incensed** (*adj.*) angry

__ **incessant** (*adj.*) never ending

__ **incompetent** (*adj.*) incapable

__ **inconspicuous** (*adj.*) hidden

__ **incriminate** (*v.*) to accuse

__ **indecent** (*adj.*) offensive

__ **indifferent** (*adj.*) not caring

__ **indispensable** (*adj.*) necessary

__ **induct** (*v.*) to put in office

__ **induce** (*v.*) to cause or start

__ **inert** (*adj.*) not moving

__ **inevitable** (*adj.*) unavoidable

__ **infamous** (*adj.*) bad reputation

__ **infinite** (*adj.*) without limit

__ **infringe** (*v.*) violate

__ **inordinate** (*adj.*) excessive

__ **insinuate** (*v.*) to imply

__ **insipid** (*adj.*) dull

__ **insolent** (*adj.*) disrespectful

__ **instigate** (*v.*) to initiate, to plot

__ **instill** (*v.*) to firmly establish

__ **instinctively** (*adj.*) automatic

__ **intact** (*adj.*) in one piece

__ **integrity** (*n.*) honesty

__ **interfere** (*v.*) to intervene

__ **intimidate** (*v.*) to frighten

__ **intricate** (*adj.*) detailed

__ **intriguing** (*adj.*) interesting

__ **intrusive** (*adj.*) unwelcomed

__ **inundate** (*v.*) to overload

__ **invigorate** (*v.*) to give energy to

__ **invincible** (*adj.*) can't be defeated

__ **irate** (*adj.*) angry

__ **irrational** (*adj.*) nonsensical

__ **irrelevant** (*adj.*) beside the point

__ **isolate** (*v.*) to separate

J

__ **jeer** (*v.*) to mock

__ **jeopardize** (*v.*) to put at risk

__ **jovial** (*adj.*) happy

__ **jubilant** (*adj.*) showing joy

K

__ **keen** (*adj.*) smart, quick

__ **knoll** (*n.*) small hill

L

__ **lament** (*v.*) to mourn, to grieve

__ **latitude** (*n.*) space to move

__ **legitimate** (*adj.*) valid, real

__ **lethargic** (*adj.*) without energy

__ **linger** (*v.*) to stay around

__ **listlessness** (*n.*) sluggishness

__ **livid** (*adj.*) enraged

__ **loathe** (*v.*) to hate

__ **lucid** (*adj.*) easy to understand

__ **lucrative** (*adj.*) well paid

M

__ **maintain** (*v.*) to continue

__ **malcontent** (*adj.*) unhappy

__ **malice** (*n.*) desire to harm

__ **malignant** (*adj.*) dangerous

__ **malleable** (*adj.*) able to be changed

__ **mandate** (*v.*) to order

__ **mar** (*v.*) to damage

__ **meager** (*adj.*) inadequate

__ **meander** (*v.*) wander aimlessly

__ **mediocre** (*adj.*) adequate

__ **melancholy** (*adj.*) sad

__ **merit** (*n.*) praise, excellence

__ **meticulous** (*adj.*) finicky

__ **misconception** (*n.*) wrong idea

__ **miscreant** (*n.*) villain

__ **mitigate** (*v.*) to lesson

__ **modify** (*v.*) to change, adjust

__ **monotonous** (*adj.*) boring

__ **moral** (*adj.*) ethical

__ **morose** (*adj.*) gloomy

__ **mundane** (*adj.*) usual, ordinary

__ **municipality** (*n.*) community

__ **mythical** (*adj.*) existing in myth

N

__ **naive** (*adj.*) trusting

__ **negligent** (*adj.*) careless

__ **nimble** (*adj.*) moving with ease

__ **nocturnal** (*adj.*) happening at night

__ **noisome** (*adj.*) offensive

__ **nomad** (*n.*) one who moves often

__ **nomadic** (*adj.*) wandering

__ **nonchalant** (*adj.*) easygoing

__ **notorious** (*adj.*) infamous

__ **novice** (*n.*) beginner

__ **noxious** (*adj.*) deadly

O

__ **objective** (*adj.*) unbiased

__ **obliterate** (*v.*) to eliminate

__ **oblivious** (*adj.*) unaware

__ **obstruct** (*v.*) to block

__ **obscure** (*v.*) to conceal

__ **obsolete** (*adj.*) outdated

___ **ominous** (*adj.*) foretelling

___ **omnipotent** (*adj.*) all powerful

___ **opaque** (*adj.*) cloudy

___ **opulent** (*adj.*) luxurious

___ **oration** (*n.*) sermon

___ **ornate** (*adj.*) fancy, decorated

___ **ostracize** (*v.*) to exclude

P

___ **pacify** (*v.*) to calm

___ **palatable** (*adj.*) pleasant in taste

___ **parched** (*adj.*) thirsty

___ **passive** (*adj.*) not aggressive

___ **pathetic** (*adj.*) sad, pitiful

___ **patron** (*n.*) sponsor, advocate

___ **pedigree** (*n.*) line of descent

___ **perceptive** (*adj.*) quick to notice

___ **perpetual** (*adj.*) ongoing

___ **perturb** (*v.*) to upset

___ **peruse** (*v.*) to look over

___ **petite** (*adj.*) small

___ **philanthropy** (*n.*) generosity

___ **pinnacle** (*n.*) peak

___ **pious** (*adj.*) religious

___ **pivotal** (*adj.*) important

___ **placate** (*v.*) to calm or pacify

___ **placid** (*adj.*) calm

___ **plausible** (*adj.*) believable

___ **plethora** (*n.*) excess

___ **plight** (*n.*) unfortunate condition

___ **poised** (*adj.*) balanced

___ **ponder** (*v.*) to think about

___ **potent** (*adj.*) powerful

___ **precocious** (*adj.*) mentally mature

___ **predominant** (*adj.*) great in number

___ **preface** (*n.*) introduction

___ **premonition** (*n.*) hunch

___ **prerogative** (*n.*) an official right

___ **preserve** (*v.*) to keep, to safeguard

___ **pretentious** (*adj.*) overly important

___ **prevalent** (*adj.*) widespread

___ **preview** (*v.*) to view before

___ **prior** (*adj.*) before

___ **principal** (*n.*) main

___ **proclaim** (*v.*) to announce

___ **procrastinate** (*v.*) to put off

___ **proficient** (*adj.*) skillful

___ **prohibit** (*v.*) to forbid

___ **prolific** (*adj.*) creative, productive

___ **prolong** (*v.*) to lengthen

___ **prompt** (*adj.*) on time

___ **provoke** (*v.*) to anger

___ **prudent** (*adj.*) careful

___ **pungent** (*adj.*) sharp smelling

___ **pilot** (*v.*) to steer

Q

___ **quandary** (*n.*) dilemma

___ **quarrelsome** (*adj.*) disagreeable

___ **quench** (*v.*) to put out

___ **querulous** (*adj.*) complaining

R

___ **radiant** (*adj.*) beaming

___ **rampant** (*adj.*) widespread

___ **ratify** (*v.*) to approve

___ **rational** (*adj.*) normal, sane

___ **ravenous** (*adj.*) starving

___ **recalcitrant** (*adj.*) disobedient

___ **reclusive** (*adj.*) isolated

___ **reconcile** (*v.*) to resolve

___ **rectify** (*v.*) to fix

___ **recuperate** (*v.*) to recover

___ **redundant** (*adj.*) repetitious

___ **reimburse** (*v.*) to pay back

___ **reflective** (*adj.*) automatic

___ **refurbish** (*v.*) to fix up

___ **refute** (*v.*) to contradict

___ **rejuvenate** (*v.*) to make new again

___ **relinquish** (*v.*) to release

___ **reluctance** (*n.*) hesitation

___ **remorse** (*n.*) sense of guilt

___ **replenish** (*v.*) to refill, to put back

___ **reprimand** (*v.*) to scold

__ **reproach** (*v.*) to express disapproval

__ **reprisal** (*n.*) retaliation

__ **reputable** (*adj.*) distinguished

__ **resume** (*v.*) to continue

__ **resolve** (*v.*) to decide, to agree

__ **restore** (*v.*) to make new

__ **reticent** (*adj.*) quiet

__ **retract** (*v.*) to take back

__ **revere** (*v.*) to admire

__ **rickety** (*adj.*) flimsy

__ **rigorous** (*adj.*) harsh, exact

__ **robust** (*adj.*) strong, healthy

__ **routine** (*adj.*) ordinary, normal

S

__ **sage** (*adj.*) wise

__ **sage** (*n.*) a wise person

__ **salvage** (*v.*) save from

__ **satiate** (*v.*) to fill, to satisfy

__ **saunter** (*v.*) to linger, to stroll

__ **scrutinize** (*v.*) to inspect, to analyze

__ **sedentary** (*adj.*) need for sitting

__ **serene** (*adj.*) calm

__ **sever** (*v.*) to cut off

__ **severe** (*adj.*) harsh

__ **shrewd** (*adj.*) clever

__ **significant** (*adj.*) important

__ **simulate** (*v.*) to imitate

__ **skeptical** (*adj.*) doubtful

__ **slovenly** (*adj.*) dirty, careless

__ **solace** (*n.*) comfort

__ **somber** (*adj.*) gloomy

__ **sparse** (*adj.*) scarce, limited

__ **spontaneous** (*adj.*) impulsive

__ **sporadic** (*adj.*) intermittent

__ **squander** (*v.*) to waste

__ **stagnant** (*adj.*) not moving

__ **staunch** (*adj.*) loyal

__ **stealthy** (*adj.*) secretive, quiet

__ **sterile** (*adj.*) germ-free

__ **stimulate** (*v.*) to provoke

__ **strife** (*n.*) a struggle

__ **stringent** (*adj.*) rigid

__ **subsequent** (*adj.*) following

__ **subtle** (*adj.*) indirect, faint

__ **succinct** (*adj.*) to the point, brief

__ **sullen** (*adj.*) gloomy

__ **superficial** (*adj.*) near the surface

__ **superfluous** (*adj.*) excessive

__ **suppress** (*v.*) to prevent, to constrain

__ **surge** (*n.*) a rush

__ **sustain** (*v.*) to keep going

__ **swelter** (*adj.*) sweat

T

__ **taciturn** (*adj.*) quiet

__ **tactile** (*adj.*) relative to touch

__ **taint** (*v.*) to pollute

__ **tangible** (*adj.*) able to be touched

__ **taunt** (*v.*) to tease

__ **tedious** (*adj.*) dull, annoying

__ **temperate** (*adj.*) mild, moderate

__ **tempest** (*n.*) a violent windstorm

__ **tense** (*adj.*) nervous, anxious

__ **tenuous** (*adj.*) weak, fragile

__ **terse** (*adj.*) to the point

__ **tenacious** (*adj.*) persistent

__ **thrive** (*v.*) to do well

__ **throb** (*v.*) pulse

__ **timid** (*adj.*) shy

__ **tirade** (*n.*) a long outburst

__ **tolerant** (*adj.*) accepting

__ **toxic** (*adj.*) poisonous

__ **trance** (*n.*) stupor

__ **transform** (*v.*) to change completely

__ **transient** (*adj.*) passing quickly

__ **translucent** (*adj.*) clear

__ **traverse** (*v.*) to cross

__ **tremble** (*v.*) to shake

__ **trivial** (*adj.*) unimportant

__ **tycoon** (*n.*) one with money

__ **tyrant** (*n.*) an unjust ruler

U

__ **ultimate** (*adj.*) last, highest

__ **undaunted** (*adj.*) not discouraged

__ **undermine** (*v.*) weaken

__ **uniform** (*adj.*) the same

__ **unkempt** (*adj.*) messy

__ **unorthodox** (*adj.*) not traditional

__ **unique** (*adj.*) the only one

__ **unsung** (*adj.*) overlooked

__ **usurp** (*v.*) to take over

__ **utilize** (*v.*) to use

__ **utmost** (*adj.*) highest, best

V

__ **vacant** (*adj.*) empty

__ **vague** (*adj.*) unclear

__ **vain** (*adj.*) egotistical

__ **valid** (*adj.*) right, genuine

__ **validate** (*v.*) to approve

__ **verbose** (*adj.*) wordy

__ **verge** (*n.*) brink

__ **viable** (*adj.*) reasonable

__ **vigilant** (*adj.*) watchful

__ **vigorous** (*adj.*) energetic

__ **vindicate** (*v.*) to confirm

__ **virtually** (*adj.*) essentially

__ **vital** (*adj.*) essential

__ **vitality** (*n.*) energy, spirit

__ **volatile** (*adj.*) quickly changing

__ **voracious** (*adj.*) hungry

__ **vulnerable** (*adj.*) defenseless

W

__ **wage** (*n.*) compensation, pay

__ **wage** (*v.*) to do or to conduct

__ **wary** (*adj.*) cautious

__ **waver** (*v.*) to go back and forth

__ **weary** (*adj.*) exhausted

__ **whimsical** (*adj.*) carefree

__ **wily** (*adj.*) crafty, sly

Y

__ **yearn** (*v.*) to want

__ **youthful** (*adj.*) young

Z

__ **zeal** (*n.*) eager desire

__ **zealot** (*n.*) fanatic

__ **zenith** (*n.*) the top, peak

WRAP IT UP WITH PRACTICE

You now have a better understanding of the importance of vocabulary and how to expand your own. Let's summarize how to improve your vocabulary.

- Reading will introduce you to new words and allow you to see the words in context.
- Using new words in conversation will remind you of the context of the word.
- Apps can be a fun way to learn new words.
- The Internet is a powerful resource and can be used to quickly look up definitions, synonyms, and antonyms.
- Search for word lists for other standardized tests designed for similar grades.
- Categorize new words as positive, negative, or neutral.
- Understanding roots, prefixes, and suffixes can help you with unfamiliar words.
- Each time you study for the HSPT, begin by reviewing your vocabulary list.
- Narrow the definition of a new word to a single synonym if possible.

VOCABULARY PRACTICE

After you've had a chance to review the word lists in this chapter, try the practice questions that follow. You will also have opportunities to practice your vocabulary in Chapter 4, "Verbal Skills" and in Chapter 6, "Reading," and of course in the practice HSPT tests in this book.

Match the Word with the Definition Practice

On the left are vocabulary words and on the right are definitions. Next to each vocabulary word, place the correct letter of the definition that belongs with it.

____	1. embark	A.	careful
____	2. gaunt	B.	compensation
____	3. enigma	C.	to put off
____	4. immaculate	D.	happening at night
____	5. prudent	E.	to do well
____	6. ostracize	F.	quiet
____	7. wage	G.	valid, real
____	8. stagnant	H.	satisfied
____	9. thrive	I.	begin a journey
____	10. reticent	J.	sturdy, strong
____	11. procrastinate	K.	intervene
____	12. nocturnal	M.	ordinary
____	13. mundane	N.	angry
____	14. incensed	O.	not moving
____	15. legitimate	P.	necessary
____	16. interfere	Q.	thin, bleak
____	17. embellish	R.	puzzle
____	18. durable	S.	decorate
____	19. content	T.	clean, spotless
____	20. crucial	U.	exclude

(Answers are on page 48.)

Positive, Negative, or Neutral Practice

Next to each vocabulary word, mark a plus symbol (+) if the word is considered a positive word or a negative symbol (–) the word is considered negative. For words that are neither, write the letter N for neutral.

_____ 1. abhor

_____ 2. mar

_____ 3. ailment

_____ 4. acclaim

_____ 5. robust

_____ 6. altruistic

_____ 7. congenial

_____ 8. intimidate

_____ 9. indecent

_____ 10. petite

_____ 11. arrogant

_____ 12. unethical

_____ 13. insolent

_____ 14. benevolent

_____ 15. consolidate

_____ 16. animosity

_____ 17. sage

_____ 18. zeal

_____ 19. amicable

_____ 20. dormant

(Answers are on page 48.)

Roots, Prefixes, and Suffixes Practice

For each set of words below, there is a word part that is shared. Read each word in the list, consider the meaning of each, then describe the meaning of the root, prefix, or suffix.

1. sub_____
   submerge
   submarine
   submissive
   subterranean
   subordinate

2. gen_____
   genuine
   genealogy
   generation
   genocide
   genesis
   genetics

3. uni_____
   universe
   unicycle
   unicorn
   united
   unanimous

4. re_____
   revisit
   rewind
   recall
   reheat
   recant

5. anim_____
   animal
   animated
   animosity
   animator
   inanimate

6. less_____
   motionless
   tasteless
   thoughtless
   careless
   penniless

7. mort_____
   mortician
   mortify
   mortuary
   mortal
   immortal

8. mag_____
   magnanimous
   magnify
   magnificent
   magnitude
   magnum

9. tract_____
   attract
   retract
   subtract
   tractor
   extract

10. path_____
    antipathy
    sympathy
    apathetic
    pathology
    empathy

(Answers are on page 48.)

ANSWERS FOR CHAPTER 3

Categorizing: Positive, Negative, or Neutral (pages 30–31)

1. (–) abdicate (*n.*) to give up power
2. (–) abnormal (*adj.*) not normal, average
3. (+) adept (*adj.*) skillful
4. (+) adorn (*v.*) to decorate
5. (–) adverse (*adj.*) opposing
6. (–) affront (*n.*) deliberate act
7. (–) aggravate (*v.*) to make worse
8. (+) alleviate (*v.*) to lessen
9. (+) altruistic (*adj.*) unselfish
10. (–) animosity (*n.*) hostility
11. (N) arduous (*adj.*) difficult
12. (+) astute (*adj.*) sharp
13. (+) authentic (*adj.*) real
14. (–) banal (*adj.*) boring
15. (–) belligerent (*adj.*) given to waging war
16. (+) benign (*adj.*) favorable
17. (+) benevolent (*adj.*) charitable
18. (+) bolster (*v.*) to support
19. (+) candid (*adj.*) frank, open
20. (+) congenial (*adj.*) pleasing
21. (N) concise (*adj.*) to the point
22. (N) conspicuous (*adj.*) easily seen
23. (–) contaminate (*v.*) to make impure
24. (N) contrive (*v.*) to devise
25. (N) contrite (*adj.*) sorry
26. (N) conventional (*adj.*) traditional
27. (–) debilitating (*adj.*) weakening
28. (N) defer (*v.*) to put off
29. (N) delicate (*adj.*) fragile
30. (+) diligent (*adj.*) persevering
31. (N) discrete (*adj.*) separate or distinct
32. (N) dubious (*adj.*) doubtful; unsure
33. (+) embellish (*v.*) to beautify
34. (N) enigma (*n.*) a puzzle
35. (+) elite (*adj.*) the best
36. (+) essential (*adj.*) necessary
37. (N) exhibit (*v.*) to display
38. (–) fallacy (*n.*) false belief
39. (–) feeble (*adj.*) weak
40. (–) feign (*v.*) to pretend
41. (–) forfeit (*v.*) to give up
42. (–) futile (*adj.*) ineffective
43. (–) gullible (*adj.*) easily deceived
44. (–) hamper (*v.*) to hinder or slow
45. (–) hapless (*adj.*) unlucky
46. (–) hindrance (*n.*) something in the way
47. (–) impede (*v.*) to obstruct
48. (N) indispensable (*adj.*) necessary
49. (N) induct (*v.*) to put in office
50. (–) irate (*adj.*) angry
51. (+) jubilant (*adj.*) showing joy
52. (–) listlessness (*adj.*) sluggishness
53. (+) lucid (*adj.*) easy to understand
54. (–) mar (*v.*) to damage
55. (–) meager (*adj.*) inadequate
56. (N) mediocrity (*adj.*) state of being adequate
57. (+) merit (*n.*) praise, excellence
58. (–) morose (*adj.*) gloomy
59. (–) mundane (*adj.*) usual, ordinary
60. (+) nimble (*adj.*) moving with ease
61. (N) nomad (*n.*) one who moves often
62. (N) opaque (*adj.*) cloudy
63. (N) petite (*adj.*) small
64. (N) pilot (*v.*) to steer
65. (–) prohibit (*v.*) to forbid
66. (–) pungent (*adj.*) a sharp smell
67. (–) reprimand (*v.*) to scold
68. (N) ratify (*v.*) to approve
69. (N) rickety (*adj.*) flimsy

70. **(N)** sever (*v.*) to cut off

71. **(–)** severe (*adj.*) harsh

72. **(–)** superficial (*adj.*) near the surface

73. **(N)** taciturn (*adj.*) quiet

74. **(–)** tempest (*n.*) a violent windstorm

75. **(N)** tenacious (*adj.*) persistent

76. **(–)** tirade (*n.*) a long outburst

77. **(–)** tremble (*v.*) fear

78. **(–)** tyrant (*n.*) an unjust ruler

79. **(+)** unique (*adj.*) one of a kind

80. **(–)** unkempt (*adj.*) messy

81. **(N)** verbose (*adj.*) wordy

82. **(+)** vigilant (*adj.*) watchful

83. **(+)** zeal (*n.*) eager desire

84. **(–)** zealot (*n.*) fanatic

Match the Word with the Definition Practice (page 44)

1. **(I)**
2. **(Q)**
3. **(R)**
4. **(T)**
5. **(A)**
6. **(U)**
7. **(B)**
8. **(O)**
9. **(E)**
10. **(F)**
11. **(C)**
12. **(D)**
13. **(M)**
14. **(N)**
15. **(G)**
16. **(K)**
17. **(S)**
18. **(J)**
19. **(H)**
20. **(P)**

Positive, Negative, or Neutral Practice (page 45)

1. **(–)** abhor
2. **(–)** mar
3. **(–)** ailment
4. **(+)** acclaim
5. **(+)** robust
6. **(+)** altruistic
7. **(+)** congenial
8. **(–)** intimidate
9. **(–)** indecent
10. **(N)** petite
11. **(–)** arrogant
12. **(–)** unethical
13. **(–)** insolent
14. **(+)** benevolent
15. **(N)** consolidate
16. **(–)** animosity
17. **(+)** sage
18. **(+)** zeal
19. **(+)** amicable
20. **(N)** dormant

Roots, Prefixes, and Suffixes Practice (pages 45–46)

1. sub– **under**
2. gen– **birth**
3. uni– **one**
4. re– **again**
5. anim– **living**
6. –less **without**
7. mort– **death**
8. mag– **great, large**
9. tract– **to pull**
10. path– **relating to feelings**

Verbal Skills

4

The Verbal Skills subtest is the first of the five HSPT subtests. There will be 60 questions in this subtest and you will be given 18 minutes to complete them. Without practice and study, most students have difficulty finishing the Verbal Skills subtest on time. In this chapter, you will learn strategies and tips that will allow you to not only finish the Verbal Skills subtext but also to score a higher percent of answers correctly.

The most important thing in this subtest of the HSPT is vocabulary. There are five types of questions in Verbal Skills, four of which rely heavily on vocabulary. You will be asked to find synonyms and antonyms of vocabulary words. You will also see questions that involve analogies and other questions involving groups of words. In each of these four question types, you will have a significant advantage if you possess a strong vocabulary. If you have not already done so, read Chapter 3 and begin improving your vocabulary right away.

THE LAYOUT

The HSPT has five distinct Verbal Skills question types as shown below.

Verbal Skills Subtest—18 Minutes and 60 Questions

Question Type	Example	Number of Questions
Synonym	Gigantic most nearly means . . .	12
Antonym	Compel is the *opposite* of . . .	9
Analogy	Drizzle is to rain as breeze is to . . .	10
Verbal Logic	If the first two statements are true, the third is . . .	12
Verbal Classification	Which word does *not* belong with the others?	17

Let's look at some general strategies and review each question type. After you learn about each, there will be a brief summary for the Verbal Skills subtest. At the end of the chapter is a full-length subtest, where you can practice the strategies that you have learned.

GENERAL STRATEGIES FOR VERBAL SKILLS

Timing is everything in this subtest. With only 18 minutes, you will have to be mindful of the time. It's okay if you spend a little extra time on one question, since there are some questions that will take you only a few seconds. Just remember to keep moving and never spend too long on a single question. Every question is worth the same amount, just one point.

> In Chapter 2, "Preparing for the HSPT," you can find general test strategies that will help you improve your score. These apply to all of the subtests. If you have not already read this list, then make sure you do so before taking the practice at the end of this chapter.

Timing and Selecting Questions

You will want to move quickly through this section, answering about four questions each minute. The vocabulary-based questions (synonyms, antonyms, analogies, and verbal classifications) can usually be answered quickly, so be certain to read each one of these questions and answer as many as you can. The logic questions take a little more time, but the good thing is that you can ALWAYS get the right answer if you have enough time.

Categorize Questions That Involve Vocabulary

TIP

When learning vocabulary, keep in mind that you are going for *quantity* and *not quality*. You only have to match the word to a synonym or antonym to find the correct answer.

Most of the questions in the Verbal Skills subtest, as well as about thirty questions in the Reading subtest, involve vocabulary. These include words that fall into one of three categories: words you know very well, words you recognize but cannot define, and those you have never seen. Each of these categories will dictate which type of strategy you should use.

This Is Not English Class

In your English class, you likely learn very specific and detailed definitions for vocabulary words. This is a great way to learn and remember new words. However, your definitions for the purpose of this test must be flexible. You will have to find meanings of words, or synonyms, that are not exactly the same as the question prompt. You are always looking for the *best* answer choice and not necessarily the perfect one. Often times you are simply ruling out all of the bad answers and choosing the one that is left.

Don't Eliminate Words You Don't Know

It is important that you *do not* rule out words that you don't recognize. The word you are not familiar with may well be the correct answer. Only rule out answer choices that you know to be incorrect.

Underline or Circle Reversal Words

When you are taking a standardized test, it is very easy to rush and forget things instantly. If a question asks, "Stingy does *not* mean . . . ," you should immediately underline or circle the word *not* (even though it is already italicized). This will help you reinforce that you are looking for what the word does *not* mean. It can be easy to mistakenly choose a synonym, such as *cheap*, if you are not careful.

Extra Time

If you have extra time, spend it on the logic questions. You will learn more about logic questions in this chapter. These questions all have the answer right in the question, so if you didn't get the answer the first time through and you have extra time, go back to these and find the right answer. Extra time is not usually much help with vocabulary, since you either know the word or you don't. You'll have already used your strategies to make a guess so there is no need to revisit these later.

TYPES OF VERBAL SKILLS QUESTIONS

By now you have the idea that vocabulary is very important. Let's see the types of questions where having a good vocabulary will really pay off. As mentioned, there are five different question types in the Verbal Skills subtest. The question types are mixed together and will not be in order of increasing difficulty. For this reason it is important to spend very little time on the questions that you feel are difficult. If you spend too much time on difficult questions, you may miss out on the easier questions that may follow later in the subtest. Let's look at each type of question separately, and then we'll put them all together in a practice subtest.

TIP

Never change an answer unless you *know* it is incorrect. Even if you guessed, there was a reason you chose that answer, so only change it if you know it is wrong.

SYNONYMS

Synonym questions ask you to identify a word that means the same, or nearly the same, as the word in the question prompt. You will have about 12 synonym questions out of the total 60 Verbal Skills questions, worded in one of three ways:

Example	Number of Questions
An enigma is a(n) . . .	1–2
Duress most nearly means . . .	9–10
To be an exception is to be a(n) . . .	1–2

The questions are brief and direct. Each will be followed by four single word choices: (a), (b), (c), or (d). Vocabulary words in the HSPT Verbal Skills subtest are not given in context, making these questions quite difficult. This means that you will have to rely on your vocabulary, the answer choices, and the strategies you're learning here to answer the synonym questions.

General Strategies for Synonym Questions

Remember there are three categories of vocabulary words:

- Words you know well
- Words you recognize but cannot define
- Words you've never seen

Let's look at these three categories and learn how best to find the correct answer choice for each.

WORDS YOU KNOW WELL

If you know the meaning of the word, or at least have a very good idea, then these questions should be very easy for you. *The stronger your vocabulary is, the easier the questions will be!* The only thing you have to worry about here is making a careless mistake. You can avoid that by thinking of a synonym *before* you look at the answer choices. When you look at the answer choices, you should be looking for a word that means the same as the synonym in your head and not necessarily the word in the prompt. This will help you avoid jumping at a wrong answer choice. Take a look at the following examples.

➡ Example 1

Banter most nearly means

(a) praise.
(b) teasing.
(c) flattery.
(d) work.

Think for a second of what the word *banter* means. Maybe you know that banter has an annoying connotation. Now look for the answer choice that most nearly means to *annoy* rather than the word that means *banter*. This will help you avoid answer choices for words that look like, sound like, or rhyme with *banter*. Lastly, look at your answer choices, keeping in mind you are looking for a word that means *to annoy*. You can easily see that *teasing* is the closest match to *annoying*, so you can safely choose (b) as your answer. Now try a couple questions using this strategy.

➡ Example 2

Vain most nearly means

(a) talented.
(b) confident.
(c) jealous.
(d) conceited.

TIP

When selecting your answer, ALWAYS read each of the answer choices. Don't be tempted to select the first answer that sounds like or looks like the word you have in mind. It must have a similar meaning to be correct.

In Example 2, *vain* means to be *conceited*. If you go right to the answer choices without first forming your own definition in your mind, you may end up choosing the first answer that is similar. In this case, you may incorrectly choose *confident* or even *talented*. If you first form your own definition, which will most likely be *conceited*, you can avoid this costly mistake. The correct answer is choice (d) *conceited*.

➡ Example 3

Gale most nearly means

(a) dance.
(b) wind.
(c) turn.
(d) whisk.

Sometimes, you may know the prompt word but cannot find a synonym. In this case, make sure you are using the word in the correct context. For example, if the word is *wind*, and you are thinking "I can *wind* the string onto the spool" instead of "the *wind* was very strong against the sail of the boat," you will not find the synonym because you have the wrong word in mind. Ask yourself if one of the answer choices may have more than one meaning or may be pronounced differently. For Example 3, the correct answer is choice (b) *wind*.

WORDS YOU RECOGNIZE BUT CANNOT DEFINE

You will come across words on the HSPT that you recognize but cannot define. You can increase the likelihood of answering these questions correctly by using the following strategies.

Eliminate Any Answers You Know Are Incorrect

Throughout the HSPT, you should always eliminate answer choices you know to be incorrect. This will help you focus on the possible correct answers.

➡ Example 4

Jubilant most nearly means

(a) feeble.
(b) elated.
(c) zealot.
(d) tyrant.

The word *jubilant* may be one you recognize but cannot define. If you use the first strategy, which you should *always* use, you can begin to eliminate words that you know to be incorrect. You may know that *jubilant* means to be happy; however, if you don't know what the word *elated* means, then you will have some trouble. If you know that *feeble* means weak you can eliminate it. Jubilant is an adjective and both *zealot* and *tyrant* are nouns, so you can also rule those out because the synonym must be a grammatical match. Your test question now looks like this:

Jubilant most nearly means

(a) feeble
(b) elated
(c) zealot
(d) tyrant

Even if you don't know what *elated* means, you can safely choose (b) as your answer.

Categorize Words as Positive, Negative, or Neutral

Let's look at another example where you may recognize the word but don't know the meaning. Try to determine if the word is positive, negative, or neutral and find a word that is similar.

TIP

When eliminating answers, draw a thin line through incorrect answer choices. Don't scribble out any words, however, in case you need to look at them again later.

➡ Example 5_____

To be belligerent is to be

(a) polite.
(b) argumentative.
(c) violent.
(d) sympathetic.

Say you heard your teacher ask a student to not be so belligerent when debating. You remember that since the student was asked to NOT behave that way, that belligerent may be a negative word. In looking at the answer choices, you can see that two are negative (*argumentative* and *violent*) and two are positive words (*polite* and *sympathetic*), so you have already narrowed this down to a fifty-fifty guess. Looking at the negative words, *argumentative* and *violent*, you will most likely choose the word *argumentative* because you remember the setting in which you heard the word.

Word parts may also be helpful when using the positive–negative–neutral strategy. A–, anti–, dis–, and mis– are often associated with words that have negative meanings, while ben– and pro– can indicate words with a positive meaning. You can find more on word parts in Chapter 3, "Vocabulary."

Rule Out Answer Choices That Have Similar Meanings

There will never be a question on the HSPT that has more than one correct answer, so if two of the answer choices have the same, or similar meanings, then neither can be the correct answer.

➡ Example 6_____

Luscious most nearly means

(a) sweet.
(b) sour.
(c) bland.
(d) boring.

In Example 6, let's assume that you have heard the word luscious before but are uncertain of the meaning. Look to see if any of the answer choices are synonyms of each other. You'll notice that *bland* and *boring* have very similar meanings, so you can rule them both out. Next, decide if *luscious* most nearly means *sweet* or *sour*. The correct answer is choice (a) *sweet*. *Luscious* means appetizing, or *sweet*.

WORDS YOU'VE NEVER SEEN

No matter how much time you spend learning vocabulary (and you should spend lots!), there will be some words on the HSPT that you have never seen.

If you don't know the meaning of the word, then you will have to guess, but it doesn't have to be an uneducated guess. You should try to narrow your answer choices to two. Here are some strategies to use when you are faced with an unfamiliar word.

Rule Out Answer Choices That Are Similar

This strategy can work, even if you have no idea what the word means.

➡️ **Example 7**_____

Candid most nearly means

(a) sweet.
(b) open.
(c) deceitful.
(d) tricky.

Say that you have never heard the word *candid*. You can see that two answer choices have similar meanings: *deceitful* and *tricky*. Because you will never be presented with a question that has more than one correct answer, the answer can be neither of these. This leaves you with two choices (*sweet* and *open*). *Sweet* may be there because *candid* has part of the word *candy* in it, making this a distractor. The correct answer is choice (b) *open*.

Find Clues in the Prefix, Suffix, or Root of the Word

If you don't recognize a word, you may be able to find clues in the word prompt. You can find more on roots, as well as prefixes and suffixes, in vocabulary review in Chapter 3. Let's consider an example where looking at parts of words can be helpful.

➡️ **Example 8**_____

Regenerate most nearly means

(a) discourage.
(b) damage.
(c) produce.
(d) destroy.

The word *regenerate* has the prefix "re–," which means "*again.*" Maybe you realize that the root "gen" means birth or kind. Now you have enough information to piece together the correct answer choice.

Reproduce is most likely a word that you know and makes sense as *regenerate* means to grow, so the correct answer is choice (c) *produce*. Remember, the prompt states "most nearly means," so the correct answer does not have to be the exact definition.

Look for Answers That Are Opposites

If you have no idea what the word means, you can try to narrow down the answer choices if you look for antonyms in the answer choices. This strategy is only to be used as a last resort if you have to guess.

➡ Example 9

Forthright most nearly means

(a) sweet.
(b) honest.
(c) deceitful.
(d) first.

If you don't know what *forthright* means, look at the answer choices for clues. Check for answer choices that are antonyms. You can see that answer choices (b) *honest* and (c) *deceitful* are opposites. It may not always be the case, but if you have to guess, you should narrow down the answer choices to these two answers. Test writers often put antonyms and synonyms in the answer choices to see if you really understand the vocabulary word. Narrow the choices to *deceitful* and *honest*, then look at the question again. Hopefully the root "right" makes you think of good rather than bad, and you choose the correct answer, choice (b) *honest. Forthright* means to be open and *honest*.

Consider Another Language

Many words in our language come from other languages. If you grew up speaking more than one language in your home, you will have an advantage in the vocabulary questions of the HSPT. When you come across an unknown word, consider what it means in another language. It may mean the same or similar to one of the answer choices. If not, then the root of the word may be a help.

➡ Example 10

Amicable most nearly means

(a) strong.
(b) friendly.
(c) secretive.
(d) troubled.

The French word for friend is *ami* and in Spanish it is *amigo*. Amicable has the root *ami* in it and therefore means friendly. The correct answer is choice (b) *friendly*.

Make a Guess and Move On

After exhausting all of these strategies (in 30 seconds or less), if you still cannot find the correct answer, it's time to make a guess and move on. Trust your instincts and choose an answer. It is unlikely that you will know every vocabulary word, so it's okay to make your guess and move on to easier questions.

Synonyms Practice

Now that you have learned strategies for answering synonym questions, try the following practice set of questions and then check your answers. If you come across words that are unfamiliar, add them to your vocabulary list.

1. Adverse most nearly means

   (a) friend.
   (b) helpful.
   (c) opposing.
   (d) assist.

2. An orator is a

   (a) dentist.
   (b) speaker.
   (c) therapist.
   (d) mechanic.

3. To be stealthy is to be

   (a) fit.
   (b) angry.
   (c) quiet.
   (d) heavy.

4. To resume a conversation is to

   (a) end.
   (b) apply.
   (c) begin.
   (d) continue.

5. Culminate most nearly means

   (a) finish.
   (b) commence.
   (c) begin.
   (d) bottom.

6. Animate most nearly means

   (a) friendly.
   (b) color.
   (c) enliven.
   (d) help.

7. An abolitionist is a(n)

   (a) activist.
   (b) runner.
   (c) researcher.
   (d) teacher.

8. To be vile is to be

   (a) disgusting.
   (b) strong.
   (c) angry.
   (d) amiable.

9. To modify a drawing is to

   (a) begin.
   (b) change.
   (c) create.
   (d) paint.

10. Diction most nearly means

    (a) peruse.
    (b) read.
    (c) end.
    (d) articulate.

(Answers are on page 80.)

ANTONYMS

Antonym questions on the HSPT ask you to identify a word that means the *opposite* of the word that is given. Like synonym questions, they test your knowledge of vocabulary. However, antonym questions also test your mental skills because you must not only know the meaning of the word but also be able to find the word that is its opposite. The antonym questions are worded in one of these two ways:

Example	Number of Questions
A _____ is *not* a(n) . . .	1–2
_____ means the *opposite* of . . .	7–8

The words *not* and *opposite* will always be italicized to remind you that you are looking for the opposite of the prompt word. Always circle or underline the words *not* and *opposite* to help avoid mistakes.

General Strategies for Antonyms

Antonym questions can be tricky and as such, it is easy to make mistakes. Read the strategies here to learn valuable tips in answering these questions.

SIMILAR STRATEGIES AS SYNONYMS

Strategies for answering antonyms questions are very similar to those used for synonyms. These strategies will not be repeated in detail here but only summarized. Read the prior section on SYNONYMS if you have not already.

- Cross out any answer choices you know to be incorrect.
- Eliminate answer choices that are similar in meaning to each other.
- Look for clues in prefixes, suffixes, and roots.
- When guessing, narrow down answer choices to two opposites if possible.

UNDERLINE OR CIRCLE REVERSAL WORDS—NOT AND OPPOSITE

When reading an antonym question, always underline or circle the reversal word *not* or *opposite*. This won't take any time, since your pencil is already in hand and should be pointing at the question. Underlining the reversal word will help your brain resist the temptation of choosing a word similar to the word prompt. This is an easy mistake to make but also an easy one to avoid.

LOOK FOR THE OPPOSITE

You are looking for the opposite of the word prompt. If the true opposite is not an answer choice, you must find one that is closest to its opposite. For example, if the word prompt is *hot* then you will be looking for the word *cold*. If *cold* is not an answer choice, you have to find a word that is the furthest away in temperature relative to the other answer choices:

➡ Example 1 _____

Hot means the *opposite* of

- (a) warm.
- (b) scalding.
- (c) tepid.
- (d) boiling.

The true opposite, *cold*, is not an answer choice. In this case, you must look for the word that is closest to the opposite, which is choice (c) *tepid.*

As with synonyms, let's look at the three word types and learn how best to find the correct antonym for each.

WORDS YOU KNOW WELL

Once you have read the question and underlined or circled the reversal word, you should get the *opposite* word in your head *before* looking at your answer choices. If you skip this step, you may be tempted to choose the synonym. This is surprisingly easy to do when taking a timed test. Let's see how this works.

➡ Example 2 _____

Meager means the *opposite* of

- (a) sparse.
- (b) shy.
- (c) abundant.
- (d) subtle.

Meager means to be scant or *sparse*. Think of word that means the opposite of *sparse*. It doesn't have to be a vocabulary word necessarily but just anything that gets the opposite idea in your head. Maybe you are thinking of *a lot of something*. Now when you look at the answer choices, you are not searching for *meager*, or even its antonym, but rather a word that means *a lot of something.*

Notice one of the answer choices is *sparse*. If you rush through this question, it will be very easy for you to accidentally jump to the word *sparse*, which of course is the synonym and not the antonym. The word that most nearly means *a lot of something* is choice (c) *abundant.*

WORDS YOU RECOGNIZE BUT CANNOT DEFINE

If you recognize the prompt word, then you're off to a good start. If you don't quite know the meaning of the word, you'll have to rely on the answer choices to guide you. Let's look at Example 2 again, only this time we'll assume that you don't know the meaning of the word *meager.* This question is going to be a little more difficult, but it is still entirely possible to select the correct answer. In the example below, there is a line through the prompt word to show that you don't know its meaning.

➡ Example 3

Meager means the *opposite* of

(a) sparse.
(b) shy.
(c) abundant.
(d) subtle.

What do you notice about the answer choices? *Sparse* and *subtle* are similar, so you should rule out both of these. Now you have narrowed it down to *shy* or *abundant* and have greatly increased your odds of correctly guessing the answer. In this example, the correct answer is choice (c) *abundant.*

LOOK FOR ROOTS, PREFIXES, OR SUFFIXES FOR CLUES

If you recognize the prompt word but cannot find the answer, then try looking for roots, prefixes, or suffixes. For example, the word incredible has the prefix *in–*, which means *not.* It may be that you think *incredible* means awesome or wonderful and cannot find the correct answer choice. However, if you look at the prefix and root this knowledge will help.

➡ Example 4

Incredible means the *opposite* of

(a) trustworthy.
(b) plausible.
(c) inconceivable.
(d) untenable.

Knowing that the prefix, *in–*, means *not*, you can figure out that the word *incredible* means *not* something. If you know that the root *cred* means believable, then you are all set; but if you do not, you can still get the correct answer. Choice (a) *trustworthy*, doesn't seem to be a word that means *not* something. Answer choices (c) and (d) both have *in–* or *un–* for prefixes, so they may be synonyms to *incredible* and not antonyms. At this point, you are safe to choose the correct answer is choice (b) *plausible* (even if you don't know that plausible means believable, which is the opposite of *incredible*).

You will have to resist the temptation to choose answers that you know are different from the prompt word but may NOT be an antonym.

➡ Example 5

Inconspicuous is the *opposite* of

(a) evil.
(b) invisible.
(c) noticeable.
(d) faint.

You may not know the exact definition of *inconspicuous*, but if you realize that *invisible* means something different from *inconspicuous*, you are correct. *Inconspicuous* means to be hidden or camouflaged. *Invisible* is different from *inconspicuous*, because it means unable to be seen. However, *invisible* is not the opposite of *inconspicuous*. The better answer is choice (c) *noticeable*. Make sure you look at each answer choice carefully before choosing. Do not select an answer choice that is simply different but one that is the *opposite* of the word prompt.

WORDS YOU HAVE NEVER SEEN

If you are given a prompt word you have never seen before, you will have to make a guess. You can eliminate answer choices the same way you did with synonyms. Rule out any answer choices that are similar to each other. Try to narrow down you answer choices to two opposites.

Eliminate any answer choices that you can, trust your instinct, choose an answer and move on. There will be easier questions ahead.

Antonyms Practice

Now that you've learned some helpful strategies for answering the antonym questions, let's practice. If you come across words that are unfamiliar, add them to your vocabulary list.

1. Estrange is the *opposite* of

    (a) alienate.
    (b) unite.
    (c) withdraw.
    (d) separate.

2. An ailment is *not* a(n)

    (a) malady.
    (b) illness.
    (c) complaint.
    (d) strength.

3. Congenial is the *opposite* of

    (a) pleasant.
    (b) kind.
    (c) unfriendly.
    (d) consistent.

4. Prolific does *not* mean

    (a) productive.
    (b) barren.
    (c) bountiful.
    (d) abundant.

5. Debilitate is the *opposite* of

    (a) enable.
    (b) ignore.
    (c) cripple.
    (d) exhaust.

6. Diligent is the *opposite* of

    (a) attentive.
    (b) studious.
    (c) careless.
    (d) eager.

7. Vitality is *not* a(n)

    (a) energy.
    (b) idleness.
    (c) spunk.
    (d) life.

8. Brisk is the *opposite* of

    (a) slow.
    (b) fast.
    (c) cold.
    (d) active.

9. Bleak does *not* mean

    (a) barren.

    (b) empty.

    (c) abundant.

    (d) sad.

10. Alleviate is the *opposite* of

    (a) lighten.

    (b) find.

    (c) ease.

    (d) burden.

(Answers are on page 80.)

ANALOGIES

An analogy is a relationship shared by two pairs of words. There will be 9–10 analogy questions as part of the Verbal Skills subtest, with each having the same format. Analogy questions on the HSPT have only one-word answer choices. See below for an example.

➡ Example 1 _____

Paint is to brush as sweep is to

    (a) floor.

    (b) broom.

    (c) dirt.

    (d) wind.

Your goal with analogy questions is to determine the relationship that exists between the first two words and then use that relationship to find the word that belongs with the prompt. In Example 1, you know a brush is used to paint in the same way a broom is used to sweep, so the answer is choice (b) *broom*. There are a variety of relationships in analogy questions. Before we look at each, let's go over some general strategies for analogies.

General Strategies for Analogies

Many of the analogies will be easy for you to figure out, and you won't need anyone's advice on how to answer these correctly. An example of an easy analogy would be "boy is to man as girl is to _____." The word that belongs in the blank is *woman*. If you come across a simple analogy like this, don't be nervous—just take the easy point. There will definitely be one or two of these on the HSPT. It is the more difficult analogy questions where a good strategy can help.

MAKE A CONNECTION

When faced with a more challenging analogy question, you should first make your own sentence that forms a connection between the first pair of words. Each analogy will have the words "is to" between the first pair of words, as in the following example.

➡ Example 2_____

Finger is to hand as toe is to

    (a) leg.

    (b) foot.

    (c) ankle.

    (d) shoe.

Use the steps below to answer this question, along with other analogy questions.

- Cross out the words "is to" and replace them with words that will make a sentence to explain the relationship between finger and hand. Finger *is part of a* hand.
- Next, make a new sentence by replacing the first word of your sentence with the first word in the next pair: "Toe *is part of a* _____."
- Before you look at your answer choices, think of a word that would make that sentence perfect. In this case, you would be thinking of "foot."
- Look at your answer choices to see which word is the same or closest to the one you have in mind and that works with your sentence. "Toe *is part of a* foot." The correct answer is choice (b) *foot.*

MAKE A STRONGER CONNECTION

If there is more than one answer choice that works with your sentence, you'll have to find a more specific sentence and try again. The stronger your connection is, the easier it will be to find the correct answer choice.

➡ Example 3_____

Hand is to finger as foot is to

(a) toe.
(b) nail.
(c) heel.
(d) shoe.

Example 3 is similar to Example 2; however, you'll notice the sentence that you used for Example 2, will not work here. Hand and finger have been switched. If you tried the sentence "finger is part of a hand" then plugged in your answer choices into the new sentence "_____ *is part of a* foot," you'll find there are three answers that work. If you come across this situation, try a more specific sentence. "A hand *has five* fingers." Now only one answer choice is going to work. "A foot *has five* toes."

ANALOGIES HAVE DIRECTION

Analogies have direction, so keep that in mind when looking for your answer. "Finger is to hand" is very different than "hand is to finger." You must keep the same direction in both of your sentences.

GRAMMAR MATTERS

The part of speech, or type of word, (noun, verb, adjective, etc.) plays an important role in analogies. If the prompt is *foot* is to *running*, you have to look for a word pair that has a *noun* first and *verb* last.

WORK BACKWARDS

If you don't understand one of the words in the first pair, you will have difficulty making a connection between them. In this case, you can work backwards by first making a connection between an answer choice and the word prompt. You may be able to rule out some answer choices by doing this.

➡ Example 4_____

~~Excerpt~~ is to whole as piece is to

(a) test.
(b) puzzle.
(c) exclusion.
(d) vital.

Excerpt is crossed out to show that this is a word that you've never seen. You will not be able to make a connection between *excerpt* and *whole*, so instead look at the word *piece* and the answer choices. Try to make a connection there. The word that makes sense is *piece*, "a *piece* of the puzzle." The correct connection here is excerpt is *part of* the whole the same as piece *is part of* a puzzle. Don't give up if you don't know a word.

VERB TENSE

You must also keep the same verb tense in an analogy. "Foot is to kick" does not work with "fist is to punching," but it would work with "fist is to punch."

Analogy Relationships

If you have a strong vocabulary and use the General Strategies for Antonyms, you'll have an advantage with these questions. In Chapter 3, you learned how to improve your vocabulary, so now let's get familiar with all of the possible analogy relationships that you may have to decipher. We'll examine each type of analogy relationship. Each description is followed by an example to help you familiarize yourself with the various analogy relationships you will see on the Verbal Skills subtest.

ANTONYMS

In antonym analogies, you will be given two words that mean the opposite of each other. You then have to find the opposite, the antonym, of the word prompt. Form the description or the definition of the word you are looking for *before* you check the answer choices.

➡ Example 5_____

Hot is to cold as quick is to

(a) warm.
(b) icy.
(c) slow.
(d) fast.

The correct answer is choice (c) *slow*. Hot *is the opposite of* cold. Quick *is the opposite of* slow.

SYNONYMS

Synonym analogies involve words that are similar in meaning. You won't have to make a sentence for these. Once you've identified that it is a synonym analogy, all you have to do is find the word that is closest in meaning to the word prompt. As with antonyms, form a definition in your mind *before* you check the answer choices.

➡ Example 6

Lethargic is to listless as energetic is to

(a) tired.
(b) active.
(c) deadly.
(d) slow.

Lethargic means to lack energy. *Listless* means the same thing, so you are dealing with a synonym analogy. You must find a word that means the same as *energetic*. The word or words you have in mind may be *to be full of energy*. Now look at your answer choices and find the word that means *to be full of energy*. The correct answer is choice (b) *active*.

EXTREMES

In extreme synonyms, you are looking for words that may have similar meanings but are in different extremes, for example warm and hot, run and sprint, etc.

➡ Example 7

Pink is to red as gray is to

(a) red.
(b) light.
(c) black.
(d) dark.

Remember that analogies have direction. For example, "Pink is to red" would *not* work with "black is to gray." Pink is a light red, but black is not a light gray. The correct answer is choice (c) *black*. Pink *is a light shade of* red and gray *is a light shade of* black.

CHARACTERISTIC/PERSONALITY

In this type of analogy, you will be given a relationship in which one word is a noun and the other is an adjective describing that noun, such as "comedian is to funny" or "ghost is to scary." When you read the word prompt, remember to finish the sentence in your head before looking at the answer choices.

➡ Example 8

Slow is to turtle as wise is to

- (a) owl.
- (b) elephant.
- (c) eagle.
- (d) rabbit.

The correct answer is choice (a) *owl.* A turtle *has a reputation of being* slow and an owl *has a reputation of being* wise.

CAUSE AND EFFECT

These can encompass many topics; for example, "vitamin is to health," "swim is to wet," "cold is to freeze," etc. Answer choices may not always be exact, so remember to cross out any answer choices that don't make sense. This way if you have to guess, you will have a better chance of choosing the correct answer.

➡ Example 9

Clumsy is to accident as organized is to

- (a) order.
- (b) neatly.
- (c) clutter.
- (d) expensive.

Clumsy *people tend to have* accidents and organized *people tend to have* (looking for a noun) *order,* choice (a).

EFFECT AND CAUSE

This is very similar to the above analogy type; however, the effect will be given before the cause. So remember that "ice is to cold" would not work with "warm is to melt." Make sure you keep the same relationship and direction in each word pair. Cause and effect cannot be paired with effect and cause and vice versa.

➡ Example 10

Ice is to freeze as steam is to

- (a) heat.
- (b) stove.
- (c) boil.
- (d) cook.

The correct answer is choice (c) *boil.* Ice *is caused by* freezing and steam *is caused by* boiling. *Freeze* is the verb that means to create *ice,* and *boil* is the verb that means to create *steam.*

PROFESSION

You may see examples that involve occupations. Instructors teach, waitresses serve, fortune tellers predict, etc. Remember to keep the same grammar. For example, "teacher is to student" cannot be paired with "leader is to lead." A teacher teaches a student, but a leader doesn't lead a lead. To make this correct, one of the relationships would have to be changed to "a teacher teaches a student" and "a leader leads a follower."

➡ Example 11 _____

Plumber is to pipes as electrician is to

(a) house.
(b) wires.
(c) tools.
(d) heat.

The correct answer is choice is (b) *wires*. A plumber *is a professional that works with* pipes and an electrician *is a professional who works with* electrical wires. They both use tools, may work in a house, and a plumber may work on heating systems, but none of these answer choices works with the same sentence structure.

SEQUENCE

You may see a sequence or a relationship that exists between days of the week, months of the year, or numbers. Five is to four as May is to April, for example. The sentence connecting these could be "four is the number before five" and "April is the month before May."

➡ Example 12 _____

February is to April as Tuesday is to

(a) weekday.
(b) Friday.
(c) Thursday.
(d) Monday.

The correct answer is choice (c) *Thursday. There is one month between* February and April just as *there is one day between* Tuesday and Thursday. Keep in mind that sentences have to have the same relationship but don't have to use all of the same words. For example, "Monday is to Tuesday as January is to February." The sentence for this would be "Monday is the *day* before Tuesday just as January is the *month* before February."

USE

Use analogies have to do with how one person, object, or group of objects uses something. A pencil uses lead, a chef may use flour, a candle uses wax, etc. Keep in mind that direction and grammar are important. "Envelope is to letter" does not work with "money is to wallet"; however, it would work with "wallet is to money."

➡ Example 13_____

Electricity is to lamp as oil is to

(a) television.
(b) furnace.
(c) peanut.
(d) can.

Electricity *is the fuel that powers a* lamp and oil *is the fuel that powers a* furnace. The correct answer is choice (b) *furnace.*

PART IS TO WHOLE

Many analogies involve parts of things. They may have to do with objects, people, or locations. A donut is part of a dozen, a classroom is made up of students, a murder is a group of crows, atoms grouped together are molecules, etc. See the following example.

➡ Example 14_____

Knuckle is to finger as knee is to

(a) ankle.
(b) shin.
(c) joint.
(d) leg.

The correct answer is choice (d) *leg.* A knuckle *is the middle part of the* finger and the knee *is the middle part of the* leg. If there is more than one correct answer (such as shin), then make the sentence more specific. A knuckle *is the part of the* finger *that bends* and the knee *is the part of the* leg *that bends.* Now you can see that there is only one right answer choice.

WHOLE IS TO PART

Relationships in analogies have to be consistent, so Part is to Whole is different from Whole is to Part. Here is an example.

➡ Example 15_____

Pack is to wolf as school is to

(a) zebra.
(b) fish.
(c) teacher.
(d) tiger.

The correct answer is choice (b) *fish. A group of* wolves *is called a* pack and *a group of* fish *is called a* school.

Analogies Practice

You've learned about several different types of analogy questions in this chapter. Now take a few minutes to try some on your own. Use the strategy of making a sentence with the prompt words. Then check your answers and read the explanations for any that you did not answer correctly or found to be difficult. The explanations can give you valuable tips that will help you with other verbal skills questions.

1. Vaccine is to disease as sunblock is to

   (a) sun.
   (b) tan.
   (c) sunburn.
   (d) skin.

2. Dig is to hole as sew is to

   (a) thread.
   (b) tear.
   (c) seam.
   (d) needle.

3. Fan is to zealot as hobbyist is to

   (a) intermediate.
   (b) beginner.
   (c) toddler.
   (d) expert.

4. Ocean is to lobster as ranch is to

   (a) cow.
   (b) beef.
   (c) rodeo.
   (d) dogs.

5. Monday is to Wednesday as August is to

   (a) month.
   (b) summer.
   (c) June.
   (d) October.

6. Water is to liquid as ice is to

   (a) cold.
   (b) cube.
   (c) wet.
   (d) solid.

7. Concur is to agree as debate is to

   (a) argue.
   (b) list.
   (c) criticize.
   (d) appease.

8. Towel is to dry as broom is to

   (a) straw.
   (b) sweep.
   (c) dirt.
   (d) floor.

9. Donkey is to stubborn as sloth is to

   (a) wet.
   (b) gross.
   (c) slow.
   (d) tall.

10. Strong is to durable as weak is to

    (a) feeble.
    (b) bleak.
    (c) calm.
    (d) lanky.

(Answers are on page 81.)

VERBAL LOGIC

The Verbal Logic questions are the most unique of the questions on the HSPT. Most students who do not prepare for this test will be surprised to see these questions and may be unsure of how to approach them. There are about 12 of these out of the 60 questions in the Verbal Skills subtest. The good news is that all of the information you need to answer these correctly is in the question. You just need time and a good note-taking method. You've already learned several strategies that will help you to be efficient with your time in this subtest so now let's focus on some good note-taking skills that will help you answer all of the logic questions correctly.

For each of these questions, the directions are part of the question. You will first read three sentences explaining a specific situation, and then the fourth and final sentence reads as follows: "If the first two statements are true, the third is . . . ."

Most verbal logic questions involve comparisons or reasoning. Occasionally a question may involve specific numbers. We'll look at each separately and review examples of each.

TIP

Since the 4th sentence is always the same for logic questions, read only the first 3 sentences to save time.

TIP

On your answer sheet, you will have answer bubbles for choices (a)–(d), so make sure you never guess (d) on Verbal Logic questions.

General Strategies for Verbal Logic

The answer choices are always the same for this type of question. This is the only question type on the HSPT that has three choices, which therefore increases your chances of answering correctly. The answer choices are: (a) true, (b) false, and (c) uncertain.

Once you learn about this type of question, you will not have to read the fourth statement because it is always the same. Read the first three sentences and then look at your notes to select the correct answer. When practicing, remember the answer choices are always in the same order.

PRACTICE MAKES PERFECT

It is important to practice this type of question. There is no reason to get these questions wrong, because you don't actually have to know anything to answer them correctly—no vocabulary, no math formulas, nothing. All of the information you need is right in the question—you just have to practice!

MAKE NOTES FOR VERBAL LOGIC QUESTIONS

As with other question types in the Verbal Skills subtest, there will be some verbal logic questions that you find to be easy. Practice will help you to know the difference between questions that require notes and those that you can answer without notes.

The best strategy for the logic questions is to make notes as you read the problem and remember not to waste time reading the last statement because it is always the same. When you read the first two sentences, you should make a diagram with the information because they are the facts and are always true. The third sentence may or may not be true, and it is your task to decide. Let's look at three examples of comparisons.

COMPARISONS WHERE THE THIRD SENTENCE IS TRUE

For questions with a correct answer of (a) *true*, you will be able to put your notes in just one line as shown in the following example.

➡ Example 1 _____

Karyn can shuck corn faster than Debbie. Debbie can shuck corn faster than Wendy. Karyn can shuck corn faster than Wendy. If the first two statements are true, the third is

(a) true.
(b) false.
(c) uncertain.

Use the first initial, to save time. If more than one person or thing in the question has the same first initial, then use the first two letters of the name. The first sentence is "Karyn can shuck corn faster than Debbie." Let's write a note that shows this relationship (Karyn = K, Debbie = D, W = Wendy).

$$K - D$$

You don't have to use the < or > symbols if you find them confusing. You are just trying to get a visual of the relationship of the three statements. Just remember that the fastest person is on the left.

The second sentence states that Debbie is faster than Wendy. Because Debbie is already in the first sentence and we are referring to Debbie again, we can keep the sentence going.

$$\textbf{K} - D - \textbf{W}$$
Fastest → Slowest

It should now be easy to see from our notes that K *must be* faster than Wendy. The correct answer is choice (a) *true*. You can see by the bold letters that Karyn is to the left of (faster than) Wendy. The question and the notes are summarized in the table below.

Sentence	Note
Karyn can shuck corn faster than Debbie.	K – D
Debbie can shuck corn faster than Wendy.	K – D – W
Karyn can shuck corn faster than Wendy.	K – D – W
Third sentence is . . .	True

COMPARISONS WHERE THE THIRD SENTENCE IS FALSE

For questions with a correct answer of (b) *false*, you will also be able to put your notes in just one line as shown in the following example. You will see when looking at your notes that the third sentence must be false.

➡ Example 2_____

Karyn can shuck corn faster than Pam. Pam can shuck corn faster than Donna. Donna can shuck corn faster than Karyn. If the first two statements are true, the third is

(a) true.
(b) false.
(c) uncertain.

Let K = Karyn, D = Donna, and P = Pam. We start out with sentence one, "Karyn can shuck corn faster than Pam."

$$K - P$$

In the second sentence, we learn that Pam is faster than Donna. Here is what our notes look like now:

$$K - P - D$$
Fastest → Slowest

The last statement says that Donna is faster than Karyn, but since Donna and Karyn are on the same line, we can easily see that this statement cannot be true. The correct answer is choice (b) *false*. Here is a table summarizing Example 2.

Sentence	Note
Karyn can shuck corn faster than Pam.	K – P
Pam can shuck corn faster than Donna.	K – P – D
Donna can shuck corn faster than Karyn.	K – P – D
Third sentence is . . .	False

COMPARISONS WHERE THE THIRD SENTENCE IS UNCERTAIN

These can often be the most difficult of the logic questions. When the third sentence is *uncertain*, you'll find that you cannot put the information on just one line without duplication.

➡ Example 3_____

Kim can shuck corn faster than Pam. Donna can shuck corn faster than Pam. Kim can shuck corn faster than Donna. If the first two statements are true, the third is

(a) true.
(b) false.
(c) uncertain.

Let K = Kim, P = Pam, and D = Donna. Looking at the first sentence, we see that Kim is faster than Pam.

$$K - P$$

In the second sentence, we learn that Donna is faster than Pam, but we don't know if she is faster than Kim. When you are unsure of where to put a note, you should put it in two places as shown below.

$$_D K _D - P$$
Fastest → Slowest

Here we see that Donna could be faster or slower than Kim (shown on either side of Kim) because either way, she will be faster than Pam. Since you don't know if Donna is faster or slower than Kim, the correct answer is choice (c) *uncertain*. Below is the summary table for Example 3.

Sentence	Note
Kim can shuck corn faster than Pam.	K – P
Donna can shuck corn faster than Pam.	D K D – P
Kim can shuck corn faster than Donna.	D K D – P
Third sentence is . . .	Uncertain

REASONING LOGIC QUESTIONS

Another type of a Verbal Logic question involves reasoning rather than comparisons. There are only a couple of these on the HSPT, but it will help your score if you practice them here.

➡ Example 4

All kids in Girl Scouts went to the parade. Jill did not go to the parade. Jill is not a Girl Scout. If the first two statements are true, the third is

(a) true.
(b) false.
(c) uncertain.

We don't need a drawing for this type, just a quiet setting and concentration. The question states that ALL kids in Girl Scouts went to the parade. That means that if someone is a Girl Scout, then she definitely went to the parade. The next sentence states that Jill did not go. If Jill was a Girl Scout, she would have been there, so Jill must not be a Girl Scout. The correct answer is then choice (a) *true*. Let's try one more like this.

➡ Example 5

All kids in Girl Scouts went to the parade. Jill went to the parade. Jill is a Girl Scout. If the first two statements are true, the third is

(a) true.
(b) false.
(c) uncertain.

Can you see how this question is different from Example 4? This question states that *all* kids in Girl Scouts went to the parade. If Jill was at the parade, it only means that she *could* be a Girl Scout. It may be there were other people, besides the Girl Scouts, who were at the parade, making the correct answer choice (c) *uncertain*.

OVERLAPPING

Another type of Verbal Logic question that you may see is one with overlapping time frames.

➡ Example 6

In Maine, it snowed five days last week. Larry walks to work in Maine five days each week. Larry walked to work in the snow at least three days last week. If the first two statements are true, the third is

(a) true.
(b) false.
(c) uncertain.

To solve this type of question, you should make a note showing the time frame involved. Take the first condition (snow) and start that at the earliest possible time (Sunday) and count forward for the number of days given (five). Take the second condition (Larry walking to work) and start that on the last day and count back the number of days that were given (five). You can see from the diagram below that they must overlap at *least three days*. It is possible that they overlap for five days, but they have to overlap at least three days of the week.

	1	2	3	4	5		
Snow:	Sun –	Mon –	Tues –	Wed –	Thu		
Larry:			Tues –	Wed –	Thu –	Fri –	Sat
			5	4	3	2	1

NUMERICAL QUESTIONS

There is one last type of Verbal Logic question that occasionally appears on the HSPT. At most there will be one of these, and they can be solved by plugging in your own numbers.

➡ Example 7

Mr. Pingry has 8 more plants in his garden than Mrs. Hastings. Mrs. Monroe has 5 more plants in her garden than Mr. Pingry. Mrs. Hastings has 10 fewer plants than Mrs. Monroe. If the first two statements are true, the third is

(a) true.
(b) false.
(c) uncertain.

To answer this, simply make up your own number for the first person and figure out the rest as you go. Let's begin with Mr. Pingry. Let's say that he has 10 plants (put a 10 above his name). Since he has 8 more than Mrs. Hastings, that means that Mrs. Hastings has 2 plants (so write the number 2 above Mrs. Hastings). Mrs. Monroe has 5 more plants than Mr. Pingry, so she must have 15 plants. Now you know that Mrs. Monroe has 13 more plants than Mrs. Hastings, the third sentence must be choice (b) *false*.

You are now familiar with the various types of Verbal Logic questions that you will see on the Verbal Skills subtest. Now practice a few on your own. Take your time. Remember that everything you need to answer them correctly is right in the question, so if you take your time you should be able to answer them all perfectly.

Verbal Logic Practice

1. Sparky is older than Sunny. Spike is younger than Sunny. Sparky is older than Spike. If the first two statements are true, the third is

   (a) true.
   (b) false.
   (c) uncertain.

2. Ann has been dancing longer than Denise. Bob has been dancing longer than Denise. Bob has been dancing longer than Ann. If the first two statements are true, the third is

   (a) true.
   (b) false.
   (c) uncertain.

3. All of the students in statistics class have an iPad. Chris does not have an iPad. Chris is a student in the statistics class. If the first two statements are true, the third is

   (a) true.
   (b) false.
   (c) uncertain.

4. Mrs. Joyce teaches a ballet dance class five days a week. Mrs. Joyce teaches a tap dance class four days a week. Mrs. Joyce teaches two different dance classes at least two days a week. If the first two statements are true, the third is

   (a) true.
   (b) false.
   (c) uncertain.

5. Mrs. Philips has more windows in her house than Mrs. Rama. Mrs. Rama has fewer windows in her house than Mrs. Carleton. Mrs. Philips has more windows than Mrs. Carleton. If the first two statements are true, the third is

   (a) true.
   (b) false.
   (c) uncertain.

6. Kate weighs more than Toby or Randall. Jack weighs more than Randall. Toby weighs more than Jack. If the first two statements are true, the third is

   (a) true.
   (b) false.
   (c) uncertain.

7. All of the houses on Creamery Street are white. Bruce and Diana live in a beige house. Bruce and Diana live on Creamery Street. If the first two statements are true, the third is

   (a) true.
   (b) false.
   (c) uncertain.

8. Kyle has more CDs than Ben. Randy has fewer CDs than Ben. Randy has fewer CDs than Kyle. If the first two statements are true, the third is

   (a) true.
   (b) false.
   (c) uncertain.

9. The biology test has 3 more questions than the chemistry test. The math test has 7 more questions than the chemistry test. The math test has 4 more questions than the biology test. If the first two statements are true, the third is

   (a) true.
   (b) false.
   (c) uncertain.

10. Olivia attended St. Mary's High School longer than Kristen. Kristen attended St. Mary's High School longer than Grace. Grace attended St. Mary's High School longer than Olivia. If the first two statements are true, the third is

    (a) true.
    (b) false.
    (c) uncertain.

(Answers are on page 81.)

VERBAL CLASSIFICATIONS

Verbal Classifications are the most common type of question on the Verbal Skills subtest. You can expect to see about 17 of these questions. Each will begin with the prompt, "Which word does *not* belong with the others?" The answer choices will be four single words. Your task is to find the one word that does not belong with the others. Sometimes all four answer choices will have something in common, so you will have to identify the one that is somehow different.

As with the other types of questions, your strong vocabulary is going to help you here. If you know what the four words mean, you will have a significant advantage in choosing the word that doesn't belong. Verbal Classification questions will include vocabulary words that are verbs, adjectives, and nouns. There is another type of verbal classification where three of the answer choices belong together and are part of the fourth answer choice, such as: elephant, giraffe, lion, animals. Clearly, the first three are part of the fourth. These are not so much vocabulary questions as they are reasoning and deduction questions. You will likely see only one or two at most of these questions on the Verbal Skills subtest.

Classification Type	Number of Questions
Nouns	1–2
Adjectives	8–10
Verbs	5–6
Three are part of the fourth	1–2

ADJECTIVES, VERBS, AND NOUNS

The majority of the verbal classification questions involve only vocabulary words. If you know the meaning of each word (and that may not always be the case), you will have no difficulty finding the one word that does not belong. If the answer is not obvious to you right away, try these simple steps to identify the correct answer choice:

- Define each word and write the description next to the answer; keep it short and simple, so you don't waste too much time.
- Look at your descriptions and try to see what they have in common.
- If you still don't find a connection, make your descriptions more specific.
- If you can't find anything in common, make a guess and move on.

➡ Example 1. Adjectives _____

Which word does *not* belong with the others?

(a) unique
(b) specific
(c) conventional
(d) distinct

Remember you are looking for the word that does *not* belong with the other three, so find what the words have in common. Even if you only know two of the words in the choices, that may be enough for you to choose the correct answer. *Unique* means one of a kind and *distinct* means specific or unmistakable, so they belong together. It should be clear now that those three words, *unique*, *specific*, and *distinct*, are all similar. Even if you don't know what *conventional* means, you can still safely choose (c) *conventional* as the correct answer. *Conventional* means traditional or ordinary.

➡ Example 2. Verbs

Which word does *not* belong with the others?

(a) jump
(b) hop
(c) skip
(d) slide

Here we have a question that involves verbs. *Jump*, *hop*, and *skip* are all things you do with your feet; however, the first three involve moving your body up and down as you do when you jump. *Slide* is the only verb that is done while either sitting or lying down, so the correct answer is choice (d) *slide*.

MAKE A SENTENCE

If you come across a question that is more challenging or one where there may seem to be more than one correct answer choice, try to make a sentence using three of the answer choices. For example: "A *pen*, *pencil*, and *marker* are all things you use to write."

➡ Example 3. Verbs

Which word does *not* belong with the others?

(a) taint
(b) mar
(c) restore
(d) tarnish

In this example, the correct answer is choice (c) *restore*. The other answer choices are all verbs that involve destroying something in some way. *Restore* is the opposite, and therefore does not belong. Putting answer choices in a sentence is helpful. "If I *taint*, *mar*, or *tarnish* something, then I am ruining it but if I *restore* it, then I am fixing it." If you are uncertain of the meaning of one or more of the answer choices, putting them into a sentence may help you find the one that doesn't belong.

➡ Example 4. Nouns

Which word does *not* belong with the others?

(a) fallacy
(b) deceit
(c) misconception
(d) reality

A *fallacy* and a *misconception* are both untruths. *Deceit* is an intentional untruth. The only word that is different is *reality*. The correct answer is choice (d).

DON'T OVERTHINK IT—CHOOSE THE MOST OBVIOUS

You may also see noun questions that involve objects such as animals or food items where you will have to have some knowledge of the objects to answer the question.

➡ Example 5. Nouns

Which word does *not* belong with the others?

(a) pumpkin
(b) squash
(c) orange
(d) broccoli

If you know your fruits and vegetables, you'll realize that orange is the only fruit in the answer choices. The correct answer is choice (c) *orange*. These questions are typically very easy if you don't overthink them. Always look for the obvious commonality among the answer choices. You may consider the answer to be *broccoli* because it is the only green item, but *squash* can also be green.

THREE ARE PART OF THE FOURTH

Another type of word classification that you may see on the HSPT is one where three of the answer choices represent parts of the fourth. These are less common; at most, you may have one or two of these questions, but they can be easy if you recognize them.

➡ Example 6

Which word does *not* belong with the others?

(a) run
(b) walk
(c) exercise
(d) swim

At first glance, you can see that these all have something in common, but you have to choose that one that doesn't belong. Running, walking, and swimming are all forms of exercise, so the correct answer choice here is (c) *exercise*. The answer is the category.

➡ Example 7

Which word does *not* belong with the others?

(a) baseball
(b) sports
(c) football
(d) soccer

You can see that these all have something in common. *Baseball, football,* and *soccer* are all types of sports so the correct answer is choice (b) *sports*.

Verbal Classifications Practice

Now it's time for you to try some Verbal Classification questions on your own.

1. Which word does *not* belong with the others?

   (a) reticent
   (b) shy
   (c) timid
   (d) talkative

2. Which word does *not* belong with the others?

   (a) diminish
   (b) augment
   (c) improve
   (d) amplify

3. Which word does *not* belong with the others?

   (a) shepherd
   (b) labrador
   (c) dog
   (d) poodle

4. Which word does *not* belong with the others?

   (a) vacant
   (b) empty
   (c) occupied
   (d) deserted

5. Which word does *not* belong with the others?

   (a) weary
   (b) rejuvenate
   (c) stimulate
   (d) invigorate

6. Which word does *not* belong with the others?

   (a) prolific
   (b) abundant
   (c) ample
   (d) reclusive

7. Which word does *not* belong with the others?

   (a) incensed
   (b) loathe
   (c) harmonious
   (d) irate

8. Which word does *not* belong with the others?

   (a) window
   (b) shade
   (c) drape
   (d) curtain

9. Which word does *not* belong with the others?

   (a) piano
   (b) guitar
   (c) violin
   (d) drum

10. Which word does *not* belong with the others?

    (a) car
    (b) airplane
    (c) train
    (d) bus

(Answers are on page 82.)

ANSWERS EXPLAINED FOR CHAPTER 4

Synonyms (page 57)

1. **(c)** *Adverse* means to be *opposing*. An adversary is a rival. Notice that the other three answer choices are all positive in meaning.

2. **(b)** An oration is a speech, and an *orator* is one who speaks. Oral means to be *of the mouth*. If you know this, you can narrow it down to *orator*.

3. **(c)** *Stealthy* means to be cautious, not seen or heard. The answer that is closest is *quiet*.

4. **(d)** To *resume* is to pick up where you left off or to *continue*.

5. **(a)** *Culminate* means to end or to *finish. Commence* and *begin* are synonyms, and so these can each be eliminated.

6. **(c)** *Animate* means to bring to life or to *enliven*. If you recognize the root *anim*, you may know that it means life. This will help you to know that the meaning of the word must have to do with life.

7. **(a)** Here is an example of a word that you may recognize although you may not know what it means. Remember the context if you've heard the word before. Maybe in history class you learned that President Lincoln *abolished* slavery. This should be enough for you to rule out the other answer choices and narrow your answer to an *activist*, one who makes a change.

8. **(a)** If you don't know what *vile* means, you can still find the correct answer by knowing that it is a negative word. Then you can eliminate *strong* and *amiable*, and you've narrowed your choices to just two. *Vile* means to be *disgusting*.

9. **(b)** *Modify* means to *change*.

10. **(d)** *Diction* means a type of speech. The root *dic* means to say or to tell. The only answer choice that has to do with speech is *articulate*. You may notice that *peruse* and *read* are very similar to each other in meaning and therefore can both be eliminated.

Antonyms (pages 61–62)

1. **(b)** *Estrange* is to disunite or to destroy a relationship. This is similar to *withdraw* or *alienate. Unite* is the opposite.

2. **(d)** An *ailment* is a negative condition, a sickness. A *malady* is a synonym of *ailment*. The opposite must be positive, making the answer *strength*.

3. **(c)** *Congenial* means *pleasant* or friendly. The opposite of friendly is *unfriendly*.

4. **(b)** *Prolific* is an adjective meaning to be fruitful or *productive. Abundant* and *bountiful* are similar in meaning. *Barren* means unable to be fruitful and is the opposite of *prolific*.

5. **(a)** *Debilitate* is a verb that means to incapacitate or disable. The opposite of this is to *enable. Cripple* and *exhaust* are similar in meaning while *ignore* is unrelated.

6. **(c)** *Diligent* means to be hard-working. The opposite would be to be *careless. Studious*, and *attentive* are similar in meaning while *eager* is also a positive word.

7. **(b)** *Vitality* means *energy*. The opposite of that would be lack of *energy*. The word that is closest is *idleness*. The other choices are all about having *energy*.

8. **(a)** *Brisk* means to be *active*. The opposite would be idle or *slow*. Sometimes *brisk* is used to refer to the weather being *cold*.

9. **(c)** *Bleak* means to be *barren* or depressing. *Bleak* is a negative word just as *barren*, *empty*, and *sad*. *Abundant* is the only positive word.

10. **(d)** *Alleviate* means to *lighten* or to make less. The opposite of this is *burden*.

Analogies (page 69)

1. **(c)** This is a use analogy. A *vaccine* is used to prevent a *disease* the same as *sunblock* is used to prevent a *sunburn*.

2. **(c)** This is a cause-and-effect analogy. If you *dig* you will make a *hole* and if you *sew* you will make a *seam*.

3. **(d)** This is an extreme analogy. A *zealot* is an extreme or serious *fan* and an *expert* is an extreme *hobbyist*.

4. **(a)** This is an example of a whole-is-to-part analogy. The *ocean* is home for *lobsters* and a *ranch* is home for *cows*.

5. **(d)** This is a sequence analogy. *Monday* is two days before *Wednesday* just as *August* is two months before *October*. You could also say there is a day between *Monday* and *Wednesday* just as there is a month between *August* and *October*.

6. **(d)** This is a characteristic analogy. *Water* is in the form of a *liquid* (all things are either a liquid, solid, or a gas) just as *ice* is in the form of a *solid*. Ice is also a cold, wet, cube however none of those describe the chemical form.

7. **(a)** This is a synonym analogy. *Concur* is a verb that means *to agree* just as *debate* is a verb that means *to argue*.

8. **(b)** This is a use analogy. A *towel* is used to *dry something* and a *broom* is used to *sweep something*. Floor, dirt, and straw are all related to a broom in some way, but sweep is the only verb.

9. **(c)** This is a characteristic analogy. A *donkey* is often described as *stubborn* and a *sloth* is often described as *slow*.

10. **(a)** This is a synonym analogy. *Durable* means to be *strong* just as *feeble* means to be *weak*.

Verbal Logic (page 75)

1. **(a)** The first three statements can be combined into one: Sparky – Sunny – Spike. Therefore Sparky is the oldest and must be older than Spike.

2. **(c)** There is no connection between Ann and Bob. Bob has been dancing longer than Denise, but he may or may not have been dancing longer than Ann as shown in the following diagram. $_B$ A $_B$ – D.

3. **(b)** Because all of the students in statistics class have an iPad, Chris must *not* be a student in statistics.

4. **(a)** Assign days of the week to each class to help picture this scenario. If she teaches ballet Sunday through Thursday (five days) and teaches tap Wednesday through Saturday (make the overlap as small as possible), then it is clear that she must teach two different classes on Wednesday and Thursday.

Ballet:	Sun	–	Mon	–	Tues	–	Wed	–	Thu				
Tap:							Wed	–	Thu	–	Fri	–	Sat

5. **(c)** Mrs. Philips, P, has more windows than Mrs. Rama, R, but it is uncertain if she has more than Mrs. Carleton, C, as shown in the diagram: $_C P_C$ – R. The diagram shows that while C has more than R, the amount may be more *or* less than P.

6. **(c)** Kate weighs more than Toby or Randall. We know that Jack weighs more than Randall, but we don't know if Toby weighs more or less than Jack. There is no sentence connecting Toby to Jack.

7. **(b)** Because ALL of the houses on Creamery Street are white, Bruce and Diana must not live on Creamery Street since they live in a beige house.

8. **(a)** Kyle has more CDs than Ben. Randy has fewer CDs than Ben. Randy has fewer CDs than Kyle. K – B – R . Kyle must have more CDs than Randy.

9. **(a)** Plug in numbers to figure this one out. Assume the biology test has 10 questions. If the chemistry test has 3 less, it must have 7 questions. If the math test has 7 more questions than the chemistry test, it must have 14 questions. Therefore the math test (14) has 4 more questions than the biology test (10).

10. **(b)** If Olivia attended school longer than Kristen and Kristen attended longer than Grace, it's not possible for Grace to have attended longer than Olivia. O – K – G.

Verbal Classification (page 79)

1. **(d)** *Reticent* means to be of few words. Synonyms for this would be *shy* and *timid*, so *talkative* is the word that does not belong.

2. **(a)** *Augment* is to make greater, to *improve*, or *amplify*. *Diminish* is the opposite of these words and means to reduce.

3. **(c)** A *shepherd*, a *labrador*, and a *poodle* are all types of dogs, so *dog* is the word that does not belong.

4. **(c)** To be *vacant* is to be *empty* or *deserted*. *Occupied* means to *not* be vacant and does not belong.

5. **(a)** *Weary* means to be tired or worn. The other three words all mean to give life or energy to something. Notice also that the other three words are all verbs and end in –*ate*. This is a clue that the word *weary* does not belong.

6. **(d)** *Prolific, abundant,* and *ample* are all similar and imply a large quantity. *Reclusive* is unrelated to the other three answer choices.

7. **(c)** *Harmonious* is the only answer choice that is positive in nature. The others all mean to be angry or full of hate.

8. **(a)** A *shade*, a *curtain*, and a *drape* are all things that are used to cover a *window*. *Window* is the word that does not belong.

9. **(d)** A *piano*, a *guitar*, and a *violin* all make sound through strings. A *drum* is the only instrument of the four that does not have strings.

10. **(b)** An *airplane* is the only one of the four that does not provide ground transportation.

WRAP IT UP WITH PRACTICE

Take a few minutes here to review the Verbal Skills strategies before you complete the Verbal Skills practice subtest.

General Verbal Skills Strategies

- Vocabulary, vocabulary, vocabulary!
- Remember the timing and answer 3–4 questions per minute.
- If you have any extra time, spend it on the logic questions.
- Use your watch to keep an eye on time, and check your progress when the proctor calls time halfway through.
- When eliminating answer choices, do not eliminate words you do not know.

Synonyms

- Read the word in the prompt, and think of a word that means the same thing.
- Determine if the word is positive or negative, and then look for a similar answer.
- Rule out answer choices that have similar meanings.
- Narrow down your choices to two opposites.
- Look at the word's root, prefix, or suffix for clues.

Antonyms

- Always underline reversal words *not* and *opposite*.
- *Before* looking at your answer choices, have your own answer in mind.
- You should look for a word that is the opposite of the prompt word.

Analogies

- Make a sentence using the given words, and then make a similar sentence with the prompt word and the correct answer choice.
- Direction matters with antonyms: "part is to whole" is different from "whole is to part."
- Grammar and verb tense matters: "noun is to verb" is not the same as "verb is to noun."

Verbal Logic

- Practice makes perfect with logic questions.
- For comparison questions, make notes to help you compare information.
- When answering *overlapping* questions, always start your list at opposite ends to determine the least amount of overlap
- When answering questions involving a numbered difference, make up a number and plug it into the question.

Verbal Classifications

- Look for the most obvious answer.
- Form a sentence with the words to find what they have in common.
- Watch for "three are part of the fourth" questions.

18 MINUTES

Samples:

A. Hurl most nearly means

   (a) run.
   (b) fall.
   (c) throw.
   (d) drop.

B. Baby is to adult as cub is to

   (a) mother.
   (b) bear.
   (c) dog.
   (d) infant.

Correct marking of samples:

A. Ⓐ Ⓑ ● Ⓓ

B. Ⓐ ● Ⓒ Ⓓ

---

1. Solemn most nearly means

    (a) honest.
    (b) serious.
    (c) unselfish.
    (d) sincere.

2. Which word does *not* belong with the others?

    (a) incredulous
    (b) questionable
    (c) farfetched
    (d) plausible

3. Which word does *not* belong with the others?

    (a) battery
    (b) steam
    (c) plug
    (d) water

4. West Newbury has a higher population than Groveland. Groveland has a smaller population than Georgetown. Georgetown has a higher population than West Newbury. If the first two statements are true, the third is

    (a) true.
    (b) false.
    (c) uncertain.

5. A debut is *not* a(n)

    (a) ending.
    (b) appearance.
    (c) initiation.
    (d) introduction.

6. Thread is to needle as chain is to

    (a) hoist.
    (b) link.
    (c) necklace.
    (d) lock.

7. Which word does *not* belong with the others?

    (a) reticent
    (b) boisterous
    (c) mute
    (d) taciturn

8. Which word does *not* belong with the others?

    (a) sad
    (b) happy
    (c) feeling
    (d) frustrated

GO TO THE NEXT PAGE ➡

9. Belittle means the *opposite* of

   (a) accuse.
   (b) antagonize.
   (c) acclaim.
   (d) admonish.

10. A hurdle is a(n)

    (a) advantage.
    (b) opening.
    (c) group.
    (d) complication.

11. Wrath most nearly means

    (a) peace.
    (b) fury.
    (c) decoration.
    (d) calm.

12. Gasoline is to car as food is to

    (a) farm.
    (b) person.
    (c) store.
    (d) apple.

13. Which word does *not* belong with the others?

    (a) maple
    (b) birch
    (c) oak
    (d) evergreen

14. Vigilant most nearly means

    (a) observant.
    (b) energetic.
    (c) opposing.
    (d) lazy.

15. Nefarious means the *opposite* of

    (a) atrocious.
    (b) respectable.
    (c) vile.
    (d) dreadful.

16. Eraser is to chalk as sponge is to

    (a) dish.
    (b) animal.
    (c) dirt.
    (d) soap.

17. Kaylee is older than Elizabeth. Charles is younger than Elizabeth. Kaylee is older than Charles. If the first two statements are true, the third is

    (a) true.
    (b) false.
    (c) uncertain.

18. Which word does *not* belong with the others?

    (a) hydrogen
    (b) sodium
    (c) nitrogen
    (d) water

19. Altruistic is to selfish as frivolous is to

    (a) necessary.
    (b) generous.
    (c) charitable.
    (d) greedy.

20. Which word does *not* belong with the others?

    (a) abdicate
    (b) reign
    (c) forfeit
    (d) overthrow

21. A saga is a(n)

    (a) test.
    (b) chronicle.
    (c) illness.
    (d) quote.

22. Country is to state as state is to

    (a) ocean.
    (b) planet.
    (c) continent.
    (d) county.

GO TO THE NEXT PAGE ➡

23. President is to country as governor is to

    (a) mayor.
    (b) state.
    (c) govern.
    (d) selectmen.

24. Which word does *not* belong with the others?

    (a) belligerent
    (b) feisty
    (c) sedentary
    (d) argumentative

25. Peter paddles faster than Sandra and Meghan. Hannah paddles faster than Meghan. Hannah paddles faster than Peter. If the first two statements are true, the third is

    (a) true.
    (b) false.
    (c) uncertain.

26. An emblem is a(n)

    (a) ticket.
    (b) insignia.
    (c) defect.
    (d) blister.

27. Test is to knowledge as odometer is to

    (a) car.
    (b) distance.
    (c) miles.
    (d) direction.

28. Chagrin means the *opposite* of

    (a) triumph.
    (b) shame.
    (c) embarrassment.
    (d) discomfort.

29. Congenial means the *opposite* of

    (a) polite.
    (b) aloof.
    (c) sociable.
    (d) pleasing.

30. Which word does *not* belong with the others?

    (a) clouds
    (b) snow
    (c) rain
    (d) drizzle

31. Roger has more tools than any of his brothers. Lucien is one of Roger's brothers. Lucien has fewer tools than Roger. If the first two statements are true, the third is

    (a) true.
    (b) false.
    (c) uncertain.

32. Which word does *not* belong with the others?

    (a) fertilize
    (b) nurture
    (c) encourage
    (d) deter

33. Karla owns more shoes than Colleen. Colleen owns more shoes than Sandra. Sandra owns more shoes than Karla. If the first two statements are true, the third is

    (a) true.
    (b) false.
    (c) uncertain.

34. Toy is to play as shovel is to

    (a) dirt.
    (b) dig.
    (c) hole.
    (d) tool.

35. Opaque most nearly means

    (a) clear.
    (b) transparent.
    (c) cloudy.
    (d) solid.

GO TO THE NEXT PAGE ➡

36. Docile means the *opposite* of

    (a) meek.
    (b) gentle.
    (c) obedient.
    (d) stubborn.

37. Zealot is to fan as hurricane is to

    (a) rain.
    (b) weather.
    (c) ocean.
    (d) tornado.

38. Kathleen ate six more peanuts than Stella. Stella ate nine fewer peanuts than Muriel. Kathleen ate fewer peanuts than Muriel. If the first two statements are true, the third is

    (a) true.
    (b) false.
    (c) uncertain.

39. To circumvent is to

    (a) cut.
    (b) avoid.
    (c) fan.
    (d) draw.

40. Alleviate is the *opposite* of

    (a) float.
    (b) worsen.
    (c) pacify.
    (d) mitigate.

41. Kelan is younger than Chris. Chris is older than Beth. Beth is older than Kelan. If the first two statements are true, the third is

    (a) true.
    (b) false.
    (c) uncertain.

42. To contrive is to

    (a) concoct
    (b) destroy
    (c) apologize
    (d) neglect

43. Which word does *not* belong with the others?

    (a) apex
    (b) summit
    (c) incline
    (d) peak

44. Which word does *not* belong with the others?

    (a) malignant
    (b) detrimental
    (c) benign
    (d) fatal

45. Tenacious most nearly means

    (a) afraid.
    (b) uncertain.
    (c) determined.
    (d) busy.

46. Shondra is taller than Tyson. Tyson is taller than Darren. Darren is taller than Shondra. If the first two statements are true, the third is

    (a) true.
    (b) false.
    (c) uncertain.

47. Jackson runs faster than Siri. Siri runs faster than Finch. Finch is slower than Jackson. If the first two statements are true, the third is

    (a) true.
    (b) false.
    (c) uncertain.

48. Larry's dog sleeps 18 hours a day. Gregory's dog sleeps eight hours a day. Larry and Gregory's dogs sleep at the same time at least two hours during a day. If the first two statements are true, the third is

    (a) true.
    (b) false.
    (c) uncertain.

GO TO THE NEXT PAGE ➡

49. Presume is the *opposite* of

    (a) suppose.
    (b) distrust.
    (c) surmise.
    (d) conjecture.

50. Homage most nearly means

    (a) residence.
    (b) respect.
    (c) cheese.
    (d) penance.

51. Rodney made more money than anyone in his family. Doug and Dan are Rodney's brothers. Dan made less money than Doug. If the first two statements are true, the third is

    (a) true.
    (b) false.
    (c) uncertain.

52. Which word does *not* belong with the others?

    (a) equate
    (b) balance
    (c) level
    (d) sum

53. Which word does *not* belong with the others?

    (a) release
    (b) expel
    (c) absorb
    (d) disperse

54. Baker is to yeast as blacksmith is to

    (a) horseshoe.
    (b) horses.
    (c) swords.
    (d) iron.

55. Which word does *not* belong with the others?

    (a) conventional
    (b) typical
    (c) unique
    (d) ordinary

56. All of the horses went into the barn. Nelly did not go into the barn. Nelly is not a horse. If the first two statements are true, the third is

    (a) true.
    (b) false.
    (c) uncertain.

57. Which word does *not* belong with the others?

    (a) rappel
    (b) meander
    (c) promenade
    (d) shuffle

58. Which word does *not* belong with the others?

    (a) encourage
    (b) prolong
    (c) extend
    (d) retract

59. To be pensive is to be

    (a) happy.
    (b) thoughtful.
    (c) cheap.
    (d) ignorant.

60. Consolidate does *not* mean

    (a) centralize.
    (b) scatter.
    (c) strengthen.
    (d) develop.

STOP

ANSWERS EXPLAINED FOR PRACTICE VERBAL SKILLS SUBTEST

1. **(b)** *Solemn* means intense or *serious*. (Synonym)

2. **(d)** *Plausible* means to be believable or likely. *Incredulous*, *farfetched*, and *questionable* all indicate that something is not believable or is unlikely. (Classification)

3. **(c)** *Battery*, *steam*, and *water* are all things that provide power or that act as fuel. They can also be considered things that make an object move, whereas a *plug* is used to stop something. Words can have multiple meanings. Even if plug, in this instance, means an electrical cord, it is still the electricity and not the plug that is providing power. (Classification)

4. **(c)** West Newbury (W) and Groveland (Gr) are in one sentence and Groveland and Georgetown (Ge) are in a separate sentence. There is no sentence connecting Georgetown to West Newbury, so the answer is uncertain. Georgetown's population may be more or less than West Newbury's. ($_{Ge}$ W $_{Ge}$ – Gr). (Logic)

5. **(a)** A *debut* is a first appearance, so it is the opposite of an *ending*. *Appearance*, *initiation*, and *introduction* are all types of beginnings. (Antonym)

6. **(a)** A *thread* is put through a *needle* for sewing and a *chain* is put through a *hoist* for lifting. (Analogy)

7. **(b)** *Reticent* and *taciturn* both mean quiet, while *mute* means unable to speak. *Boisterous* means noisy and is the opposite of these. (Classification)

8. **(c)** *Sad*, *happy*, and *frustrated* are all types of *feelings*. (Classification)

9. **(c)** *Belittle* means to put down or insult. *Acclaim* means to praise or build up. (Antonym)

10. **(d)** A *hurdle* is an obstacle such as a *complication*. (Synonym)

11. **(b)** *Wrath* most nearly means *fury*. *Peace* and *calm* mean the opposite, and *decoration* is possibly a wreath but not *wrath*. (Synonym)

12. **(b)** *Gasoline* is what fuels a *car*'s motion and the *food* is what fuels a *person*'s growth. (Analogy)

13. **(d)** A *maple* tree, a *birch* tree, and an *oak* tree are all specific types of trees, whereas *evergreen* is a category of tree. (Classification)

14. **(a)** *Vigilant* means to be watchful and alert, which are synonyms for *observant*. (Synonym)

15. **(b)** *Nefarious* means corrupt or vicious, both of which are the opposite of *respectable*. *Atrocious*, *vile*, and *dreadful* are all synonyms of *nefarious*. (Antonym)

16. **(c)** An *eraser* is used to remove *chalk* and a *sponge* is used to remove *dirt*. A sponge can be an *animal* and is used with *dishes* and *soap*; however, they are not things that a sponge removes. (Analogy)

17. **(a)** Kaylee > Elizabeth > Charles, so Kaylee must be older than Charles. (Logic)

18. **(d)** *Hydrogen*, *sodium*, and *nitrogen* are all atoms or elements and *water* is a molecule made up of atoms. Also, *hydrogen*, *sodium*, and *nitrogen* are all gases, while *water* is a liquid. (Classification)

19. **(a)** *Altruistic* is the opposite of *selfish* just as *frivolous* is the opposite of *necessary*. To be *frivolous* is to be foolish or superficial. (Analogy)

20. **(b)** To *reign* is to rule. *Abdicate* means to give up ruling as in to "*abdicate* the throne." *Forfeit* and *overthrow* are also ways to give up or take away power. (Classification)

21. **(b)** A *saga* is a story that takes place over a long time like a *chronicle*. The other answer choices have nothing to do with a story. (Synonym)

22. **(d)** A *state* is usually made up of *counties* in the same way that *countries* are usually made up of *states*. Be careful, county and country look alike. (Analogy)

23. **(b)** A *president* is the figurehead for a *country* and a *governor* is the figurehead for a *state*. Mayors and selectmen are associated with cities and towns rather than states. (Analogy)

24. **(c)** *Belligerent* and *argumentative* are very close to the same meaning, both being negative. *Feisty* is more closely related to *argumentative* than *sedentary*, so *sedentary* is the word that does not belong. (Classification)

25. **(c)** Peter is faster than both Sandra and Meghan. Hannah is faster than Meghan, but we are uncertain if Hannah is faster than Peter. There is no sentence that compares Hannah to Peter. $_H$P$_H$ > S, M. (Logic)

26. **(b)** An emblem is a badge or *insignia*. The other answer choices are unrelated to *emblem*. (Synonym)

27. **(b)** A *test* is used to measure *knowledge* and an *odometer* is used to measure *distance*. *Miles* are the units but *distance* is the thing being measured. (Analogy)

28. **(a)** *Chagrin* is synonymous with *shame* or *embarrassment*. *Discomfort* is similar in meaning. *Triumph* is the opposite of these. (Antonym)

29. **(b)** *Congenial* means to be *polite*, *sociable*, or *pleasant*. *Aloof* means uncaring or unknowing. (Antonym)

30. **(a)** *Rain*, *snow*, and *drizzle* are all types of precipitation that fall from the sky. *Clouds* do not fall from the sky. (Classification)

31. **(a)** This is a reasoning question. Roger has more tools than all of his brothers. So if Lucien is his brother, then Lucien has fewer tools than Roger. (Logic)

32. **(d)** *Fertilize*, *nurture*, and *encourage* are all positive things that promote growth or development. *Deter* means to slow down or interfere. (Classification)

33. **(b)** Your notes should be all on one line: K > C > S. Therefore Sandra cannot have more shoes than Karla. (Logic)

34. **(b)** A *toy* is used to *play* and a *shovel* is used to *dig*. *Dirt*, *hole*, and *tool* are all related to *shovel*, but they are not verbs. Notice the relationship of noun to verb. (Analogy)

35. **(c)** *Opaque* means milky or cloudy and is the opposite of *clear* or *transparent*. (Synonym)

36. **(d)** *Docile* is to be *gentle* or *meek*, conforming or *obedient*. *Stubborn* is an antonym of *docile*. (Antonym)

37. **(a)** A *zealot* is an extreme *fan*. Similarly, a *hurricane* is an extreme *rain*. The sentence will not work with the other words. *Hurricane* is extreme *weather* but that is not specific enough. *Rain* is the better choice. (Analogy)

38. **(a)** Make up numbers to help with this one. For example, if Stella ate 10 peanuts (Stella = 10), then Kathleen = 16, so Muriel must be 19. Therefore Kathleen ate fewer peanuts than Muriel. (Logic)

39. **(b)** *Circumvent* most nearly means to go around something or to *avoid*. The other choices are unrelated to *circumvent*. (Synonym)

40. **(b)** *Alleviate* means to lessen or to make lighter. *Float, pacify*, and *mitigate* all have similar meanings. *Worsen* is an antonym of *alleviate*. (Antonym)

41. **(c)** K < C. Because Chris is older than Beth, we know that Beth must be to the left of Chris in the notes: $_{Be}$ K $_{Be}$ – C. Beth could be older or younger than Kelan and still be younger than Chris, so this is uncertain. (Logic)

42. **(a)** *Contrive* is to devise. *Concoct* is a synonym for devise. (Synonym)

43. **(c)** *Apex, summit*, and *peak* all represent the location of the top of something, the highest point. *Incline* refers to the slope and not a place. (Classification)

44. **(c)** *Malignant, detrimental*, and *fatal* are all negative words. *Benign* is a positive word meaning good or favorable. (Classification)

45. **(c)** *Tenacious* means to be *determined*. *Afraid* and *uncertain* are antonyms of *tenacious* and *busy* is unrelated. (Synonym)

46. **(b)** Darren is the shortest and cannot be taller than Shondra. S > T > D. (Logic)

47. **(a)** Jackson is the fastest, and Finch is the slowest, so Finch is slower than Jackson. J > S > F. (Logic)

48. **(a)** This is a reasoning question. If Larry's dog sleeps 18 hours a day (say from midnight to 6 P.M.) and Gregory's dog sleeps from 4 P.M. to midnight that is the least overlap that will exist and will be two hours, between 4 P.M. and 6 P.M. (Logic)

49. **(b)** *Presume* means to assume or *surmise*. Synonyms are *suppose* and *conjecture*. *Distrust* is the opposite of *suppose*. (Antonym)

50. **(b)** *Homage* is a tribute or an honor. To pay *homage* to is to show *respect*. The other answer choices are unrelated. (Synonym)

51. **(c)** Rodney made the most money of all of his family. Therefore, both Doug and Dan made less than Rodney, but there is no information given that lets us know if Dan made more or less than Doug. (Logic)

52. **(d)** *Equate, balance*, and *level* all involve making things equal. *Sum* is the addition of things and therefore does not belong. (Classification)

53. **(c)** *Release, expel*, and *disperse* all mean to give off or to spread out. *Absorb* means the opposite and refers to taking something in. (Classification)

54. **(d)** A *baker* uses *yeast* to bake and a *blacksmith* uses *iron* to forge. A blacksmith often makes *horseshoes* and *swords*, and sometimes may even work with *horses*; however, the material he works with is *iron*. (Analogy)

55. **(c)** To be *unique* is to be one of a kind. *Conventional, typical,* and *ordinary* are all opposites of *unique*. (Classification)

56. **(a)** If all of the horses went into the barn and Nelly did not go into the barn, then Nelly must not be a horse; if she were, she would be in the barn. (Logic)

57. **(a)** *Meander, promenade,* and *shuffle* are all manners of walking. *Rappel* means to move down a steep incline using ropes. (Classification)

58. **(d)** *Encourage, prolong,* and *extend* all mean to lengthen something or to move something along. *Retract* means to take something back and is therefore the opposite and does not belong. (Classification)

59. **(b)** *Pensive* means to be deep in thought. The other word choices are unrelated to *pensive*. (Synonym)

60. **(b)** *Consolidate* means to gather together. *Centralize* and *strengthen* are synonyms of *consolidate* and *scatter* is an antonym of *consolidate*. (Antonym)

SCORING YOUR PRACTICE VERBAL SKILLS SUBTEST

Now that you have reviewed the answers and explanations, let's see how well you are doing. Go through the explanations again and count up the number of each question type you answered correctly. Then fill in the chart below.

	Logic	Analogy	Classification	Antonym	Synonym	Total
Number of each question type you answered correctly						
Total of each question type	12	10	17	9	12	60

First, add up the total number of questions you answered correctly. Then divide that number by 60 and multiply by 100 to determine your raw score for the Verbal Skills subtest:

$$\text{Raw Score} = \frac{\text{Total Number Correct}}{60 \text{ Total Questions}} = \frac{\quad\quad}{60} \times 100 = \underline{\quad\quad}\%$$

Next, to determine your raw score for each question type, take the number of questions you answered correctly in each category and divide that number by the total number of questions in each question type. Multiply each answer by 100 to convert to a percent.

$$\text{Logic} = \frac{\text{Total Number Correct}}{12 \text{ Total Questions}} = \frac{\quad\quad}{12} \times 100 = \underline{\quad\quad}\%$$

$$\text{Analogy} = \frac{\text{Total Number Correct}}{10 \text{ Total Questions}} = \frac{\quad\quad}{10} \times 100 = \underline{\quad\quad}\%$$

$$\text{Classification} = \frac{\text{Total Number Correct}}{17 \text{ Total Questions}} = \frac{\quad\quad}{17} \times 100 = \underline{\quad\quad}\%$$

$$\text{Antonym} = \frac{\text{Total Number Correct}}{9 \text{ Total Questions}} = \frac{\quad\quad}{9} \times 100 = \underline{\quad\quad}\%$$

$$\text{Synonym} = \frac{\text{Total Number Correct}}{12 \text{ Total Questions}} = \frac{\quad\quad}{12} \times 100 = \underline{\quad\quad}\%$$

How well did you do? Make sure to go back and review any areas that you can improve upon.

Quantitative Skills

5

There are two nonverbal subtests of the HSPT. Quantitative Skills is the second subtest of the HSPT and the Mathematics subtest is the fourth. As in other standardized tests, this section will include a variety of math concepts. Unlike other tests, however, this section has only three specific question types: sequences, comparisons, and computations. If you become familiar with each of these question types, you will not only have an easier time finishing the subtest on time, but you will also boost your score.

The Quantitative Skills subtest of the HSPT will assess your knowledge of general mathematics and will include the following operations and concepts:

> **MATH TIP**
>
> Keep your eye on the prize! While you study for the HSPT, your main goal is to IMPROVE YOUR SCORE. So leave the more complicated math problems for math class. All you need to know for the Quantitative Skills subtest is right in this chapter.

Mathematics

Addition/subtraction
Multiplication/division
Operations involving fractions
Fraction comparisons
Operations involving decimals
Distributive property
Exponents and scientific notation

Algebra

Distributive property with variables
Slope of a line
Evaluating equations with variables

Geometry

Sum of angles
Angles in a triangle
Transversal and vertical angles
Right angles

Miscellaneous

Roman numerals
Comparing objects
Measurements
Graphs and charts

This may seem like a long list, but chances are, you already know many of these concepts well. The purpose of this subtest is to not only assess your understanding of these concepts but also to test your ability to apply these concepts in questions of reasoning. For example, you will have to know your times tables, but you will also have to recognize a sequence that is increasing by 7 with each term. You may understand how to calculate a percent, but can you also compare three different percents and place them in increasing order? In this chapter, you will become familiar with the format for each question type and will learn strategies to help you answer them quickly and accurately.

THE LAYOUT

The Quantitative Skills subtest of the HSPT is made up of 52 questions numbered 61–112. You will have 30 minutes to complete the subtest. Calculators are not allowed at any time during the HSPT. Although this subtest covers a variety of concepts, it has just three question types.

Quantitative Skills Subtest—30 Minutes and 52 Questions

Question Type	Example	Number of Questions
Sequence	In the sequence: 1, 2, 3, . . . , what number should come next?	22–23
Comparison	Examine (A), (B), and (C) and find the best answer . . .	19–20
Computation	What number subtracted from 20 is half of 36?	10–11

You will see examples of each question type and format in this chapter. Now that you have an idea of the types of questions you'll see, let's get to work on some general strategies that will save you time and improve your score on the Quantitative Skills subtest.

GENERAL STRATEGIES FOR QUANTITATIVE SKILLS

The Quantitative Skills subtest is very structured, consisting of three different types of questions. You can and should definitely use this to your advantage. Visually, each of the three question types looks very different. Once you become familiar with the different types, you'll be able to spot each without even reading the question. Let's look at some strategies that are sure to help you perform your best.

General HSPT Strategies

If you have not already done so, review the general HSPT strategies found in Chapter 2. There you will learn how to avoid mistakes, work more efficiently, and maximize your test score.

Timing Is Everything

You will have 30 minutes to answer 52 questions, which means you will have to complete about two questions per minute. Many of the questions will be easy, and you will do them in just seconds, so it is okay to occasionally spend a minute on one problem, but only occasionally. As you practice, try to get a sense of your timing. If you are taking too long on a particular question, circle the question number, make a guess, and move on. You may have time at the end of the subtest to come back to it.

Recognize Problem Types

There are sequence, comparison, and computation questions in this subtest. It is very simple to see which type is which.

The sequencing questions all begin with "In the sequence:" so they are easy to spot. They are very short, typically just two lines, and make up a third of the Quantitative Skills questions. The computation questions are also very brief. You can recognize the comparison questions, since they always have three items labeled with capital letters (A), (B), and (C).

You'll notice that the questions typically take up more room on the page. Take a minute to flip through the practice subtest at the end of this chapter to see if you can quickly identify each question type.

Do What You Like

TIP

You are calling the shots. Feel free to skip questions that are difficult and come back to them if you have extra time. But make a guess as you go, in case you run out of time.

One of your goals in this chapter is to learn which of the three types of questions you like best. Once you figure this out, make sure you DO ALL OF THESE! You'll most likely do very well on those questions, so you don't want to miss even one. Maybe, for example, you are very skilled at the sequencing questions. If it seems like you are running out of time, flip through the subtest and make sure you do any problems in which you see the word "sequence" (always remembering *Touch–Touch–Bubble*). If you have extra time after you finish, go back and answer the remaining questions.

Easy Does It

Do the easy questions first, and don't waste time on the more challenging questions until the end. There are only a few difficult questions in this section. The real challenge is in answering all 52 questions in less than 30 minutes. When you see a difficult question, or one you think may take a while, you should make a guess, circle the question number, and move on to an easier question. If you have extra time, come back to the question numbers you circled. Both the very easiest and the most challenging questions are each worth just one point.

This Is Not Math Class

Unfortunately, or fortunately, no human is going to look at your answers. No one is going to say "Wow, I love the way you solved question 6—you used a great approach!" Things that may get you in trouble in math class may be your best strategies here. DO AS LITTLE MATH AS POSSIBLE! In this chapter, you will learn about each question type as well as strategies that will help you do as little math as possible.

When You Find the Right Answer—Move On

Once you find the answer, stop looking! There is only one right answer choice. In the comparison questions, you will be asked to find the *best* answer, but even there you will find only one answer that is correct. There is no need to check the other answer choices unless you are unsure that your answer is correct.

Answer Choices as Clues

On the HSPT, the answer choices may not be in numerical order. Check the answer choices for clues as you work through the question. If you see the answer choices are all large numbers, it may indicate that that you have to multiply rather than divide in a computation problem. Look to see if the answer choices are fractions or decimals. There are often valuable clues in the answers choices. Perhaps you are solving a quotient and you know there is a remainder. This means you can rule out any integers. You should always cross out answer choices you know are false as you work through the problem.

Do Your Work on the Test

You are allowed to write in the test booklet, so do all of your work right next to the question in the booklet. If you do your work on scrap paper, you will lose precious time going back and forth. If you have extra time at the end, the work on the scrap paper will be useless to you. If you do the work right next to the problem, you can easily see this work when you are reviewing your answers.

If You See Your Answer, Feel Good About It

Here is some good news! In this subtest, the wrong answer choices, sometimes called the distractors, are not usually carefully planned values put there to trap you. For example, if the correct answer choice is 5 the answer choices may be 5, –5, 50, –50. If, after determining your answer, you see it as one of the answer choices, you should feel good because you are most likely correct.

TYPES OF QUANTITATIVE SKILLS QUESTIONS

The Quantitative Skills subtest has only three different questions types. If you become familiar with each, you will be comfortable on test day with the content of the questions and the format of each. Let's review each type of question in detail.

SEQUENCES

A sequence is simply a list of numbers, or letters, in a pattern separated by commas. The items in the sequence are called terms. Your task is to figure out the pattern in the given list of terms and then to find the next or missing term. Some sequences are very easy, while others are more difficult. Do not to spend too much time on one problem, or else risk missing out on easier questions. In this type of question, you will see sequences that involve only numbers, some with only letters, some with both numbers and letters and maybe one, at most two, with Roman numerals.

Here are the types of sequence questions, and the approximate quantity of each, that you can expect to see in the Quantitative Skills subtest.

Sequence Type	Example	Number of Questions
Numbers Only	2, 4, 6, 8, . . .	14–15
Letters Only	AC, BD, CE, . . .	0–1
Letters and Numbers	3C, 4E, 5G, . . .	4–5
Roman Numerals	I, IV, VII, . . .	1–2

In total, you can expect to see 22–23 sequence questions in the Quantitative Skills subtest. There are more of these questions than there are of the other two types, so it is important that you read this section carefully and complete the practice set of questions at the end of this section. Let's take a look at the makeup of a sequence question.

What the Questions Look Like

In each of these questions, you will first be given a sequence. Your task is to figure out the pattern in the sequence and answer the question posed. These questions are worded in several different ways. Below are some examples.

> In the sequence: 1, 2, 3, . . . , what number comes next?
> In the sequence: A, B, C, . . . , what letter should come next?
> In the sequence: 1, 2, 3, ___, ___, what numbers belong in the blank?
> In the sequence: 1, 2, 3, . . . , what *two* numbers should come next?
> In the sequence: 1, ___, 3, 4, what number should fill in the blank?
> In the sequence: 1, 2, 4, 4, . . . , one number is *wrong*. That number should be . . . .

These questions all look a little different, but they are asking you to do the same thing: figure out the pattern and find either the next or missing term(s).

Types of Sequence Patterns

Let's look at the different sequences and review strategies that will help you.

ADDITION AND SUBTRACTION SEQUENCES

About half of the sequence questions will involve simple addition and subtraction. When trying to figure out a pattern, you should *always try addition first then subtraction*. Below is an easy sequence to demonstrate the method of finding the pattern.

➡ Example 1 _____

In the sequence: 11, 15, 19, 23, . . . , what number comes next?

(a) 11   (b) 20   (c) 27   (d) 32

TIP

If you don't find a pattern when reading from left to right, try reading it from right to left instead. This is helpful for descending sequences.

Look at the sequence and determine what number must be added to 11 to get 15. This number is known as the difference. Because 15 – 11 = 4, you can see that the difference is 4. This sequence is generated by simply adding four. Now check that pattern on the next numbers in the sequence to verify. Add 4 to the last number given for a correct answer of choice (c) 27.

➡ Example 2_____

In the sequence: 5,634, 5,625, 5,616, 5,607, . . . , what comes next?

(a) 5,608   (b) 5,626   (c) 5,598   (d) 5,518

Even though the numbers are larger, this is still an easy subtraction sequence with – 9, – 9, – 9. Since 5,607 – 9 = 5,598, the correct answer is choice (c) 5,598.

Try the next example that involves negative numbers.

⇒ Example 3_____

In the sequence: 27, 12, –2, _____, –31, –46, what number belongs in the blank?

(a) –14   (b) –17   (c) 17   (d) –26

If you have trouble seeing the sequence when looking from left to right, then try going from right to left. Look at –2 then 12. How much greater is 12 than –2? It takes 12 to get back to zero and then another 2 to get to –2, so the difference is 14.

$$\begin{array}{ccccccc} & -15 & -14 & -15 & -14 & -15 \\ 27, & 12, & -2, & \underline{\quad}, & -31, & -46 \end{array}$$

Now look between 12 and 27. The difference here is 15. The pattern seems to be –15, –14. If you subtract 15 from –2, you'll get –17. Then subtract 14 to get –31. The missing number is –17 for a correct answer of choice (b) –17.

If you don't like subtracting negative numbers, here is a trick you may use. When each number in the sequence is negative, and the sequence starts and ends far from zero, you can ignore the negatives when finding the pattern.

⇒ Example 4_____

In the sequence: –50, –45, –40, –35, . . . , what number should come next?

(a) –28   (b) –30   (c) –7   (d) 30

This negative sequence begins with 50 and decreases by 5 with each term, so the next term must be 30. Because the values in the sequence are all negative, your answer must also be negative. The correct answer is choice (b) –30.

SEQUENCES WITH A PATTERN IN THE DIFFERENCES

If you come across a sequence that is difficult to figure out, it may be because the pattern exists in the differences between the terms. See if you can figure out the following sequence then read the explanation for a helpful strategy.

⇒ Example 5_____

In the sequence: 3, 4, 6, 9, 13, . . , what comes next?

(a) 15   (b) 26   (c) 16   (d) 18

This is an example where there is a pattern in the numbers that are being added each time. The numbers being added represent the differences between each term.

$$\begin{array}{ccccc} & +1 & +2 & +3 & +4 \\ 3, & 4, & 6, & 9, & 13, \ldots \end{array}$$

You can see that the difference between 3 and 4 is 1, the difference between 4 and 6 is 2, and so on. The next difference is + 5. The correct answer is 13 + 5, choice (d) 18.

➡ Example 6_____

In the sequence: 8, 10, 13, 15, 18, . . . , what two numbers come next?

  (a) 20, 23   (b) 21, 23   (c) 21, 24   (d) 20, 22

Sometimes you will be asked to determine the next *two* numbers. Usually in these questions there is a more complicated pattern involving the differences, which is why you have to show two numbers to demonstrate that you figured out the pattern.

  In Example 6, the differences are + 2, + 3, + 2, + 3, etc., so the next two differences will be + 2, + 3.

$$\begin{array}{ccccccccc} & +2 & & +3 & & +2 & & +3 & \\ 8, & & 10, & & 13, & & 15, & & 18, \ldots \end{array}$$

Therefore the last two terms will be 20, 23 for a correct answer of choice (a) 20, 23.

  You may come across a question where you have to find the missing number in a sequence. Don't worry, these questions tend to be simple addition sequences. Try Example 7 and then read the explanation that follows to learn different strategies for this type of sequence.

➡ Example 7_____

In the sequence: 4, _____, 32, 46, . . . , what number should fill in the blank?

  (a) 20   (b) 57   (c) 36   (d) 18

You can approach this in a couple of different ways. If you look at the end of the sequence, you can see the numbers are 32 followed by 46, so the pattern could be + 14. Try adding 14 to 4 to see if the pattern works. Another approach is to look at the number on either side of the blank and find the average: $(4 + 32) \div 2 = 18$. Then put 18 in place of the blank space and check to see if the pattern is complete. You will see that it is, and the correct answer is choice (d) 18.

SEQUENCES WITH MULTIPLICATION AND DIVISION

Always try addition first in any sequence, then subtraction. If you don't find the pattern, then try multiplication and division. In the next example, look at the easiest or smallest numbers first to help you find the pattern.

➡ Example 8_____

In the sequence: 320, 160, 40, 20, 5, . . . , what number comes next?

  (a) 0.5   (b) 1.25   (c) 0.25   (d) 2.5

You'll notice in the sequence above that the pattern is $\div 2, \div 4, \div 2, \div 4$, as shown.

$$\begin{array}{ccccccccc} & \div 2 & & \div 4 & & \div 2 & & \div 4 & \\ 320, & & 160, & & 40, & & 20, & & 5, \ldots \end{array}$$

Don't be afraid of fractions and decimals. 5 divided by 2 is more than 2, so rule out answer choices (a), (b), and (c). The answer is $\frac{5}{2}$ which is $2\frac{1}{2}$, which is the equivalent of choice (d) 2.5.

TIP

Skip over large numbers, decimals, or fractions at the beginning of a sequence. Instead look at the easier numbers at the end.

Example 9

In the sequence: 220, 110, 120, 60, 70, . . . , what number comes next?

(a) 35   (b) 80   (c) 65   (d) 30

The sequence in Example 9 involves division and addition. The pattern is $\div 2, +10, \div 2, +10$, as shown.

$$\begin{array}{cccccccc} & \div 2 & & +10 & & \div 2 & & +10 \\ 220, & & 110, & & 120, & & 60, & & 70, \ldots \end{array}$$

The next number will be $70 \div 2$, choice (a) 35.

You may also come across a question where you will be asked to find the number that is incorrect in the given sequence. At most, there will be only one of these questions, but if you don't read the question carefully, you may waste a lot of time trying to figure out the next number instead of the wrong one, so be on the lookout and read each question carefully. Here is an example:

TIP

Always read the entire question and not just the values. You may waste time looking for the next number when you are supposed to be finding the error in the sequence!

Example 10

In the sequence 10, 12, 23, 24, 34, 36, . . . , one number is *wrong*. That number should be

(a) 26   (b) 22   (c) 32   (d) 30

Remember one number is incorrect, so look for a pattern that works for all but one number. In this case, the pattern is $+2, +10, +2, +10$. The incorrect number is 23 and should be replaced with 22, making the correct answer choice (b) 22.

SEQUENCES WITH FRACTIONS AND/OR DECIMALS

If you are like many students, you probably aren't crazy about fractions and decimals. The good news is there are very few of these in the Quantitative Skills subtest. You may see a question with a fraction or decimal in it, but you can often find the pattern by looking at the other whole numbers. Here are a couple of examples.

Example 11

In the sequence: 0.25, 1, 4, 16, . . . , what number comes next?

(a) 0.5   (b) 64   (c) 32   (d) 0.16

It is much easier to see the pattern by looking at the last three terms: 1, 4, 16. You can recognize the pattern is multiplying by 4. The next term would be 16 times 4 or 64 for a correct answer of choice (b).

➥ Example 12 _____

In the sequence: $\frac{1}{3}$, 1, 3, 9, . . . , what number comes next?

(a) $\frac{1}{2}$ (b) 12   (c) 27   (d) 54

The correct answer is choice (c) 27. By ignoring the first term, you can see that the sequence is simply multiplying by 3. In Examples 11 and 12, you can realize that each term is multiplied by a whole number and that the fractions and decimals are not too intimidating.

Here are some common fractions and decimals that you should know well and may see in the HSPT sequences.

$$\frac{1}{2} = 0.5 \qquad \frac{1}{4} = 0.25 \qquad \frac{1}{5} = 0.20 \qquad \frac{1}{8} = 0.125$$

➥ Example 13 _____

In the sequence: 0.125, 0.25, 0.5, 1, . . . , what number comes next?

(a) 0.1   (b) 5   (c) 2   (d) 1.25

The pattern here is a simple doubling that may look more complicated because of the decimals. If you find this to be too difficult, just look at the last two numbers to see that 1 is twice as much as $\frac{1}{2}$. No other answer choice makes sense except for choice (c) 2. If decimals are not your favorite, then you can multiply each term by 100 to eliminate some or all of the decimals. If you multiply each term by 100 you will have: 12.5, 25, 50, 100. From here you can easily see that the sequence is doubling. Remember not to double 100 to get the next term but instead double the last term. $1 \times 2 = 2$.

SEQUENCE IN A SEQUENCE

Not all sequences have just one pattern. Try to figure out this next sequence. You'll see from the explanation that it is actually quite simple.

➥ Example 14 _____

In the sequence: 3, 8, 6, 12, 9, 16, . . . , what number comes next?

(a) 12   (b) 5   (c) 20   (d) 15

If you try addition, you'll see that the differences between every term are $+ 5, - 2, + 6, - 3, + 7$ as shown below.

$$\begin{array}{ccccccccc} & +5 & & -2 & & +6 & & -3 & & +7 \\ \mathbf{3,} & & 8, & & \mathbf{6,} & & 12, & & \mathbf{9,} & & 16, \ldots \end{array}$$

Clearly this is not a simple addition sequence. It can be challenging to find a pattern in the differences; however, if you look at *every other* term, beginning with 3, you'll see an easy pattern: 3, 6, 9, . . . so the next term must be 12. The correct answer is choice (a) 12. This is a simple version of a sequence within a sequence.

SEQUENCE WITH MULTIPLE PATTERNS

Not all sequences have just one pattern. Can you see how this sequence is more complicated than the sequences above?

➡ Example 15 _____

In the sequence: 4, 8, 11, 16, 20, _____, _____, what numbers belong in the blanks?

(a) 24, 25   (c) 25, 31
(b) 24, 29   (d) 26, 31

If you are having trouble, here is a clue. This is an example of a challenging sequence within a sequence. If you first try addition, you will see that the sequence is + 4, + 3, + 5, + 4. Now look at every other number in the differences. The differences below are separated to show that there are two patterns within the one sequence. This makes the sequence easier to decipher.

$$
\begin{array}{cccccccc}
& +4 & & +5 & & +6 & & \\
& & +3 & & +4 & & +5 & \\
4, & 8, & 11, & 16, & 20, & \_\_\_\_, & \_\_\_\_, &
\end{array}
$$

You'll see + 4, + 5. You can assume the next difference will be + 6. If you start with the + 3 and look at every other difference, you will see + 3, + 4, etc. The next two numbers should be 20 + 6 then 26 + 5 for an answer of choice (d) 26, 31.

➡ Example 16 _____

In the sequence 5, 9, 17, 29, 45, . . . , what number comes next?

(a) 54   (b) 65   (c) 56   (d) 66

If you try adding, you will get + 4, + 8, + 12, + 16. Do you see a pattern in the differences? The number you add to the last term of 45 should be 20 since the differences are increasing by 4, giving you a correct answer of choice (b) 65.

$$
\begin{array}{cccccc}
& +4 & +8 & +12 & +16 & +20 \\
5, & 9, & 17, & 29, & 45, . . . &
\end{array}
$$

➡ Example 17 _____

In the sequence: 10, 22, 17, 27, 23, 31, . . . , what three numbers come next?

(a) 20, 33, 27   (c) 28, 34, 32
(b) 34, 28, 32   (d) 41, 33, 20

This sequence involves both addition and subtraction and also has a pattern in the differences. If you are having trouble figuring it out, look for a pattern in the differences.

$$
\begin{array}{ccccccc}
& & -5 & & -4 & & -3 & & -2 \\
& +12 & & +10 & & +8 & & +6 & \\
10, & 22, & 17, & 27, & 23, & 31, . . . &
\end{array}
$$

Look at every other difference. Start with 12 and you will see + 12, + 10, + 8, . . . , so the next difference will be + 6. Then look at – 5, – 4, and you can see the next will be – 3. To continue the pattern, you must – 3, + 6, – 2 for a correct answer of choice (c) 28, 34, 32.

SEQUENCES WITH SQUARE ROOTS

A square root, also known as a radical expression, such as $\sqrt{4}$, is an operator asking you "what number when multiplied by itself will give you a value of 4?" This can be written as a perfect square as well. A perfect square is the product of a number multiplied by itself. Here are a few common perfect squares and square roots.

Perfect Square	Square Root
$2^2 = 4$	$\sqrt{4} = 2$
$3^2 = 9$	$\sqrt{9} = 3$
$4^2 = 16$	$\sqrt{16} = 4$
$5^2 = 25$	$\sqrt{25} = 5$
$6^2 = 36$	$\sqrt{36} = 6$
$7^2 = 49$	$\sqrt{49} = 7$
$8^2 = 64$	$\sqrt{64} = 8$
$9^2 = 81$	$\sqrt{81} = 9$
$10^2 = 100$	$\sqrt{100} = 10$

At most, you may see a question or two that involves perfect squares or square roots, as shown in the following example.

➡ Example 18 _____

In the sequence: 100, 10, 81, 9, 64, . . . , what number comes next?

(a) 10   (b) 49   (c) 8   (d) 7

The sequence here is $\sqrt{100}$, 10, $\sqrt{81}$, 9, etc. The correct answer is the square root of 64, which is choice (c) 8.

SEQUENCES WITH LETTERS AND NUMBERS

There may be a handful of sequence questions on the HSPT that involve a combination of letters and numbers. You can think of this type as another "sequence within a sequence" question. To figure these out, first find the pattern in the numbers and then the pattern in the letters. Treat them as if they were two separate sequences. You often only have to figure out one of the sequences in order to find the correct answer.

TIP

In sequences with letters and numbers, you may only have to find one of the two patterns in order to find the correct answer.

→ Example 19 _____

In the sequence: 2A, 4B, 6C, 8D, . . . , what comes next?

(a) 10F   (b) 10E   (c) 8E   (d) 8F

Looking at the numbers, first you see 2, 4, 6, 8. The next number is 10 so you have already narrowed it down to choices (a) or (b). Next look at the letters A, B, C, D, ... The next letter should be E, meaning that the correct answer is choice (b) 10E.

TIP

It may be helpful to write the alphabet on your scratch paper to use for finding letter patterns.

→ Example 20 _____

In the sequence: 3A, 6C, 7E, 14G, 15I, . . . , what comes next?

(a) 10K   (b) 10E   (c) 30K   (d) 16J

Once again, begin with the numbers: 3, 6, 7, 14, 15. You can see that the pattern is double, plus one, double, plus one, so the next number should be 30.

```
       ×2   +1   ×2   +1              B   D   F   H
      3,   6,   7,   14,   15,...    A,  C,  E,  G,  I,...
```

Look at your answer choices. There is only one answer choice with a 30—so STOP! On test day, there is nothing to be gained by trying to figure out the rest of the sequence. This will only waste time. For now, go ahead and find the pattern in the letters. A, C, E, G, I, . . . , the pattern is every other letter, and the next letter should be K. The correct answer is choice (c) 30K.

THREE PATTERNS

You may see a sequence with three different patterns; one pattern in the numbers, a second pattern for the first letter, and a third pattern for the next letter.

TIP

In sequence questions with letters and numbers, pull the sequence apart by looking at the first item of each term, then the second, etc.

→ Example 21 _____

In the sequence: 22AH, 20BG, 18CF, 16DE, . . . , what comes next?

(a) 14DE   (b) 14ED   (c) 24EH   (d) 24EF

The first sequence is the number in each term.

```
        -2   -2   -2
      22,  20,  18,  16, . . . the next number is 14
```

The second sequence is the first letter in each term.

A, B, C, D, . . . the next letter is E

This narrows your answer to choice (b).
The third sequence is the second letter in each term.

H, G, F, E, . . . the next letter is D

The correct answer is choice (b) 14ED.

This type of question has also been on the HSPT written in a slightly different way, but don't panic if you see this—it's the same question as in Example 21.

➡ Example 22 _____

In the sequence: 22 × AH, 20 × BG, 18 × CF, 16 × DE, . . . , what comes next?

(a) 14 × DE   (b) 14 × ED   (c) 24 × EH   (d) 24 × EF

The × sign in this example does NOT mean multiplication; it is just another symbol. You can ignore it completely and treat this sequence in the exact same way you did in Example 21. The correct answer is choice (b). You may also see this question with an addition sign (+) but like the × sign, it will mean nothing.

TIP

Some sequencing questions may have "×" or "+" in the terms. If you see these, don't worry—just ignore them! In sequences, the × symbol does not mean multiplication and the + does not mean addition.

SEQUENCES WITH ROMAN NUMERALS

If you have never seen Roman numerals before, don't worry. You'll learn here how to read them. At most, you will only have two questions involving Roman numerals on the HSPT, so we won't spend too much time on them. If Roman numerals are new to you, read the review. If you feel that you already understand Roman numerals, skip the lesson and go right to Example 23.

The Quantitative Skills section is the only subtest on the HSPT that has Roman numerals. The following is everything you need to know about Roman numerals in order to answer the sequence questions of the HSPT.

The table below shows five Arabic numbers and their corresponding Roman numerals.

Arabic Number	Roman Numeral
1	I
5	V
10	X
50	L
100	C

Roman Numeral Rules to Know:

1. Symbols that are the same and next to each other are added together.
   For example, XX (10 + 10) = 20 and XXX (10 + 10 + 10) = 30.
2. You can use no more than three of the same symbol next to each other.
   For example, I = 1, II = 2, and III = 3. IIII is NOT the correct way to write the number 4.
3. If a Roman numeral is followed by a smaller value on the right, the two are added together. For example, VI = 6 because I is on the right of and has a lesser value than V. 5 (V) + 1 (I) = 6.
4. When a smaller Roman numeral is to the left of a larger Roman numeral, subtract the smaller number on the left from the larger number on the right. For example, IX = 9 because 10 (X) – 1(I) = 9, and XC = 90 because 100 (C) – 10 (X) = 90.
5. Never subtract more than one symbol. For example, IX = 9 but 8 ≠ IIX (8 = VIII).

For practice, translate the following Roman numerals into Arabic numbers, 1, 2, 3, etc., then check your answers.

Roman Numeral	Arabic Number
III	
IV	
IX	
XVI	
XXVII	
XLIII	
XLV	

(Answers are on page 131.)

If you had more than one wrong answer, review the rules once more and try again. It is unlikely that you will see L (50) or C (100) on the HSPT, but it doesn't hurt to be a little over prepared. When working with Roman numerals, convert each value in the sequence to an Arabic number, determine the next value, then convert your answer back to a Roman numeral.

TIP

When working with Roman numerals, first convert the value to its Arabic number (1, 2, 3, etc.) and write the number above the Roman numeral. Then look at the numbers you've written to decipher the pattern.

➡ Example 23 _____

In the sequence: III, V, VII, IX, . . . , what number comes next?

(a) X   (b) XI   (c) XV   (d) XII

$$
\begin{array}{ccccc}
 & +2 & +2 & +2 & \\
3 & 5 & 7 & 9 & \\
\text{III,} & \text{V,} & \text{VII,} & \text{IX, ...} &
\end{array}
$$

The sequences is III = 3, V = 5, VII = 7, IX = 9, so the next number is 11, which is XI. The correct answer is choice (b) XI.

➡ Example 24 _____

In the sequence: III, VI, VII, XIV, XV, . . . , what number comes next?

(a) XXI   (b) XI   (c) XXX   (d) XXXI

This sequence is 3, 6, 7, 14, 15. The pattern is shown below.

$$
\begin{array}{ccccc}
\times 2 & +1 & \times 2 & +1 & \\
3 & 6 & 7 & \cdot 14 & 15 \\
\text{III,} & \text{VI,} & \text{VII,} & \text{XIV,} & \text{XV, ...}
\end{array}
$$

The next number would then be 30, so the correct answer is choice (c) XXX.

Sequences Practice

Now you're ready to review all that you have learned. Let's practice a mix of sequencing problems.

1. In the sequence: 1000, 200, 40, 8, . . . , what number comes next?

   (a) $\frac{8}{5}$ (c) $\frac{8}{3}$

   (b) 1   (d) 4

2. In the sequence: Q × 36, S × 27, U × 18, W × 9, . . . , what comes next?

   (a) Y × 1   (c) X × 0
   (b) Y × 0   (d) X × 9

3. In the sequence: 4, 16, 5, 25, 6, 36, . . . , what number comes next?

   (a) 49   (c) 40
   (b) 7   (d) 16

4. In the sequence: –82, –73, –64, –55, . . . , what number comes next?

   (a) –46   (c) 44
   (b) –44   (d) –40

5. In the sequence: 22, 20, 10, 8, 4, . . . , what number comes next?

   (a) 0   (c) 2
   (b) 16   (d) 14

6. In the sequence: 2, 4, 5, 8, 10, . . . , what two numbers should come next?

   (a) 12, 15   (c) 7, 11
   (b) 14, 17   (d) 13, 15

7. In the sequence: 1.3, 3.9, 11.7, . . . , what number comes next?

   (a) 35.1   (c) 13.9
   (b) 17.1   (d) 37.1

8. In the sequence: 9, 11, 10, 14, 12, 18, 15, . . . , what two numbers should come next?

   (a) 17, 16   (c) 17, 20
   (b) 23, 19   (d) 22, 25

9. In the sequence: AZ1, DY3, GX5, . . . , what comes next?

   (a) IW7   (c) JW7
   (b) HX3   (d) IY9

10. In the sequence: 7, 3, 12, 6, 17, 9, . . . , what number comes next?

    (a) 11   (c) 19
    (b) 12   (d) 22

(Answers are on page 131.)

COMPARISONS

There will be about 20 comparisons in the Quantitative Skills subtest. The comparison questions all have the obvious commonality of asking you to compare things. There are two categories of comparison questions: geometric and non-geometric. For the geometric questions, you'll be comparing shapes or areas, and in some cases, you'll have to count objects. Non-geometric questions involve everything else. The expressions and diagrams that you will be asked to compare will include the following:

Mathematical Expressions

Fractions, decimals, and percents
Associative and distributive properties
Exponential expressions
Scientific notation

Algebra

Distributive property in algebraic
   expressions
Slope of linear equations

Geometry

Angles in triangles
Transverse and intersecting angles
Perimeter, area, and volume of polygons

Measurements

Shaded objects such as circles or rectangles
U.S. coins such as pennies, nickels,
   and dimes
Hourglasses
Measuring cups

What the Questions Look Like

Each of the comparison questions will have the same prompt: Examine (A), (B), and (C) and find the *best* answer. The answer choices are expressed in words such as "(A) is greater than (B) which is greater than (C)" or with mathematical symbols such as "(A) > (B) > (C)." You may also see descriptions such as "(A) is more shaded than (B)" or "more time has passed in hourglass (A) than in hourglass (B)."

Many of the comparison questions will include mathematical symbols, so let's make sure you are familiar with the symbols you will see in both the questions and answer choices.

Symbol	Meaning
+	add
–	subtract
÷	divide
fraction bar —	divide
×	multiply
>	is greater than
<	is less than
=	is equal to
≠	is not equal to
∠A	angle A
⌐	right angle or 90 degrees
5^2	5 squared or 5 times 5
$\sqrt{4}$	square root of 4

Mathematical Concepts for the Comparison Questions

The Quantitative Skills subtest has a limited number of mathematical concepts within the three question types. You've already reviewed some math content in the sequence questions, so now let's review what you need to know to answer comparison questions.

FRACTIONS AND DECIMALS

In the comparison questions, you will not be asked to add and subtract but rather just multiply or compare fractions and decimals. Below are some key points to help compare fractions or decimals.

Comparing Fractions

- When comparing fractions with equal denominators and different numerators, the fraction with the largest numerator is the largest fraction.

$$\frac{2}{3} \text{ of a pizza is } more\ than\ \frac{1}{3} \text{ of a pizza}$$

- When comparing fractions with equal numerators and different denominators, the fraction with the largest denominator is the smallest fraction.

$$\frac{1}{4} \text{ of a pizza is } more\ than\ \frac{1}{8} \text{ of a pizza}$$

- For a fraction to be equal to $\frac{1}{2}$, the numerator must be half the value of the denominator $\left(\frac{4}{8} = \frac{1}{2}\right)$. The fraction $\frac{3}{7}$ is less than $\frac{1}{2}$ because the numerator, 3, is less than 3.5 (half of 7). The fraction $\frac{5}{9}$ is more than $\frac{1}{2}$ because the numerator, 5, is more than 4.5 (half of 9).

- When comparing fractions, always DO AS LITTLE MATH AS POSSIBLE! If you rewrite the fractions with common denominators, you may be wasting precious time.

- Another way to order fractions is the cross-up method. Let's compare $\frac{1}{2}$ and $\frac{2}{3}$. Multiply the numerator of $\frac{2}{3}$ with the denominator of $\frac{1}{2}$ and put the product over $\frac{2}{3}$. This looks like: $\frac{1}{2} \overset{4}{\diagup} \frac{2}{3}$. Then multiply the numerator of $\frac{1}{2}$ with the denominator of $\frac{2}{3}$ and put that product above $\frac{1}{2}$. This looks like: $\overset{3}{\underset{}{\frac{1}{2}}} \times \overset{4}{\frac{2}{3}}$. The fraction that has the larger number on top is the larger fraction, which means $\frac{2}{3} > \frac{1}{2}$.

Try putting the fractions $\frac{3}{8}$, $\frac{1}{2}$, and $\frac{2}{7}$ in increasing order using the cross-up.

First you should notice that $\frac{3}{8}$ and $\frac{2}{7}$ are both smaller than $\frac{1}{2}$, so you only have to compare two fractions. Using the cross-up method you will multiply 3 and 7 and place the product, 21, above $\frac{3}{8}$. Then, multiply 8 and 2 and place the product, 16, over $\frac{2}{7}$. This looks like: $\overset{21}{\frac{3}{8}} \times \overset{16}{\frac{2}{7}}$.

Since $\frac{3}{8}$ has the larger number above it, that is the larger fraction. In increasing order, the fractions are $\frac{2}{7}, \frac{3}{8}, \frac{1}{2}$.

Let's look at some comparison questions involving fractions.

➡ Example 1 _____

Examine (A), (B), and (C) and find the *best* answer.

(A) $\frac{5}{24}$

(B) $\frac{7}{20}$

(C) $\frac{1}{4}$

(a) (A) < (C) < (B)
(b) (A) = (B)
(c) (C) > (A) > (B)
(d) (B) = (C)

Compare each fraction to one fourth. $\frac{7}{20}$ is more than one fourth because $\frac{5}{20} = \frac{1}{4}$; therefore, $\frac{7}{20}$ must be larger. You know that 6 is one fourth of 24, so $\frac{5}{24} < \frac{1}{4}$. Do not take the time to convert these to like denominators. The correct answer is choice (a) (A) < (C) < (B).

➡ Example 2 _____

Examine (A), (B), and (C) and find the *best* answer.

(A) $\frac{2}{3}$

(B) $\frac{27}{28}$

(C) $\frac{3}{7}$

(a) (A) is greater than (B).
(b) (B) is greater than (A) which is greater than (C).
(c) (C) is greater than (A) or (B).
(d) (A) is greater than (B) which is greater than (C).

This is a good comparison to answer using the one half comparison. You can see that (A) $\frac{2}{3}$ is more than $\frac{1}{2}$, (B) is more than one half and very close to one, and (C) is less than $\frac{1}{2}$. The correct answer is (b), (B) is greater than (A) which is greater than (C).

➡ **Example 3**_____

Examine (A), (B), and (C) and find the *best* answer.

(A) $\dfrac{7}{9}$

(B) $\dfrac{2}{3}$

(C) $\dfrac{6}{11}$

(a) (A) is greater than (B) is less than (C).
(b) (B) is greater than (A) which is greater than (C).
(c) (C) is greater than (A) or (B).
(d) (A) is greater than (B) which is greater than (C).

Let's see how the cross-up method can help here.

$$\overset{21}{}\dfrac{7}{9}\times\overset{18}{}\dfrac{2}{3}\qquad\overset{22}{}\dfrac{2}{3}\times\overset{18}{}\dfrac{6}{11}$$

$\dfrac{7}{9}$ is larger than $\dfrac{2}{3}$ (because 21 is larger than 18) and $\dfrac{2}{3}$ is larger than $\dfrac{6}{11}$ (because 22 is larger than 18). The correct answer is (d), (A) is greater than (B) which is greater than (C).

Comparing Decimals

For comparison questions, all that you have to know about decimals is how to compare them to other numbers. For example, you should know that $0.6 = \dfrac{6}{10}$, or that $0.16 = \dfrac{16}{100}$. You should be able to recognize that 0.16 is greater than $\dfrac{1}{10}$.

PERCENTS

You will see a few questions that involve comparing or multiplying percents in the comparison questions. These will not be multistep problems such as figuring out discounts but rather simple calculations. Here is all you need to know to answer these questions correctly.

■ To change a decimal to a percent, move the decimal point two places to the right and add a percent sign. For example, 0.16 is equal to 16% and 2 is equal to 200% (remember 2 is the same as 2.00).
■ The word *of* means to multiply. You may be asked to multiply a percent in this subtest. For example, 10% of 50 = 0.10 × 50 = 5.0.

Try the examples below. Read the explanations to learn some valuable strategies.

FRACTIONS TIP

To compare two fractions, write the product of the numerator and the other fraction's denominator above each fraction. The fraction with the largest value above it is the larger of the two fractions.

---

15 PERCENT TIP

Don't multiply by 15% but rather multiply by 10% then add half to that result. For example:

0.15 × 300 = 45

First multiply by 0.10:

0.10 × 300 = 30

Half of 30 = 15.
Add the two values:

30 + 15 = 45

➡ Example 4_____

Examine (A), (B), and (C) and find the *best* answer.

(A) 10% of 70

(B) $\frac{1}{7}$ of 49

(C) 70% of 10

(a) (A) > (C)
(b) (A) < (B) < (C)
(c) (B) > (C)
(d) (A) = (B) = (C)

The answer is choice (d). Convert each of these expressions to a number. (A) 10% of 70 = 7, (B) $\frac{1}{7}$ of 49 = 7, (C) 70% of 10 = 7. Now you can see they are all equal.

➡ Example 5_____

Examine (A), (B), and (C) and find the *best* answer.

(A) $\frac{1}{4}$

(B) 26%

(C) 0.23

(a) (A), (B), and (C) are equal.
(b) (B) is greater than (A) which is greater than (C).
(c) (C) is less than (A) or (B).
(d) (A) and (C) are greater than (B).

The answer is choice (b). One fourth is 25%. (C) 0.23 = 23%, so (B) > (A) > (C).

➡ Example 6_____

Examine (A), (B), and (C) and find the *best* answer.

(A) 10% of 25
(B) 15% of 30
(C) 20% of 10

(a) (A) = (C)
(b) (B) > (A) > (C)
(c) (C) > (B) > (A)
(d) (C) = (B)

Your task is to compare (A), (B), and (C) and NOT to figure out percent problems as you would in math class. 10% of 25 is 2.5, however if you are consistent, you can forget about worrying whether it is 2.5 or 0.25 or 250. Ignore the percent sign (because there is one in each and each number is a two-digit integer) and look only at the numbers. Take a look:

(A) 10% of 25 → 10 × 25 = 250
(B) 15% of 30 → 15 × 30 = 450
(C) 20% of 10 → 20 × 10 = 200

Keep in mind that the statements above are INCORRECT values for the expressions. Any math teacher would cringe at these statements. But it gets the job done! This shortcut will allow you to quickly determine the correct comparison of choice (b) (B) > (A) > (C).

You will find the same correct answer if you calculate the percents, but it will take longer.

(A) 10% of 25 = 0.10 × 25 = 2.5
(B) 15% of 30 = 0.15 × 30 = 4.5
(C) 20% of 10 = 0.20 × 10 = 2.0

ASSOCIATIVE PROPERTY, DISTRIBUTIVE PROPERTY, AND PEMDAS

If you are familiar with these three rules and concepts, they will help you to evaluate expressions in the comparison questions.

The *associative property* states that one can add values regardless of where the parentheses are placed, for example $(2 + 3) + 4 = 2 + (3 + 4)$. The same is true for multiplication: $(2 \times 3) \times 4 = 2 \times (3 \times 4)$.

The *distributive property* is used when a number (or variable) is multiplied by the sum or difference of two numbers (or variables). The number outside of the parentheses must be multiplied by each of the values inside the parentheses. These two products are then added or subtracted as shown.

$$A(B + C) = AB + AC$$
$$A(B - C) = AB - AC$$

Below are some examples of the distributive property.

$$2(3 + 4) = (2 \times 3) + (2 \times 4)$$
$$2(3 - 4) = (2 \times 3) - (2 \times 4)$$
$$4(x + y) = 4x + 4y$$
$$3(x - y) = 3x - 3y$$

Now let's see how to answer a comparison question using the distributive property.

➡ **Example 7**_____

Examine (A), (B), and (C) and find the *best* answer when x and y are both positive.

(A) $9x + 5y$
(B) $9(x + y)$
(C) $9x + y$

(a) (B) and (C) are equal.
(b) (A) is less than (C).
(c) (B) is greater than (C).
(d) (C) is greater than (A).

Use the distributive property to rewrite expression (B), $9(x + y) = 9x + 9y$.

Since each expression has a $9x$, you only have to compare the y terms to see that (B) is the largest expression for positive numbers x and y. The correct answer is (c), (B) is greater than (C).

PEMDAS (Please Excuse My Dear Aunt Sally) is used to determine order of operations and is an acronym for **P**arentheses, **E**xponents, **M**ultiplication and **D**ivision, and **A**ddition and **S**ubtraction. The only part of this that you will have to remember in this section is that the operations inside the parentheses are performed first, before completing the rest of the equation.

TIP

Don't try to simplify in your head. If you get right to work and use the distributive property, you can simplify these questions in seconds.

➡ **Example 8**_____

Examine (A), (B), and (C) and find the *best* answer.

(A) $6 \times (4 + 3)$
(B) $(6 \times 4) \div 3$
(C) $6 + (4 \times 3)$

(a) (A) is greater than (C) which is greater than (B).
(b) (B) is greater than (A) which is greater than (C).
(c) (A) is equal to (B) and (C).
(d) (C) is greater than (A).

The solution look like this:

$$(A) \quad 6 \times (4 + 3) = 6 \times 7 = 42$$
$$(B) \quad (6 \times 4) \div 3 = 24 \div 3 = 8$$
$$(C) \quad 6 + (4 \times 3) = 6 + 12 = 18$$

The correct answer is choice (a), (A) is greater than (C) which is greater than (B).

EXPONENTIAL AND RADICAL EXPRESSIONS

There are many rules involving exponents; however, if you understand the meaning of an exponent, then you will do well on the one or two exponent comparison questions. An exponential expression has the form 3^4. In this example, 3^4 means 3 multiplied by itself 4 times, $3^4 = 3 \times 3 \times 3 \times 3 = 81$.

➡ Example 9_____

Examine (A), (B), and (C) and find the *best* answer.

(A) 2^3
(B) 2^4
(C) 4^2

(a) (A) is equal to (B).
(b) (B) is equal to (C).
(c) (B) is less than (A).
(d) (C) is less than (B).

Simplify each exponential expression to an integer.

$$(A)\ 2^3 = 2 \times 2 \times 2 = 8$$
$$(B)\ 2^4 = 2 \times 2 \times 2 \times 2 = 16$$
$$(C)\ 4^2 = 4 \times 4 = 16$$

You can now see that (B) is equal to (C) for a correct answer of choice (b).

➡ Example 10 _____

Examine (A), (B), and (C) and find the *best* answer.

(A) 3×2^2
(B) 2×3^2
(C) 2×3^3

(a) (A) = (B) = (C)
(b) (A) > (B) > (C)
(c) (C) > (B) > (A)
(d) (A) = (B) > (C)

When you see a question with exponents, you should determine the value of each expression and write it next to each letter.

$$(A)\ 3 \times 2^2 = 3 \times 4 = 12$$
$$(B)\ 2 \times 3^2 = 2 \times 9 = 18$$
$$(C)\ 2 \times 3^3 = 2 \times 27 = 54$$

Once you simplify (B) you can STOP. Do you see that you already have your answer? Just by looking at (A) and (B), you can rule out answer choices (a), (b), and (d). The correct answer is choice (c) because (C) is the greatest of the three, $2 \times 27 = 54$.

Example 11

Examine (A), (B), and (C) and find the *best* answer.

(A) $\sqrt{10}$

(B) $\sqrt{5 \times 2}$

(C) $\sqrt{5} + \sqrt{2}$

(a) (A) = (B) = (C)

(b) (A) = (B) ≠ (C)

(c) (A) ≠ (B) ≠ (C)

(d) (A) ≠ (B) = (C)

You will not be expected to know the value of radicals that do not involve perfect squares. All you have to know here is that (A) and (B) are equal and that you cannot add unlike terms. In (C) $\sqrt{5}$ and $\sqrt{2}$ cannot be added because they are unlike terms; therefore, that answer expression is *different* from the other two. You will not have to know if it is more or less, since that type of problem is more complicated than what you will see on the HSPT. The correct answer is choice (b).

SCIENTIFIC NOTATION

Scientific notation is a means of expressing very large and very small numbers in a concise manner. Numbers written in scientific notation are made up of a decimal part and an exponent part with a base of 10. To convert a number from scientific notation to a decimal, move the decimal point to the right the same number of places that is the exponent of 10. You can see this in the following examples:

$$3.45 \times 10^3 = 3.45 \times 1{,}000 = 3{,}450$$

$$0.0023 \times 10^4 = 0.0023 \times 10{,}000 = 23$$

$$568.2308 \times 10^3 = 568.2308 \times 1{,}000 = 568{,}230.8$$

REMEMBER

The exponent in a number written in scientific notation tells you the number of places to move the decimal point to the right.

Example 12

Examine (A), (B), and (C) and find the *best* answer.

(A) 1,740

(B) 1.74×10^2

(C) 0.174×10

(a) (A) is equal to (B).

(b) (B) is equal to (C).

(c) (B) is greater than (A).

(d) (C) is less than (B).

Convert the expressions that are in scientific notation to a decimal. (B) $1.74 \times 10^2 = 174$ and (C) $0.174 \times 10 = 1.74$. The correct answer is choice (d), (C) is less than (B).

CHARTS, DRAWINGS, AND GEOMETRIC COMPARISONS

On the HSPT, you may see one or two questions where you are simply counting. Put a value under each diagram, and you will answer these quickly and accurately. You may have to compare coins, bar graphs, the number of hearts on cards, dots on dominos, time that has passed in an hourglass, or other visual images. Keep in mind these are just different ways of showing you numerical values. These are easy if you follow the tips below:

- Label each diagram with a number if you are counting.
- Do NOT rush. These are easy, but if you rush it will be easy to make a mistake.
- If the drawings are shaded, then under each drawing, write the fraction of shaded pieces. The number of shaded pieces is the numerator (top part of the fraction) and the total number of pieces is the denominator (bottom part of the fraction).

➡ Example 13 _____

Examine the number of dots in (A), (B), and (C) and find the *best* answer.

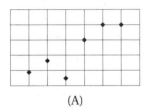 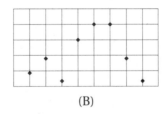 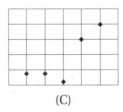

| (A) | (B) | (C) |

(a) (B) is greater than (A) and equal to (C).
(b) (B) is greater than (A) or (C).
(c) (A) is greater than (B).
(d) (A) is equal to (C).

This is an example of a geometric comparison. Count CAREFULLY and write the number under each image. Read the answer choices and cross out the wrong answers as you go. (A) = 6, (B) = 8, (C) = 5. The correct answer is choice (b), (B) is greater than (A) or (C).

➡ Example 14 _____

Examine (A), (B), and (C) and find the *best* answer.

 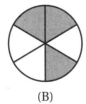 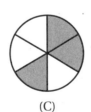

| (A) | (B) | (C) |

(a) (A) is shaded more than (B).
(b) (A), (B), and (C) are shaded equally.
(c) (C) is shaded more than (B).
(d) (A) is shaded more than (B) or (C).

For this geometric comparison, put a fraction beneath each picture to represent the shaded area. (A) is $\frac{2}{4} = \frac{1}{2}$, (B) is $\frac{3}{6} = \frac{1}{2}$, and (C) is also $\frac{3}{6} = \frac{1}{2}$. You can see that they are all equal to $\frac{1}{2}$, making the correct answer choice (b).

➡ Example 15 _____

Examine (A), (B), and (C) and find the *best* answer.

     (A)   (B)   (C)

(a) (C) − (B) > (A)
(b) (A) − (C) > (B)
(c) (C) + (B) < (A)
(d) (A) − (B) = (C)

For this comparison write 10 under the dime, 5 under the nickel, and 25 under the quarter. This is an easy question, but your brain may play tricks on you if you are rushed. Labeling each coin will help to ensure that you do not make the mistake of thinking a nickel is *larger* than a dime. As you read each answer choice, cross out the letter of the answers you find to be false. The correct answer is choice (a), (C) − (B) > (A).

GEOMETRY

It is not necessary to have had a course in geometry to do well on the HSPT. Most questions in the Quantitative Skills subtest that involve geometry can be answered easily by knowing just a few concepts. You will not be asked to define an object in this subtest; however, a comparison question may make reference to certain polygons. To do well on these questions, you should understand the following:

- The sum of the interior angles of a triangle always add to 180° as seen in the below example.

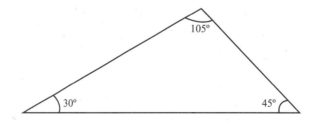

- In a triangle, the side opposite the largest angle is the longest side, and the side opposite the smallest angle is the smallest side.
- A right triangle has one 90° angle.
- In an isosceles triangle, two of the angles are equal in measure, making two sides of equal length.
- In an equilateral triangle, all three angles are equal making all three sides equal.
- A trapezoid is a four-sided polygon with only two parallel sides.

NOTE

You will learn more math concepts in Chapter 7 "Mathematics." For now, you are focusing only on what you need to know to answer Comparison questions in the Quantitative Skills subtest.

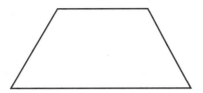

- Straight angles that make up a line add to 180°.

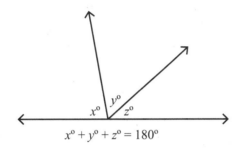

$$x° + y° + z° = 180°$$

- Transversal angles are created by passing a line through two parallel lines. Transversal angles have the same measure. In the following diagram, angles are represented by capital letters A and D as well as B and C, which are pairs of transversal angles. $A = D$, $B = C$, $E = H$, $F = G$; in addition, $A = E$, $B = F$, $C = G$, and $D = H$.

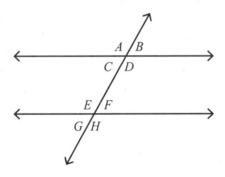

Now review some comparison examples involving basic geometry to see how you do.

➡ Example 16

Examine angles *A*, *B*, and *C* and find the *best* answer.

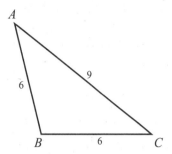

- (a) *A* is greater than *C*.
- (b) *A* is equal to *B*.
- (c) *B* is less than *C*.
- (d) *A* is equal to *C*.

Angles that are opposite smaller sides are smaller than angles opposite larger sides. Angles *A* and *C* are the same measure, since they are opposite sides of the same length. They are both smaller than angle *B* which is opposite the largest side. The correct answer is choice (d), *A* is equal to *C*.

➡ Example 17

Examine angles *A*, *B*, and *C* and find the *best* answer.

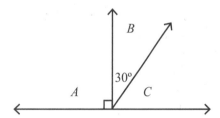

- (a) *C* is greater than *A*.
- (b) *C* is equal to *B*.
- (c) *A* is greater than *C* which is greater than *B*.
- (d) *A* is greater than *B* which is greater than *C*.

Angles that make up a line or a triangle add to 180 degrees. Figure out the measure of the missing angle, and write the measure next to the letter *A*, *B*, or *C* then read the answer choices. Angle *A* is 90 degrees as indicated by the right angle symbol and angle *B* is 30 degrees. Therefore, angle *C* must be 180 − 90 − 30 = 60 degrees. An easier solution is to recognize that two right angles add up to 180, and since you already have one right angle, then the other two angles must add to 90 degrees. 60 + 30 = 90. The correct answer is choice (c), *A* is greater than *C* which is greater than *B*.

ALGEBRA

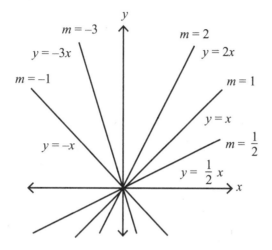 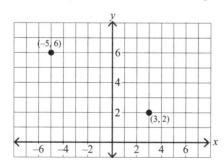

Algebra questions on the Quantitative Skills subtest involve either slopes of linear equations or the distributive property using variables. Here is what you should know to answer these questions correctly.

- $y = mx + b$ is a linear equation in slope-intercept form. For example $y = 2x + 5$.
- The letter, m, in front of the variable, x, represents the slope of the line, and the letter that is alone, b, is the constant and represents the y-intercept, where the line intersects the y-axis.
- If m is a negative number, the line has a negative slope; if it is positive, the line has a positive slope. In the diagram below, m represents the slope of each line. Notice that steep lines have larger values for m than lines that are less steep.

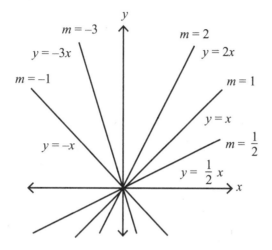

- Coordinate points are always labeled (x, y). x is the horizontal axis and y is the vertical axis.
- To figure out the slope by looking at a graph, pick two points (x_1, y_1) and (x_2, y_2) and put the difference in the heights (y-values) over the difference between the horizontal values (x-values) according to the formula below. This fraction is referred to as "rise over run" and represents the slope of a line.

$$m = \frac{y_2 - y_1}{x_2 - x_1}$$

Look at the diagram below to see how you can calculate the slope from two points on a graph.

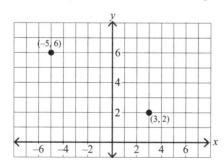

To determine the slope, note the two points $(-5, 6)$ and $(3, 2)$, and use the formula above.
Slope $= \frac{6-2}{-5-3} = \frac{4}{-8} = -\frac{1}{2}$.

➡ Example 18 _____

Examine the slopes of lines *A, B,* and *C* and find the *best* answer.

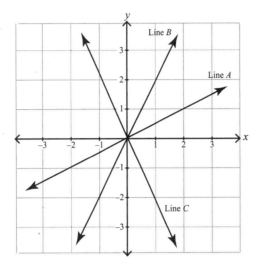

(a) $A = 2$

(b) $B = 2$

(c) $B < A$

(d) $C = 2$

Looking at line *A*, compare the points $(0, 0)$ and $(2, 1)$. The rise, *up*, from the first to second point is 1 and the run, *over*, is 2. This gives a slope of $\frac{1}{2}$. Likewise, the slope of line *B* is 2, and the slope of line *C* is -2 since the line heads downwards when going from $(0, 0)$ to $(1, -2)$. The correct answer is choice (b), $B = 2$.

When answering algebraic questions with variables in the questions, replace the variable with a small number such as 2. Avoid choosing the numbers 0 and 1 as these two numbers have unique characteristics and may give more than one correct answer.

➡ Example 19 _____

Examine (A), (B), and (C) and find the *best* answer when *x* is positive.

(A) $x + (4 - 1)$

(B) $4 + x$

(C) $10 + (1 + x)$

(a) (A) is greater than (B).

(b) (A) is less than (B) which is greater than (C).

(c) (C) is greater than (A) or (B).

(d) (B) is greater than (C) which is greater than (A).

Substitute a small number such as 2 for each *x* that you see, and then evaluate as shown below.

(A) $x + (4 - 1) \rightarrow 2 + (4 - 1) = 5$
(B) $4 + x \rightarrow 4 + 2 = 6$
(C) $10 + (1 + x) \rightarrow 10 + (1 + 2) = 13$

The correct answer is choice (c), (C) is greater than (A) or (B). You may have noticed that when you simplify each expression you have (A), $x + 3$, (B) $x + 4$, (C) $x + 11$, also indicating the answer of (c).

Comparisons Practice

It's time to practice what you have learned about comparison questions. Here are ten questions for you to try.

1. Examine (A), (B), and (C) and find the *best* answer.

   (A) $(3 \times 9) + 5$
   (B) $5 + (3 \times 9)$
   (C) $3 \times (9 + 5)$

   (a) (B) is equal to (A) and less than (C).
   (b) (B) is equal to (C) which is greater than (A).
   (c) (B) is greater than (A) which is greater than (C).
   (d) (B) is greater than (C) which is greater than (A).

2. Examine (A), (B), and (C) and find the *best* answer.

   (A) $\dfrac{1}{3}$
   (B) 34%
   (C) 0.34

   (a) (A), (B), and (C) are equal.
   (b) (B) is more than (A) and equal to (C).
   (c) (C) is less than (A) or (B).
   (d) (A) and (C) are greater than (B).

3. Examine (A), (B), and (C) and find the *best* answer when *x* and *y* are both positive.

   (A) $7x + 5y$
   (B) $5(x - y)$
   (C) $7x + y$

   (a) (B) and (C) are equal.
   (b) (B) is greater than (C).
   (c) (A) is more than (C).
   (d) (C) is greater than (A).

4. Examine (A), (B), and (C) and find the *best* answer.

   (A) $\dfrac{21}{23}$
   (B) $\dfrac{21}{30}$
   (C) $\dfrac{2}{3}$

   (a) (C) > (A) > (B)
   (b) (A) > (B) > (C)
   (c) (A) > (B) = (C)
   (d) (B) > (C) > (A)

5. Examine (A), (B), and (C) and find the *best* answer.

   (A) 20% of 60
   (B) 60% of 30
   (C) 30% of 50

   (a) (A) > (B)
   (b) (B) = (C)
   (c) (B) > (C)
   (d) (C) < (A)

6. Examine (A), (B), and (C) and find the *best* answer.

   (A) 2 meters
   (B) 18 inches
   (C) 1 yard

   (a) (A) > (B) > (C)
   (b) (C) < (A) < (B)
   (c) (B) < (C) = (A)
   (d) (A) > (C) > (B)

7. Examine (A), (B), and (C) and find the *best* answer.

   (A)   (B)   (C)

   (a) (A) is shaded more than (B).
   (b) (A), (B), and (C) are shaded equally.
   (c) (B) is shaded more than (C).
   (d) (C) is shaded more than (A).

8. Examine the triangle and find the best answer.

   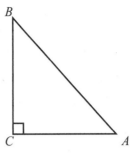

   (a) ∠A is greater than ∠C.
   (b) All angles are equal.
   (c) ∠C is greater than (∠A + ∠B).
   (d) ∠C is equal to (∠A + ∠B).

9. Examine (A), (B), and (C) and find the *best* answer.

   (A)   (B)   (C)

   (a) (C) has twice as many as (A).
   (b) (B) has more than (C) and less than (A).
   (c) (C) has two more than (A).
   (d) (B) has fewer than (A).

10. Examine (A), (B), and (C) and find the *best* answer.

    (A) 200% of 42
    (B) 100% of 67
    (C) 300% of 20

    (a) (A) < (B) < (C)
    (b) (B) = (C)
    (c) (A) < (C)
    (d) (A) > (B) > (C)

    (Answers are on page 132.)

COMPUTATIONS

There are 9–10 computation questions on the Quantitative Skills subtest, and they can be very easy with a little practice and some helpful strategies. As the name implies, these questions involve only computations, in other words, addition, subtraction, multiplication, and division.

What the Questions Look Like

The computation questions will all have the words "what number" either in the beginning or middle of the question. If you like these questions, you're probably good at them, so make sure you complete them all.

The questions will all be similar in format, following one of these two examples.

Question Prompt	Example	Answer
What number is . . . ?	What number is $\frac{1}{5}$ of 40 percent of 200?	The correct answer is 16.
_____ of what number is _____?	$\frac{1}{3}$ of what number is two more than 18?	The correct answer is 60.

Strategies for the Computation Questions

SOLVING COMPUTATIONS ALGEBRAICALLY

If you have had algebra and know how to *quickly* answer the computation questions by writing an equation, then do that. Below each example that follows, the equation that represents the question is listed. There is no need to use algebra to solve these, so don't worry if the equation is confusing to you. If it is, just ignore it, and answer the questions working from right to left.

READ LEFT TO RIGHT, BUT SOLVE FROM RIGHT TO LEFT

The trick to these questions is to do them in small pieces. Read the question from left to right, but when you solve it, you should solve it from right to left, in small pieces. Read the example below from left to right as you normally would.

➡ Example 1 _____

2 times what number is 10 times 5?

(a) 5   (b) 15   (c) 25   (d) 45

Now solve the problem in pieces starting at the right. What is 10 times 5? The product is 50. The question now reads, "2 times what number is 50?" You'll quickly figure out the correct answer is choice (c) 25. The equation that represents this is $2x = 10 \times 5$.

TIP

Read the question from left to right, then solve it in pieces from right to left. Write the answers on top of the question as you work, so you won't forget each piece.

Here are some additional examples of computation questions that you may see on the HSPT. Try each example and then read the answers and explanations that follow.

➡ Example 2

What number subtracted from 36 makes 7 more than 15?

  (a) 8   (b) 14   (c) 15   (d) 38

Let's work backwards here. 7 more than 15 is 22, 7 + 15 = 22. Next, subtract 22 from 36 to get the answer. 36 − 22 = 14. The correct answer is choice (b) 14. The equation that represents this is 36 − x = 7 + 15.

➡ Example 3

What number multiplied by 4 is 3 less than 43?

  (a) 2   (b) 4   (c) 10   (d) 8

Three less than 43 is 40. Now the question is "What number multiplied by 4 is 40?" 40 divided by 4 is 10. The correct answer is choice (c) 10. The equation that represents this is 4x = 43 − 3.

➡ Example 4

TIP

Tackle percents in tens. Calculate 10% by moving the decimal point one place to the left and then double that answer for 20%. You can also triple it for 30%.

What number subtracted from 7^2 is 20% of 50?

  (a) 39   (b) 25   (c) 49   (d) 40

Ten percent of 50 is 5, so double that to find 20% which is 10. You can also remember that 20% is $\frac{1}{5}$. Next, $\frac{1}{5}$ of 50 is 10. Then move on to 7^2, which is 7 × 7 = 49. Now the question reads "What number subtracted from 49 is 10?" 10 subtracted from 49 is 39, making the correct answer choice (a) 39. The equation that represents this is $7^2 − x = 0.20 × 50$.

➡ Example 5

What number is 11 more than $\frac{1}{7}$ of 35?

  (a) 28   (b) 5   (c) 14   (d) 16

From right to left, 35 times $\frac{1}{7}$ is the same as 35 divided by 7, which equals 5. The new question reads "What number is 11 more than 5?" The correct answer is choice (d) 16. The algebraic equation that represents this is $x = 11 + \frac{1}{7} × 35$.

USE THE ANSWER CHOICES TO SAVE YOU TIME

If you have to guess on a question, you will have a 25% chance of guessing correctly. If you eliminate one or two answer choices, you will greatly increase the probability of guessing correctly. Look at the following example to see how the answer choices can save you time.

➡ Example 6_____

What number is $\frac{1}{5}$ of 9 times 7?

(a) 10   (b) 16   (c) $12\frac{3}{5}$ (d) 63

Working from the right, 9 times 7 is 63. Since 63 is not a multiple of 5, the answer is going to have a remainder, so you are done! The answer has to be choice (c) $12\frac{3}{5}$, since it is the only answer choice that is not a whole number. $\frac{1}{5}$ of 63 is $12\frac{3}{5}$.

If you come across a question that you don't understand or don't know how to answer, then you may have to guess. Don't waste too much time, but take a quick look at the answer choices before you guess. Chances are that if there are two answers that are close, as in the example below, it will be one of those two. This is not always true, but it's worth a try if you really are stuck.

➡ Example 7_____

What number subtracted from 4^2 is 25% of 36?

(a) 7   (b) 8   (c) 18   (d) 25

REMEMBER

Knowing your perfect squares will help you in the non-verbal sections of the HSPT. For a list of perfect squares, see page 105.

If you are running out of time, then choose either 7 or 8, since they are close to each other. One fourth or 25% of 36 is 9. Then $16 - 9 = 7$. The correct answer for this example is choice (a) 7. The equation that represents this is $4^2 - x = 0.25 \times 36$.

YOU KNOW YOURSELF BEST

It is important to remember that no one knows you as well as you do. Hints and strategies are very useful if you do not otherwise know how to solve the problem quickly and accurately. However, if you are more comfortable solving computation problems another way, such as writing an algebraic equation, AND you are getting the questions correct in a timely manner, then you should continue to do what you are doing. The nice thing about mathematics is that there are often many different ways to solve the problem, but only one correct answer.

Now you are ready to complete a practice set of computation problems. Remember the skills you have learned while you answer the questions.

Computations Practice

1. What number is 8 more than 20% of 50?

   (a) 12   (b) 18   (c) 36   (d) 42

2. What number is 18 less than $\frac{2}{3}$ of 120?

   (a) 28   (b) 46   (c) 62   (d) 68

3. What number subtracted from 97 leaves 7 more than 3 times 8?

   (a) 10   (b) 63   (c) 66   (d) 24

4. What number is twice as much as $\frac{1}{4}$ of 250?

   (a) 100   (b) 125   (c) 50   (d) 150

5. What number is 7 more than 14% of 200?

   (a) 800   (b) 20   (c) 35   (d) 28

6. What number multiplied by 11 is equal to 15 more than 73?

   (a) 4   (b) 12   (c) 6   (d) 8

7. What number multiplied by 5 is 15 less than 35?

   (a) 5   (b) 4   (c) 7   (d) 8

8. What number subtracted from 37 makes 5 more than 10?

   (a) 22   (b) 13   (c) 15   (d) 35

9. What number subtracted from 5^2 is 20% of 75?

   (a) 14   (b) 6   (c) 5   (d) 10

10. What number is $\frac{1}{3}$ of 7 times 6?

    (a) 42   (b) 14   (c) $11\frac{1}{4}$ (d) 12

(Answers are on page 132.)

ANSWERS EXPLAINED FOR CHAPTER 5

Roman Numerals (page 108)

III = 3, IV = 4, IX = 9, XVI = 16, XXVII = 27, XLIII = 43, XLV = 45

Sequences Practice (page 109)

1. **(a)** The pattern here is to divide by 5. The last term would be 8 ÷ 5, which is equal to $\frac{8}{5}$. Remember to look at your answer choices so you don't waste time turning this fraction into a mixed number.

2. **(b)** Ignore the × signs completely! Solve this one in pieces, beginning with the first letter of each term. Q, skip R, S, skip T, so the next term begins with a Y, which narrows the answer down to either choice (a) or (b). Next, look at the numbers, which are decreasing by 9 with each term. The last number is 9 less than 9 which is 0. So the correct answer is Y × 0.

3. **(b)** If you look at every other term you'll see 4, 5, 6, . . . , so the next term will be 7. The pattern (which you do not have to decipher here) is 4, 4^2, 5, 5^2, 6, 6^2.

4. **(a)** This pattern is + 9 for each term. The next term will be –55 + 9 = –46.

5. **(c)** The pattern is – 2, ÷ 2, – 2, ÷ 2, etc. The next term is 4 ÷ 2 = 2.

6. **(b)** This is an example of a pattern in the differences. Write the differences between each term: + 2, + 1, + 3, + 2, then look at every other difference. The first is + 2, skip the next, then + 3, skip the next, the next difference should be + 4. To find the next term, add 4 to the 10 to get 14. This means the answer must be choice (b)14, 17. The second difference pattern is + 1, skip the next, then + 2, skip the next, then the last difference would be + 3. Add 3 to 14 to get 17.

$$\begin{array}{ccccccccc} & \mathbf{+2} & & +1 & & \mathbf{+3} & & +2 & \\ 2, & & 4, & & 5, & & 8, & & 10, \ldots \end{array}$$

7. **(a)** This pattern is multiplying by 3. The last term would be 11.7 times 3 which is 35.1.

8. **(b)** Look at the differences in this sequence: + 2, – 1, + 4, – 2, + 6, – 3. Then look at every other difference to discover the pattern. The addition pattern is increasing by 2 each time and the subtraction is increasing by 1. The next two operations will be + 8 then – 4.

$$\begin{array}{ccccccccccccc} & \mathbf{+2} & & -1 & & \mathbf{+4} & & -2 & & \mathbf{+6} & & -3 & \\ 9, & & 11, & & 10, & & 14, & & 12, & & 18, & & 15, \ldots \end{array}$$

9. **(c)** You should look at each item in the terms separately beginning with the first letter, A, D, G, (skipping 2 letters each time). The next term will begin with J which narrows the answer to only one. There is no need to find the remaining pattern.

10. **(d)** Addition or subtraction doesn't seem to work, so try looking at every other term. This is a sequence within a sequence. First 7, 12, 17 (add 5). Look at the other terms, 3, 6, 9 (add 3), but this sequence is not needed since the next term is plus 5, so 17 + 5 = 22.

Comparisons Practice (pages 125–126)

1. **(a)** Simplify each expression. (A) $27 + 5 = 32$, (B) $5 + 27 = 32$, (C) $3 \times 14 = 42$, and compare your values. As soon as you simplify (A) and (B), you are done; there is only one possible answer.

2. **(b)** One third is equal to 33.33%. (C) $0.34 = 34\%$ so (A) < (B) = (C).

3. **(c)** Use the distributive property to rewrite (B), $5(x - y) = 5x - 5y$. Looking at the x variable you can see that (B) is the smallest with only $5x$, while (A) and (C) both have $7x$. (B) also has a negative y, so it must be the smallest of the three choices. Since (A) has $5y$ and (C) only has $1y$, (A) is the larger of the two.

4. **(b)** It is too much work to create a common denominator. Instead, compare each fraction to $\frac{2}{3}$. $\frac{21}{30}$ is just over $\frac{2}{3}$ while $\frac{21}{23}$ is very close to 1. $\frac{2}{3} < \frac{21}{30} < \frac{21}{23}$.

5. **(c)** This is an example where you can ignore the percent symbols and the trailing zeros as they are the same in each value. This leaves (A) $2 \times 6 = 12$, (B) $6 \times 3 = 18$, and (C) $3 \times 5 = 15$ for a correct answer of choice (c), (B) > (C).

6. **(d)** A meter is approximately 3 feet or 36 inches, so 2 meters is about 72 inches, making (A) > (C) > (B).

7. **(d)** Convert each of the diagrams to a fraction. In each fraction the numerator is the number of shaded rectangles and the denominator is the number of total rectangles. Now you can see that (B) = (C) and both are greater than (A).

8. **(d)** In a right triangle (designated by the symbol at angle C) the largest angle, $\angle C$, is equal to the sum of the other two angles.

9. **(c)** Count the number of dots and write the number below each domino. Then read each answer to determine the correct answer.

10. **(d)** Convert each expression to a value, ignoring all of the trailing zeros in each percent. (A) $2 \times 42 = 84$, (B) $1 \times 67 = 67$, and (C) $3 \times 20 = 60$.

Computations Practice (page 130)

1. **(b)** Working from the right, first take 20%, or one fifth, of 50 which is 10. Then 8 more than 10 is 18. The equation is $x = 8 + (0.2 \times 50)$.

2. **(c)** $\frac{2}{3}$ of 120 is 80 (first take one third then double it), then subtract 18 from 80 to get 62. The equation is $x = \left(\frac{2}{3} \times 120\right) - 18$.

3. **(c)** Multiply 3 times 8 to get 24 then add 7 to make 31. Next ask "what number subtracted from 97 is 31?" $97 - 31 = 66$. The equation is $97 - x = 7 + (3 \times 8)$.

4. **(b)** The easiest way to solve this is to double one fourth to get one half. Then take half of 250 which is 125. The equation is $x = 2\left(\frac{1}{4} \times 250\right)$.

4. **(b)** The easiest way to solve this is to double one fourth to get one half. Then take half of 250 which is 125. The equation is $x = 2\left(\frac{1}{4} \times 250\right)$.

5. **(c)** 14% of 200 is 28. Here's a shortcut—just multiply 2 times 14 to get 28. 200% of 14 is the same as 14% of 200, only much easier to see. Seven more than 28 is 35. The equation is $x = 7 + (0.14 \times 200)$.

6. **(d)** Begin by adding 15 and 73 to get 88. 11 times what number is 88? The answer is 8. The equation is $11x = 15 + 73$.

7. **(b)** Find the difference of 35 and 15 (which is 20). Five times what number is 20? The answer is 4. The equation is $5x = 35 - 15$.

8. **(a)** Begin by adding 5 and 10 to get 15. What number when subtracted from 37 is equal to 15? ($37 - 15 = 22$.) The equation is $37 - x = 5 + 10$.

9. **(d)** Twenty percent of 75 is 15 (0.2 times 75). What number subtracted from 25 is 15? ($25 - 15 = 10$.) The equation is $5^2 - x = 0.20\,(75)$.

10. **(b)** Multiply 7 times 6 for a product of 42. One third of 42 is 14. The equation is $x = \frac{1}{3}(7 \times 6)$.

WRAP IT UP WITH PRACTICE

Summary of General Quantitative Skills Strategies

Review these strategies once more before trying the practice subtest at the end of this chapter.

- You have about 30 seconds to complete each question.
- Recognize the question type so you know which strategy to use.
- If you find yourself running out of time, try to answer the question type that you like the most and guess on the rest.
- Do as little math as possible. Whenever you can, solve the problem the easy way.
- Use the answer choices as clues.
- When you see the correct answer move on.
- Do all of your work on the test itself and not on the scrap paper.

Summary of the Sequence Strategies

When answering the sequence questions, keep the following strategies and tips in mind.

- First, try addition and/or subtraction to figure out the pattern.
- Next, try multiplication and/or division.
- If you have trouble finding the pattern when looking from left to right, try it from right to left.
- Write the differences or the ratios above the sequence and look for the pattern in the differences.
- Look for a sequence within a sequence.
- If the terms include one or more letters, then treat each position in the term as its own sequence.
- Convert Roman numerals to their Arabic counterparts, write the number above each term, and then follow the strategies above.

Summary of the Comparison Strategies

- Use the one-half rule to compare fractions.
- In percents, if each value has the same number of trailing zeros, ignore the trailing zeros in each.
- When comparing diagrams, place a numerical value beneath each diagram.
- To answer questions with variables, replace the variables with a small number.

Summary of the Computation Strategies

- Begin solving the question at the right. If you work the problem in small pieces you will be much less likely to make a mistake.

30 MINUTES

Samples:

A. What number added to 3 makes 2 plus 5?

   (a) 3   (b) 4   (c) 5   (d) 7

B. In the sequence: 1, 2, 3, 4, 5, . . . , what number should come next?

   (a) 3   (b) 6   (c) 5   (d) 4

C. Examine (A), (B), and (C) and find the *best* answer.

   (A) (3 – 2) – 1
   (B) (3 – 1) – 2
   (C) 3 – (2 – 1)

   (a) (A) is greater than (B).
   (b) (A), (B), and (C) are equal.
   (c) (C) is greater than (A) and (B).
   (d) (B) is greater than (A).

D. Examine the hourglasses (A), (B), and (C) and find the *best* answer.

   (A)   (B)   (C)

   (a) (A) shows the most time passed.
   (b) (B) shows the most time passed.
   (c) (C) shows the most time passed.
   (d) (A) and (B) show the same time has passed.

Correct marking of samples:

A. Ⓐ ● Ⓒ Ⓓ
B. Ⓐ ● Ⓒ Ⓓ
C. Ⓐ Ⓑ ● Ⓓ
D. Ⓐ Ⓑ ● Ⓓ

---

61. In the sequence: 25, 5, 36, 6, . . . , what number should come next?

   (a) 49   (b) 12   (c) 7   (d) 16

62. Examine (A), (B), and (C) and find the *best* answer.

   (A)   (B)   (C)

   (a) (B) – (C) = (A)
   (b) (A) + (C) > (B)
   (c) (C) – (B) < (A)
   (d) (A) + (B) = (C)

63. In the sequence: 0.6, 1.2, 2.4, 4.8, . . . , what number should come next?

   (a) 6.0   (b) 1.75 (c) 9.6   (d) 5.5

64. What number subtracted from 28 makes 5 more than 8?

   (a) 8   (b) 13   (c) 15   (d) 35

65. In the sequence: 37, 28, 19, . . . , what number should come next?

   (a) 38   (b) 10   (c) 27   (d) 9

GO TO THE NEXT PAGE ➡

66. Examine (A), (B), and (C) and find the *best* answer.

(A) $\frac{3}{4}$ of 36

(B) $\frac{1}{3}$ of 60

(C) $\frac{2}{5}$ of 55

(a) (A) < (B) < (C)
(b) (A) = (B)
(c) (A) > (C) > (B)
(d) (B) = (C)

67. In the sequence: K15, N13, Q26, T24, . . . , what comes next?

(a) T22   (b) O11   (c) P9   (d) W48

68. What number subtracted from 6^2 is 25% of 44?

(a) 10   (b) 9   (c) 26   (d) 25

69. Examine the angles A, B, and C in the isosceles triangle and find the *best* answer.

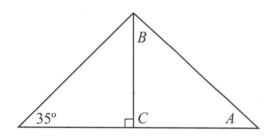

(a) $A > C$
(b) $B > A = C$
(c) $B = C$
(d) $C > B > A$

70. In the sequence: 1,280, 320, 80, 20, . . . , what number should come next?

(a) 5   (b) 10   (c) 4   (d) 60

71. In the sequence: 8, 4, 2, 1, . . . , what number should come next?

(a) 0.2   (b) 0.5   (c) 2   (d) $\frac{1}{5}$

72. Examine (A), (B), and (C) and find the *best* answer.

(A) $\frac{3}{8}$

(B) $\frac{3}{11}$

(C) $\frac{3}{13}$

(a) (A) < (B) < (C)
(b) (A) = (B)
(c) (A) > (B) > (C)
(d) (B) = (C)

73. In the sequence: 576, 144, 36, 9, . . . , what number should come next?

(a) 2.25   (b) 1.75   (c) 2.1   (d) 4.5

74. In the sequence: 180, 60, 30, 10, 5, . . . , what number should come next?

(a) 1   (b) 6   (c) $\frac{5}{2}$ (d) $\frac{5}{3}$

75. In the sequence: II, IV, V, X, XI, . . . , what numeral should come next?

(a) XXXI   (c) XX
(b) XXII   (d) XII

76. Examine (A), (B), and (C) and find the *best* answer when x and y are both positive.

(A) $2x + 5y$
(B) $2(x + y)$
(C) $2x + y$

(a) (B) and (C) are equal.
(b) (A) is less than (C).
(c) (B) is greater than (C).
(d) (C) is greater than (A).

77. In the sequence: 26H, 31F, 36D, . . . , what comes next?

(a) 41C   (b) 31B   (c) 31C   (d) 41B

GO TO THE NEXT PAGE ➡

78. In the sequence: 17FH, 20GI, 23HJ, . . . , what comes next?

    (a) 26IK   (c) 20KM

    (b) 26KM   (d) 20KI

79. What number is 6 more than $\frac{1}{6}$ of 36?

    (a) 42   (b) 37   (c) 36   (d) 12

80. In the sequence: 88, 44, 52, 26, 34, . . . , what two numbers should come next?

    (a) 42, 21   (c) 16, 24

    (b) 17, 25   (d) 66, 33

81. What number is 12 less than $\frac{2}{3}$ of 90?

    (a) 30   (b) 46   (c) 48   (d) 68

82. Examine (A), (B), and (C) and find the *best* answer.

    (A) $(3 \times 8) + 7$

    (B) $3 + (8 \times 7)$

    (C) $3 \times (8 + 7)$

    (a) (B) is equal to (A) and greater than (C).

    (b) (B) is equal to (C) which is greater than (A).

    (c) (B) is greater than (A) which is greater than (C).

    (d) (B) is greater than (C) which is greater than (A).

83. Examine (A), (B), and (C) and find the *best* answer.

(A)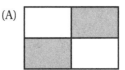

(B)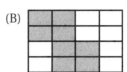

(C)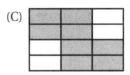

    (a) (A), (B), and (C) are equally shaded.

    (b) (C) is shaded less than (B) and more than (A).

    (c) (B) and (C) are shaded equally.

    (d) (A) and (B) are shaded equally.

84. What number subtracted from 84 leaves 9 more than 2 times 8?

    (a) 19   (b) 57   (c) 59   (d) 27

85. In the sequence: 64, 60, 68, 62, 72, 64, . . . , what two numbers should come next?

    (a) 76, 66   (c) 72, 66

    (b) 63, 72   (d) 66, 60

86. In the sequence: −56, −49, −42, −35, . . . , what number should come next?

    (a) −28   (b) −5   (c) −7   (d) $\frac{1}{7}$

GO TO THE NEXT PAGE ➡

87. Examine (A), (B), and (C) and find the *best* answer.

(A) 10% of 60
(B) 50% of 30
(C) 30% of 50

(a) (A) > (B)
(b) (B) = (C)
(c) (B) > (C)
(d) (C) < (A)

88. In the sequence: 181, 177, 171, 167, 161, . . . , what number should come next?

(a) 155 (b) 158 (c) 157 (d) 177

89. Examine (A), (B), and (C) and find the *best* answer.

(A) 1680
(B) 1.68×10^2
(C) 0.168×10

(a) (A) is equal to (B).
(b) (B) is equal to (C).
(c) (B) is greater than (A).
(d) (C) is less than (B).

90. What number is twice as much as $\frac{1}{5}$ of 250?

(a) 100 (b) 25 (c) 50 (d) 150

91. In the sequence: ZA, YB, XC, WD, . . . , what comes next?

(a) VE (b) EV (c) UE (d) UF

92. What number subtracted from 36 makes 18 more than 4?

(a) 14 (b) 18 (c) 60 (d) 58

93. In the sequence: Q7, P14, O28, . . . , what should come next?

(a) M56   (c) N56
(b) N14   (d) N35

94. Examine (A), (B), and (C) and find the *best* answer.

(A) 0.13
(B) 13%
(C) $\frac{1}{8}$

(a) (A), (B), and (C) are equal.
(b) (C) is greater than (B) and equal to (A).
(c) (C) is less than (A) or (B).
(d) (A) and (C) are greater than (B).

95. In the sequence: 75, 13, 70, 16, . . . , what number should come next?

(a) 19 (b) 65 (c) 11 (d) 67

96. What number is 8 more than 12% of 100?

(a) 10 (b) 20 (c) 32 (d) 108

97. In the sequence: 2, 16, 10, 80, 74, 592, . . . , what number should come next?

(a) 3,552   (c) 98
(b) 582   (d) 586

98. Examine the bar graph and find the *best* answer.

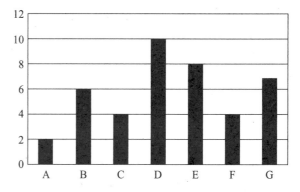

(a) A plus E equals G.
(b) B plus C equals D.
(c) G plus A plus F equals E.
(d) A, C, and F are equal.

GO TO THE NEXT PAGE ➡

99. In the sequence: 13, 16, 18, 22, 25, . . . , one number is *wrong*. That number should be

(a) 30   (b) 58   (c) 98   (d) 19

100. In the sequence: 46HK, 57IL, 68JM, 79KN, . . . , what should come next?

(a) 90LO   (c) 98LO
(b) 89OP   (d) 90OP

101. Examine the trapezoid below and find the *best* answer.

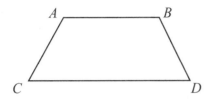

(a) *AB* is greater than *CD*.
(b) *AB* is parallel to *CD*.
(c) *AB* and *BD* equal *CD*.
(d) *AC* is equal to *BD*.

102. What number multiplied by 11 is equal to 15 more than 73?

(a) 4   (b) 12   (c) 6   (d) 8

103. Examine (A), (B), and (C) and find the *best* answer.

(A) 5^2
(B) 2^5
(C) 5^3

(a) (A) is equal to (B).
(b) (C) is greater than (A) or (B).
(c) (B) is less than (A).
(d) (A), (B), and (C) are all equal.

104. In the sequence: 6, 11, 17, 24, . . . , what number should come next?

(a) 34   (b) 27   (c) 32   (d) 6

105. Examine (A), (B), and (C) and find the *best* answer.

(A) $(36 \div 2) \times 3$
(B) $(36 \div 3) \times 2$
(C) $36 \div (2 \times 3)$

(a) (A) is equal to (B).
(b) (A) is greater than (C).
(c) (B) is greater than (A).
(d) (C) is equal to (B).

106. Examine (A), (B), and (C) and find the *best* answer.

(A) $\dfrac{63}{65}$

(B) $\dfrac{21}{30}$

(C) $\dfrac{1}{3}$

(a) (C) > (A) > (B)
(b) (A) > (B) > (C)
(c) (A) > (B) = (C)
(d) (B) > (C) > (A)

107. What number multiplied by 7 is 6 less than 41?

(a) 5   (b) 4   (c) 7   (d) 8

GO TO THE NEXT PAGE ➡

108. Examine the slopes of lines *A*, *B*, and *C* and find the *best* answer.

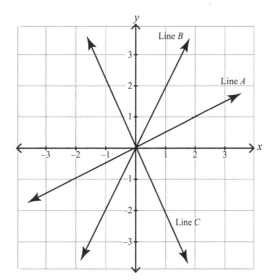

(a) *A* = *B*
(b) *C* > *A*
(c) *B* > *A*
(d) *A* > *B*

109. Examine (A), (B), and (C) and find the *best* answer.

(A) 20% of 40
(B) 40% of 20
(C) 8

(a) (A) is equal to (B) and greater than (C).
(b) (A), (B), and (C) are equal.
(c) (C) is greater than (A) or (B).
(d) (B) is greater than (A).

110. What number is $\frac{1}{4}$ of 9 times 5?

(a) 10   (b) 20   (c) $11\frac{1}{4}$ (d) 45

111. Examine (A), (B), and (C) and find the *best* answer.

(A) $(11 + 6) \times 3$
(B) $(3 \times 11) + (3 \times 6)$
(C) $(11 \times 6) + 3$

(a) (A) and (B) are equal.
(b) (A) and (C) are equal.
(c) (B) is greater than (A).
(d) (C) is less than (B).

112. Examine (A), (B), and (C) and find the *best* answer.

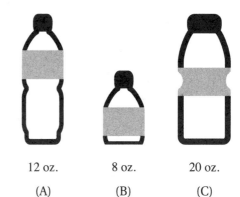

| 12 oz. | 8 oz. | 20 oz. |
| (A) | (B) | (C) |

(a) (B) – (C) = (A)
(b) (A) < (B) + (C)
(c) (C) – (B) = (A)
(d) (B) + (A) > (C)

STOP

NOTE

Answer explanations in this section are labeled with their corresponding question types. You will need this for the scoring chart on page 145.

ANSWERS EXPLAINED FOR PRACTICE QUANTITATIVE SKILLS SUBTEST

61. **(a)** This is a sequence in a sequence. 5^2, skip the next, 6^2, skip the next, 7^2 is 49. You can ignore the other sequence, which is 5 plus one, 6, plus one, etc. (Sequence)

62. **(b)** (A) is a dime, ten cents; (B) is a nickel, five cents; (C) is a quarter, twenty-five cents. (A) + (C) > (B) or 10 cents plus 25 cents is more than 5 cents. (Geometric Comparison)

63. **(c)** The sequence is doubling. 0.6 times 2 is 1.2, times 2 is 2.4, times 2 is 4.8, and times 2 is 9.6. (Sequence)

64. **(c)** Work this from right to left in pieces. 5 more than 8 is 13. 28 minus 13 is 15. The algebraic equation representing this is $28 - x = 5 + 8$. (Computation)

65. **(b)** The pattern is $- 9, - 9, - 9$, so $19 - 9 = 10$. (Sequence)

66. **(c)** The best way to answer this is to evaluate each product. $\frac{3}{4}$ of 36 is 27 ($36 \div 4 = 9$, then $9 \times 3 = 27$); $\frac{1}{3}$ of 60 is 20; $\frac{2}{5}$ of 55 is 22 ($55 \div 5 = 11$, then $11 \times 2 = 22$). So (A) > (C) > (B). (Non-geometric Comparison)

67. **(d)** This is a sequence within a sequence. Look at the letters first and rule out answer choices. **K**, skip L, M, **N**, skip O, P, **Q**, skip R, S, **T**, skip U, V. The next letter must be W. Don't waste time figuring out the number sequence because only one answer choice begins with W. (Sequence)

68. **(d)** Work this problem from right to left. 25% is the same as one fourth. One fourth of 44 is 11. Now look at the next piece. Six squared is 36. Subtract 11 from 36 to get 25. The algebraic equation is $6^2 - x = .25 \times 44$. (Computation)

69. **(d)** As a supplementary angle next to a right angle, C is a 90-degree angle. This is an isosceles triangle, so angle A must be 35 degrees. Lastly, all interior angles in a triangle add to 180 degrees, so angle B must be 55 degrees ($180 - 90 - 35 = 55$). The correct answer is choice (d). (Geometric Comparison)

70. **(a)** The pattern here is $\div 4$, $\div 4$, etc. If you don't see it right away, try looking at it from right to left, and you should quickly see that 20 times 4 is 80, and 80 times 4 is 320. Going the other way from left to right, perform the inverse of multiplication, which is division, $20 \div 4 = 5$. (Sequence)

71. **(b)** The pattern is $\div 2$, $\div 2$, etc. One divided by two is one half or 0.5. (Sequence)

72. **(c)** Because the numerators are all the same, you only have to compare the denominators. Remember that if you cut a pizza into 13 pieces, each piece will be smaller than the pieces of a pizza that is cut into only 8 pieces. So $\frac{3}{8}$ is larger than $\frac{3}{11}$, which is larger than $\frac{3}{13}$. You can rule out anything with an equal sign. (Non-geometric Comparison)

73. **(a)** The pattern is $\div 4$, $\div 4$, etc. It is easier to see the pattern if you look from right to left and see that it is $\times 4$, $\times 4$. So, left to right must be $\div 4$. If you divide 9 by 4, you will have a number that is $2\frac{1}{4}$ or 2.25. (Sequence)

74. **(d)** The pattern is ÷ 3, ÷ 2, ÷ 3, ÷ 2, etc. So 5 ÷ 3 would come next in the pattern to give you a value of $\frac{5}{3}$. (Sequence)

75. **(b)** Translate the Roman numerals to find the sequence. II = 2, IV = 4, V = 5, X = 10, XI = 11. Now you have the Arabic numbers, you can see that the pattern is × 2, + 1, × 2, + 1. The next number is 22. In Roman numerals, 22 is XXII. (Sequence)

76. **(c)** Before looking at the answer choices, simplify (B) using the distributive property. $2(x + y) = 2x + 2y$. Now you can compare the three more easily to see that (A) > (B) > (C). If you don't see this right away, try making up a number for x and y. If $x = 2$ and $y = 3$ then (A) = 19, (B) = 10, and (C) = 7. (Non-geometric Comparison)

77. **(d)** The sequence has numbers and letters, so look at each separately beginning with the numbers. 26 + 5 = 31, 31 + 5 = 36, so the next term will be 36 + 5 = 41. There are two choices with 41, so now look at the letters. They are going backwards every other letter. **H**, skip G, **F**, skip E, **D**, skip C, making the next letter B. (Sequence)

78. **(a)** The sequence has numbers and letters, so look at each pattern separately. 17 + 3 = 20, 20 + 3 = 23, so 23 + 3 = 26. Since there are two answer choices with 26, look at the first letter in each term: F, G, H, etc. The next letter will be I, making the correct answer choice (a). Don't waste time figuring out the remaining pattern! (Sequence)

79. **(d)** Working from right to left, you see that $\frac{1}{6}$ of 36 is 6. What number is 6 more than 6? The answer is 12. The algebraic equation is $x = 6 + \frac{1}{6}$ (36). (Computation)

80. **(b)** The pattern is, ÷ 2, + 8, ÷ 2, + 8. The next two terms will be 34 ÷ 2 = 17, and then 17 + 8 = 25. (Sequence)

81. **(c)** Working from right to left, multiply 90 by $\frac{2}{3}$. If you are unsure, just write it out and reduce the fraction. $90 \times \frac{2}{3} = 60$ (one third of 90 is 30, then double 30 to make 60). The number 12 less than 60 is 48. The algebraic equation is $x = \frac{2}{3}$ (90) – 12. (Computation)

82. **(d)** Simplify each expression before looking at the answer choices and remember to always do what's in the parentheses first. (A) 24 + 7 = 31; (B) 3 + 56 = 59; (C) 3 × 15 = 45. Since they are all different, you can quickly rule out (a) and (b). The correct answer is choice (d) (B) > (C) > (A). (Non-geometric Comparison)

83. **(d)** Convert each shaded area to a reduced fraction before looking at the answer choices. (A) = $\frac{2}{4} = \frac{1}{2}$, (B) = $\frac{8}{16} = \frac{1}{2}$, (C) = $\frac{8}{12} = \frac{2}{3}$. Since $\frac{2}{3} > \frac{1}{2}$, the only correct choice is (A) = (B). (Geometric Comparison)

84. **(c)** Working from right to left, multiply 2 and 8, and then add 9 to make 25. 84 minus what number makes 25? 84 – 25 = 59. The algebraic equation is 84 – x = 9 + (2 × 8). (Computation)

85. **(a)** The pattern is – 4, + 8, – 6, + 10, – 8, etc. Look at every other difference beginning with + 8, + 10, so the next term will be found by adding 12, 64 + 12 = 76. The next pattern is – 4, – 6, – 8, so the last term will be 76 –10 = 66. (Sequence)

86. **(a)** The pattern is + 7, + 7. Then, −35 + 7 = −28. Since all of the numbers are negative, you can ignore the negative signs and look at the numbers descending by 7, making the next answer 28. Now put the negative back, −28. (Sequence)

87. **(b)** Because each number is one digit followed by a zero, you can ignore the trailing zeros and multiply the remaining whole number. Remember you are just making a comparison. (A) = 6, (B) = 15, and (C) = 15, so (B) = (C). (Non-geometric Comparison)

88. **(c)** The pattern is − 4, − 6, − 4, − 6. Then, 161 − 4 = 157. (Sequence)

89. **(d)** Simplify each. (A) = 1,680, (B) = 168, and (C) = 1.68, so (C) < (B). (Non-geometric Comparison)

90. **(a)** Working from right to left, $\frac{1}{5}$ of 250 is 50. The number that is twice the amount of 50 is 100. The algebraic equation is $x = 2\,(\frac{1}{5} \times 250)$. (Computation)

91. **(a)** Look at the first letter in each term to see they are going backwards: Z, Y, X, W; therefore, V is next. Since there is only one choice that begins with V, you don't have to figure out the rest. (Sequence)

92. **(a)** Working from right to left, add 18 and 4 to make 22. Then subtract 22 from 36 to get 14. The algebraic equation is $36 - x = 18 + 4$. (Computation)

93. **(c)** Look at the letters first: going backwards Q, P, O, etc., making the next letter N. Next look at the numbers: + 7 is not the pattern, so try multiplication. 7 doubled is 14, doubled again is 28, then double 28 to get the next number, 56. (Sequence)

94. **(c)** Percent means to divide by 100. (B) 13% = 0.13. (C) $\frac{1}{8}$ = 0.125 is the smallest. (Non-geometric Comparison)

95. **(b)** This is a sequence within a sequence. Ignore the 13 and 16, and you see 75 − 5 = 70. 70 − 5 = 65 and you're done. Don't waste time on the rest. If you do, you may incorrectly pick choice (a). (Sequence)

96. **(b)** Working from right to left, first take 12 percent of 100 which is 12. Then 8 more than 12 is 20. The algebraic equation is $x = 8 + (0.12 \times 100)$. (Computation)

97. **(d)** The sequence is × 8, −6, × 8, −6, × 8, etc. To get the correct answer, subtract 6 from 592 to get 586. If you are rushed, don't check 74 × 8. (Sequence)

98. **(b)** The height of each column represents the frequency (the number of items). Bar A is 2, Bar B is 6, etc. B (6) plus C (4) is equal to D (10). (Geometric Comparison)

99. **(d)** Remember you are looking for the *wrong* number so you can replace it with the correct one. The pattern is + 3, + 3, etc., so the 18 should be a 19 to complete the sequence properly. (Sequence)

100. **(a)** Look at the numbers first. The pattern here is + 11, + 11, etc., so the next number will be 90. Next, look at the first letter in each term, H, I, J, K, etc., the next letter will be L. The correct answer is choice (a). Do NOT waste time figuring out the last letter pattern! (Sequence)

101. **(b)** The top and bottom sides of trapezoids are parallel, so *AB* must parallel to *CD*. Sides *AC* and *BD* are not necessarily the same length. (Geometric Comparison)

102. **(d)** Working right to left in pieces, add 15 and 73 to make 88. $88 \div 11 = 8$. The algebraic equation is $11x = 15 + 73$. (Computation)

103. **(b)** Simplify each expression to a whole number. (A) = 25, (B) = 32, and (C) = 125. Since none are equal, you can eliminate answer choices (a) and (d). (Non-geometric Comparison)

104. **(c)** The pattern is + 5, + 6, + 7. The next increase will be + 8. $24 + 8 = 32$. (Sequence)

105. **(b)** Simplify each expression, remembering to simplify inside the parentheses first. (A) $18 \times 3 = 54$, (B) $12 \times 2 = 24$, and (C) $36 \div 6 = 6$. Since none are equal, eliminate answer choices (a) and (d) and select choice (b), (A) > (C). (Non-geometric Comparison)

106. **(b)** It is too much work to create a common denominator, so use the $\frac{1}{2}$ rule. Since $\frac{1}{3}$ is less than $\frac{1}{2}$ and the other two are more than $\frac{1}{2}$, you can eliminate answer choices (a) and (d). Neither (A) nor (B) is equal to (C), so you can eliminate answer choice (c); therefore the answer must be choice (b). (Non-geometric Comparison)

107. **(a)** Working right to left, subtract 6 from 41 to make 35. Divide 35 by 7 to get 5. The algebraic equation is $7x = 41 - 6$. (Computation)

108. **(c)** Looking at the slope of each line, notice that both A and B are increasing, so they both have a positive slopes. Line C has a negative slope. This is enough to rule out answer choices (a) and (b). Because line B is steeper than A, it has a greater slope making B > A. (Non-geometric Comparison)

109. **(b)** The word *of* means multiply. 20% of 40 = 40% of 20, or $0.20 \times 40 = 0.40 \times 20$, and both are equal to 8. (A), (B), and (C) are all equal. (Non-geometric Comparison)

110. **(c)** Working right to left, 9 times 5 is 45. As soon as you realize 45 is not divisible by 4, you know the answer is not a whole number so it must be answer choice (c). The algebraic equation is $x = \frac{1}{4} (9 \times 5)$. (Computation)

111. **(a)** Simplify each working inside the parentheses first. (A) $17 \times 3 = 51$, (B) $33 + 18 = 51$, and (C) $66 + 3 = 69$; therefore, (A) = (B). (Non-geometric Comparison)

112. **(c)** This diagram is labeled in ounces beneath each image. After verifying that each number has the same units (ounces), compare the numbers. $20 - 8 = 12$. (Geometric Comparison)

SCORING YOUR PRACTICE QUANTITATIVE SKILLS SUBTEST

Now that you have reviewed the answers and explanations, let's see how well you are doing. Go through the explanations again and count up the number of each question type you answered correctly. Then fill in the chart below.

	Sequence	Geometric Comparison	Non-geometric Comparison	Computation	Total
Number of each question type you answered correctly					
Total of each question type	22	6	13	11	52

First, add up the total number of questions you answered correctly. Then divide that number by 52 and multiply by 100 to determine your raw score for the Quantitative Skills subtest.

$$\text{Raw Score} = \frac{\text{Total Number Correct}}{52 \text{ Total Questions}} = \frac{}{52} \times 100 = \underline{}\%$$

Next, to determine your raw score for each question type, take the number of questions you answered correctly in each category and divide that number by the total number of questions in each question type. Multiply each answer by 100 to convert to a percent.

$$\text{Sequence} = \frac{\text{Total Number Correct}}{22 \text{ Total Questions}} = \frac{}{22} \times 100 = \underline{}\%$$

$$\text{Geometric Comparison} = \frac{\text{Total Number Correct}}{6 \text{ Total Questions}} = \frac{}{6} \times 100 = \underline{}\%$$

$$\text{Non-geometric Comparison} = \frac{\text{Total Number Correct}}{13 \text{ Total Questions}} = \frac{}{13} \times 100 = \underline{}\%$$

$$\text{Computation} = \frac{\text{Total Number Correct}}{11 \text{ Total Questions}} = \frac{}{11} \times 100 = \underline{}\%$$

Look at your highest score of the four above. This is the question type that you do best so make sure you ALWAYS finish each of these. You should read each explanation for questions that you answered incorrectly. You should also read the explanations for any questions that you feel took a long time to answer to see if there may have been an easier way to solve it.

Reading

6

Reading comprehension is part of most standardized tests and is considered to be an indicator as to how well you may perform in school. To some, reading comes naturally and is enjoyable, but for others, reading can be slow, unenjoyable, and laborious. In this chapter, you will learn strategies that can help you increase your reading speed and reading comprehension. On the HSPT, you will have to read passages and answer questions after each. The passages will be appropriate for your age and grade and will not be more than a few paragraphs in length. The challenge in this subtest is to read carefully, identify key information, and finish on time.

THE LAYOUT

The Reading Subtest is the third subtest on the HSPT. You will have 25 minutes to complete the 62 questions. This subtest is made up of two different sections: READING—Comprehension and READING—Vocabulary. Each section will be labeled as such. The Comprehension section is made up of four reading passages, each followed by 10 questions for a total of 40 questions. The Vocabulary section is made up of 22 questions.

Reading Subtest—25 Minutes and 62 Questions

Question Type	Example	Number of Questions
Comprehension—General	What is the *best* title for the passage?	14–16
Comprehension—Vocabulary	Hinder, as underlined and used in the passage, means . . .	8
Comprehension—Specific	According to the passage, what event began the war?	14–16
Vocabulary	The novice performer	22

Each subtest begins with sample questions that demonstrate the directions for each type of question. Because Reading is the third subtest, your test booklet will be open while the proctor reads the instructions. The proctor will read sample questions aloud before beginning the timed part of your test. There is an example of this at the beginning of the practice Reading subtest.

Let's review and practice each type of question. Afterwards, there will be a brief summary to remind you of key strategies for the Reading subtest. At the end of the chapter is a full-length practice subtest, where you can practice the strategies you have learned here.

GENERAL STRATEGIES FOR READING

If you ask any reading specialist how to improve your reading comprehension skills, they will undoubtedly reply, "Read more!" When answering questions in the reading subtest, you will be expected to understand the overall intent of the passage as well as to find specific details in the reading. Reading more often will improve your ability to do both. Below are some general strategies to guide you in this subtest.

Do Not Let Your Mind Wander

Have you ever read a book, and as you turn the page, you realize that you have no idea what you just read? This happens to everyone. If it happens to you on the HSPT, it can cost you valuable time. Get in the habit of checking in with yourself after each paragraph. You don't have to review the paragraph, but just ask yourself if you are still focused. If the answer is *yes* then keep reading. If the answer is *no* then reread that paragraph and keep going. Don't wait until the end of the passage to do this or you may end up having to reread the entire passage. Get in the habit of doing this as you practice, and it will pay off on test day.

Do Not Move Your Lips!

Subvocalizing is the act of muttering or mouthing words as you read. Many of us do this, and it isn't always a bad thing; however, it does slow you down. Let your brain focus on the task at hand, which is reading not talking. If you subvocalize habitually, then do your best to break this habit before test day. Try chewing gum to help you to stop. Of course you cannot chew gum on test day, but perhaps you can put a finger over your lips while you read. Use this strategy when taking the practice tests.

Do Not Study the Passage

You have only one goal here and it is not to understand everything you are reading. Your only goal is to answer as many questions correctly as possible. There is no extra credit for thoroughly understanding what you read.

Move Quickly Through the Reading Passages and Questions

This is a difficult subtest to finish in the time allowed. You will have four passages to read and 62 questions to answer in only 25 minutes. It is important to practice for this subtest so you can improve your reading speed.

You ONLY Know What Is Written

When answering questions, remember to use only the information you read about in the story. Forget everything you may already know on that subject or tale.

Use Process of Elimination for Comprehension Questions

It is important that you read every answer choice to find the best one. When you read an answer choice you know is incorrect, cross it out. All of the answers are in the passage, so if you can eliminate one or more answer choices, you will have an easier time when you look through the passage for the correct answer.

Save Time for Vocabulary

You should plan to spend about 20 minutes in the Reading—Comprehension part of the subtest (5 minutes for each passage), and the remaining 5 minutes answering the Reading—Vocabulary questions. If you struggle with finishing on time, do the vocabulary first.

Extra Time

If you have extra time, spend it on Comprehension questions and NOT Vocabulary. Chances are if you didn't know the meaning of a vocabulary word the first time, you will not know it on your second pass. The answers to the Comprehension questions are in the passage, so use your extra time looking for answers that you missed earlier.

Important Note on Timing

If in your practice you are consistently finishing the Reading subtest in the 25 minutes allowed, you are in great shape. You can read the passages in the order given and use any extra time to check your work. If, instead, you are not finishing this subtest on time, then you should answer the Vocabulary questions first. You will only need 5 minutes, at most, to get through these. The 22 questions can be answered quickly, unlike the Comprehension questions. You should try this in the practice section at the end of the chapter.

HOW TO IMPROVE READING SPEED

The single best way to improve the speed at which you read, as well as your reading comprehension, is to practice, practice, practice. Read as much as you can before test day. Establish a baseline of your reading speed, then try to increase the number of words you can read and comprehend in one minute. This is something that you can improve simply by reading more. Here are some additional tips that can help you improve your reading speed.

> **READING SPEED**
>
> If you found that you finished the Reading subtest of the first practice test with time remaining, then feel free to skip over this part. If you find later that you need to improve your reading speed, then come back to this section.

Establish a Baseline

Most people over the age of 14 can read about 200 words per minute. If you cannot read at this speed, spend some time practicing reading to increase your speed. Let's try an exercise to determine your reading speed. Below is a sample passage. Set a stopwatch, read the passage at a pace that is comfortable, and when finished record your time. As you read, try to remember key points and the overall meaning of the passage. Set your timer and read the passage on the following page.

"And always be careful when you choose your friends. There are lots of bad men in the army, Henry. The army makes them wild. They like nothing better than taking a young fellow like you, who has never been away from home much and has always had a mother, and teaching him to drink liquor and curse. Stay away from them, Henry. I don't want you ever to do anything, Henry, that you would be ashamed to tell me about. Just act as if I were watching you. If you keep that in your mind always, I guess you'll come out all right.

"You must always remember your father, too, child. And remember he never drank a drop of liquor in his life, and seldom cursed, either.

"I don't know what else to tell you, Henry, except that you must never avoid your duty, child. If a time comes when you have to be killed or do a bad thing, Henry, don't think of anything except what's right. Many women have to endure such things in these times, and the Lord will take care of us all.

"Don't forget your shirts, child, and try and keep warm and dry. Good-bye, Henry. Be careful, and be a good boy."

– excerpt from *The Red Badge of Courage* by Stephen Crane

Time to read the passage: _____ seconds

How long did it take you to finish the passage? The passage contains 200 words and if you are reading at the right speed, you should have completed it in about one minute. If you spent more than 60 seconds reading this passage than you should work to improve your speed. Try reading the passage again, but this time make a conscious effort to read more quickly.

Time to read the passage: _____ seconds

Did you finish the passage in less time? Sometimes knowing that you have to read more quickly is all it takes to improve your speed.

Use a Pointer

TIP

After each paragraph you read, make a mental check to see if you are focused. Try to focus on the passage and nothing else.

When you read, try using your finger or a pencil to keep your focus. If you move the pencil along at a faster pace than you typically read, your brain will instinctively try to keep up and in turn force you to read faster. Try to practice before test day to see if this technique works for you. Practicing this technique will help you to feel comfortable, so it won't end up being a distraction. As you get better, try putting the pencil under the second word in each sentence rather than the first and ending with the second to last word. Your peripheral vision will help you to see these words, but you won't be making a conscious effort to read them. This will reduce the amount of words, and in turn, the time you spend on this passage. Can you start three words in? Practice this technique to see if it works for you.

Get an App

There are some great apps available on smartphones and tablets. ReadMe! and BeeLine Reader are a couple of apps that can help you to improve your reading efficiency. These incorporate features, such as color coding sentences, to help you develop good reading habits.

Track Your Progress

Tracking your progress as you actively work to improve your reading speed, will be a valuable motivator for you. There is no need to become a speed reader. Your goal is to finish the Reading subtest in the time allowed—not to finish it in record time.

TYPES OF READING QUESTIONS

There are two sections in this subtest: Comprehension and Vocabulary. The Comprehension questions can be categorized as general, specific, or vocabulary (words in the context of the passage). You learned about vocabulary in Chapters 3 and 4, and hopefully are continually adding to your vocabulary journal as you study, so let's focus now on reading comprehension. Here you will learn about each question type in more detail and learn specific strategies you can use for each.

READING—COMPREHENSION

The Reading Comprehension portion of this subtest will assess how well you understand the material you read. It will test your ability to make inferences as well as your understanding of the author's intent and tone in writing the passage. These questions are categorized as Comprehension, Structure, and Integration. There are 40 Reading Comprehension questions in the Reading subtest. Below is a list of the concepts you will see in the Comprehension section.

Comprehension	Structure	Integration
Main ideas	Vocabulary in context	Compare and contrast
Details and events	Purpose of the passage	Compare paragraphs
Inferences	Plot	Fact versus fiction
Conclusions	Setting	Make predictions
Passage title		
Cause and effect		

 TIP

Answer questions in order. Resist the temptation to skip around— this may cause confusion. Skim questions before reading; after you read the passage, answer the questions in the order they are asked.

Let's look at how to read a passage in a timely manner and answer questions based on these concepts. It is important that you decide on an approach for the reading portion of this subtest. You should practice your approach when taking the sample tests in this book, adjust it if it's not ideal, and then use this approach on test day. Below are steps outlining an approach that is recommended for this subtest.

1. Make a note of the time and check the clock often. Spend only 5 minutes on each passage including the 10 questions that follow. If you have difficulty managing your time, then write the time at the bottom of each page to remind you. For example, if the subtest begins at 9:24, write 9:29 at the bottom of the first passage, 9:34 at the bottom of the second passage, etc.

2. Skim the questions, but not the answer choices, before reading the passage, paying particular attention to the specific questions about vocabulary or questions about a particular person or thing.

3. Read the passage without studying it. Get a general idea of each paragraph as you read through. If making labels is helpful to you, then make brief notes, just a couple of words, next to each paragraph.

4. As you see information that you know is needed to answer a specific question, circle it so you can find it quickly when you are done reading.

5. Underline anything you think may be important in answering the questions.

6. Before looking for answers to specific questions, eliminate as many wrong answer choices as possible. Skim the passage to find answers specific to the story and look at words that you have underlined or circled.

7. If you feel that you are spending too long on one question, then make a guess, circle the question number, and move on. If you have extra time, come back to the questions you circled.

8. Check the time and make sure to move on to the next passage within 5 minutes.

General Questions

General questions are often the most difficult. To answer these correctly, you must have an overall understanding of the author's intent in writing the passage. You must also understand the flow of the passage, so you can predict what may happen next. Here are some examples of the format for the general questions.

> The author's style of writing can best be described as . . .
>
> What is the best title for the passage?
>
> Who is most likely to agree with the author's point of view?
>
> In which of the following publications would this passage most likely be printed?
>
> What is the main idea of the passage?
>
> The passage is an example of . . .
>
> If Napoleon were alive today . . .
>
> The author of this passage is most likely a . . .
>
> From this passage, you can infer that . . .

USING LABELS

Some readers find it helpful to make notes as they read. This can help in answering the general questions. Brief labels can show the overall flow of the passage or direct you to the correct paragraph when looking for specific information. If you can make labels without taking too much time, *and* you find them to be helpful, then you should use this technique throughout your practice. Do not use labels if they are not helpful or take too much time. When doing the practice questions in this chapter, try writing labels and using them to answer the general questions and as a roadmap to guide you to the right paragraph. You know yourself better than anyone else does so you decide if label making is helpful for you.

PROCESS OF ELIMINATION

When reading general questions you must consider each answer choice before choosing the best one. The process of elimination is your best strategy for general questions. When reading answer choices, eliminate any of the following:

- Answer choices that you know are incorrect
- Answers choices that are too broad in scope (ex: history of the world, global warming)
- Answer choices that are absolute (ex: never, always)
- Answers choices that contain information that may be true but is not in the passage

Let's do a practice passage to see if you will benefit from taking notes. Read the following passage and make a brief note after each paragraph in the boxes on the side.

Reading Passage 1
Refer to this passage when answering Examples 1–6.

Yosemite National Park, located in the state of California, is one of the United States' most revered parks. Yosemite was formed millions of years ago when uplifting changed the area's elevation forming deep canyons, wide rivers, and powerful waterfalls. During the glacial era, ice thickness in Yosemite is estimated to have been thousands of feet thick. The melting of the glaciers created what are now some of the most breathtaking granite formations in our country.

> Paragraph 1

The most widely known rock formation in Yosemite is known as El Capitan, which in Spanish means The Captain or The Chief. This monolith is over 3,000 feet high along its tallest side. It is composed almost entirely of granite carved by glacial action 100 million years ago. Rock climbers from all over the world have scaled the face of El Capitan.

> Paragraph 2

Another of the park's beloved treasures is Mariposa Grove. In the grove are hundreds of Giant Sequoia trees. One of the oldest known living trees is the Grizzly Giant estimated to be 2,700 years in age.

> Paragraph 3

In addition to hiking, rock climbing, and sightseeing, other activities are widespread and include horseback riding, stargazing, rafting, and camping. There is something to interest every visitor at Yosemite.

> Paragraph 4

Your notes should look something like this:

Paragraph 1	Paragraph 2	Paragraph 3	Paragraph 4
History of Yosemite	El Capitan—granite	Sequoia trees	Lots to do at Yosemite

Now let's see if you can answer these general questions simply by looking at your labels. If you have to reread parts of the passage, first try using just the labels. Each of the examples represent a type of general question.

BEST TITLE AND MAIN IDEAS

Rule out answer choices that are broader in scope than the passage. Look at your labels for clues. Ask yourself what was discussed most in the passage. If you are still unsure, read the last sentence of the passage again. Usually the main idea and purpose of the passage are summarized in the first or last sentences.

➡ Example 1

The best title for this passage is

(a) "Yosemite—A National Treasure."
(b) "The History of the National Park System."
(c) "America's National Parks."
(d) "How Mountains Are Formed."

Looking at your labels, you should see the words "History," "El Capitan," "Trees," and "Lots to Do" and realize that this is an article about the various sites specific to Yosemite. While this passage does mention some of the history, the National Parks, and mountain formation, the overall intent of the passage is to discuss the wonder of Yosemite. The correct answer is choice (a) "Yosemite—A National Treasure."

➡ Example 2

What is the main idea of the passage?

(a) how El Capitan got its name
(b) the many ways to reach the top of El Capitan
(c) an introduction to Yosemite National Park
(d) how glaciers create mountains

This is a commonly asked general question. Remember to use process of elimination whenever the correct answer isn't obvious to you. You may notice that this question is very similar to that in Example 1 but a bit more direct. This passage discusses various things about Yosemite and not just El Capitan. The correct answer choice is choice (c) an introduction to Yosemite National Park.

AUTHOR'S TONE OR PROFESSION

When answering questions about the author, you must have an overall sense of the author's opinion of the passage topic. Was the author being light-hearted or matter-of-fact? Did the author appear to be an expert, a scientist, a student, or a novelist (one who writes fiction)? Eliminate as many unlikely answers as you can, then choose the most obvious of the remaining answers.

➡ Example 3

The author is most likely a

(a) scientist.
(b) park ranger.
(c) a sports writer.
(d) a novelist.

The author is clearly knowledgeable about Yosemite, and while there is some mention of glaciers and how they impacted mountain formation, there is not enough science to indicate an expert. The passage is nonfiction, so you can rule out a novelist. While hiking and rock climbing can be considered sports, the passage is more broad. The correct answer is choice (b) park ranger.

➡ Example 4

The author's tone is best described as

(a) critical.
(b) sarcastic.
(c) matter-of-fact.
(d) somber.

The passage was written in an informational article. There is no evidence in the passage of sarcasm or seriousness (somber). There were no criticisms made, so the only remaining answer is choice (c) matter-of-fact.

PREDICTIONS

Some general questions ask you to predict an event. Use your labels to answer this type of question. If you don't write labels, then ask yourself how the story flows and what would be the natural progression if the passage continued. You may also be asked about how the author or a character in the passage feels either in general or about a particular event. Rule out anything extreme, and if you have more than one possible answer choice, look back at the story for evidence.

➡ Example 5

The author would agree that

(a) all national parks offer similar attractions as Yosemite.
(b) everyone should climb El Capitan.
(c) Mariposa Grove is the oldest place on Earth.
(d) Yosemite would be a good vacation destination.

It is important that you read each answer and find the *best* one. While all of these answers may be true, the only one that can be inferred from the passage is choice (d) Yosemite would be a good vacation destination. Oftentimes you can find clues to this answer in the last couple of sentences. In this passage, the author states clearly that there is something for everyone, implying that Yosemite would make a nice place for a vacation.

CONCLUSIONS

General questions may ask you to determine the conclusion of the passage. This is very similar to the main purpose. If you use labels, these may help you with this type of question. To answer this, first identify the flow of the story. Is the author trying to convince you of something? Are the events in the story leading you to a particular opinion? Or perhaps they are leading up to a particular event. Read each answer choice and eliminate incorrect answer choices.

➡ **Example 6**_____

What is the conclusion of this passage?

(a) People should appreciate the wonder of Yosemite.
(b) Families should plan their vacations carefully.
(c) Hiking granite cliffs can be very dangerous.
(d) To preserve the beauty of Yosemite, visitors should not litter.

For general questions, refer to the last paragraph. Answer choices (b), (c), and (d) are all very specific and are not addressed in the passage. While the reader was not asked to appreciate the beauty of Yosemite, its wonder was described throughout the passage, making the best answer choice (a) People should appreciate the wonder of Yosemite.

You should now have a better idea of how to answer the general questions you'll see in the reading comprehension section. Now let's look at the questions that focus on specific facts from the passage.

Specific Questions

When reading specific questions, you also must read each answer choice. The answers to each specific question are in the passage—you just need the time to find them. Here are some examples of specific questions.

> According to the passage . . .
> In this passage, it is implied that . . .
> Why did the boy hide his shoe?
> The main character is best known for . . .
> Which word best describes Robert?
> Comparing the first and second paragraph, the second is . . .
> It is probably true that . . .
> The word swift, as underlined and used in the passage, means . . .

REMEMBER KEY WORDS

You should skim the questions prior to reading the passage, looking for the specific questions. When you see a specific question, try to remember key words or ideas from the question, so that you can keep an eye out for them when reading. If you see a word in the reading that you think relates to one of the specific questions, underline the word. When you read the specific questions later, you will have an easy time finding the answers.

LABELING

If you find labels helpful, keep using them. They can act as a guide when looking for answers to specific questions.

ANSWER THE QUESTION

The answers to specific questions are in the passage, and your task is simply to find them. Be careful though; some answer choices may contain correct information or details that were taken directly from the story, but they do not specifically answer the question.

PROCESS OF ELIMINATION

The process of elimination is a useful strategy for specific questions about the passage. When reading answer choices, eliminate any of the following:

- Answer choices that while correct, do not answer the question
- Answer choices that contain information you know to be incorrect
- Answer choices that are absolute (ex: never, always)

Now that you have learned some strategies for specific questions, let's look at some examples of specific questions you may find in the Reading—Comprehension section. Before reading the passage, skim the questions in Examples 7–14 (not the answer choices—just the questions). Try to remember key words as you read the passage. Read the passage and make brief labels in the boxes on the side of each paragraph.

Reading Passage 2
Refer to this passage when answering Examples 7–14.

Resetting a dislocated shoulder is hard work, even seconds after an injury. When attempted on a large young man hours later, it requires considerable strength because the muscles are swollen and pulling on the joint. The job took all the strength Marie had. There was a fire burning close by, and she hoped they wouldn't both topple in if the shoulder popped in too quickly. All of a sudden, the shoulder joint gave a soft crunching *snap* as it popped back into place. The young man looked amazed as he explored his much improved shoulder.

Paragraph 1

"It isn't broken anymore!" he exclaimed. A smile of relief came across his face, and the group of men broke out in cheers. Marie was sweating from the task, but she was smugly pleased with her accomplishment. "It will be sore and swollen for about a week. You must not use your shoulder for a while and when you do, move slowly."

Paragraph 2

Although the young man looked upon her with admiration, the others were studying Marie with suspicious glares. "I'm a healer, you see," Marie told them, feeling very nervous. The men exchanged looks and whispers. Their leader, Gregory, approached Marie. "Can you secure the boy's arm, so he will be able to ride a horse?" "Indeed, I can," Marie replied with asperity. "But why should I want to help you anyway?" Gregory ignored her and turned to his men instead.

Paragraph 3

ACCORDING TO THE PASSAGE

Questions that begin with *According to the passage* are often asking about a particular event or character in the passage. The answers to these questions can be found in the passage. If you believe you know the answer, then you can select it and move on to another question. If you are even a little uncertain then go back to the passage and find the answer, spending just a few seconds to do so. You will be pressed for time, so if you think you know the answer, trust your instinct and move on to the next question.

➡ Example 7

According to the passage, resetting a dislocated shoulder is

(a) easy if done on a large man.
(b) usually hard work.
(c) doesn't cause pain to the patient.
(d) just a part of the recovery.

The first paragraph states that resetting a shoulder is hard work even seconds after an injury. The best answer is choice (b) usually hard work.

IN THIS PASSAGE, IT IS IMPLIED THAT

The answer to this type of question is not specifically stated in the passage but rather implied. These can be a little difficult because you are not looking for something that was mentioned specifically.

➡ Example 8

In the passage, it is implied that the men

(a) are outlaws.
(b) know Marie very well.
(c) are planning to ride on horseback.
(d) are all injured.

Because the men look at Marie with suspicion and she has to explain that she is a healer, it appears that they do not know her very well. The men may be outlaws but there is no mention of that in the passage. They ask Marie if she can secure the boy's arm in order to ride a horse, so it is implied that they (c) are planning to ride on horseback. Notice that although they never say they're going to ride on horseback, the question they ask Marie makes that implication.

QUESTIONS ABOUT A SPECIFIC DETAIL

There may be a few of these after each passage. These are usually very easy to answer. If you do not remember the answer from your reading, then look at your labels or quickly scan the passage to find the necessary information.

Example 9

Marie's profession is

(a) horse trainer.
(b) housekeeper.
(c) healer.
(d) physical therapist.

In Paragraph 3, Marie announces that she is a healer when the men eye her suspiciously. While she may be a housekeeper who is helping out, there is no mention of that in the passage. You must be careful not to make assumptions and use ONLY the information that is given in the passage. The correct answer is choice (c) healer.

DESCRIPTIVE WORDS

You may be asked to describe a character or event from the passage. To find the correct answer, look for words in the passage that may be similar in meaning to one of the answer choices, as in the following example.

Example 10

Which word best describes the men in the room?

(a) angry
(b) lazy
(c) cautious
(d) friendly

In the passage, Marie seems to be in an unfamiliar setting and does not know the men she is helping. They are *suspicious* of her when she fixes the boy's shoulder in the third paragraph. They appear to be very untrusting, exchanging looks and whispers. They are not described as friendly, lazy, or angry. The correct answer is (c) cautious.

COMPARING PARAGRAPHS

At most, twice on your test you will see a question asking you to compare two paragraphs. These are specific questions and usually just refer to one of the two paragraphs in question. Read the question and look at the particular paragraph in question. While the questions involves two paragraphs it will usually ask specifically about only one.

Example 11

Comparing the second and third paragraph, the third paragraph

(a) reveals the outcome of fixing the shoulder.
(b) outlines the recovery of the injured man.
(c) is more about the injured man than Marie.
(d) reveals the nature of Marie's relationship with the men.

You can see that the question is really about Paragraph 3 only. Before reading the answer choices, quickly scan the third paragraph. This will take just a few seconds, then you will be ready to read the answer choices and select the correct one. If you are unsure of your answer, then scan over the second paragraph as well. You can see that the second paragraph is all about resetting the injured shoulder while the third paragraph gives insight as to the cautious relationship between the men and Marie. The correct answer, choice (d), reveals the nature of Marie's relationship with the men.

IT IS PROBABLY TRUE THAT

You may be asked to make assumptions about situations or characters based on clues given in the passage. These are similar to the prediction questions you saw in the general questions. Look for key words in the question then find a similar sentence in the paragraph.

➡ Example 12 _____

It is probably true that the injured man

(a) is angry with Marie for causing his injury.
(b) is grateful to Marie.
(c) is relieved that he can ride a horse.
(d) already knew that Marie is a healer.

Because there is no mention of how the injured man feels toward Marie you will have to use process of elimination for this one. While the passage did says he feels *relief*, after his shoulder is fixed, this is not an answer choice. Let's rule out answers. While the injured man may be able to ride a horse, there is no indication that he is relieved about it. Gregory is the person asking about riding a horse and not the young man. It may be that the man is very disappointed in this news. There is no indication that the injured man is angry with Marie, especially given that he is relieved. Marie announced after fixing the shoulder that she is a healer, so it appears that this was unknown to them before that. The best and only answer choice remaining is choice (b) is grateful to Marie.

WORDS IN CONTEXT

You have learned many strategies from Chapter 3 and 4 regarding vocabulary words. Here you have the advantage of seeing the word in context. If you are uncertain of the correct answer, try replacing the underlined word in the passage with the answer choices and rule out any that do not make sense.

➡ Example 13 _____

Smugly, as underlined and used in the passage, means

(a) embarrassed.
(b) feeling pride.
(c) quietly.
(d) angry.

If you are not sure what it means to be smug, then consider the context. Marie has just done what is described as difficult work: "Marie was sweating from the task, but she was smugly pleased with her accomplishment." Notice the word *but* is used as a reversal word. If the words before the *but* are negative (sweating, exertion), then what follows must be positive. The only positive answer is choice (b) feeling pride.

➡ Example 14 _____

The word asperity, as underlined and used in the passage, means

(a) harshness of tone.
(b) generosity.
(c) politeness.
(d) humble.

Let's look at the word *asperity* in context.

> . . . "Can you secure the boy's arm, so he will be able to ride a horse?" "Indeed, I can,"
> Marie replied with asperity. . . .

If you don't know what asperity means, this will be a difficult one. Generosity doesn't make sense if replacing the underlined word, but the other three answers all make sense. Marie appears to be defiant and not necessarily polite or humble (as seen in the last paragraph) so the best answer is choice (a) harshness of tone.

You have now become familiar with the Reading—Comprehension portion of this subtest. You should be able to complete the 40 reading questions that will be in this subtest. Next, let's review some of the vocabulary strategies that you learned earlier in this book as well as some new strategies to answer questions about vocabulary in context.

READING—VOCABULARY

There will be 22 vocabulary questions on the last page of the Reading subtest. They are numbered 153–174 and will be followed by the word **STOP**. It is important that you get to the vocabulary questions. Many students, when taking the HSPT for the first time, do not finish this section and miss out on the Vocabulary questions. Perhaps this happened to you when taking the practice test. If so, don't worry just yet. In this chapter you will learn strategies to help you to finish on time.

The vocabulary words in this section, unlike those in the Verbal Skills subtest, will be given with another word in context. You will not see the word in a full sentence; however, even a word or two can help you remember the meaning of a word. Below is an example of a Reading—Vocabulary question.

> Vocabulary is very important on the HSPT, so make sure you read Chapter 3 to expand your vocabulary and Chapter 4 to learn strategies that are helpful in answering synonym questions.

➥ Example 15 _____

Directions: Choose the word that means the same as the underlined word.

an <u>invincible</u> hero

(a) strong
(b) undefeatable
(c) insensitive
(d) kind

In each question, the vocabulary word will be underlined. *Invincible* means unable to be defeated, so the correct answer is choice (b) *undefeatable*. While heroes are often strong and kind, neither of those have the same meaning as *invincible*.

Here are some strategies to help you to maximize your score in the Reading—Vocabulary section.

TIMING

Because the vocabulary questions can be answered quickly, you will only need a few minutes to answer all 22. You MUST save time to answer these questions, even if it means skipping a reading passage. You can come back to the reading comprehension questions if you have extra time. Not getting to the Vocabulary section is a costly mistake. Even if you blindly guess at them you are likely to get five or six correct, so imagine what you can do if you actually read and answer them all!

SYNONYMS

Because you are looking for a synonym, all of the answer choices will be just one word. In Chapter 4 you learned several strategies to help you identify synonyms. You should review Chapter 4 before taking the practice Reading subtest at the end of this chapter. You may remember there are three types of vocabulary words: Words you know well, Words you recognize but cannot define, and words you've never seen. See pages 51–57 for a review on synonyms.

Unlike the Verbal Skills Vocabulary, the Reading—Vocabulary questions are in context, which means you can replace the underlined word with an answer choice to see if your choice makes sense in context.

➥ Example 16 _____

reach the <u>summit</u>

(a) end
(b) total
(c) peak
(d) kind

If you do not know what *summit* means, or perhaps only have a general idea, try replacing the word *summit* with the words in the answer choices. Reach the *end* makes sense but not reach the *kind* or reach the *total*. Reach the *peak* makes sense, so now you have narrowed down your answer to two possible choices. Make a guess now that you have increased your odds, and move on. The correct answer is choice (c) *peak*.

Because you already learned quite a bit about vocabulary in Chapters 3 and 4, you should be ready to try some vocabulary questions in context. Put all of your good strategies to use here. The only difference in the Reading subtest is now you will have a little context for each word.

Take a few minutes and see how you do on the following vocabulary questions. Ten questions should take you no more than three minutes. Time yourself to see how you do.

READING—Vocabulary Practice

Directions: Choose the word that means the same as the underlined word.

1. a ravenous customer

   (a) angry
   (b) starving
   (c) problematic
   (d) new

2. a severe scolding

   (a) mild
   (b) loud
   (c) deserved
   (d) harsh

3. the noisome intruder

   (a) noisy
   (b) loud
   (c) offensive
   (d) quiet

4. a monotonous lecture

   (a) single
   (b) boring
   (c) brief
   (d) interesting

5. to enhance the output

   (a) reduce
   (b) decorate
   (c) improve
   (d) confuse

6. to exhibit the art

   (a) value
   (b) destroy
   (c) frame
   (d) display

7. the clandestine friendship

   (a) secret
   (b) only
   (c) lengthy
   (d) failing

8. an abrupt ending

   (a) surprise
   (b) sudden
   (c) interrupted
   (d) sad

9. to aggravate the situation

   (a) ease
   (b) analyze
   (c) make worse
   (d) entertain

10. my small abode

   (a) couch
   (b) home
   (c) office
   (d) family

(Answers are on page 164.)

ANSWERS EXPLAINED FOR CHAPTER 6

READING—Vocabulary Practice (page 163)

1. **(b)** *Ravenous* means to be *starving*.

2. **(d)** *Severe* means to be *harsh*.

3. **(c)** *Noisome* does not have to do with noise but with personality. *Noisome* means to be *offensive* in manner.

4. **(b)** To be *monotonous* is to be *boring*.

5. **(c)** *Enhance* means to *improve*.

6. **(d)** To *exhibit* art is to *display* it, not to *value* or *frame* it.

7. **(a)** *Clandestine* means *secretive*.

8. **(b)** *Abrupt* means *sudden*. An *abrupt* ending is one that happened *suddenly*.

9. **(c)** *Aggravate* is a verb meaning to make something *worse*.

10. **(b)** An *abode* is a residence or a *home*.

WRAP IT UP WITH PRACTICE

Before taking the practice Reading subtest, take a few minutes to review what you have learned in this chapter.

Approach for READING—Comprehension

- Make a note of the time and check the clock often.
- Skim over the questions first.
- Read, don't study, the passage and make labels as you read.
- As you read, underline information that you remember from skimming the questions.
- Answer questions in order, referring to the passage as necessary.
- Eliminate wrong answers choices.
- For general questions, read the first and last sentences.

Approach for READING—Vocabulary

- Replace the prompt word with each of the answer choices.
- If you know the meaning of the prompt word, form a synonym in your mind before reading the answer choices.
- Rule out answer choices that are synonyms.
- Narrow down your answer choices to two antonyms if possible.
- Eliminate answers you believe are incorrect.

Now that you are familiar with the format and the strategies for the Reading Subtest, it's time to you put your skills and strategies to the test. Read the following instructions and practice with the following Reading subtest.

25 MINUTES

READING—Comprehension

Questions 113–122 refer to the following passage.

When she first saw the flying creature, Sarah was terrified. She didn't know what had awakened her and was startled when she saw a bat flying <u>erratically</u> around her room, as if in a panic itself. Sarah slipped quietly from her bed and crawled towards the door. Once safely on the other side, she slammed the door shut and breathed a sigh of relief.

Sarah heard the noise of the trapped bat searching for a way out to the darkness of the night. Questions raced through her tired mind. Were there more bats in the house? Should she try to help the bat? What if it bites her? Sarah tried to sleep on the couch but answers to her questions were filling her thoughts. She wondered if the bat was afraid like her.

In the morning, Sarah put on a winter hat and <u>donned</u> a heavy sweatshirt and long gloves, looking very out of season. She found a tennis racket and a butterfly net and held them as she tip-toed into the bedroom. Opening the window, Sarah saw to her amazement, the tiniest little bat hanging upside down on the drape. With its webbed arms tucked in, it bore no resemblance to the giant creature from hours earlier. She tapped the drape and the bat fell gently onto the tennis racket and she quickly covered it with the net. Sarah carried the racket with its passenger to the open window and waited patiently for the bat to wake and fly away. As it did, she smiled and began to breathe again.

GO TO THE NEXT PAGE ➡

113. According to Sarah, the bat

  (a) had been in the house for days.
  (b) was trying to bite her.
  (c) has webbed arms.
  (d) was very quiet.

114. The passage is mostly about

  (a) the dangers of bats.
  (b) the many ways to catch a bat.
  (c) the events of one night.
  (d) the life of a bat.

115. The word erratically, as underlined and used in the passage, most nearly means

  (a) softly.
  (b) irregularly.
  (c) heavily.
  (d) slowly.

116. What best describes Sarah's reaction upon seeing the bat?

  (a) sleepy
  (b) dazed
  (c) terrified
  (d) indifferent

117. The word donned, as underlined and used in the passage, most nearly means

  (a) put on.
  (b) took off.
  (c) burned.
  (d) ironed.

118. The passage can best be described as

  (a) a children's book.
  (b) a comic book.
  (c) an instruction manual.
  (d) a narrative.

119. It can be implied from the passage that

  (a) the event takes place in the summertime.
  (b) there were more bats in the house.
  (c) the bat bit Sarah while she slept.
  (d) Sarah's memory is bad.

120. What did Sarah do with the tennis racket?
  (a) She swung it at the bat.
  (b) She played tennis.
  (c) She used it to open the drapes.
  (d) She used it carry the bat.

121. Which of the following best describes Sarah's feeling towards the bat?

  (a) indifference
  (b) anger
  (c) concern
  (d) hatred

122. According to the passage, Sarah did which of the following?

  (a) She kept the bat as a pet.
  (b) She screamed when she saw the bat.
  (c) She crawled from her room in the night.
  (d) She slept soundly on the couch.

GO TO THE NEXT PAGE ➡

Questions 123–132 refer to the following passage.

Pipelines exist <u>virtually</u> everywhere. Is your home heated by gas or oil? Does it have electric lights or a kitchen stove with gas burners for cooking? Do you drive a car that uses gasoline? Have you ever wondered how that fuel gets to the place where you use it? There is a vast network of underground pipelines in America. These pipes provide crude oil, petroleum products, natural gas, and fuel used to generate your electricity.

Natural resources are found all over our country and often in locations very different from where the fuel is actually consumed. America has over two million miles of underground pipelines that safely transport fuel from these locations to utility companies, airports, military bases, and industries every day. Pipelines are similar to highways and are either interstate or intrastate. Interstate pipelines carry materials from one state to another and sometimes straight across the country. Intrastate pipelines carry fuel within one particular state.

Pipelines were first used in America back in the early 1800s to transport oil. They were made of wood and used to take oil from wells to local refineries. The population of America grew and fuel was needed in places further away from the energy sources. By the late 1800s, pipelines were made of steel and began to span across the country.

Today our pipeline system is an <u>indispensable</u> part of our infrastructure, incorporating state of the art computer technology, advanced materials, and sophisticated safety features. It can be considered the unsung hero of our energy consumption.

123. This author of the passage is most likely

    (a) a historian.
    (b) a supporter of the pipeline.
    (c) a kindergarten teacher.
    (d) an environmental activist.

124. The author refers to the pipeline as the unsung hero because

    (a) it is unseen but important.
    (b) no one cares about it.
    (c) no one believes in it.
    (d) it saves lives.

125. The word <u>indispensable</u>, as underlined and used in the passage, most nearly means

    (a) underground.
    (b) trivial.
    (c) outdated.
    (d) necessary.

126. The passage is mostly about

    (a) the use of fossil fuels.
    (b) the pipeline system in America.
    (c) the safety considerations of the pipeline.
    (d) the pros and cons of the pipeline.

GO TO THE NEXT PAGE ➡

127. The pipeline system can best be described as

    (a) obvious.
    (b) widespread.
    (c) controversial.
    (d) deplorable.

128. It is implied from the passage that

    (a) pipelines are always located under highways.
    (b) gas pipelines are more narrow than oil pipelines.
    (c) the same pipeline is used to transport different materials.
    (d) pipelines make up a system similar to our road system.

129. The word virtually, as underlined and used in the passage, most nearly means

    (a) not real.
    (b) more than.
    (c) almost.
    (d) abundant.

130. According to the passage, the first pipeline was used to transport

    (a) natural gas.
    (b) oil.
    (c) well water.
    (d) sewage.

131. Interstate pipelines are used

    (a) to transport fuel within a state.
    (b) to deliver fuel to peoples' homes.
    (c) to transport fuel from one state to another.
    (d) for delivering gas only.

132. What is the author's main purpose in writing this passage?

    (a) to provide an overview of the pipeline system in America
    (b) to convince readers to oppose a new pipeline
    (c) to educate readers of the dangers of natural gas
    (d) to discuss homeowners' energy consumption

GO TO THE NEXT PAGE ➡

Questions 133–142 refer to the following passage.

Our brains are constantly creating thousands of opinions and thoughts each day. The brain spends countless hours confirming those ideas and creating reasons for those opinions. We believe that we think independently and control these thoughts and opinions, when in reality we do not. We jump to conclusions without even taking the time to think first.

We look at a person and instantly create a story that suits their appearance. We do this with images as well. If we see 1 + 1, we <u>instinctively</u> answer it and see the number 2. We didn't tell our brain to do this, but we did it anyway. There are reflexes in our brain that we do not control. Confirmation bias is a term that refers to the tendency of our brains to pick information that suits our preconceived ideas. For example, if you were asked "Is your sister friendly?" images of your sister's friendly acts would come to mind. If you were asked "Is your sister unfriendly?" you would perhaps start thinking of examples of how your sister is unfriendly.

The major <u>consequence</u> of the confirmation bias is that if we make the wrong assumption, we will often believe it. For example, a person may falsely believe that one who is poorly dressed is a delinquent and will treat them differently than they would treat a well-dressed person. In the medical profession, confirmation bias can have serious consequences for patients. If a doctor makes a wrong diagnosis, they can often find symptoms to support their false idea and the patient may suffer the consequences.

133. This passage would be best titled

    (a) "Doctors Make Mistakes Too."
    (b) "Confirmation Bias and the Brain."
    (c) "Psychology Disorders."
    (d) "We Can Control Our Brain."

134. Confirmation bias can best be described as

    (a) always false.
    (b) an illness.
    (c) an instinctive opinion.
    (d) affecting adults only.

135. The word <u>consequence</u>, as underlined and used in the passage, most nearly means

    (a) result.
    (b) punishment.
    (c) decision.
    (d) drawback.

136. According to the passage, people often

    (a) spend hours confirming ideas.
    (b) are misdiagnosed by doctors.
    (c) have full control over their brain.
    (d) jump to conclusions without thinking.

137. It can be inferred from the passage that

    (a) everyone is subject to confirmation bias.
    (b) some people control their brains fully.
    (c) confirmation bias was just discovered.
    (d) doctors do not have confirmation bias.

138. This passage was most likely written by a

    (a) surgeon.
    (b) college student.
    (c) novelist.
    (d) math teacher.

GO TO THE NEXT PAGE ➡

139. The tone of this passage can best be described as

    (a) grave.

    (b) informative.

    (c) sarcastic.

    (d) light-hearted.

140. The word instinctively, as underlined and used in the passage, most nearly means

    (a) slowly.

    (b) with prejudice.

    (c) automatically.

    (d) reluctantly.

141. This passage is an example of

    (a) a journal article.

    (b) an autobiography.

    (c) mythology.

    (d) fiction.

142. Which of the following is an example of confirmation bias?

    (a) a doctor performing an allergy test

    (b) asking a person to solve a math problem

    (c) judging a book by its cover

    (d) wearing nice clothes to school

GO TO THE NEXT PAGE ➡

Questions 143–152 refer to the following passage.

The Civil War in America resolved two basic questions for our country: Should the United States be a dissolvable confederation of states or an indivisible nation with a national government? And should the practice of slavery be allowed to continue? Seven states from the South had already seceded and together formed the Confederate States of America. The Union was made up of the northern states. The day after Lincoln's inauguration in 1861, the Confederacy demanded that he surrender Fort Sumter or face an imminent attack.

Presented with a dilemma, Lincoln decided to neither attack nor surrender. On April 12, the fort was attacked by South Carolinians and bombarded with over 4,000 rounds of ammunition, forcing the fort's commander, Major Anderson, to surrender. President Lincoln called for volunteers from the North to serve for three months in the Union military. Both the Union and the Confederacy believed the war would be brief and victorious.

The Union's advantages included more resources than the Confederacy, a railroad system, and President Lincoln as its leader; however, the Confederacy had a strong military with highly motivated soldiers. As the war began, the Union had a strategy to blockade the southern ports to prevent the export of cotton and the import of vital supplies. The Union also planned to send boats down the Mississippi River to divide the Confederate states, then to capture the capital of Virginia. The Confederacy's plan was one based primarily on defense.

By the end of that year, almost a million men battled each other from Virginia to Missouri. The real fighting would not begin until 1862 and would last until the spring of 1865.

143. The Civil War resolved the question of whether

    (a) slavery should be allowed to continue in the United States.
    (b) Washington DC should be the nation's capital.
    (c) the United States should have a Declaration of Independence.
    (d) there should be an indivisible confederation of states.

144. The best title for this passage is

    (a) "The Civil War."
    (b) "The Battles of the Civil War."
    (c) "The Beginning of the Civil War."
    (d) "Military Strategies of the Confederacy."

145. The word imminent, as underlined and used in the passage, most nearly means

    (a) dangerous.
    (b) about to happen.
    (c) possible.
    (d) important.

146. According to the passage, which of the following statements is true?

    (a) Both the Union and the Confederacy believed the war would be brief.
    (b) The war was fought for three months.
    (c) The Confederacy had the railroad as an advantage over the North.
    (d) The sole reason for the Civil War was the debate on slavery.

GO TO THE NEXT PAGE ➡

147. According to the passage, the Civil War began

    (a) at President Lincoln's inauguration.
    (b) when the southern states seceded.
    (c) with the battle at Fort Sumter.
    (d) as soon as slavery began in the United States.

148. It is inferred by the passage that

    (a) the southern states had an offensive plan of attack.
    (b) the export of cotton was important to the Confederacy.
    (c) Major Anderson was in support of slavery.
    (d) the attack on Fort Sumter was a surprise.

149. This passage is an example of a

    (a) critique.
    (b) biography.
    (c) political statement.
    (d) historical account.

150. The word vital, as underlined and used in the passage, most nearly means

    (a) military.
    (b) important.
    (c) extra.
    (d) minimal.

151. This passage would most likely be found in a

    (a) newspaper.
    (b) high school textbook.
    (c) novel.
    (d) science book.

152. Which statement is true of the battle at Fort Sumter?

    (a) It was the battle that ended the Civil War.
    (b) Close to a million rounds were fired.
    (c) The fort was bombarded by South Carolinians.
    (d) The Confederate major surrendered in the morning.

GO TO THE NEXT PAGE ➡

READING—Vocabulary

153. a moral dilemma

    (a) sad
    (b) ethical
    (c) quarrelsome
    (d) unfair

154. an inordinate amount

    (a) excessive
    (b) similar
    (c) minute
    (d) equal

155. a volatile situation

    (a) large
    (b) new
    (c) stable
    (d) changing

156. to avert disaster

    (a) cause
    (b) embrace
    (c) avoid
    (d) watch

157. destitute conditions

    (a) unusual
    (b) desirable
    (c) poor
    (d) healthy

158. to deviate from course

    (a) stray
    (b) remain
    (c) create
    (d) run

159. the verge of insanity

    (a) topic
    (b) brink
    (c) idea
    (d) course

160. to culture curiosity

    (a) find
    (b) love
    (c) purchase
    (d) breed

161. to berate a child

    (a) believe
    (b) scold
    (c) deliver
    (d) praise

162. a shrewd decision

    (a) unanimous
    (b) rushed
    (c) clever
    (d) poor

163. aspire to greatness

    (a) push
    (b) share
    (c) decline
    (d) strive

164. a tenacious clerk

    (a) persistent
    (b) beginner
    (c) sales
    (d) young

GO TO THE NEXT PAGE ➡

165. a candid discussion

    (a) sweet
    (b) open
    (c) long
    (d) funny

166. a merit award

    (a) employment
    (b) excellence
    (c) financial
    (d) trophy

167. to ensure success

    (a) destroy
    (b) consider
    (c) guarantee
    (d) explain

168. a trivial task

    (a) quick
    (b) easy
    (c) unimportant
    (d) challenging

169. an amicable agreement

    (a) friendly
    (b) difficult
    (c) frustrating
    (d) written

170. to disregard rules

    (a) create
    (b) watch
    (c) examine
    (d) ignore

171. quench a thirst

    (a) encourage
    (b) put out
    (c) dry
    (d) suggest

172. a jubilant winner

    (a) historic
    (b) questionable
    (c) joyous
    (d) recurring

173. to prolong a speech

    (a) enjoy
    (b) promote
    (c) record
    (d) lengthen

174. to recuperate from loss

    (a) recover
    (b) suffer
    (c) struggle
    (d) remove

STOP

NOTE

Answer explanations in this section are labeled with their corresponding question types. You will need this for the scoring chart on page 179.

ANSWERS EXPLAINED FOR PRACTICE READING SUBTEST

113. **(c)** In the third paragraph, Sarah states how small the bat looked with its webbed arms tucked in. (Specific)

114. **(c)** While the story involves a bat, it is just about one night and its events. While bats are dangerous, there was no mention of this in the passage. (General)

115. **(b)** *Erratically* most nearly means to be irregular and unpredictable. (Vocabulary)

116. **(c)** The opening line clearly states Sarah is terrified. (General)

117. **(a)** *Donned* means to *put on*, to dress. (Vocabulary)

118. **(d)** The passage is a narrative told in story form, a written account. (General)

119. **(a)** When Sarah puts on a winter hat and a sweatshirt she is "out of season," implying it's a warm weather season such as summer. (Specific)

120. **(d)** Sarah tapped at the drape and then used the racket to hold the bat and carry it to the window. (Specific)

121. **(c)** While she was afraid of the bat, Sarah is also concerned that it may also be afraid. (Specific)

122. **(c)** In the first paragraph, Sarah slips from the bed and crawls toward the door. (Specific)

123. **(b)** While the author may be a historian, there is no evidence of this in the passage. It is clear that the author is a supporter of pipelines as there is no mention of anything negative about the pipeline system. (General)

124. **(a)** *Unsung* means to be not celebrated. Someone who is *unsung* is not recognized but usually performs good deeds. In this case, pipelines are unsung because they are below ground, unseen, yet an important system that many never think about. (Specific)

125. **(d)** *Indispensable* means to be vital or *necessary*. (Vocabulary)

126. **(b)** This passage gives a brief overview of the pipeline system in America. While it does discuss its importance, pros, there is no mention of any negative attributes of the system. (General)

127. **(b)** The pipeline system can be described as vast or widespread. The passage makes mention of how it is spread across the country and compares it to our highway system which is widespread. While pipelines may be controversial, there was no mention of this in the passage. (Specific)

128. **(d)** Pipelines were compared to our highway system, but the passage did not say that all of the pipes are located under roads. The passage discussed various types of fuel but never said that one pipe carries different fuels. The width of the pipes was not mentioned. (Specific)

129. **(c)** *Virtually* means *almost* or nearly. (Vocabulary)

130. **(b)** In the third paragraph, the first pipeline is described as being used to transport oil. (Specific)

131. **(c)** In the second paragraph, the author describes interstate pipelines as transporting fuel from one state to another. (Specific)

132. **(a)** The passage provides an overview of the pipeline system. There is no mention of dangers so choices (b) and (c) can be eliminated. While use of energy in homes is mentioned in the first paragraph, it is not the purpose of the passage. (General)

133. **(b)** This passage is about confirmation bias. While it does mention that doctor's may make mistakes, this was only a small part of the passage. (General)

134. **(c)** Confirmation bias is described in the second paragraph as the tendency of our brains to pick information that suits a preconceived idea; the passage then goes on to say that we don't control it, therefore, this is instinctive. (Specific)

135. **(a)** A *consequence* is a *result* of an action or decision. (Vocabulary)

136. **(d)** The passage is all about jumping to conclusions, often incorrectly. (Specific)

137. **(a)** Because we can't control our brains, as stated in the first paragraph, we can assume that confirmation bias affects everyone. (General)

138. **(b)** The passage is not scientific enough to be written by a doctor for a medical journal and involves almost no math. It is most likely written by a college student or possibly a professor. (General)

139. **(b)** The passage does not convey much emotion and can be described as informational. (General)

140. **(c)** *Instinctively* means done without thought, *automatically*. (Vocabulary)

141. **(a)** This passage is most likely a journal article or a term paper. If you are unfamiliar with a journal article, you can still get this correct using process of elimination. The other choices are all inaccurate. (General)

142. **(c)** Judging a book by its cover is the description of confirmation bias. Wearing nice clothes is related—you may want people to think well of you. However, judging you based on your clothes is confirmation bias, not choosing those clothes. (Specific)

143. **(a)** Slavery was one of the two issues that was resolved in the Civil War as stated in the first paragraph. (Specific)

144. **(c)** While this passage is about the Civil War, there is very little mentioned about the actual war other than the beginning. (General)

145. **(b)** *Imminent* is an adjective that means *about to happen*, or soon. (Vocabulary)

146. **(a)** As stated at the end of the second paragraph, both sides believed the war would be brief and that they would be victorious. (Specific)

147. **(c)** The first action of the Civil War, as mentioned in the second paragraph, was the battle at Fort Sumter. (Specific)

148. **(b)** While cotton was not mentioned as an advantage for the South, it is implied since the Union had plans to stop its export. (Specific)

149. **(d)** This is an historic account. There is little mention of politics and does not contain enough personal information to be a biography about Lincoln or Anderson. (General)

150. **(b)** *Vital* most nearly means *important* or critical. (Vocabulary)

151. **(b)** Newspapers typically contain current events. This article is nonfiction so it would most likely be found in a textbook. (General)

152. **(c)** This battle *began* the war and didn't end it. Close to 4,000 rounds were fired, not a million. The *Union* major surrendered in the morning not the Confederate. The fort was bombarded by South Carolinians. (Specific)

153. **(b)** *Moral* means to be *ethical* or good. Notice that *sad, quarrelsome*, and *unfair* are all negative words while *ethical* is the only positive word. (Vocabulary)

154. **(a)** *Inordinate* means *excessive* and usually refers to a quantity or an amount. Rule out *similar* and *equal* as they are synonyms. Notice that *minute* and *excessive* are antonyms. (Vocabulary)

155. **(d)** A *volatile* situation is one that is *changing* quickly, unstable. *Stable* is an antonym while *large* and *new* are unrelated. (Vocabulary)

156. **(c)** *Avert* is a verb meaning to *avoid* or to go around. (Vocabulary)

157. **(c)** *Destitute* is an adjective meaning very *poor*. If you recognize that *destitute* is a negative word, you can rule out three answers. *Desirable* and *healthy* are both positive words and *unusual* is neither positive nor negative. (Vocabulary)

158. **(a)** To *deviate* is to *stray* or veer away. (Vocabulary)

159. **(b)** *Verge* is a noun meaning the edge or the *brink* of something. (Vocabulary)

160. **(d)** *Culture*, when used as a verb, means to *breed* or grow. (Vocabulary)

161. **(b)** *Berate* is a verb that means to *scold*. If you know that *berate* has a negative meaning, you can rule out *praise* and *believe* since they are positive. *Deliver* is neither positive nor negative. (Vocabulary)

162. **(c)** A *shrewd* decision is one that is *clever* or well thought. (Vocabulary)

163. **(d)** To *aspire* to greatness is to *strive* for it. (Vocabulary)

164. **(a)** *Tenacious* is an adjective meaning to be *persistent*. (Vocabulary)

165. **(b)** *Candid* means to be *open* or honest. (Vocabulary)

166. **(b)** *Merit* can be a verb but here is used as an adjective meaning *excellence*. The award itself can be a *trophy* or *financial* gain; however, the underlined word is *merit* and not award. (Vocabulary)

167. **(c)** *Ensure* is a verb meaning to *guarantee* or to make certain. (Vocabulary)

168. **(c)** *Trivial* is an adjective used to refer to something that is insignificant, unnecessary, or *unimportant*. (Vocabulary)

169. **(a)** An *amicable* agreement is one that is *friendly*. (Vocabulary)

170. **(d)** To *disregard* something is to *ignore* it. If you know any French, you'll know that *regarder* translates to watch. *Dis-regard* means the opposite of watch—*ignore*. (Vocabulary)

171. **(b)** *Quench* is a verb meaning to extinguish or to *put out*, and is usually refers to feelings such as desire or thirst. (Vocabulary)

172. **(c)** *Jubilant* means to be *joyous* or happy. (Vocabulary)

173. **(d)** To *prolong* something means to make it longer, to extend, or *lengthen*. (Vocabulary)

174. **(a)** When someone is *recuperating*, they are *recovering* from something such as a loss or an injury. (Vocabulary)

SCORING YOUR PRACTICE READING SUBTEST

Now that you have reviewed the answers and explanations, let's see how well you are doing. Go through the explanations again and count up the number of each question type you answered correctly. Then fill in the chart below.

	Vocabulary	Specific	General	Total
Number of each question type you answered correctly				
Total of each question type	30	18	14	62

First, add up the total number of questions you answered correctly. Then divide that number by 62 and multiply by 100 to determine your raw score for the Reading subtest:

$$\text{Raw Score} = \frac{\text{Total Number Correct}}{62 \text{ Total Questions}} = \frac{\rule{2em}{0.4pt}}{62} \times 100 = \rule{4em}{0.4pt}\%$$

Next, to determine your raw score for each question type, take the number of questions you answered correctly in each category and divide that number by the total number of questions in each question type. Multiply each answer by 100 to convert to a percent.

$$\text{Vocabulary} = \frac{\text{Total Number Correct}}{30 \text{ Total Questions}} = \frac{\rule{2em}{0.4pt}}{30} \times 100 = \rule{4em}{0.4pt}\%$$

$$\text{Specific} = \frac{\text{Total Number Correct}}{18 \text{ Total Questions}} = \frac{\rule{2em}{0.4pt}}{18} \times 100 = \rule{4em}{0.4pt}\%$$

$$\text{General} = \frac{\text{Total Number Correct}}{14 \text{ Total Questions}} = \frac{\rule{2em}{0.4pt}}{14} \times 100 = \rule{4em}{0.4pt}\%$$

How well did you do? Make sure to go back and review any areas that you can improve upon.

Mathematics

7

THE LAYOUT

The Mathematics subtest is the fourth and the longest of the five subtests on the HSPT. Because the Mathematics subtest is made up of many different types of mathematics questions, the directions will be part of each question. Here is what you can expect to see in this subtest.

Mathematics Subtest—45 Minutes and 64 Questions

Question Type	Example	Number of Questions
Basics and Conversions	Six hundredths can be written as . . . 3 quarters are equivalent to what fraction of 2 dollars?	16–18
Fractions, Decimals, Percents, and Ratios	30 is 40% of what number? Solve: $34.5 \times 18.6 =$ Solve: $\dfrac{3}{5} \div \dfrac{2}{15} =$	5–6
Geometry, Logic, and Word Problems	What is the area of a triangle with a base of 3 and a height of 8? If Jim can drive 20 miles in 30 minutes, how far can he travel in 2 hours?	16–18
Exponents, Radicals, and Algebra	The product of 2 times a number and 18 is 72. What is the number? What number is equal to $\sqrt[3]{64}$? Simplify $(4.32 \times 10^2) + (1.2 \times 10^3)$	13–15
Statistics and Probability	Find the median of this set of numbers. What is the probability of choosing a red marble if . . . ?	7–8

GENERAL STRATEGIES FOR MATHEMATICS

Below are some general strategies to use throughout the Mathematics subtest. While there are many different question types, these strategies should be kept in mind for each.

Timing

You must answer 64 questions in just 45 minutes, so you should be answering approximately one question per minute. If you are thinking that it would take you over an hour to finish at that rate, you are correct; however, there are lots of easy questions that will take just seconds.

So move along, and if there is a more difficult question, feel free to spend a minute working on it. If you find yourself spending longer, you should circle the question number, make your guess, and move on. You don't want to miss out on three easy questions, while you are solving one difficult problem. They are all worth the same one point.

Work in Your Test Booklet

Do your work in your test booklet. You are allowed to write in the booklet and may be given scratch paper as well. If you do your work in the margins of the test booklet, this will save you time, since you will not be going back and forth between scratch paper and the test booklet. This will also help you if you come back to review a problem, since the work will be right where you need it.

Know Your Math Facts

You can greatly reduce your time in answering math questions if you have a good foundation of math facts. Take the time to brush up on them if you know you are rusty. A set of math multiplication facts can be found below.

0	1	2	3	4	5	6	7	8	9	10	11	12
1	1	2	3	4	5	6	7	8	9	10	11	12
2	2	4	6	8	10	12	14	16	18	20	22	24
3	3	6	9	12	15	18	21	24	27	30	33	36
4	4	8	12	16	20	24	28	32	36	40	44	48
5	5	10	15	20	25	30	35	40	45	50	55	60
6	6	12	18	24	30	36	42	48	54	60	66	72
7	7	14	21	28	35	42	49	56	63	70	77	84
8	8	16	24	32	40	48	56	64	72	80	88	96
9	9	18	27	36	45	54	63	72	81	90	99	108
10	10	20	30	40	50	60	70	80	90	100	110	120
11	11	22	33	44	55	66	77	88	99	110	121	132
12	12	24	36	48	60	72	84	96	108	120	132	144

If you are not 100% confident in your math facts, you can make some flashcards and practice them each day until you can answer any of the multiplication questions from the above table. The shaded diagonal represents perfect squares between 0 and 144. Each value in the table represents the product of the number at the top of the column and the left of the row.

Avoid Calculators

Between now and the day you take your HSPT, you should avoid using calculators for basic math. Practice mental math whenever possible. This will improve both your timing and your confidence when you get to the Mathematics subtest.

Show Your Work

On test day, do your work in your test booklet rather than in your head, particularly with questions involving two and three digit numbers. This will help you to avoid careless math errors and will allow you to quickly check your work if you have extra time.

Estimate and Check Answers

Remember to check the answer choices often to see if you can estimate rather than calculate. Cross out answer choices you know to be too big or too small. Look for clues in your answer choices, such as the last digit in a multiplication question, to save time. If you read through the example explanations in this section, you will learn time-saving tips for each question type.

TYPES OF MATHEMATICS QUESTIONS

In this chapter you will be provided with an overview of the basic skills needed to answer the specific types of questions in the Mathematics subtest. If there is a concept that you find difficult, ask your teacher or parent to explain it in more detail and find additional questions for practice. If you feel very confident with the topic of a particular question type feel free to skip over the review and go straight to the example questions.

> **KNOW IT? SKIP IT**
>
> If you are confident with a particular topic, feel free to skip over the review and go straight to the practice questions. Always try the practice questions before moving to a new section.

THE BASICS

There are some basic math skills that you must know to be successful on the HSPT. If you know you are a strong math student, then skip the review and focus on the examples. There will be anywhere from 3 to 8 basic math questions on the HSPT, so it is worthwhile to review them before trying the more advanced questions.

Adding and Subtracting Positive and Negative Numbers

Here is a song to help with adding and subtracting positive and negative numbers. It can be sung to the melody of "Row, row, row your boat."

> "Same signs add 'em up, opposites subtract, ♫ take the sign of the larger one, then you'll be exact ♫."

Let's see how to use this song to add and subtract positive and negative numbers.

ADDING

1. If both numbers have the same sign, you can add them together, and the sign will remain the same as it is for each number (same sign add 'em up ♫). For example, $4 + 3 = 7$ or $(-3) + (-8) = -11$.

2. If you are adding two numbers where one is positive and the other is negative, you should ignore the signs, positive or negative, at first and find the difference between the two values. The final answer will have the same sign as the number with the larger absolute value (the number furthest from zero). For example, for $4 + (-20)$, the difference between 4 and 20 is 16. Because 20 has the largest absolute value and it is negative, your final answer will also be negative. $4 + (-20) = -16$.

> **NOTE**
>
> On the actual HSPT exam, the negative sign in front of negative numbers is often shown higher than normal: $^-4$ rather than -4. Don't be confused if you see it written this way on test day!

SUBTRACTING

1. When subtracting a smaller number from a larger one, simply find the difference and your answer will be positive. For example, 7 – 3 = 4.

2. Never subtract unless both numbers are positive and the first number is larger than the second. If the second number is larger than the first use the "*Keep–Change–Change*" rule and add instead. Here's how it works.

To change a subtraction question to one of addition, you can *Keep* the first value, *Change* the subtraction symbol to addition, *Change* the second value to the opposite sign (negative to a positive or positive to a negative). Look at the example below:

Keep   Change
$$4 - (-3) = 4 + 3 = 7$$
Change

In the example, *Keep* the 4, *Change* the subtraction symbol to addition and *Change* the negative 3 to a positive 3. *Keep–Change–Change.*

The Number Line

Numbers to the left on a number line are less than numbers to the right. At most, you will see just one number line question. You may be asked to find the distance between two points. For example, given the following number line, what is the distance between the point on the left and the point on the right?

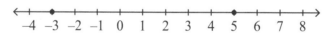

To answer this, you have only to count the spaces between the two values using your finger or pencil. Begin at –3 and count the spaces until you get to 5. The answer is 8. If you prefer to set up a math question, you can subtract the number on the left of the line from the number on the right, 5 – (–3) → *Keep–Change–Change* → 5 + 3 = 8.

➡ **Example 1** _____

According to the number line, what it the distance from point *A* to point *B* to the nearest whole number?

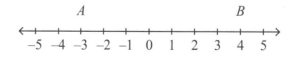

(a) –7   (b) 7   (c) 4   (d) 8

The correct answer is choice (b). Count the spaces between –3 and 4 to arrive at 7. You may also find the difference between 4 and –3 as shown: 4 – (–3) = 4 + 3 = 7.

Multiplication and Division

Numbers are either positive, negative, or zero. Each number is made up of two parts: the value of the number itself, and the sign of the number (positive or negative). When multiplying or dividing numbers, you must keep track of how many negative numbers you have in the question. If there is an even number of negatives or no negatives at all, then your answer will be positive. If there are an odd number of negative numbers, then your answer will be negative. When multiplying or dividing, you can begin by ignoring the sign of each number until the end. Carry out the operation then decide if your answer is positive or negative. If there is a zero in a multiplication problem the answer will always be zero. You cannot divide by zero; however, you can have zero as the dividend or numerator. If you do, the quotient will be zero. Look at the examples below. Remember to ignore the sign until after you multiply or divide.

Question	Answer
$4 \times 2 \times 3 =$	24
$4 \times (-2) \times 3 =$	–24
$4 \times (-6) \times (-3) =$	72
$(-14) \div (-2) =$	7
$(-14) \times 1 \times (-1) \times (-2) =$	–28
$(-2) \times (-5) \times 1 \times (-1) \times (-2) =$	20
$(-20) \div 1 \times (-2) \div (-2) =$	–20
$(-2) \times (-5) \times 1 \times (-1) \times (-2) \times 0 =$	0
$0 \div 4 =$	0

Most likely you know how to multiply two and three-digit numbers. If you need a refresher, review the explanations to see the detailed process or ask your teacher for a quick lesson. Remember when dividing whole numbers, the leftover becomes the remainder. To express a remainder as a fraction, place the remainder over the divisor (the denominator or the number outside of the long division symbol).

Greatest Common Factor and Least Common Multiple

A *multiple* is a number that is found by multiplying one number by another. *Factors* are numbers that are multiplied to make another number. The *greatest common factor* of a set of numbers is the largest *factor* that is common to each number. The greatest common factor of 27 and 18 is 9. To find this common factor, first consider all of the factors of 27 (1, 3, **9**, 27) and the factors of 18 (1, 2, 3, 6, **9**, 18). Which is the largest factor that 27 and 18 have in common? You can see the greatest common factor is 9. On the HSPT you do not have to figure out all of the factors. Instead, look at the answer choices and determine the largest value that is a factor of both.

The *least common multiple* of a set of numbers is the smallest number that has each of the given values as factors. It is a *multiple* of the values. The least common multiple of 27 and 54 is 54 because 54 is the smallest number that is divisible by both 27 and 54. On the HSPT you can look at your answer choices and find the smallest number that is a multiple of the two given values.

To determine the *Greatest Common Factor*, start with the largest answer choice. When you find one choice that is a factor of both values, you're done!

For the *Least Common Multiple*, start with the smallest answer choice. The choice that is a multiple of both values is the correct answer.

➥ Example 2

Find the greatest common factor of 36 and 12.

(a) 18   (b) 6   (c) 9   (d) 12

Start with the largest answer choice that is not larger than 12. The largest factor they have in common is 12. The correct answer is choice (d).

➥ Example 3

Find the least common multiple of 27 and 9.

(a) 54   (b) 36   (c) 27   (d) 18

Use the answer choices to help. Beginning with the smallest number that is not less than 27, find the value that is divisible by both 27 and 9. The correct answer is choice (c).

Absolute Value

Straight bars placed on either side of a number indicate absolute value. The absolute value of a number is the positive value of the number that is inside the bars and represents the distance that the number is from 0. For example: $|-4| = 4$, $|4| = 4$, both 4 and −4 are 4 units away from zero.

Order of Operations

PEMDAS, also known as Please Excuse My Dear Aunt Sally, represents **P**arentheses, **E**xponents, **M**ultiplication and **D**ivision from left to right, and **A**ddition and **S**ubtraction from left to right. Most questions on the HSPT do not involve many different operations. The most important thing to remember is *parentheses first*. For example $4 \times 9 + 4 \neq 4 \times (9 + 4)$, because $36 + 4 \neq 4 \times 13$.

The Basics Practice

Now it's time for you to practice. Try each problem below to become familiar with the type of questions you will see that involve basics math skills.

1. Solve: $-8 + (-18) =$

    (a) −26   (c) −10
    (b) 26   (d) 20

2. Solve: $-4 + 12 =$

    (a) 8   (c) 16
    (b) −8   (d) −16

3. Solve: $-212 - (-11) =$

    (a) 232   (c) − 232
    (b) −201   (d) 201

4. Solve:

$$
\begin{array}{r}
4 \\
656 \\
18 \\
+\,2{,}876 \\
\hline
\end{array}
$$

    (a) 3,426   (c) 3,450
    (b) 3,544   (d) 3,554

5. Solve:

6,829
− 3,679

(a) 3,050   (c) 3,150
(b) 2,350   (d) 3,250

6. Solve: −6 × −2 × 9 =

(a) −84   (c) −108
(b) 96   (d) 108

7. Solve: −6 ÷ −2 =

(a) 12   (c) 3
(b) −3   (d) −12

8. Solve: 36 × 72 =

(a) 324   (c) −2,596
(b) 2,592   (d) 218

9. Solve:

2,765
× 28

(a) 77,420   (c) 77,413
(b) 76,420   (d) 77,302

10. Solve: 36)4,793 =

(a) 116 R2   (c) 133 R1
(b) 103   (d) 133 R5

(Answers are on page 230.)

FRACTIONS, DECIMALS, PERCENTS, AND RATIOS

Below is a brief summary of what you need to know about fractions, decimals, percents, and ratios. Each subject is followed by examples of questions you are likely to see in the Mathematics subtest of the HSPT. You can expect to see about 5 or 6 of these questions in this subtest. You learned about decimals, fractions, and percents in Chapter 5, "Quantitative Skills." If you need to review the operations involved more thoroughly, go back to Chapter 5.

As you read through this review, try each example then read each explanation carefully to learn time-saving tips.

Fractions

A fraction is a division problem that expresses a value in terms of a *part* and a *whole*. The fraction $\frac{5}{7}$ represents 5 pieces out of a total of 7. The numerator, the top of the fraction, represents the *part*, and the denominator, the bottom, represents the *whole*. Both the numerator and the denominator are always whole numbers. You should be comfortable working with fractions; that is, you should be able to add, subtract, multiply and divide them. You will have a chance to practice these skills in the examples at the end of this section. You will see a few questions and four or five word problems involving fractions in this subtest.

REDUCING FRACTIONS

To reduce a fraction, divide the numerator and denominator by the same number. Don't waste time trying to figure out what is the greatest common factor—just try easy numbers such as 2, 3, and 5 then keep reducing. If you happen to already know the greatest common factor, then certainly use it, but if not, then just start reducing as in the example below.

$$\frac{96}{24} \div \frac{3}{3} = \frac{32}{8} \text{ then } \frac{32}{8} \div \frac{4}{4} = \frac{8}{2} \text{ then } \frac{8}{2} = 4$$

MIXED NUMBERS AND IMPROPER FRACTIONS

An improper fraction is one where the numerator is a higher number than the denominator, making the value greater than 1 such as $\frac{9}{4}$. A mixed number is one with a whole number part and a fraction part such as $4\frac{5}{7}$. To convert an improper fraction to a mixed number, divide the numerator by the denominator to get the largest whole number. The remainder is then placed over the denominator. For example:

$$\frac{15}{7} = 2 \text{ R}1 = 2\frac{1}{7}$$

To change a mixed number to an improper fraction, you must multiply the whole number by the denominator and then add the numerator of the fraction. That total becomes the new numerator and the denominator remains the same.

$$2\frac{1}{7} = \frac{2 \times 7 + 1}{7} = \frac{15}{7}$$

COMPARING FRACTIONS

You learned how to compare fractions using the cross-up method in Chapter 5 on page 111. Feel free to go back and review if you need a refresher.

ADDITION AND SUBTRACTION

Only fractions with the same denominators can be added or subtracted. This is also true of the fraction portion when adding or subtracting mixed numbers.

➡ **Example 1** _____

Solve: $9 - 6\frac{5}{7} =$

(a) $\frac{5}{7}$ (b) $2\frac{2}{7}$ (c) $3\frac{2}{7}$ (d) $2\frac{5}{7}$

To find the difference, you must borrow one from the 9 as shown below.

$$
\begin{array}{cc}
9 & 8\frac{7}{7} \\
-6\frac{5}{7} \rightarrow & -6\frac{5}{7} \\
\hline
& 2\frac{2}{7}
\end{array}
$$

You can also look at your answer choices and estimate your answer. Because you are subtracting more than 6 and less than 7 your answer will be between 2 and 3. That narrows your answer to choices (b) and (d). Because you are taking away $\frac{5}{7}$, the remaining portion must be $\frac{2}{7}$ making answer choice (b) $2\frac{2}{7}$ the correct answer.

MULTIPLICATION AND DIVISION

To multiply proper or improper fractions, multiply the numerators together to form the numerator of the product, and then multiply the denominators together to form the denominator of the product. You should always reduce as much as possible before multiplying. To multiply mixed numbers, first convert them to improper fractions as shown.

$$\frac{3}{25}\times1\frac{3}{7}=\frac{3}{25}\times\frac{(1\times7+3)}{7}=\frac{3}{\overset{}{\underset{5}{25}}}\times\frac{\overset{2}{10}}{7}=\frac{3}{5}\times\frac{2}{7}=\frac{3\times2}{5\times7}=\frac{6}{35}$$

Never divide fractions! There is no reason to divide when you can multiply instead. To change a division problem into a multiplication one, you can use *Keep–Change–Change. Keep* the first number, *Change* the operation symbol from division to multiplication, and then *Change* the second fraction by flipping it over (taking the reciprocal). Here is an example:

$$\frac{3}{5}\div\frac{2}{15}\to\frac{3}{\underset{1}{5}}\times\frac{\overset{3}{15}}{2}\to\ \text{reduce}\ \frac{3}{1}\times\frac{3}{2}=\frac{9}{2}$$

Decimals

You must have a basic understanding of decimals for this subtest. There are usually about four questions involving decimals in the Mathematics subtest. A decimal is a fraction whose denominator is a power of ten. The number to the left of the decimal point is the whole number part and the numbers to the right of the decimal point represents the fraction part. Decimals, when written as fractions, always have denominators that are multiples of 10, for example $0.8 = \frac{8}{10}$ and $0.88 = \frac{88}{100}$. Let's review what each decimal place represents. Below is the number 168,259.743 with a label shown for each place.

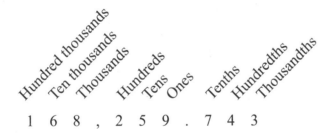

Let's review a couple of examples to demonstrate how to read decimals.

➡ Example 2

In the number 267.417, in what place is the number 4?

(a) tens   (b) hundredths   (c) tenths   (d) hundreds

In the number 267.417, the 4 is in the tenths place. Do not confuse this with the tens place, which is two places to the left of the decimal point. The correct answer is choice (c).

➡ Example 3

Three one hundredths can be written as

(a) 0.3   (b) 300   (c) 0.03   (d) 0.003

Three one hundredths is the equivalent of $\frac{3}{100}$. Dividing by 100 is the same as moving the decimal point two places to the left to make 0.03. The correct answer is choice (c).

ADDITION AND SUBTRACTION

To add and subtract decimals, first line up the decimal points of each number. When working with whole numbers and decimals, you can make the whole number a decimal by placing a decimal point after the number then adding zeros to the right. For example:

$$3 - 2.56 = 3.00 - 2.56 = \begin{array}{r} 3.00 \\ -\ 2.56 \\ \hline 0.44 \end{array}$$

MULTIPLICATION AND DIVISION

To multiply decimals, move each decimal point all the way to the right, counting how many times you move over. For example: 42.61×0.112 will look like 4261×112 when you move the decimal point on the first number 2 places and on the second number 3 places. You have moved the decimal point a total of 5 places to the right. Multiply the two new numbers.

$$42.61 \times 0.112 \ \rightarrow \ \begin{array}{r} 4261 \\ \times\ \ 112 \\ \hline 477232 \end{array}$$

Now put the decimal point of the product back by moving from the right, the total number of 5 places. Your final answer will be 4.77232.

When dividing with decimals, make each number an integer by moving the decimal point to the right for both the dividend and the divisor. *You must move the decimal point the same number of places in each number.* This means you may have to add a zero to one of the numbers. For example: $4.86 \div 0.6 = 486 \div 60 = 8.1$.

If you do not have an integer answer, you can write the quotient as a fraction and reduce to the simplest form.

$$0.84 \div 0.6 = 84 \div 60 = \frac{84}{60} = \frac{7}{5}$$

If you are not able to reduce the fraction, find the quotient using long division. When doing long division, move the decimal point in the same way as was done in the example above.

CONVERTING FRACTIONS AND DECIMALS

Moving a decimal point one place to the right is the same as multiplying by 10, two places to the right is the same as multiplying by 100, etc.

$$0.8 \times 10 = 8.0 \quad \text{or} \quad 0.08 \times 100 = 8.0$$

Likewise, moving the decimal point to the left is the same as dividing by 10, two places will be dividing by 100, etc.

$$2.0 \div 10 = \frac{2}{10} = 0.2 \quad \text{likewise} \quad 2.0 \div 100 = \frac{2}{100} = 0.02$$

To change a fraction to a decimal you may have to use long division as shown below.

$$\frac{7}{8} = 8\overline{)7} = 8\overline{)7.000}$$
$$ 0.875$$

$$
\begin{array}{r}
-64 \downarrow \\
\hline
60 \\
-56 \downarrow \\
\hline
40 \\
-40 \\
\hline
0
\end{array}
$$

If the quotient repeats itself, a bar is placed over the number that repeats, as in $\frac{1}{3} = 0.\overline{3}$. Below, you will find a list of some common fractions and their equivalent decimals. You should become familiar with these to save time in the Mathematics subtest.

Percents

There may only be a couple of questions that ask you about percents; however, there will be another few word problems that also test your understanding of percents, so let's review how to calculate percent. Here you will see each type of format involving percents. Each may look slightly different but will involve similar concepts.

The term *percent* can be split into two parts: *per*, which means division, and *cent* which means 100. The value, 8 *percent*, 8%, can be written as $\frac{8}{100}$ where the fraction bar represents the *per* and the denominator of 100 represents *cent*. A shortcut for changing a percent to a decimal is to move the decimal point two places to the left, then remove the % sign. For example, 8% is 8.0 *per-cent* or 0.08 when written as a decimal. To convert a percent to a fraction, first write the percent as a fraction over 100 then reduce. For example, 70% = $\frac{70}{100}$ = $\frac{7}{10}$.

TIP

To convert a percent to a decimal, remove the % sign, and move the decimal point two places to the left.

Look at the following table to become familiar with some common equivalent values for each.

Fraction	Decimal	Percent
$\frac{1}{8}$	0.125	12.5%
$\frac{1}{5}$	0.2	20%
$\frac{1}{4}$	0.25	25%
$\frac{1}{3}$	$0.\overline{3}$	$33.\overline{3}$%
$\frac{1}{2}$	0.5	50%
$\frac{3}{4}$	0.75	75%
1	1.00	100%

To find other common equivalents, multiply the values from the table by the numerator. For example, $\frac{3}{8} = 0.125 \times 3 = 0.375$. Look at the following examples to become familiar with percent and decimal conversions.

➡ Example 4_____

As a percent, 0.156 can be written as

(a) 15.6%   (b) 156%   (c) 0.00156%   (d) 1.56%

To convert a decimal to a percent, move the decimal point two places to the right and add the percent symbol, 0.156 = 15.6%. The correct answer is choice (a).

➡ Example 5_____

In a classroom of 20 students, 5 are girls. What percent of the students are girls?

(a) 5%   (b) 10%   (c) 60%   (d) 25%

Percent is part over the whole, in this case girls over students, $\frac{5}{20} = \frac{1}{4} = 25\%$. Because percent means to divide by 100, you can change $\frac{5}{20}$ into a fraction with a denominator of 100.

$\frac{5 \times 5}{20 \times 5} = \frac{25}{100} = 25\%$. The correct answer is choice (d).

OF MEANS MULTIPLY

Now that you know what *per-cent* means, let's combine it with the word *of*. The expression "8 percent of 20" is the same as writing any of these expressions.

$$8\% \times 20 = \frac{8}{100} \times 20 = 0.08 \times 20$$

You can often find the correct answer by estimating, using 10% as a benchmark. To calculate 10 percent, move the decimal point one place to the left, dividing by 10. For example, 10% of 20 is 2. If you can quickly figure out 10% then you may be able to estimate the correct answer choice.

Read the following example and notice it is the same question as shown above. What is 8% of 20? Do not be intimidated by word problems.

➡ Example 6_____

What is your savings if you bought a $20 book at an 8% discount?

(a) $2.00   (b) $18.40   (c) $16.00   (d) $1.60

Use estimation to answer this question. Since 2 is 10% of 20, the answer has to be less than 2 because we want just 8%. There is only one choice less than $2.00, so you are all done! If you calculate the exact value, 0.08×20, you can see the only two numbers that matter are the 8 and the 2, so when you multiply, you will end up with 16. The only answer choices are (c) and (d) but (c) is much too large. The correct answer is choice (d) $1.60.

DISCOUNTED PRICE

Calculating discounted price can be a two-step problem. You must first figure out the percent of the discount and then subtract that amount from the original price. You can, however, solve this in just one step. If you buy a $70 sweater at a 30% discount, what percent are you actually paying? The answer is 70%, because 100% − 30% = 70%. Figure out 70% of the original price rather than having to do multiplication then subtraction. 70% of $70 is $49.

⇥ Example 7_____

A dress is discounted at 20% off the full price of $80. What is the discounted purchase price?

(a) $16   (b) $64   (c) $74   (d) $56

If you have a 20% discount, this means you are paying 80% of the original cost. 80% of $80 is choice (b) $64.

FINDING THE ORIGINAL VALUE

In this type of question, you are told the percent and asked to find the original value. To answer this, you could set up an algebraic expression, but there is no need when the answer is right below the question. Just plug in each answer choice until you find the right one.

⇥ Example 8_____

24 is 6% of what number?

(a) 240   (b) 800   (c) 4000   (d) 400

6% of 400 is 24 because 0.06 × 400 = 24. The algebraic expression that represents this is $24 = 0.06x$. To solve for x, divide both sides by 0.06.

$$24 = 0.06x$$
$$\frac{24}{0.06} = \frac{0.06x}{0.06}$$
$$\frac{2400}{6} = x$$
$$400 = x$$

You could also estimate and find both 5% and 10% of each answer choice looking for the answer whose values are on either side of 24. The only answer choice that has 24 between 5% and 10% of the value is choice (d) 400.

Ratios

You can expect to see about 4 or 5 questions involving ratios in this subtest. In addition, there will be questions about probability, a very similar topic. You will need only a basic understanding of ratios to be successful in answering these questions.

A ratio is a relationship between two amounts and describes the proportion of how the two are combined. A proportion is an equation made up of two ratios. For example, a fruit company wants to sell baskets of fruit and wants their baskets to be made up of apples and oranges. Regardless of the size of the basket, they want to have 4 apples for every 3 oranges. They could express this as a ratio: $\frac{4 \text{ apples}}{3 \text{ oranges}}$ OR $\frac{3 \text{ oranges}}{4 \text{ apples}}$. A ratio may also be written horizontally as 4 apples : 3 oranges, or without the fruit labels it is written as 4 : 3. A valid proportion of apples to oranges could be written as $\frac{4}{3} = \frac{12}{9}$. This would indicate that a fruit basket with 4 apples and 3 oranges is the same ratio, or the same proportion, as a basket having 12 apples and 9 oranges. When setting up a ratio, is it important that the relationship on the left of the equal sign mimics the relationship on the right, $\frac{4 \text{ apples}}{3 \text{ oranges}} = \frac{12 \text{ apples}}{9 \text{ oranges}}$ and not $\frac{4 \text{ apples}}{3 \text{ oranges}} \neq \frac{9 \text{ oranges}}{12 \text{ apples}}$.

SET UP A PROPORTION

When faced with a ratio question with one piece of missing information, you should set up a similar set of fractions using x to represent the unknown value.

➡ **Example 9**_____

If 4 skeins of yarn are required to knit 3 mittens, how many skeins of yarn will be required to make 15 mittens?

(a) 60   (b) 20   (c) 24   (d) 12

You should start first by setting up a proportion, using x to represent the missing information.

$$\frac{4 \text{ skeins}}{3 \text{ mittens}} = \frac{x}{15 \text{ mittens}}$$

Now you must figure out the ratio factor. Look at the two pieces of information that you have, either two numerators, or in this case the two denominators. What is 3 multiplied by to make 15? If the answer is not obvious then just divide 15 by 3 to find 5. The ratio factor is 5, so to maintain the proportion, you must multiply the top and bottom of the left fraction, each by 5 to arrive at $x = 4 \times 5 = 20$. To confirm your answer, check that the following proportion is true: $\frac{4}{3} = \frac{20}{15}$. You can also plug in the answer choices for x and see which answer choice makes the proportion true. You may choose to cross multiply, although this may be more work than you need do. But if you are comfortable with this method, use it for these questions.

$$\frac{4 \text{ skeins}}{3 \text{ mittens}} = \frac{x}{15 \text{ mittens}}$$
$$4 \times 15 = 3x$$
$$\frac{60}{3} = \frac{3x}{3}$$
$$20 = x$$

The correct answer is choice (b) 20.

GIVEN A TOTAL, FIND THE MISSING INFORMATION

Another ratio question you may encounter is one where you are given the total amount and then asked to find a missing piece of information.

➡️ **Example 10** _____

If the ratios of dogs to cats in a kennel is 5 to 3 and there are a total of 40 dogs and cats, how many cats are in the kennel?

(a) 24   (b) 15   (c) 8   (d) 12

Because there are 5 dogs for every 3 cats that means that for every 5 dogs and 3 cats there are 8 animals. The correct proportion that represents this question is $\frac{3 \text{ cats}}{8 \text{ total}} = \frac{x}{40}$. Because $40 \div 8 = 5$, the ratio factor is 5. Multiply the number of cats by 5 to determine the number of cats there would be if 40 were the total. $3 \times 5 = 15$, or answer choice (b). The correct proportion is now $\frac{3 \text{ cats}}{8 \text{ total}} = \frac{15 \text{ cats}}{40 \text{ total}}$; notice that 15 is 5 times 3 and 40 is 5 times 8.

Fractions, Decimals, Percents, and Ratios Practice

1. What fraction of a day is 10 hours?

    (a) $\frac{5}{12}$ (c) $\frac{1}{24}$

    (b) $\frac{5}{6}$ (d) $\frac{1}{3}$

2. Solve: $\frac{2}{3} - \frac{1}{5} =$

    (a) $-\frac{1}{2}$ (c) $\frac{1}{2}$

    (b) $\frac{1}{5}$ (d) $\frac{7}{15}$

3. Solve: $28 - 9\frac{2}{3}$

    (a) $19\frac{2}{3}$ (c) $18\frac{1}{3}$

    (b) $19\frac{1}{3}$ (d) $18\frac{2}{3}$

4. Solve: $\frac{2}{7} \div \frac{3}{7} =$

    (a) $\frac{6}{49}$ (c) $\frac{3}{2}$

    (b) $\frac{6}{14}$ (d) $\frac{2}{3}$

5. If $\frac{2}{3}$ of a number is 8, what is $\frac{1}{2}$ of the same number?

    (a) 6   (c) 12

    (b) 4   (d) 16

6. What is equal to four-fifths of 6 dollars?

    (a) $4.80   (c) $2.80

    (b) $4.50   (d) $4.20

7. Four dimes are equivalent to what fraction of two dollars?

    (a) $\frac{1}{10}$ (c) $\frac{2}{100}$

    (b) $\frac{40}{2}$ (d) $\frac{1}{5}$

8. Solve $4 - 2.718 =$

    (a) 1.282   (c) 1.372

    (b) 2.318   (d) 6.718

9. Solve: $0.76 + 2.35 + 1.6 =$

    (a) 3.27   (c) 4.71

    (b) 63.37   (d) 5.76

10. To make a cake, Kimmy must spend $3.00 on flour, $2.00 on sugar, and $1.50 on eggs. What is the total cost of cake ingredients?

    (a) $6.50   (c) $5.50
    (b) $7.00   (d) $4.50

11. Solve: $2.462 \times 1.3 =$

    (a) 3.2106   (c) 3.206
    (b) 3.12   (d) 3.2006

12. Solve:

    $$27.3$$
    $$\times 1.2$$

    (a) 32.76   (c) 28.5
    (b) 32.70   (d) 31.76

13. Solve: $9.2\overline{)11.316}$

    (a) 8.27   (c) 11.23
    (b) 8.23   (d) 1.23

14. As a *simplified* fraction, 0.36 can be written as

    (a) $\frac{36}{100}$ (c) $\frac{5}{9}$

    (b) $\frac{18}{50}$ (d) $\frac{9}{25}$

15. As a decimal, $\frac{5}{6}$ can be written as

    (a) 0.83   (c) $0.\overline{83}$
    (b) $0.8\overline{3}$ (d) 8.3

16. Joseph owes 12% interest per year on his loan of $960. How much interest will he pay for one year?

    (a) $80   (c) $11.52
    (b) $1,152   (d) $115.20

17. If you spend $3,000 each month and $600 of that is spent on food, what portion of your spending goes to food?

    (a) 5%   (c) 60%
    (b) 10%   (d) 20%

18. The below pie chart shows the types of clubs at the Horace Mann School and the percent of students that join each. If there are 1,200 students in all, how many of them are in the art club?

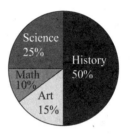

    (a) 250   (c) 180
    (b) 120   (d) 240

19. 36 is 30% of what number?

    (a) 120   (c) 140
    (b) 1.20   (d) 7.5

20. If x% of 120 is 90, what is x?

    (a) 210   (c) 75
    (b) 150   (d) 15

21. A map uses a scale of 1 cm to represent 2 miles. How many miles apart are two points that are 4.5 cm apart on the map?

    (a) 4.5 miles   (c) 4 miles
    (b) 18 miles   (d) 9 miles

22. Which is a proportion?

    (a) $1:2 = 2:4$ (c) $8:4 = 5:10$
    (b) $3:4 = 4:3$ (d) $2:5 = 10:15$

23. If one roll of wrapping paper will wrap 32 square feet, how many square feet will 2.5 roles wrap?

   (a) 80 ft.^{2} (c) 64 ft.^{2}
   (b) 90 ft.^{2} (d) 74 ft.^{2}

24. If a man burns 500 calories in 2 hours how many hours will it take to burn 625 calories ?

   (a) 3.25 hrs.   (c) 2.75 hrs.
   (b) 2.5 hrs.   (d) 3.5 hrs.

25. Arioch rakes $\frac{2}{5}$ of the yard in 2 hours. At this rate, how long will it take to rake the entire yard?

   (a) 12 hrs.   (c) 5 hrs.
   (b) 4 hrs.   (d) 10 hrs.

26. A train travels 900 miles in 9 hours. How long will it take the train to travel 1150 miles?

   (a) 1.5 hrs.   (c) 10 hrs.
   (b) 12 hrs.   (d) 11.50 hrs.

27. If a dozen donuts have 3,000 calories, how many calories are there in one donut?

   (a) 300   (c) 350
   (b) 250   (d) 275

(Answers are on page 231.)

CONVERSIONS AND PROPERTIES

In this subtest there are between 5 and 8 questions involving unit conversions. You should be familiar with the common units that you will see in the Mathematics subtest. Review the tables below and try the questions at the end of the section. Use the tables when working through the examples, but try the to memorize them before taking the practice subtest at the end of this chapter. Keep in mind that this is a short list of conversions, and includes only those you will have to know to be successful on the HSPT.

You will usually be asked to make only one conversion in a question. If you do not know the conversion, you may need to break the conversion into more pieces. Let's review one where you may have to use more than one conversion, for example, how many seconds are in two hours? See the example below:

$$2 \text{ hours} = 2 \text{ hours} \times \frac{60 \text{ minutes}}{1 \text{ hour}} \times \frac{60 \text{ seconds}}{1 \text{ minute}} = 2 \times 3{,}600 \text{ seconds} = 7{,}200 \text{ seconds}$$

Notice that all of the units except for *seconds* are canceled out by the conversion factors. By writing the solution out like this, you will not have to memorize the full conversions such as 3,600 seconds per hour. The more conversion factors you know, the fewer steps you will need.

$$2 \text{ hours} \times \frac{3{,}600 \text{ seconds}}{1 \text{ hour}} = 7{,}200 \text{ seconds}$$

Now let's look at the various conversion factors you should know for this subtest of the HSPT.

Did you know there
are 5 tomatoes
in a mile? Five—
Two—mEight—Os!
Remember there
are 5,280 feet in
a mile.

Linear Measure

There are many different types of linear measure, including old-fashioned measures such as rods and cubits, but you will only have to know a few of the more modern terms for the HSPT. They are listed for you in the table below.

Linear Measure

Inches, Feet, Yards, and Miles
1 Yard = 3 feet
1 Mile = 5,280 feet
1 Foot = 12 inches
1 Yard = 36 inches
Meters, Millimeters, Centimeters, and Kilometers
1 meter = 100 centimeters
1 meter = 1,000 millimeters
1 kilometer = 1,000 meters

REMEMBER

For Metric units, there are three prefixes that you must know:

Milli = $\frac{1}{1000}$

Kilo = 1,000

Centi = $\frac{1}{100}$

WEIGHT MEASURE

It can be easy to confuse liquid measure and weight measure because both can be measured in ounces. Keep this in mind when you read the next couple of conversion tables. Remember there are 8 ounces in a cup of liquid and 16 ounces in one pound.

Weight Measure

Ounces and Pounds
16 ounces (oz.) = 1 pound (lb.)
Milligrams, Grams, and Kilograms
1 kilogram = 1,000 grams
1 gram = 1,000 milligrams

Liquid Measure

If other conversions are needed to answer a question, they will be provided in the directions. For now, you only have to be familiar with the following table to answer questions on liquid measure.

Liquid Measure

Ounces, Cups, Pints, Quarts, and Gallons	
1 gallon = 4 quarts	1 quart = 2 pints
1 pint = 2 cups	1 cup = 8 ounces
Liters, Milliliters, and Kiloliters	
1 kiloliter = 1,000 liters	
1 liter = 1,000 milliliters	

Memorizing these liquid measures, especially cups, pints, and quarts, can be difficult. The diagram of "Mr. Gallon" will help you to remember measures of liquid amounts. There are 4 quarts in a gallon. This should be easy to remember since the word quart means in *fours*, like 4 quarters in a dollar. There are two pints in a quart, shown by the two *P*s inside the *Q*s, so therefore there must be 8 pints in a gallon. If you look inside each of the *P*s, you can see there are two *C*s indicating 2 cups in one pint, *P*, so there are 4 cups in a quart, *Q*.

Units of Time

You probably know these conversions well. It is a good idea to memorize the last, 1 hour = 3,600 seconds, to save you time. Review the table below then practice the examples at the end of the section.

Time

Seconds, Minutes, Hours, and Days	
1 day = 24 hours	1 hour = 60 minutes
1 minute = 60 seconds	1 hour = 3,600 seconds

Temperature

Converting temperatures is always difficult but the good news is you will not have to do this. You will, however, have to estimate temperatures such as a comfortable room temperature.

Remember these key conversions:

- Freezing point of water is 32°F = 0°C.
- Boiling point of water is 212°F = 100°C.
- Comfortable Indoor Temperature is 60°F to 70°F or 16°C to 22°C.

You should be familiar with the more common values for both Fahrenheit and Celsius, such as boiling and freezing points of water.

➡ Example 1 _____

Which temperature would be considered typical for the inside of a home?

(a) 30°F   (b) 50°C   (c) 0°C   (d) 65°F

Remember that 32°F is freezing as is 0°C. 100°C is the boiling point of water (212°F) so even half of that is still very hot. By process of elimination, the correct answer is choice (d) 65°F.

Other Conversions

Any other conversion factors that are necessary will be given to you within the question such as centimeters in an inch (2.54 cm = 1 in.).

Properties

You may see one question on the HSPT asking you to identify one of the properties shown in the table below. These properties can be used to answer other mathematics questions as well. For example, the commutative property is a rule that allows you to rearrange numbers to make a multiplication problem easier and you may use the distributive property when doing mental math. Take a few minutes to make sure you understand each of the properties shown.

Number Properties

Commutative Property of Addition	Commutative Property of Multiplication
A + B = B + A	A × B = B × A
4 + 6 = 10 and 6 + 4 = 10	3 × 2 = 6 and 2 × 3 = 6
Associative Property of Addition	**Associative Property of Multiplication**
A + (B + C) = (A + B) + C	A × (B × C) = (A × B) × C
2 + (6 + 7) = 15 and (2 + 6) + 7 = 15	3 × (1 × 5) = 15 and (3 × 1) × 5 = 15
Identity Property of Addition	**Identity Property of Multiplication**
A + 0 = A	A × 1 = A
8 + 0 = 8	10 × 1 = 10

Distributive Property

A(C + D) = AC + AD	A(C − D) = AC − AD
3(2 + 4) = 3 × 2 + 3 × 4 = 18	4 (6 − 2) = 4 × 6 − 4 × 2 = 16

There are more properties that you will learn about in school, but this list represents all of the properties you will have to be familiar with on the HSPT.

Example 2

What property is illustrated here?

$3 + (7 - 5) = (7 - 5) + 3$

(a) Commutative Property
(b) Associative Property
(c) Distributive Property
(d) Identity Property

Notice that the location of the term in parentheses has changed but not the values inside. This is an example of the commutative property of addition, choice (a).

Conversions and Properties Practice

It's time to practice all that you have learned about Conversions and Properties in the following questions.

1. How many inches are in 2 yards, 1 foot, and 7 inches?

   (a) 94 in.   (c) 43 in.
   (b) 91 in.   (d) 55 in.

2. What equals 2 yards?

   (a) 70 in.   (c) 36 in.
   (b) 5 ft., 12 in. (d) 2 ft., 24 in.

3. Which of the following is equal to 1.6 meters?

   (a) 16 millimeters
   (b) 1.6 millimeters
   (c) 0.0016 millimeters
   (d) 1,600 millimeters

4. Which of the following is equal to 2.1 kilometers?

   (a) 210 cm   (c) 210,000 cm
   (b) 21,000 cm   (d) 2,100 cm

5. How many meters are 612.5 kilometers?

   (a) 0.6215   (c) 61.25
   (b) 6,125   (d) 612,500

6. 5 miles is equal to 8 kilometers. What is the speed in kilometers of a car driving at 70 miles per hour?

   (a) 112   (c) 350
   (b) 40   (d) 120

7. Which is true?

   (a) 200 meters > 0.5 kilometers
   (b) 7 centimeters > 1 meter
   (c) 200 grams < 20 centigrams
   (d) 2 kilometers > 500 meters

8. A baby that weighs 6 pounds and 7 ounces weighs how many ounces?

   (a) 215 oz.   (c) 103 oz.
   (b) 55 oz.   (d) 71 oz.

9. If a dog weights 2.4 kilograms, how many grams does he weigh?

   (a) 2,400 g   (c) 24,000 g
   (b) 0.0024 g   (d) 0.240 g

10. How many cups of milk fit into a 56-ounce pitcher?

   (a) $3\frac{1}{2}$ cups   (c) 7 cups
   (b) 4 cups   (d) $4\frac{1}{2}$ cups

11. How many cups are in 5 quarts?

    (a) 10   (c) 20

    (b) 40   (d) 8

12. How many pints equal one and a half gallons?

    (a) 8   (c) 12

    (b) 6   (d) 5

13. How many liters is 2,450 milliliters?

    (a) 24.50   (c) 0.245

    (b) 2.45   (d) 245

14. 14,400 seconds equals how many hours?

    (a) 4   (c) 16.5

    (b) 12   (d) 12.5

15. What fraction of an hour is 36 minutes?

    (a) $\frac{3}{5}$ (c) $\frac{5}{7}$

    (b) $\frac{1}{2}$ (d) $\frac{7}{9}$

16. What property is illustrated here?

    $(3 + 7) + 5 = 3 + (7 + 5)$

    (a) Commutative Property

    (b) Associative Property

    (c) Distributive Property

    (d) Identity Property

(Answers are on page 234.)

GEOMETRY

Geometry is a full-year course made up of proofs and theorems. The good news is that on the HSPT you only have to know a few geometric concepts. You can expect to see about 10 questions as well as an additional 5 word problems involving geometry. Let's begin with a review of what you will have to know about various geometric concepts.

Circles

You will see only a few questions about circles on the HSPT, but if you understand just two definitions, these will be easy questions for you to answer correctly.

DIAMETER: A line passing from one side of a circle to the other and passing through the center.

RADIUS: A line passing from the center of the circle to the side. It is half of the distance of the diameter. The drawing below shows both the radius and diameter of a circle.

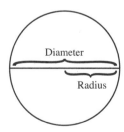

AREA OF A CIRCLE: $A = \pi r^2$ where r represents the radius and π can be approximated by 3.14.

Polygons

You should know the names of the polygons below. While parallelograms and quadrilaterals are also polygons, they will be reviewed separately.

Name of Object	Example	Number of Sides
Triangle		3
Quadrilateral		4
Pentagon		5
Hexagon		6
Heptagon		7
Octagon		8

You know the sum of interior angles of a triangle is 180°. To determine the sum of the interior angles of a polygon, you can cut it up into triangles and multiply the number of triangles you have by 180°. For example, a square can be cut into two separate triangles, so the sum of the interior angles is 2 × 180° = 360°. Similarly, a hexagon can be cut into 4 triangles, so the sum of the interior angles is 4 × 180° = 720°. There are always 2 fewer triangles than the number of sides. This is represented by the following formula, where n is the number of sides in the polygon.

$$\text{The sum of the interior angles of a polygon} = (n - 2) \times 180°$$

Parallelograms and Quadrilaterals

For the HSPT, all that you will need to know about parallelograms and quadrilaterals are the definitions. A *quadrilateral* is any four sided figure. A *parallelogram* is a four-sided polygon whose opposite sides are parallel. So every parallelogram is a quadrilateral but not every quadrilateral is a parallelogram. The sum of the four interior angles for all quadrilaterals is 360°.

Quadrilaterals and Parallelograms		
Square		All sides are equal in length. Opposite sides are parallel. All angles are 90°.
Rectangle		Opposite sides are equal in length and parallel. All angles are 90°.
Rhombus		All sides are equal in length, opposite sides are parallel, opposite angles are equal
Trapezoid		Quadrilateral with only *one* pair of parallel sides

Perimeter and Area

In the Mathematics subtest of the HSPT, you will be asked to calculate the area and the perimeter of rectangles, squares, and triangles. You can expect to see about 3 of these questions in the Mathematics subtest. Let's begin with a few definitions.

PERIMETER OF A POLYGON: The sum of the lengths of all sides.

AREA OF A RECTANGLE: Area = length × width.

AREA OF A SQUARE: Because a square is made of 4 sides of equal length the area, length × width, can be simplified to the length of one side, s, squared: $A = s^2$.

AREA OF A TRIANGLE: One half of the product of the length of the base and the height of a measure perpendicular (at a right angle to) the base. $A = \frac{1}{2}bh$. The commutative property of multiplication allows us to cut either the base in half or the height before multiplying them together. For example, if the $A = \frac{1}{2} \times 9 \times 8$, you can choose to first take one half of 8, which is 4, then multiply 4 by 9 to make 36. This is easier than trying to figure out $\frac{1}{2}$ of 9 and then multiplying it by 8.

Lines and Angles

There are a few questions in the Mathematics subtest that deal specifically with lines and angles. If you remember each of the definitions below, you will be able to answer these questions both quickly and accurately.

PERPENDICULAR LINES: Lines are perpendicular if they intersect at a 90° angle. The symbol to indicate *perpendicular* is ⊥.

ANGLE: An angle is formed when 2 lines or line segments intersect. Angle A can be represented as $\angle A$. Angles may also be described by the intersecting lines or segments that create the angle. The angle shown in the diagram below, can be expressed as ∠*KJL*, with the letter in the middle representing the point of intersection of the two line segments that form the angle.

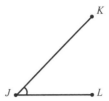

COMPLEMENTARY ANGLE: Either of two angles that when added create a sum of 90°. The angles below, 30° and 60° are complementary angles.

ACUTE ANGLE: Any angle that is less than 90°. The 45° angle below is an example of an acute angle.

OBTUSE ANGLE: Any angle that is more than 90° and less than 180°. The 130° angle below is an example of an obtuse angle.

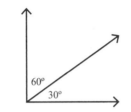

PARALLEL LINES: Lines that have the same slope and never intersect.

RIGHT ANGLE: An angle that is 90°. Right angles are created by the intersection of perpendicular lines or rays.

CONGRUENT ANGLES: Angles that have the same measure. The two angles shown below are congruent. While they are facing different directions they have the same measure.

STRAIGHT ANGLES: A straight angle is 180° and changes the direction of a ray to point the other way.

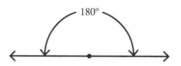

SUPPLEMENTARY ANGLE: Either of two angles that when added create a sum of 180°. The angles below, 130° and 50°, are supplementary angles.

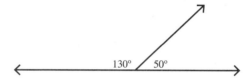

TRANSVERSAL: Any line that crosses at least two parallel lines.

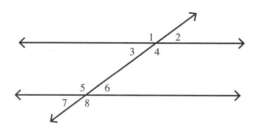

Opposite angles that are created by transversals are known as *vertical angles* and are equal in measure.

In the diagram above, the following pairs of angles are vertical angles: 1 and 4, 2 and 3, 5 and 8, 7 and 6, and therefore each pair of angles is equal in measure.

Triangles

On the HSPT you may see one or two questions that involve identifying triangles or finding missing information in a triangle. Below are the definitions you will need to know.

ACUTE TRIANGLE: One that has only acute, less than 90°, angles.

CONGRUENT TRIANGLES: Triangles that have the same measure for corresponding angles and side lengths. Line segments show that the sides and angles are congruent.

For example, the 3 line segments in the triangle on the left indicate that the length of that side, $\overline{AC}$, is equal to the side of the triangle on the right that also has 3 line segments, $\overline{DF}$. This can be expressed as $\overline{AC} \cong \overline{DF}$.

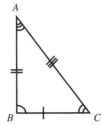
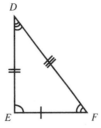

EQUILATERAL TRIANGLE: A triangle where all sides are equal in length and all angles are equal in measure.

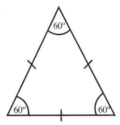

If a triangle is an equilateral, you know that all three angles are the same measure, and because they must add to 180°, each angle is 180° ÷ 3 = 60°.

ISOSCELES TRIANGLE: A triangle that has two angles of equal measure and as a result has two sides of the same length. The line segments shown on the triangle below indicate that sides *a* and *b* are the same length.

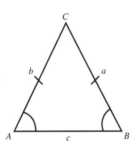

OBTUSE TRIANGLE: A triangle that contains an obtuse angle (greater than 90° and less than 180°). In the triangle shown, the 120° angle is obtuse.

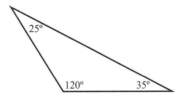

RIGHT TRIANGLE: Any triangle that contains a right (90°) angle. Below are two examples of a right triangle. Notice the symbol used to represent the 90° angle.

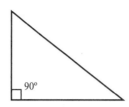 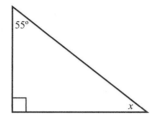

In the right figure above, angle *x* must be 35° because 180° – 55° – 90° = 35°.

If one angle in a triangle is 90° the sum of the other two must also be 90°, making them complementary angles.

SCALENE TRIANGLE: A triangle that has three unequal sides and three unequal angles.

 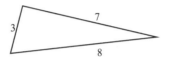

SIMILAR TRIANGLES: Triangles having the same angles and the same ratio of the sides, (same shape, not the same size). In the example below, each triangle is made up of the same angles. Each side of the larger triangle is twice the length of the corresponding sides of the smaller triangle. *ABC ~ DEF* indicates that triangle *ABC* is similar to triangle *DEF*. Notice the two triangles have the same shape, same angles, and different sizes.

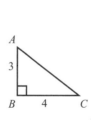 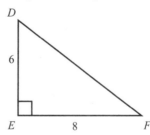

Now that you are familiar with vocabulary necessary to answer questions involving angles and triangles let's look at a couple of other questions types that you may see involving triangles.

Perimeter of Triangle Sides with Consecutive Even or Odd Integers

Consecutive means to be in order with no missing values. You may see a question that asks you to identify the length of a side of a triangle when given the perimeter. The sides will be described as consecutive integers, such as 3, 4, 5, or consecutive odd integers, such as 3, 5, 7, or consecutive even integers such as 6, 8, 10. When answering this type of question, do not set up an algebraic expression, just check your answer choices.

➡ Example 1 _____

If a triangle is made up of sides that are consecutive even integers and has a perimeter of 54, what is the length of the smallest side?

(a) 10   (b) 20   (c) 14   (d) 16

Let's start with an answer choice that is not the largest or smallest but rather one in the middle, 14. If 14 were the smallest side, then the other two sides would have to be 16 and 18. The perimeter would then be 14 + 16 + 18 = 48 which is too small. Now you know there is no need to try answer choice (a) because that will also be too small, so try 16. The perimeter must be 16 + 18 + 20 = 54. The correct answer is choice (d) 16.

PYTHAGOREAN THEOREM

It is possible that you may see one question involving the Pythagorean theorem. The Pythagorean theorem states that in a right triangle the square of the longest side, the hypotenuse, is equal to the sum of the squares of the other two sides. For example, in the triangle below, $5^2 = 3^2 + 4^2$. This is an example of a 3–4–5 triangle, which is a unique example of the Pythagorean theorem.

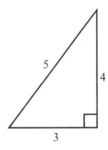

3–4–5 triangles have sides in the ratio of $3x : 4x : 5x$. One example is a right triangle with sides 6, 8, and 10 because $6 = 2 \times 3$, $8 = 2 \times 4$, and $10 = 2 \times 5$.

Three-dimensional Objects

You should be able to identify solids including cubes, cylinders, and rectangular solids, also known as rectangular prisms. You must also be able to calculate the volume and the surface area of rectangular solids. Let's review the definitions of volume and surface area for the specific objects that you will see on the HSPT.

VOLUME: The amount of space that an object occupies.

SURFACE AREA: Total area of the surface of a three-dimensional object.

RECTANGULAR PRISM: Volume = length × width × height. $V = l \times w \times h$. Surface area is the sum of the *areas* of all six sides. Opposite sides are equal in area, so once the area is determined, it can be doubled. $S = 2(w \times h) + 2(l \times w) + 2(l \times h)$

CUBE: Volume = a^3, where a is the length of a side. Because a cube is made up of sides of equal length, the volume is obtained by cubing the length of one side.

Surface area = $6a^2$. Find the area of one side, a^2, then multiply that by 6 (the number of equal-length sides on a cube).

CYLINDER: All you have to know about a cylinder is the overall shape. A can of tuna fish or soda is an example of a cylinder. You will not have to calculate volume or surface area for this object.

Geometry Practice

1. If a circle has a diameter of 18, its radius is

   (a) 36   (c) 8
   (b) 10   (d) 9

2. What is the radius of the circle?

   Diameter = 36 ft.

   (a) 72 ft.   (c) 18 ft.
   (b) 36 ft.   (d) 9 ft.

3. Name this figure.

   (a) pentagon   (c) hexagon
   (b) octagon   (d) nonagon

4. Which of the following is *not* a parallelogram?

   (a) square   (c) rectangle
   (b) circle   (d) rhombus

5. Which of the following is a parallelogram?

   (a)   (c)

   (b)   (d)

6. What is the area of the rectangle?

   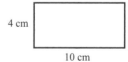

   4 cm   10 cm

   (a) 14 cm^2 (c) 40 cm^2
   (b) 28 cm^2 (d) 400 cm^2

7. If the perimeter of a square is 64 cm, what is the length of one side?

   (a) 16 cm   (c) 32 cm
   (b) 8 cm   (d) 4 cm

8. If the perimeter of a rectangle is 20 inches, what is the longest possible side of the rectangle?

   (a) 10 in.   (c) 19 in.
   (b) 18 in.   (d) 9 in.

9. If the area of a rectangle is 32 in.² and one side is 4 inches, what is the perimeter?

   (a) 20 in.   (c) 16 in.
   (b) 8 in.   (d) 24 in.

10. If a parking lot measures 32 feet in length and 10 feet in width, how many square feet are in the parking lot?

    (a) 84 ft.²   (c) 320 ft.²
    (b) 160 ft.²   (d) 3,200 ft.²

11. If floor mats cost $20 per square yard, what will it cost to buy floor mats for a gym that is 30 feet wide and 15 feet long?

    (a) $300   (c) $850
    (b) $1,000   (d) $4,500

12. What is the perimeter of the figure below?

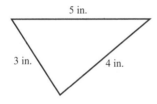

    (a) 15 in.   (c) 12 in.
    (b) 60 in.   (d) 6 in.

13. Which type of angles are shown?

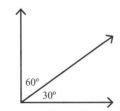

    (a) supplementary
    (b) obtuse
    (c) straight
    (d) complementary

14. What is the measure of angle x?

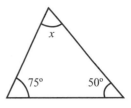

    (a) 65°   (c) 25°
    (b) 90°   (d) 55°

15. What is the area of the triangle shown?

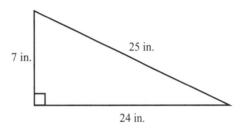

    (a) 84 in.²   (c) 198 in.²
    (b) 86 in.²   (d) 56 in.²

16. Which type of triangle is shown?

    (a) scalene   (c) isosceles
    (b) equilateral   (d) obtuse

17. A triangle is made up of sides with lengths that are consecutive odd integers. The perimeter of the triangle is 27 inches. What is the length of the longest side?

    (a) 7 in.   (c) 11 in.
    (b) 9 in.   (d) 27 in.

18. If *ABC* ~ *DEF*, what is the length of side *DE*?

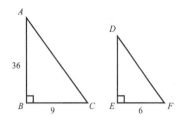

(a) 24   (c) 18
(b) 12   (d) 10

19. What object has half the area of the triangle shown?

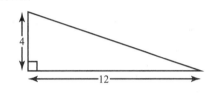

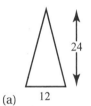   (a)   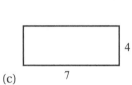 (c)

(b)   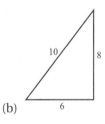   (d)

20. Find the length of the hypotenuse of the triangle.

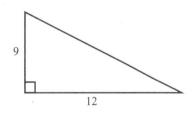

(a) 15   (c) 144
(b) 21   (d) 36

21. A can of soup is an example of what?

(a) sphere   (c) circle
(b) cylinder   (d) cube

22. What is the surface area of the rectangular prism?

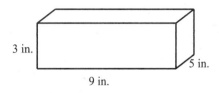

(a) 174 in.^{2} (c) 138 in.^{2}
(b) 90 in.^{2} (d) 162 in.^{2}

23. What is the volume of the rectangular prism shown below?

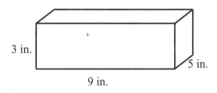

(a) 27 in.^{3} (c) 90 in.^{3}
(b) 135 in.^{3} (d) 45 in.^{3}

24. If the side of a cube has a perimeter of 32 inches, what is the volume of the cube?

(a) 64 in.^{3} (c) 24 in.^{3}
(b) 256 in.^{3} (d) 512 in.^{3}

(Answers are on page 236.)

WORD PROBLEMS

Word problems are ways of applying concepts that you learn in math class to real world situations. The challenge is to decipher the question being asked in the midst of a lot of words. In the Mathematics subtest you will see as many as 14 or 15 word problems. Most of these you have already learned about in this chapter such as those involving percents, fractions, conversions, geometry, and algebra. All of these together make up the majority of word problems. You may, however, see a couple of word problems that you have not already learned about. Let's review those here, and then you can try a few on your own.

Money

Money word problems involve simple multiplication and addition. Read this example and describe in your own words how you would figure out how much Chandler will spend.

➡ **Example 1** _____

To make New England clam chowder, Chandler must buy 3 pounds of clams and 4 pounds of potatoes. Clams cost $6.00 per pound and potatoes cost $1.25 per pound. How much will Chandler spend to make the chowder?

(a) $22.75   (b) $23.00   (c) $19.25   (d) $22.25

Imagine you had to explain this to someone. You would start by saying that Chandler has to buy 3 pounds of clams and 4 pounds of potatoes. Next you must know how much each ingredient costs. If the clams are $6.00 per pound and you need 3 pounds then you count the $6.00 three times ($6.00 × 3) AND the potatoes are $1.25 per pound and 4 pounds are needed ($1.25 × 4). Now add the cost of the two ingredients together.

$$\begin{aligned} \text{Clams: } (\$6.00 \times 3) &= \$18.00 \\ + \quad \text{Potatoes: } (\$1.25 \times 4) &= \$\ \ 5.00 \\ \hline &\ \ \ \$23.00 \end{aligned}$$

The correct answer is choice (b) $23.00.

Reasoning

Now apply the same technique to a different type of question. Imagine you had to explain to someone how to calculate how many different fruits and vegetables are in Mrs. Smith's garden.

➡ **Example 2** _____

Mrs. Smith has a garden with 16 different fruits and twice as many for vegetables. How many different fruits and vegetables are in her garden?

(a) 18   (b) 48   (c) 32   (d) 52

If Mrs. Smith has 16 different fruits and *twice* as many vegetables that means that she has 16 × 2 = 32 types of vegetables. The total is the varieties of vegetables added to the varieties of fruit, 32 + 16 = 48. The correct answer is choice (b) 48.

Below is a similar reasoning example involving money.

⇒ **Example 3**_____

If Kathleen spent $250 dollars on groceries last week and only one fifth of that the following week, how much did she spend over the two weeks?

(a) $300   (b) $400   (c) $275   (d) $50

Because one fifth of $250 is $50, Kathleen spent a total of $250 + $50 or $300 in the two week period. The correct answer is choice (a) $300.

Distance, Rate, and Time

Let's look at another common question type involving distance, rate, and time. You should be familiar with the equation below.

$$\text{Distance} = \text{rate} \times \text{time}$$

If you were told that your friend ran at a rate of 10 miles per hour for 2 hours, how far (distance) did your friend run? How did you come up with your answer?

$$\frac{10 \text{ miles}}{1 \text{ hour}} \times 2 \text{ hours} = 20 \text{ miles}$$

You can use this same formula to answer questions that ask for distance, rate, or time.

⇒ **Example 4**_____

If your friend ran a 5 mile race in 45 minutes, at what rate did he run?

(a) 6.2 mph   (b) 6.4 mph   (c) 2.5 mph   (d) 6.$\bar{6}$ mph

5 miles = Rate × 0.75 hours or $5 = \frac{3}{4}r$ where r = rate. To solve for r, multiply both sides by $\frac{4}{3}$, which is the reciprocal of $\frac{3}{4}$.

$$5 = \frac{3}{4}r$$

$$\frac{4}{3} \times 5 = \frac{3}{4}r \times \frac{4}{3}$$

$$\frac{20}{3} = r$$

$$r = 6\frac{2}{3} \text{ mph}$$

Because $\frac{2}{3} = 0.\bar{6}$, $6\frac{2}{3}$ can be written as 6.$\bar{6}$ mph. The correct answer is choice (d).

You may also see a question that seems like the logic questions in the Verbal Skills test. There are other types of word problems that you may see in this subtest, but they will all involve concepts you have learned in school and in this book. Now it's time to apply the mathematical concepts that you know to a few more word problems.

Word Problems Practice

1. Charles, Ben, and Kyle sold 27 hats at the Georgetown Craft Fair. Charles sold 5 times as many as Ben. Kyle sold 3 times as many as Ben. How many hats did Ben sell?

   (a) 9
   (b) 3
   (c) 15
   (d) 12

2. One mile is equal to 1.6 kilometers. If a bus is traveling at 60 miles per hour, what is its speed in kilometers per hour?

   (a) 7.6
   (b) 76
   (c) 9.6
   (d) 96

3. Jackson bought grass seed for his yard at $3.12 per pound and fertilizer for $1.00 per pound. Jackson bought 3 pounds of seed and 8 pounds of fertilizer. How much did he spend?

   (a) $17.36
   (b) $9.36
   (c) $11.12
   (d) $27.96

4. Jordan hiked for 2 hours at 10 miles per hour then another 30 minutes at 6 miles per hour. How far did Jordan hike?

   (a) 50 miles
   (b) 200 miles
   (c) 20.5 miles
   (d) 23 miles

5. Which is the correct formula for distance?

   (a) Rate = Distance × Time
   (b) Time = Distance × Rate
   (c) Time = Rate ÷ Distance
   (d) Distance = Rate × Time

6. Kathryn studied for 6 hours on Tuesday and half of that time on Wednesday. How many hours did she study in those two days?

   (a) 12
   (b) 18
   (c) 9
   (d) 10

7. Donna bought 12 books in March, 18 books in April, and 56 books in May. Each book cost $4.25. How much did Donna spend on books?

   (a) $86.00
   (b) $365.50
   (c) $323.00
   (d) $128.53

8. If one cup of sugar is equal to 250 grams, how many cups of sugar are needed in a recipe that calls for 750 grams of sugar?

   (a) 3 cups
   (b) 2.5 cups
   (c) 1.5 cups
   (d) 3.5 cups

(Answers are on page 237.)

EXPONENTS, RADICALS, AND ALGEBRA

The HSPT test is designed to be taken by students in the first quarter of their 8th grade year. Some 8th graders are taking math, while others are taking pre-algebra or algebra. Because of this, there are a handful of pre-algebra and algebra questions in the Mathematics subtest. You are not expected to know how to do all of these questions but if you can answer at least some of them correctly, these questions can help distinguish your score from other students. Students who score in the upper 10th or 5th percentile usually have a good understanding of a few basic algebra concepts. Each concept will be reviewed in this section. Every HSPT administration is different but you can expect to see between 5 and 10 questions involving pre-algebra or algebra skills.

Exponential Expressions

You may see 3 or 4 questions involving exponents in this subtest. Exponents are a shortcut for writing multiplication statements. For example, 4^3 can be read as *four to the power of 3* where 4 is the base and 3 is the exponent. The exponential expression, 4^3, is the equivalent of writing $4 \times 4 \times 4$ or 64. If you understand this concept, then you do not need a lot of rules to succeed in this subtest. If you prefer rules, they are shown here.

MULTIPLICATION RULE ($a^m \times a^n = a^{m + n}$)

If two exponential expressions with the *same bases* are multiplied, the exponents are added. Here are some examples of the multiplication rule:

- $m^2 \times m^3 = (m \times m) \times (m \times m \times m) = m^{(2 + 3)} = m^5$
- $3^3 \times 3^4 = (3 \times 3 \times 3) \times (3 \times 3 \times 3 \times 3) = 3^{(3 + 4)} = 3^7 = 2{,}187$
- $(-2)^2 \times (-2)^4 = [(-2)\,(-2)] \times [(-2)(-2)(-2)(-2)] = (-2)^{(2 + 4)} = (-2)^6 = 64$

DIVISION RULE ($a^m \div a^n = a^{m - n}$)

If two exponential expressions with the same bases are divided, the exponent of the denominator is subtracted from the exponent of the numerator. Here are some examples of the division rule:

- $4^5 \div 4^3 = \dfrac{4 \times 4 \times 4 \times 4 \times 4}{4 \times 4 \times 4} = 4^{(5 - 3)} = 4^2 = 16$

- $\dfrac{(-2)^3}{(-2)^2} = \dfrac{(-2)(-2)(-2)}{(-2)(-2)} = (-2)^{(3 - 2)} = (-2)^1 = (-2)$

EXPONENT OF 1 OR 0

Any number or variable raised to the power of 1 is itself.

$$4^1 = 4 \text{ and } m^1 = m$$

Any number or variable raised to the power of 0 is equal to 1. The only exception is 0, which is undefined when raised to a power of 0.

$$x^0 = 1 \text{ and } (-8)^0 = 1$$

SCIENTIFIC NOTATION

Scientific notation is a method of using exponents to express very large or very small numbers. On the HSPT you will only be using scientific notation with positive exponents and will see at most just one question like this. Numbers written in scientific notation are made up of a decimal part and an exponent part with a base of 10. To convert a number from scientific notation to a decimal, move the decimal point to the right the same number of places that is the exponent of 10.

$$3.657 \times 10^2 \text{ (move the decimal point two places to the right)} = 365.7$$

Likewise if the exponent were a 5 you would move the decimal 5 places to the right. Review the following table for some examples.

Scientific Notation	Decimal Point	Decimal
3.405×10^4	4 places to the right	34,050
1.65×10	1 place to the right	16.5
0.231×10^2	2 places to the right	23.1

Radical Expressions

There will only be one or two questions involving radical expressions. They are usually easy and based on the definition of a square root or cubed root.

RADICAL EXPRESSION: Expression that contains a radical symbol, for example $\sqrt{}$ (square root) or $\sqrt[3]{}$ (cube root).

SQUARE ROOT: The square root of a number is a value that when multiplied by itself, gives the number inside the square root. For example, $\sqrt{4} = 2$ because $2 \times 2 = 4$.

PERFECT SQUARE: A value that is the square of another number. The number 9 is a perfect square because $3 \times 3 = 9$. Perfect squares between 0 and 144 are 0, 1, 4, 9, 16, 25, 36, 49, 64, 81, 100, 121, 144.

The following table shows some common perfect squares and square root expressions that you should know.

Exponential	Radical
$2^2 = 4$	$\sqrt{4} = 2$
$3^2 = 9$	$\sqrt{9} = 3$
$4^2 = 16$	$\sqrt{16} = 4$
$5^2 = 25$	$\sqrt{25} = 5$
$6^2 = 36$	$\sqrt{36} = 6$
$7^2 = 49$	$\sqrt{49} = 7$
$8^2 = 64$	$\sqrt{64} = 8$
$9^2 = 81$	$\sqrt{81} = 9$
$10^2 = 100$	$\sqrt{100} = 10$
$11^2 = 121$	$\sqrt{121} = 11$
$12^2 = 144$	$\sqrt{144} = 12$
$13^2 = 169$	$\sqrt{169} = 13$
$14^2 = 196$	$\sqrt{196} = 14$
$15^2 = 225$	$\sqrt{225} = 15$

CUBE ROOT: The cube root of a value is a number that when multiplied by itself three times, gives the number inside the radical, $\sqrt[3]{8} = 2$ because $2 \times 2 \times 2 = 8$.

PERFECT CUBE: A value that is the product of a number cubed such as 8, since $2 \times 2 \times 2 = 8$.

The following table shows some common perfect cubes and cube root expressions that you should know.

Exponential	Radical
$2^3 = 8$	$\sqrt[3]{8} = 2$
$3^3 = 27$	$\sqrt[3]{27} = 3$
$4^3 = 64$	$\sqrt[3]{64} = 4$
$5^3 = 125$	$\sqrt[3]{125} = 5$

Algebra

NUMBER SENTENCES

In this subtest you will be asked to match a mathematical expression with its sentence form. You can expect to see two or three of these questions. Carefully read the sentence given, then read each of the answer choices to find the correct match. Once you find it, you can move on—there is only one right answer. To answer these correctly, you must know some math terms and symbols well. Review the table below to become familiar with the terms and symbols that you will see in number sentence questions.

Math Terms and Symbols

Term	Definition	Symbol
Sum	result of addition	+
Difference	result of subtraction	–
Product, of	result of multiplication	×
Quotient, per	the result of division	÷
A number	a letter or variable	x, y, z, etc.
Is, leaves	equal to	=
Is greater than	larger but not equal to	>
Is less than	less but not equal to	<
Greater than or equal to	greater and includes values equal to	≥
Less than or equal to	less than and includes values equal to	≤
Is not equal to	includes values both greater than or less than	≠

ADDITIONAL NOTES

- The *difference between a number and 2* is written as $x - 2$ and not $2 - x$.
- When answering questions regarding money and change, remember that change is what you are left with and belongs on the right side of the equal sign. For example, the equation $\$50 - \$6n = \$3.25$ might represent a person buying n number of items at $6 each and paying with $50. The change they received was $3.25.

- When multiplying a number and a letter, or variable, no multiplication symbol is needed. $4n$ is the same as $4 \times n$.
- The word *what* refers to a variable or letter. Four plus *what* is 5, can be expressed as $4 + x = 5$.

Here are some examples of questions involving number sentences that you may see on your HSPT.

EVALUATE THE EXPRESSION

Evaluate means to find the value of an expression. You may see one or two questions where you are given an expression with a variable, and you will then have to replace each variable with a number to evaluate the expression. Here is an example.

➡ Example 1 _____

If $a = 2$, $b = 15$, and $c = -3$, what is $a - 2b + c$?

(a) -23 (b) 25 (c) -31 (d) 31

To answer this question, replace each variable with the number assigned to it.
Replace each a with 2, each b with 15, and each c with -3.

$$(2) - 2(15) + (-3) = 2 - 30 - 3 = -31$$

The correct answer is choice (c) 31. (It's a good idea to use parentheses where you are replacing the variables, as this will help you to be careful with negative numbers.)

SOLVING FOR A VARIABLE

Algebra is all about using letters to represent values in mathematical expressions and figuring out what value the letters represent. You may have experience with this if you are taking algebra now, but if you are not, you can still answer these correctly because of the nature of the multiple-choice question.

The expression *Solve for x* means to get the variable, *x*, all alone on one side of the equal sign. This is often referred to as "isolating the variable." There will be at most 2 or 3 of these questions. Below is a brief review of the steps to solve this question type algebraically. If you are unfamiliar with this method, you may choose to simply plug in the answer choices to see which one makes the statement true.

Steps to isolate a variable:

1. RULE: Whatever you do to one side of the equation, you must do to the other side. You must never alter the equality.
2. Add and subtract to move all of the variables to one side and everything else to the other side. Repeat this until there are no more addition or subtraction symbols in the equation.
3. Multiply both sides by the reciprocal of a constant that is multiplied with the variable.
4. In an inequality, when multiplying or dividing by a negative number you must reverse the inequality symbol. If it was >, then you must change it to < and vice versa.
5. Once you solve for the variable, you can plug your answer into the original equation (if time allows) and check to see if the answer makes a true statement.

TIP

When asked to solve for *x*, if your answer choices are numbers, you can save time by simply plugging in each number into the expression to find the solution. You don't have to know any algebra to do this.

Solve for x: $\frac{1}{5}x + 6 = x - 2$

(a) −10   (b) 15   (c) 10   (d) 8

Plug in each answer choice to see which value makes the statement true, as that will be your answer. To solve for x using algebraic methods, follow the steps below.

First subtract $\frac{1}{5}x$ from each side and simplify.

$$\frac{1}{5}x + 6 = x - 2$$
$$-\frac{1}{5}x \qquad -\frac{1}{5}x$$
$$\overline{}$$
$$6 = \frac{4}{5}x - 2$$

Because there is still an addition or a subtraction sign, you should continue with addition by adding 2 to both sides:

$$6 = \frac{4}{5}x - 2$$
$$+2 \qquad +2$$
$$\overline{}$$
$$8 = \frac{4}{5}x$$

To isolate x, in other words, to move $\frac{4}{5}$ to the other side, multiply both sides by the reciprocal, which in this case is $\frac{5}{4}$.

$$\frac{5}{4} \times 8 = \frac{4}{5}x \times \frac{5}{4} \rightarrow 10 = x$$

The correct answer is choice (c) 10. If time allows, check your answer by plugging it into the original equation.

$$\frac{1}{5}x + 6 = x - 2$$

$$\frac{1}{5}(10) + 6 = (10) - 2$$

$$8 = 8 \quad ✔$$

Exponents, Radicals, and Algebra Practice

1. Solve: $8^3 \div 8^2 =$

    (a) 8

    (b) 8^5

    (c) 64

    (d) 1

2. Solve: $\dfrac{(-3)^8}{(-3)^5} =$

    (a) 3^3

    (b) $(-3)^3$

    (c) $(-3)^{13}$

    (d) 1

3. What number is the same as $6^2 \times 6^6$?

    (a) 6^8

    (b) 36^8

    (c) 12^8

    (d) 6^{12}

4. The number 4 has the same value as

    (a) 4^1

    (b) 4^0

    (c) 1^4

    (d) 1^0

5. Solve: $4^3 - 8 =$

    (a) 4

    (b) 32

    (c) 56

    (d) 58

6. 15 squared is equal to

    (a) 150

    (b) 225

    (c) 425

    (d) 30

7. What number is in the tens place after simplifying the following?

    $(0.2 \times 10^4) + (1.62 \times 10^3) + (0.6 \times 10^2)$
    $+ (6 + 10) =$

    (a) 3

    (b) 6

    (c) 9

    (d) 4

8. Simplify $\sqrt{196}$

    (a) 14

    (b) 12

    (c) 13

    (d) 15

9. Simplify $\sqrt[3]{64}$

    (a) 14

    (b) 16

    (c) 8

    (d) 4

10. If $x = 3$, $y = 4$, and $z = 5$, evaluate $\dfrac{\sqrt{3x} + 3y}{z}$

    (a) 15

    (b) 3

    (c) 2

    (d) 10

11. What number sentence represents the following?

    The difference of 4 and a number is 76.

    (a) $4x = 76$

    (b) $4 - x = 76$

    (c) $4 \div x = 76$

    (d) $76 - 4 = x$

12. What number sentence represents the following?

    The sum of a number and 16 is 27.

    (a) $x + 16 = 27$

    (b) $x + 27 = 16$

    (c) $16 + 27 = x$

    (d) $16 - x = 27$

13. What number sentence represents $2x + 8 < 10$?

    (a) The sum of two and a number is less than ten.

    (b) The product of two, a number, and eight is less than ten.

    (c) The product of two and a number, added to eight is less than ten.

    (d) Two times the product of a number and 8 is ten.

14. Which equation represents a car rental fee where a person is charged $70 for the first day and $20 for each additional day for a total fee of $170?

    (a) $70 + 20 = 170$

    (b) $70x + 20 = 170$

    (c) $70 + x = 170$

    (d) $70 + 20x = 170$

15. Sandra purchases apples for $1.25 each, and after paying with a $20 bill, she receives $7.50 in change. Which equation represents this transaction?

    (a) $\$1.25 + \$7.50x = \$20$

    (b) $\$20 - \$1.25x = \$7.50$

    (c) $\$20 - \$7.50x = \$1.25$

    (d) $\$20 - \$1.25 + x = \$7.50$

16. Find the value if $x = 2$, $y = 3$, and $z = 10$.

$$\frac{\sqrt{z+6}}{4-y} + x$$

(a) $\frac{4}{7}$

(c) 4

(b) $\frac{4}{3}$

(d) 6

17. Solve for x: $-9x < 27$

(a) $x < 3$ (c) $x < 3$

(b) $x > -3$ (d) $x > 3$

18. Solve for x: $9 - x > 27$

(a) $x > 36$ (c) $x < 36$

(b) $x > 18$ (d) $x < -18$

19. Solve for x: $\frac{2}{3} = \frac{x}{27}$

(a) $x = 18$ (c) $x = 3$

(b) $x = 9$ (d) $x = 51$

(Answers are on page 238.)

LINEAR EQUATIONS AND COORDINATE GEOMETRY

Coordinate geometry is a system used to locate and graph points on an x, y coordinate plane. Linear equations are expressed in terms of x and y and represent lines. You will have to know only one form of a linear equation as well as some basics about the x, y coordinate plane to answer these questions. If you graph two points, you can then connect them with a ruler to form a line, which can be represented by a linear equation.

Basics of Coordinate Geometry

NOTE

This is an algebra topic, so if you have not learned this material or find it difficult, feel free to skip this section and guess on the one or two questions that involve linear equations on the HSPT.

- The x-axis is the *horizontal* line and is labeled x, while the y-axis is the *vertical* line labeled y.
- The origin, $(0, 0)$, is the point where the x- and y-axes intersect.
- Any point on the graph can be labeled using the x- and y-coordinates (x, y). The first number in the parentheses is the x-coordinate and represents horizontal distance from the y-axis, and the second number is the y-coordinate and represents vertical distance from the x-axis.

Take a few minutes to see if you can identify the coordinates of the points on the graph below. Label each point shown then check your answers with those following the graph.

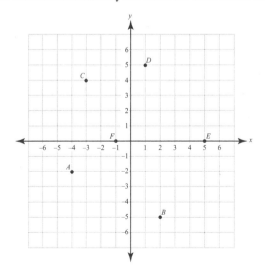

The coordinates for the points shown are as follows: $A(-4, -2)$, $B(2, -5)$, $C(-3, 4)$, $D(1, 5)$, $E(5, 0)$, $F(-1, 0)$. If you found the correct coordinates, then you know all that you have to know about coordinate geometry for the HSPT.

Basics of Linear Equations

The slope of a line tells us how steep it is and can be expressed as "rise over run." To calculate the slope of a line, first select two points on the line. Figure out the vertical difference between the two points and divide this by the horizontal difference. The slope between two points (x_1, y_1) and (x_2, y_2) is represented by the equation below.

$$\text{Slope} = \frac{y_2 - y_1}{x_2 - x_1}$$

For example, the slope of a line connecting the two points $(-2, 3)$ and $(5, 4)$ is $\frac{4-3}{5-(-2)} = \frac{1}{7}$.

The slope intercept form of a linear equation is $y = mx + b$, where m represents the slope of the line and b represents the y-intercept, which is the point where the line crosses the y-axis. Can you find the slope and y-intercept of the line shown on the graph below?

TIP

When given a line on a graph, you can find the slope by choosing a point then counting how many units you move up to reach a second point, RISE (if you move down, make the value negative). Divide this by how many units you have to move to the right to reach the second point, RUN (moving to the left is negative).

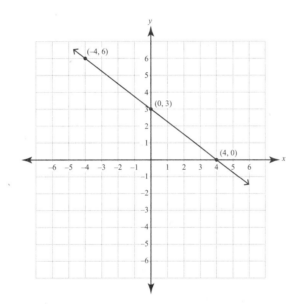

To calculate the slope, you may choose any two points on the graph, such as $(0, 3)$ and $(4, 0)$. The slope can be determined by $\frac{3-0}{0-4} = -\frac{3}{4}$. The y-intercept is 3 so the equation can be written $y = -\frac{3}{4}x + 3$.

Try the next couple of examples to apply what you have learned about linear equations.

Linear Equations and Coordinate Geometry Practice

1. What is the equation for the graph below?

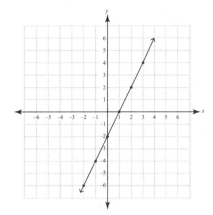

2. What is the slope of the line shown?

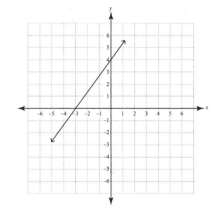

(a) $y = 2x - 2$ (c) $y = -2x - 2$

(b) $y = 2x$ (d) $y = -2x$

(a) $-\dfrac{4}{3}$ (c) $\dfrac{3}{4}$

(b) $-\dfrac{3}{4}$ (d) $\dfrac{4}{3}$

(Answers are on page 239.)

STATISTICS AND PROBABILITY

The Mathematics subtest will have a handful of questions involving statistics and probability. Don't worry if you have not learned this at school yet. These questions involve just the basics. You should be able to answer questions about mean, median, mode, and range, to read graphs and charts, and lastly to calculate basic probabilities. In all, you will see about 6 to 8 statistics and probability questions in this subtest.

Mean, Median, Mode and Range

There may be one or two questions involving mean, median, mode, or range. Here are the definitions you should know to answer these questions correctly.

MEAN: The mean is the average of a set of numbers. To calculate the mean, first add all of the values then divide that sum by the number of values. For example, the mean, or average of the data set (3, 5, 6, 2, 8, 0) is $(3 + 5 + 6 + 2 + 8 + 0) \div 6 = 24 \div 6 = 4$. Be careful with zeros. While you could leave them out of the sum in the numerator you, must remember to include them in the total number of values.

$$\text{Mean} = \frac{\text{Sum of all values}}{\text{Number of values}}$$

MEDIAN: The median is the value that is located in the middle of a data set that is in increasing order. If there is an even number of values, the median is found by averaging the middle two values. The median of the data set (2, 7, 5, 9, 11, 12, 15, 18, 20) is 11 because that is the number in the middle of the set of increasing values. The median of this data set (2, 7, 5, 9, 11, 12, 15, 18) is 10 because that is the average of the 4th and 5th values. If you are not given values in increasing order, take a few seconds to rewrite the list in increasing order before answering the question.

MODE: The mode is the value that occurs most frequently, the one that you see most often in the list. The mode of the data set (2, 7, 3, 2, 11, 2, 15, 3) is 2 because there are more 2s than any other value.

RANGE: The range of a data set is the difference between the highest terms and the lowest. The range of the data set (2, 7, 14, 9, 23, 11, 15, 18) is 23 – 2 = 21. Remember that data sets are not always given in increasing order so make sure you look for the highest and lowest values.

Graphs and Frequency Tables

In this subtest you may be asked to answer questions based on a graph or chart. Charts may include line graphs, bar graphs, pie charts or frequency tables. There will only be 2 to 4 of these questions. Let's review each type of graph.

PIE CHART

A pie chart, also known as a circle graph, shows a set of data in categories. It is important to know that these are categories. Things like money, height, temperature, etc. are not usually represented with a pie chart. Pie charts typically display data that can be counted such as the number of ice cream flavors, number of rainy days, or different types of pets. The chart displays either percents or number of items for each category.

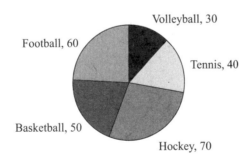

The pie chart above shows the favorite sport for a group of 250 students. To determine what percent of students favor a certain sport, divide the specific number shown in the chart by the total number of students. You can see that the percent of students who prefer basketball is $\frac{50}{250} = \frac{1}{5} = 0.20 = 20\%$.

BAR GRAPH

A bar graph, or bar chart, can be displayed with horizontal or vertical bars. The length of the bar represents the frequency, or how many items are in that category. Like a pie chart, this graph is used to represent data that is in categories but may also display changes over time.

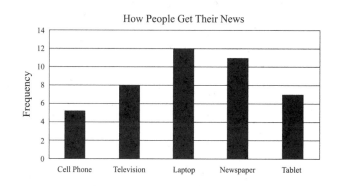

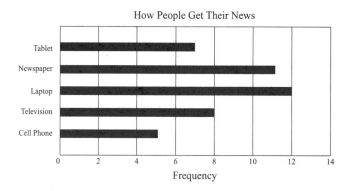

The two bar graphs above display the same data set, one shown horizontally and the other vertically. You can see that the most frequent way people get their news is using a laptop. You can also see relationships among the bars. For example, you can see that the difference between those who get their news from a laptop and the television is 12 – 8 = 4. You can also see the mode of the data set is laptop because that is the category with the highest frequency.

LINE GRAPHS

A line graph shows a set of data over a period of time. The thing that is being measured is on the vertical axis and the horizontal axis represents some measure of time. Using a line graph, you can answer questions about differences, averages, range, and mode.

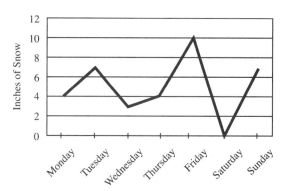

This line graph shows inches of snowfall in Bridgton, Maine for one week this winter. Which day shows the biggest increase from the day before? On Tuesday, there is an increase of 3 inches, Wednesday shows a decrease, Thursday has only a slight increase, Friday shows an increase of 6 inches, Saturday shows a decrease of 10 inches, and Sunday has an increase of 7 inches. The biggest increase from the day before is Saturday. You can also see that the range is 10 – 0 = 10. The weekly average is (4 + 7 + 3 + 4 + 10 + 0 + 7) ÷ 7 = 5 inches.

FREQUENCY TABLE

A frequency table shows data in a list rather than in a graphical display. Data is listed by category on the left and the number in each category is shown to the right. You can answer questions about mode, median, averages, and differences when given a frequency table.

Number of College Applications	Number of High School Students
0–3	10
4–7	25
8–11	50
12 or more	15

In the table above, the number of college applications made by 100 high school students is listed. The number of students, the right column, represents the frequency. You can see that most students applied to between 8 and 11 colleges, the mode. You could also answer questions such as "How many students applied to fewer than 8 colleges?" The correct answer is 35 because 10 students applied to 0–3 colleges, while an additional 25 students applied to 4–7 colleges, making a total of 35 students.

Probability

You will see a couple of questions involving probability on the HSPT. Probability can be expressed as a fraction, percent, or decimal and is always between 0 and 1. A probability of 0 means that the event is impossible, such as choosing a red marble from a jar of yellow and blue marbles. A probability of 1 is a certainty, such as flipping a coin and having it land on either heads or tails. You will only be asked questions involving events that have an equal chance of happening. When flipping a coin, you are just as likely to flip heads as tails. When selecting a marble from a jar, each marble has the same chance of being chosen.

To determine basic probability, you only have to know how many possible outcomes there are for an event and how many of those outcomes could be in your favor. For example, when reaching into a jar with 8 red candies, 4 blue, and 3 green, the probability of selecting a blue candy can be written as:

$$\text{Probability} = \frac{\text{the number of possible favorable outcomes}}{\text{number of possible outcomes}} = \frac{4 \text{ blue}}{15 \text{ marbles}} = \frac{4}{15}$$

There are 4 ways to have a favorable outcome, choosing any of the 4 blue candies. The denominator represents the 15 different candies in the jar. Do not use 3 as the denominator (for the 3 different colors), but always use the *total* number of items for the denominator (15 in this example). There are many other types of probabilities and related formulas but this is all that you need to know for the HSPT.

Statistics and Probability Practice

1. What is the mean of the data below?

   40, 52, 28, 47, 33, 5, 75

   (a) 42   (c) 40
   (b) 70   (d) 38

2. What is the median of the data?

   42, 52, 28, 47, 33, 5, 75

   (a) 47   (c) 52
   (b) 42   (d) 33

3. What is the mode of the list of data?

   28, 52, 28, 47, 33, 75, 75, 28

   (a) 28   (c) 47
   (b) 75   (d) 52

4. What is the range of the list of data?

   22, 10, 28, 47, 33, 75, 75, 28

   (a) 5   (c) 65
   (b) 50   (d) 53

5. According to the bar graph, which year showed the greatest increase in women teachers at this school?

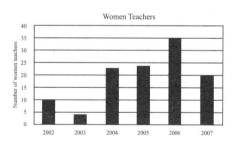

   (a) 2004   (c) 2006
   (b) 2003   (d) 2005

6. The chart shows rainfall over a 6 month period. What is the average rainfall in inches for the period?

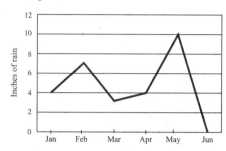

   (a) 28   (c) 6
   (b) 4   (d) $4\frac{2}{3}$

7. The following table shows the hourly rate for 26 landscapers. How many landscapers earn $9.00 or less?

Hourly Rate	Number of Landscapers
$5.00–$7.00	2
$7.01–$9.00	8
$9.01–$11.00	10
$11.01–$13.00	6

   (a) 2   (c) 10
   (b) 13   (d) 20

8. The circle graph shows car colors for 200 cars for sale. How many cars are yellow?

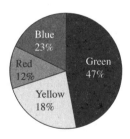

   (a) 18   (c) 72
   (b) 36   (d) 24

9. Which info is *best* displayed on a bar graph?

   (a) Height of all preschool children
   (b) Amount spent on food by families
   (c) Number of different vegetables in a garden
   (d) Income of all Americans

10. There are 8 red marbles and 13 green marbles in a bag. What is the probability that if you select one at random it will be a red marble?

   (a) $\dfrac{1}{2}$ (c) $\dfrac{8}{21}$

   (b) $\dfrac{8}{13}$ (d) $\dfrac{13}{8}$

11. Which of the following has a probability closest to 1?

   (a) Flipping a coin and having it land on tails
   (b) Not rolling a 2 on a die
   (c) Guessing correctly on a true/false question
   (d) Guessing the outcome of a school election with 3 candidates

(Answers are on page 239.)

ANSWERS EXPLAINED FOR CHAPTER 7

The Basics Practice (pages 186–187)

1. **(a)** $(-8) + (-18) = -26$. Because the values have the same sign, add the two and keep the sign the same. "Same signs add 'em up ♫."

2. **(a)** $(-4) + 12 = 8$. Since the two terms have opposite signs, you must first find the difference between 12 and 4, which is 8. The sign will be that of the number with the largest absolute value, which in this case is positive 12. " . . . opposites subtract, ♫ take the sign of the larger one, then you'll be exact ♫."

3. **(b)** $(-212) - (-11) = (-212) + 11$ (*Keep–Change–Change*). Ignore the signs and find the difference, 201. Because 212 is larger and is negative, your final answer is –201.

4. **(d)**

$$
\begin{array}{r}
{\scriptstyle 1\,1\,2} \\
4 \\
656 \\
18 \\
+\,2{,}876 \\
\hline
3{,}554
\end{array}
$$

5. **(c)**

$$
\begin{array}{r}
{\scriptstyle 7\,1} \\
6{,}8\!\!\!/29 \\
-\,3{,}679 \\
\hline
3{,}150
\end{array}
$$

6. **(d)** $(-6) \times (-2) \times 9 = 108$. Because there are an even number of negative signs, the product is positive.

7. **(c)** $(-6) \div (-2) = 3$. An even number of negative signs gives a positive quotient.

8. **(b)** Because the last digits of the two factors are 6 and 2, the product must end in 2 ($6 \times 2 = 12$). You don't actually have to multiply these numbers to find the answer, you only have to multiply 6 and 2.

9. **(a)** This product must end in a 0 because 5 times 8 is 40, narrowing your answers to either choice (a) or (b).

$$
\begin{array}{r}
2765 \\
\times\ \ 28 \\
\hline
22{,}120 \\
+\,55{,}300 \\
\hline
77{,}420
\end{array}
$$

10. **(d)**

$$\begin{array}{r} 133 \text{ R5} \\ 36\overline{)4793} \\ \underline{-36}\downarrow\, \\ 119 \\ \underline{108}\downarrow \\ 113 \\ \underline{-108} \\ 5 \end{array}$$

Fractions, Decimals, Percents, and Ratios Practice (pages 195–197)

1. **(a)** Because a day is made up of 24 hours, the fraction of a day that is 10 hours can be represented as $\frac{10}{24}$ which can be reduced by dividing the numerator and the denominator by 2.

$$\frac{10 \text{ hr.} \div 2}{24 \text{ hr.} \div 2} = \frac{5}{12}$$

2. **(d)** Make the denominators the same before adding or subtracting fractions.

$$\frac{2}{3} - \frac{1}{5} = \frac{2}{3} \cdot \frac{5}{5} - \frac{1}{5} \cdot \frac{3}{3} = \frac{10}{15} - \frac{3}{15} = \frac{7}{15}$$

Or use the cross-up method from page 111:

$$\overset{10}{\frac{2}{3}}\overset{3}{\times}\frac{1}{5} = \frac{10-3}{15} = \frac{7}{15}$$

3. **(c)** The easiest way to answer this is to recognize that when you subtract 9 from 28 the difference is 19. If you then take away an additional $\frac{2}{3}$ you will be left with $\frac{2}{3}$ less than 19 or $18\frac{1}{3}$. If you wish to carry out the subtraction problem the solution is shown here.

$$28 - 9\frac{2}{3} = \begin{array}{r} 28 \\ -9\frac{2}{3} \\ \hline \end{array} = \begin{array}{r} 27\frac{3}{3} \\ -9\frac{2}{3} \\ \hline 18\frac{1}{3} \end{array}$$

4. **(d)** Remember *Keep–Change–Change*. Reduce before multiplying the fractions together.

$$\frac{2}{7} \div \frac{3}{7} = \frac{2}{\underset{1}{\cancel{7}}} \times \frac{\overset{1}{\cancel{7}}}{3} = \frac{2}{1} \times \frac{1}{3} = \frac{2}{3}$$

5. **(a)** $\frac{2}{3}$ of a number is 8. This translates to $\frac{2}{3}x = 8$. If you can, try to guess which number when multiplied by $\frac{2}{3}$ will give you 8. If you cannot guess the number, then multiply both sides by the reciprocal of $\frac{2}{3}$ which is $\frac{3}{2}$ to find $x = 8 \times \frac{3}{2} = 12$. Now you must finish the question by figuring out half of 12, which is 6.

6. **(a)** $\frac{4}{5} \cdot \frac{6}{1} = \frac{24}{5} = 4\frac{4}{5}$. At this point, check your answer choices. You know that $\frac{4}{5}$ is larger than one half so the answer must be more than $4.50.

7. **(d)** Four dimes is the equivalent of 40 cents. Two dollars is the same as 200 cents, so the fraction can be written $\frac{40}{200}$. Then reduce to yield $\frac{1}{5}$.

8. **(a)** $4 - 2.718$ will be a value less than 2, because $4 - 2 = 2$. You are then subtracting an additional 0.718. Because this is more than 0.7, the answer must be less than 1.3. You've narrowed your answer to choice (a).

$$\begin{array}{r} 4.000 \\ -\ 2.718 \\ \hline 1.282 \end{array}$$

9. **(c)** Because the last digits on the right are 6 and 5, the sum of the two is 11, which means your final answer must end in a 1, narrowing your choices to just one. If you prefer to do the addition problem, write it out and line up the decimal points.

$$\begin{array}{r} 0.76 \\ 2.35 \\ +\ 1.60 \\ \hline 4.71 \end{array}$$

10. **(a)** $3.00 + $2.00 = $5.00. Adding an addition $1.50 makes $6.50 in total.

11. **(d)** Because your answer choices are all similar, you must multiply this out.

$$\begin{array}{r} 2.462 \\ \times\ 1.3 \\ \hline 7386 \\ +\ 24620 \\ \hline 3.2006 \end{array}$$

Remember to add the number of digits to the right of the decimal point (4) and when done, insert a decimal point 4 places from the right.

12. **(a)** The decimal point in the product must be two places from the right because in the question there are two numbers to the right of the decimal points.

$$\begin{array}{r} 27.3 \\ \times\ 1.2 \\ \hline 546 \\ +\ 2730 \\ \hline 32.76 \end{array}$$

13. **(d)** After moving the decimal place one place to the right, you can solve using long division.

$$
\begin{array}{r}
1.23 \\
92\overline{)113.16} \\
-92 \downarrow \\
\hline
211 \\
-184\downarrow \\
\hline
276 \\
-276 \\
\hline
0
\end{array}
$$

14. **(d)** Because the 6 is in the hundredths place in 0.36, the decimal can be written as a fraction $\frac{36}{100}$, which reduces to $\frac{9}{25}$.

15. **(b)** To convert a fraction to a decimal you must divide. Your answer choices are all similar, so you have to find out which number or numbers repeats. After seeing the 3 more than once, you can rule out all answers except $0.8\overline{3}$.

$$
\begin{array}{r}
.833 \\
6\overline{)5.000} \\
-48\downarrow \\
\hline
20 \\
-18\downarrow \\
\hline
20 \\
-18
\end{array}
$$

16. **(d)** You can estimate this one. Always begin with 10%. 10% of $960 is $96 (move the decimal point one place to the left). If 10% is $96 then 12% must be slightly higher, so the answer must be $115.20. If the answer choices were closer together, you would have to multiply this out: $0.12 \times 960 = \$115.20$.

17. **(d)** Use the 10% rule to estimate. 10% of 3,000 is 300, so 20% must be twice that or 600. You can also write this as a fraction and then reduce: $\frac{600}{3000} = \frac{6}{30} = \frac{1}{5} = 20\%$.

18. **(c)** 15% of the students are in the art club. 15% of 1,200 is 10% + 5%. 10% of 1,200 is 120, then half of 120 is 60, so 120 + 60 = 180.

19. **(a)** 36 is 30% of what number translates to $36 = 0.30x$. Look at your answer choices rather than try to solve this. Which answer choice makes this a true statement? 10% of 120 is 12, so 30% of 120 is 3 times that or 36.

20. **(c)** $x\%$ of 120 is 90, translates to $\frac{x}{100} \cdot 120 = 90$. You can solve this by plugging in your answer choices. 75% of 120 is 90. Or you can transform the equation $\frac{x}{100} \cdot \frac{120}{120} = \frac{90}{120} \rightarrow$ $\frac{x}{100} = \frac{3}{4}$. Three-fourths is equal to 75%.

21. **(d)** The ratio that represents this question is $\frac{1}{2} = \frac{4.5}{x}$. Since 1 is multiplied by 4.5 then 2 must also be multiplied by 4.5 to find x. $2 \times 4.5 = 9$.

22. **(a)** To be a proportion, the ratio on the left must equal the ratio on the right. You can check this for each answer choice: $\frac{1}{2} = \frac{2}{4}$. The other answer choices are not equalities.

23. **(a)** The ratio to represent this problem is $\frac{1}{32} = \frac{2.5}{x}$. Because 1 is multiplied by 2.5 to make 2.5, then 32 must be multiplied by 2.5 to get 80. If you choose to cross multiply, $1x = 2.5 \times 32 = 80$.

24. **(b)** The proportion for this question is $\frac{500}{2} = \frac{625}{x}$. The numerator, 500, was multiplied by 1.25 to make 625, so 2 must be multiplied by 1.25 to get x. You can also cross multiply, $2 \times 625 = 500x$, and then divide each side by 500 to find $x = \frac{1250}{500} = 2.5$.

25. **(c)** If Arioch needs 2 hours to rake $\frac{2}{5}$ of the yard, then he must need 5 hours to get the whole yard done. This can be written as $\frac{2}{5}x = 2$, where x represents the total time for the whole yard. If you multiply both sides by the reciprocal of $\frac{2}{5}$ you will arrive at the answer.

$$\frac{5}{2} \cdot \frac{2}{5}x = 2 \cdot \frac{5}{2} \rightarrow x = 5$$

26. **(d)** The proportion representing this is $\frac{900 \text{ miles}}{9 \text{ hours}} = \frac{1{,}150 \text{ miles}}{x}$. Rather than cross multiply or figure out the ratio factor of 900 to 1,150, look at the relationship between the numerator and denominator on the left. 9 is $\frac{1}{100}$ of 900, so x must be $\frac{1}{100}$ of 1,150. $x = 11.50$.

27. **(b)** This is a division question. If 3,000 calories are in 12 donuts, then there must be $\frac{3{,}000}{12}$ calories in one donut. $\frac{\text{calories}}{1 \text{ donut}} = 250$.

Conversions Practice (pages 201–202)

1. **(b)** There are 3 feet in a yard, so in 2 yards there will be 6 feet. Because there are 12 inches in a foot, you must multiply 6 feet by 12 inches. Lastly, add 12 inches for the additional foot and another 7 inches.

$$\left(2 \text{ yd.} \times \frac{3 \text{ ft.}}{1 \text{ yd.}} \times \frac{12 \text{ in.}}{1 \text{ ft.}}\right) + \left(1 \text{ ft.} \times \frac{12 \text{ in.}}{1 \text{ ft.}}\right) + 7 \text{ in.} = 72 \text{ in.} + 12 \text{ in.} + 7 \text{ in.} = 91 \text{ in.}$$

2. **(b)** Because one yard is equal to 3 feet, two yards is equal to 6 feet. Find the answer that is the equivalent of 6 feet, which is 5 feet and 12 inches.

3. **(d)** There are 1,000 millimeters in a meter, so in 1.6 meters there will be 1,600 millimeters.

$$1.6 \text{ m} \times \frac{1{,}000 \text{ mm}}{1 \text{ m}} = 1{,}600 \text{ mm}$$

4. **(c)** In one kilometer there are 1,000 meters and in 1 meter there are 100 centimeters.

$$2.1 \text{ km} \times \frac{1,000 \text{ m}}{1 \text{ km}} \times \frac{100 \text{ cm}}{1 \text{ m}} = 210,000 \text{ cm}$$

5. **(d)** One kilometer is equal to 1,000 meters, so $612.5 \text{ km} \times \frac{1,000 \text{ m}}{1 \text{ km}} = 612,500 \text{ m}.$

6. **(a)** This is a ratio problem in which you are given a conversion factor, $\frac{5 \text{ mi.}}{8 \text{ km}} = \frac{70 \text{ mph}}{x \text{ kph}}$. You must cross multiply to determine x.

$$\frac{5 \text{ mi}}{8 \text{ km}} = \frac{70 \text{ mph}}{x \text{ kph}}$$
$$5x = 8 \times 70$$
$$\frac{5x}{5} = \frac{560}{5}$$
$$x = 112 \text{ kph}$$

You can also solve this by first figuring out the ratio factor. Because 70 is equal to 14 times 5, x must be equal to 14 times 8 or 112.

7. **(d)** To answer this question, you must remember your conversion factors and check each answer choice. The correct answer is choice (d).

8. **(c)** One pound is equal to 16 ounces.

$$\left(6 \text{ lb.} \times \frac{16 \text{ oz}}{1 \text{ lb.}}\right) + 7 = 96 \text{ oz.} + 7 \text{ oz.} = 103 \text{ oz.}$$

9. **(a)** There are 1,000 grams in a kilogram.

$$2.4 \text{ kg} \times \frac{1,000 \text{ g}}{1 \text{ kg}} = 2,400 \text{ g}$$

10. **(c)** One cup of liquid is equal to 8 liquid ounces.

$$56 \text{ oz.} \times \frac{1 \text{ cup}}{8 \text{ oz.}} = 7 \text{ cups}$$

11. **(c)** There are 2 cups in a pint and 2 pints in a quart so there are 4 cups in each quart.

$$5 \text{ quarts} \times \frac{2 \text{ pints}}{1 \text{ quart}} \times \frac{2 \text{ cups}}{1 \text{ pint}} = 20 \text{ cups}$$

12. **(c)** Remember Mr. Gallon; there are 4 quarts in a gallon and 2 pints in a quart.

$$1.5 \text{ gal} \times \frac{4 \text{ quarts}}{1 \text{ gal}} \times \frac{2 \text{ pints}}{1 \text{ quart}} = 12 \text{ pints}$$

13. **(b)** There are 1,000 milliliters in one liter.

$$2,450 \text{ ml} \times \frac{1 \text{ liter}}{1,000 \text{ ml}} = 2.45 \text{ liters}$$

14. **(a)** There are 60 minutes in one hour and 60 seconds in one minute.

$$14,400 \text{ seconds} \times \frac{1 \text{ minute}}{60 \text{ seconds}} \times \frac{1 \text{ hour}}{60 \text{ minutes}} = 4 \text{ hours}$$

15. **(a)** Because one hour is equal to 60 minutes, you can set up a fraction of minutes.

$$\frac{36 \, \text{min.}}{1 \, \text{hr.}} = \frac{36 \, \text{min.}}{60 \, \text{min.}} = \frac{18}{30} = \frac{3}{5}$$

16. **(b)** This is an example of the Associative Property of Addition.

Geometry Practice (pages 210–212)

1. **(d)** The radius of a circle is half the length of the diameter. If the diameter is 18, then the radius is 9.

2. **(c)** The radius is half of the diameter. 36 ft. ÷ 2 = 18 ft.

3. **(c)** A six-sided polygon is called a hexagon.

4. **(b)** A circle is neither a polygon nor a parallelogram. A parallelogram has two sets of parallel sides.

5. **(d)** A parallelogram must have two, and only two, sets of opposite parallel sides as in the case of the rhombus in choice (d).

6. **(c)** The area of a rectangle is $A =$ length × width. The area is $4 \times 10 = 40 \, \text{cm}^2$.

7. **(a)** The perimeter is the sum of all of the sides. Because a square has sides of equal length, if the perimeter is 64 cm, then the side must be one fourth of that or 16.

8. **(d)** If the perimeter is 20 in. then the longest side must be less than 10 in. If one side was 10 in. then the opposite side would also be 10 in. and there would be nothing left for the other two sides. Only one answer choice is less than 10 in.

9. **(d)** If the area of the rectangle is 32 in.^{2} and one side is 4 in., the other side must be 8 in. Area = length × width. The perimeter is therefore $4 + 8 + 4 + 8 = 24$ in.

10. **(c)** Area = length × width. The area of the parking lot is 32 ft × 10 ft = 320 ft.^{2}

11. **(b)** First convert the dimensions that are in feet to yards (always convert larger numbers to smaller numbers). 30 ft. × 15 ft. = 10 yd. × 5 yd. = 50 yd.^{2} If each square yard is $20 then the total cost will be 50 yd.^{2} × $20/yd.^{2} = $1,000.

12. **(c)** The perimeter is the sum of the side lengths. $3 + 5 + 4 = 12$ in.

13. **(d)** Angles that make up a right angle, 90°, are complementary.

14. **(d)** Angles in a triangle add to 180°. $180° - 75° - 50° = 55°$.

15. **(a)** The area of a triangle is half of the base times the height.

$$A = \frac{1}{2}bh$$
$$A = \frac{1}{2} \times 24 \times 7$$
$$A = 12 \times 7$$
$$A = 84 \, \text{in.}^2$$

16. **(c)** An isosceles triangle is one with two equal sides, as indicated by the line segments.

17. **(c)** Consecutive odd integers are odd numbers in a row such as 3, 5, 7. Look at each answer choice and see which will give three sides that add up to 27 inches. $7 + 9 + 11 = 27$.

18. **(a)** Set up a ratio to answer this question. Because these are similar triangles, corresponding sides are proportional: $\frac{6}{9} = \frac{x}{36}$. Since 36 is four times 9, x must be four times 6 or 24. You can also set up the ratio as $\frac{9}{36} = \frac{6}{x}$.

19. **(d)** The area of the given triangle is $\frac{1}{2} \times 12 \times 4 = 24$, so you must select an answer choice that has an area of 12. The rectangle in answer choice (d) has an area of $3 \times 4 = 12$.

20. **(a)** This is a 3–4–5 triangle; 9 is **3** $\times$ 3, 12 is **4** $\times$ 3, so the longest sided must be **5** $\times$ 3 or 15.

21. **(b)** Typically soup comes in a cylindrical can. The top is a circle but the three-dimensional object is a cylinder.

22. **(a)** The side facing the front has an area of $3 \times 9 = 27$ in.^{2} There are two of these sides. The other two sides are 9×5 or 45 in.^{2} each. The two ends each have an area of $5 \times 3 = 15$ in.^{2} This must be doubled because there are two ends. The surface area is $(2 \times 27) + (2 \times 45) + (2 \times 5) = 54 + 90 + 30 = 174$ in.^{2}

23. **(b)** The volume is $3 \times 9 \times 5 = 135$ in.^{3}

24. **(d)** If one side of a cube has a perimeter of 32 in. then the side length must be $32 \div 4 = 8$ in. The volume is the length of the side cubed or $8^3 = 512$ in.^{3}

Word Problems Practice (page 215)

1. **(b)** Plug in the answer choices. Start with a value that is not the highest or lowest, let's try 9. If Ben sold 9, then Kyle sold 3 times as many or 27, and Charles, who sold 5 times as many as Ben must have sold 9×5 or 45. You can already see that 9 is *too large* (the sum of all of the hats sold must be 27). Now try a *lower* value, 3. If Ben sold 3, then Kyle sold 9, and Charles sold 15; $3 + 9 + 15 = 27$ so answer choice (b) is the correct answer.

2. **(d)** This is a proportion: $\frac{1 \text{ mile}}{1.6 \text{ km}} = \frac{60 \text{ mph}}{x \text{ kph}}$. To determine the value for x, multiply 1.6 by 60 to get 96.

3. **(a)** To answer this, you must calculate the total amount spent. Total = (3 lb. grass seed $\times$ \$3.12 per pound) + (8 lb. fertilizer $\times$ \$1.00 per pound) = \$9.36 + \$8.00 = \$17.36.

4. **(d)** If Jordan hiked for 2 hours at a rate of 10 miles per hour, then he hiked for 20 miles (2×10 mph). He then hiked another 30 minutes at 6 miles per hour for a total of 3 miles (0.5 hours $\times$ 6 mph = 3 miles). The total is 20 miles + 3 miles = 23 miles.

5. **(d)** Distance = Rate $\times$ Time. For example, if you travel at 60 miles per hour (rate) for 2 hours (time), your distance traveled equals 60 miles/hour $\times$ 2 hours = 120 miles.

6. **(c)** Half of 6 is 3, so Kathryn studied for 6 hours and then an additional 3 hours for a total of $6 + 3 = 9$ hours in the two days.

7. **(b)** Donna bought a total of $12 + 18 + 56 = 86$ books. If each book costs \$4.25, then she spent a total of $86 \times \$4.25 = \$365.50$. Because you know that $8 \times 4 = 32$, you can estimate

this product and know that your answer must be larger than \$320. \$323 is too close to \$320, so the only answer left is choice (b).

8. **(a)** This is a ratio question. The ratio of one cup of sugar to its weight is 1 : 250. The proportion that represents this question is $\dfrac{1 \text{ cup}}{250 \text{ g}} = \dfrac{? \text{ cups}}{750 \text{ g}}$. Because 750 is 3 times 250, the missing number of cups must be equal to 3 times 1 or 3 cups.

Exponents, Radicals, and Algebra Practice (pages 221–222)

1. **(a)** Use the division rule for exponents. $8^3 \div 8^2 = 8^{(3-2)} = 8^1 = 8$.

2. **(b)** Use the division rule for exponents. $(-3)^8 \div (-3)^5 = (-3)^{(8-5)} = (-3)^3$.

3. **(a)** Use the multiplication rule for exponents. $6^2 \times 6^6 = 6^{(2+6)} = 6^8$.

4. **(a)** Any value raised to the power of 1 is itself so $4^1 = 4$.

5. **(c)** $4^3 - 8 = 4 \times 4 \times 4 - 8 = 64 - 8 = 56$.

6. **(b)** 15 squared is equal to $15^2 = 15 \times 15 = 225$.

7. **(c)** $(0.2 \times 10^4) + (1.62 \times 10^3) + (0.6 \times 10^2) + (6 + 10) = 2{,}000 + 1{,}620 + 60 + 16 = 3{,}696$. There is a 9 in the tens place.

8. **(a)** The square root of 196 is 14 because $14 \times 14 = 196$.

9. **(d)** The cube root of 64 is 4 because $4 \times 4 \times 4 = 64$.

10. **(b)** When $x = 3$, $y = 4$, and $z = 5$:

$$\frac{\sqrt{3x} + 3y}{z} = \frac{\sqrt{9} + 12}{5} = \frac{3 + 12}{5} = \frac{15}{5} = 3$$

11. **(b)** *The difference of 4 and a number is 76* is represented by $4 - x = 76$.

12. **(a)** *The sum of a number and 16 is 27* is represented by $x + 16 = 27$

13. **(c)** The inequality $2x + 8 < 10$ can be described as *the product of two and a number, added to eight is less than ten.*

14. **(d)** The number of days is represented by x and must be multiplied by the rate of \$20. The equation is $70 + 20x = 170$.

15. **(b)** The number of apples is represented by x and must be multiplied by the cost per apple of \$1.25. The equation is $\$20 - \$1.25x = \$7.50$. Change is always on the right of the equal sign.

16. **(d)** Replacing x with 2, y with 3, and z with 10 you'll get:

$$\frac{\sqrt{10 + 6}}{4 - 3} + 2 = \frac{4}{1} + 2 = 6$$

17. **(b)** Divide both sides by –9. Remember to change the < symbol to > to find $x > -3$.

18. **(d)** Begin by adding x to both sides of the inequality. Next, subtract 27 from both sides. You now have $-18 > x$, or from the other direction $x < -18$.

19. **(a)** The easiest way to solve this is using a ratio. What was 3 multiplied by to get 27? The answer is 9, so multiply 2 by 9 to get $x = 18$. You may also plug in the answer choices to find the correct answer. If you cross multiply, you are doing too much work.

Linear Equations and Coordinate Geometry Practice (page 224)

1. **(a)** The slope between the points (1, 0) and (2, 2) is $\frac{2-0}{2-1} = \frac{2}{1} = 2$, and the y-intercept can be seen at –2. The correct equation is $y = 2x - 2$.

2. **(d)** The slope between the points (0, 4) and (–3, 0) is $\frac{4-0}{0-(-3)} = \frac{4}{3}$.

Statistics and Probability Practice (pages 228–229)

1. **(c)** The mean is $(40 + 52 + 28 + 47 + 33 + 5 + 75) \div 7 = 280 \div 7 = 40$.

2. **(b)** Arrange the data in increasing order: 5, 28, 33, 42, 47, 52, 75. The number in the middle is the 4th value, 42.

3. **(a)** The mode is 28 because it appears three times in the list, more than any other value.

4. **(c)** The range is $75 - 10 = 65$; the highest value minus the lowest value.

5. **(a)** The height of the bar is the frequency, so 2004 was the year that had the greatest increase over the prior year. You can see it is approximately 20, but you don't have to know the exact value.

6. **(d)** The average is $(4 + 7 + 3 + 4 + 10 + 0) \div 6 = 28 \div 6 = 4\frac{2}{3}$.

7. **(c)** There are two categories of wages that are $9.00 or less. $2 + 8 = 10$.

8. **(b)** 18% of 200 is 36. You can first figure out 18% of 100 (which is 18) then double it to get 36.

9. **(c)** Bar graphs are used to display data that is in categories and can be counted, such as types of vegetables.

10. **(c)** There are 8 red marbles, favorable outcomes, over 21 possible outcomes (total of all marbles).

11. **(b)** Getting tails on a coin has a probability of 50% as does guessing correctly on a true/false question. Guessing an election with three candidates has a 1 in 3 probability or 33.3%. The probability of *not* rolling a 2 is $\frac{5}{6}$ because there are 6 outcomes when rolling a die and 5 of them will *not* give you a 2.

WRAP IT UP WITH PRACTICE

Take a few minutes to review the Mathematics concepts and strategies you have learned before you complete the practice subtest.

Make sure you know:

- Math facts and conversion factors
- Formulas for area, surface area, and perimeter
- Names of polygons
- Math symbols for equalities and inequalities
- Names of angles and triangles

Be able to:

- Convert decimals to fractions
- Add, subtract, multiply, and divide fractions and decimals
- Calculate the sum of interior angles in a polygon
- Calculate mean, median, and mode
- Determine ratios and probability
- Interpret graphs

Use these methods and strategies:

- Cross-up method to compare fractions
- Ten percent rule to estimate percents
- *Keep–Change–Change* to convert subtraction to addition
- *Keep–Change–Change* to convert fraction division to multiplication
- Do as little math as possible—estimate or plug in answers to find the correct one
- Plug in answer choices when appropriate to save time
- Never spend too long on one question

45 MINUTES

Sample:

A. The number thirty-seven is also written as

(a) 27 (b) 33 (c) 37 (d) 63

Correct marking of sample:

A. Ⓐ Ⓑ ● Ⓓ

175. Solve:

2,176
1,287
+ 3,750

(a) 7,013   (c) 7,203
(b) 7,213   (d) 7,246

176. The fraction $\frac{5}{6}$ is equal to

(a) 0.83   (b) $0.8\overline{3}$ (c) $0.\overline{83}$ (d) $0.\overline{830}$

177. Solve:

1,073
$\times 128$

(a) 138,344   (c) 237,344
(b) 137,344   (d) 238,340

178. $8.2\overline{)25.502}$

(a) 0.031   (c) 0.311
(b) 3.12   (d) 3.11

179. Solve $\frac{3}{5} \div \frac{2}{15} =$

(a) $7\frac{1}{2}$ (b) $\frac{1}{5}$ (c) $4\frac{1}{2}$ (d) $\frac{2}{3}$

180. How many quarts of milk will fit in a 6-gallon container?

(a) 24   (b) 48   (c) 12   (d) 18

181. Solve: 1.67 – 0.96 =

(a) 0.72   (b) 2.63   (c) 0.71   (d) 1.73

182. How long is side x in the given triangle?

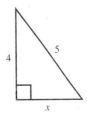

(a) 1   (b) 2   (c) 9   (d) 3

183. Solve: $\sqrt{121}$

(a) 12   (b) 11   (c) 21   (d) 6

184. 17 hundredths can be written as

(a) 1.7   (c) 0.17
(b) 1,700   (d) 0.017

185. What number is the same as $2^5 \times 2^2$?

(a) 2^7 (b) 2^{10} (c) 2^3 (d) 1^3

186. What fraction of an hour is 36 minutes?

(a) $\frac{3}{5}$ (b) $\frac{1}{3}$ (c) $\frac{36}{100}$ (d) $\frac{1}{12}$

GO TO THE NEXT PAGE ➡

187. If Joanne has 10 pencils and 20 pens in her drawer and she randomly selects one from the drawer, what is the probability that she will select a pencil?

    (a) $\dfrac{1}{2}$ (b) $\dfrac{1}{3}$ (c) $\dfrac{2}{3}$ (d) $\dfrac{1}{30}$

188. Solve for x: $\dfrac{2}{3} = \dfrac{x}{60}$

    (a) $x = 4$ (c) $x = 40$
    (b) $x = 20$ (d) $x = 30$

189. How many ounces are in $2\dfrac{1}{2}$ pounds?

    (a) 20 oz.   (c) 18 oz.
    (b) 32 oz.   (d) 40 oz.

190. 40% of what number is 80?

    (a) 200   (b) 100   (c) 320   (d) 120

191. What number is the same as $3^2 \times 3^6$?

    (a) 3^{12} (b) 6^{12} (c) 9^8 (d) 3^8

192. If 20 miles is equal to 32 km, how fast is a bus going, in kilometers per hour, when traveling at 60 miles per hour?

    (a) 40 k/hr.   (c) 96 k/hr.
    (b) 52 k/hr.   (d) 66 k/hr.

193. If Tom jogged $\dfrac{2}{5}$ of his total run in 20 minutes, how long will it take him to complete the entire run?

    (a) 40 min.   (c) 25 min.
    (b) 50 min.   (d) 60 min.

194. One gallon of paint will be enough to paint $30\dfrac{1}{3}$ square feet. What area can be painted with 3 gallons?

    (a) 91 ft.^{2} (c) $60\dfrac{2}{3}$ ft.^{2}

    (b) 60 ft.^{2} (d) $60\dfrac{1}{3}$ ft.^{2}

195. What is considered a comfortable temperature for a bedroom?

    (a) 10°F   (b) 35°F   (c) 20°C   (d) 50°C

196. The greatest common factor of 72 and 60 is

    (a) 6   (b) 12   (c) 18   (d) 16

197. What is the surface area of a cube with a side length of 4 inches?

    (a) 16 in.^{2} (c) 32 in.^{2}
    (b) 64 in.^{2} (d) 96 in.^{2}

198. Solve: $(-2) \times (-3) \times 8 =$

    (a) −24   (b) 48   (c) −48   (d) 26

199. A basketball is an example of what?

    (a) circle   (c) prism
    (b) sphere   (d) polygon

200. Solve $34\overline{)6871}$

    (a) 202 R3   (c) 202 R18
    (b) 201 R1   (d) 201 R3

201. Charles wishes to leave a waitress a tip of 15% of his food bill. If the bill is $24.20, what should he leave for a tip?

    (a) $36.30   (c) $2.42
    (b) $4.84   (d) $3.63

202. If you attend school for 10 hours each day and you are in math class for 3 hours each day, what percent of your school day is spent in math class?

    (a) 33%   (b) 10%   (c) 30%   (d) 36%

203. 6 lb. 10 oz. equals

    (a) 60 oz.   (c) 96 oz.
    (b) 58 oz.   (d) 106 oz.

GO TO THE NEXT PAGE ➡

204. What is the least common multiple of 25 and 5?

    (a) 125   (b) 50   (c) 25   (d) 5

205. Solve: $37 \times 92 =$

    (a) 3,400   (c) 407
    (b) 3,404   (d) 3,416

206. A ball pit is made up of 40 red, 60 yellow, 10 blue, and 40 green balls. If you pick one ball at random from the pit, what is the probability that the ball will be red?

    (a) $\frac{4}{150}$ (b) $\frac{4}{11}$ (c) $\frac{4}{15}$ (d) $\frac{1}{150}$

207. How much wallpaper is needed to paper a wall that is 12 feet wide and 8 feet high?

    (a) 96 ft.^{2} (c) 72 ft.^{2}
    (b) 40 ft.^{2} (d) 144 ft.^{2}

208. A rectangle has an area of 48 in.^{2} and a perimeter of 28 in., what are the dimensions of the rectangle?

    (a) 4 in. × 7 in.   (c) 6 in. × 8 in.
    (b) 14 in. × 2 in.   (d) 4 in. × 12 in.

209. Which equation best states this problem?

    The product of 6 and one number is equal to the sum of 4 and 36.

    (a) $6 + x = 4 \times 36$
    (b) $6x = 144$
    (c) $6 + x = 4 + 36$
    (d) $6x = 4 + 36$

210. Sarah is older than Will. Chris is older than Riley. Liz is the same age as Chris but younger than Sarah. Sarah is

    (a) the same age as Chris.
    (b) the oldest.
    (c) younger than Riley.
    (d) younger than Liz.

211. 68 ounces is equal to how many pounds?

    (a) $2\frac{1}{2}$ (b) $4\frac{1}{4}$ (c) $4\frac{1}{16}$ (d) $2\frac{1}{8}$

212. Seven nickels are equal to what fraction of a quarter?

    (a) 35   (b) $\frac{7}{5}$ (c) $\frac{2}{5}$ (d) $\frac{35}{7}$

213. What percent represents 0.465?

    (a) 46.5%   (c) 465%
    (b) 0.465%   (d) 4.65%

214. Solve for x: $9x < -3$

    (a) $x < \frac{1}{3}$ (c) $x > \frac{1}{3}$

    (b) $x < -\frac{1}{3}$ (d) $x > -\frac{1}{3}$

215. What is equal to the following?

    $(6 \times 10^3) + (7 \times 10^3) + (4 \times 10^2) + (5 + 10^1)$

    (a) 6,745   (c) 13,450
    (b) 1,345   (d) 13,415

216. Kathy has 18 pieces of fruit in a bowl: 5 bananas, 3 apples, and 10 oranges. If she randomly selects one piece of fruit, what is the probability that it will be an apple?

    (a) $\frac{8}{18}$ (b) $\frac{3}{15}$ (c) $\frac{1}{6}$ (d) $\frac{3}{15}$

GO TO THE NEXT PAGE ➡

217. The table shows the number of days in January that 33 towns in the Northeast had snow. How many towns had more than 10 days of snow?

Number of Snow Days	Number of Towns
0-5	2
6-10	11
11-15	15
16-20	3

(a) 18   (b) 15   (c) 12   (d) 29

218. Solve for x: $48 - 6x = 0$

(a) $x = 6$ (c) $x = 8$
(b) $x = 12$ (d) $x = 38$

219. What is the area of the rectangle when $w = 4$ cm?

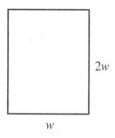

(a) 24 cm^2 (c) 16 cm^2
(b) 32 cm^2 (d) 8 cm^2

220. Roof shingles cost $80 per square yard. How much will it cost to buy shingles for a roof that is 24 feet by 15 feet?

(a) $3,200   (c) $28,800
(b) $360   (d) $4,500

221. Solve: $23 - 4\frac{2}{9} =$

(a) $19\frac{2}{9}$ (b) $18\frac{2}{9}$ (c) $18\frac{7}{9}$ (d) $19\frac{7}{9}$

222. What is the volume of a storage room with the dimensions below?

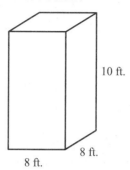

(a) 800 ft.^{3} (c) 6,400 ft.^{3}
(b) 640 ft.^{3} (d) 1,600 ft.^{3}

223. If $a < b$, $b < c$, $c < d$, then

(a) $a > d$ (c) $b < d$
(b) $b > d$ (d) $a = b$

224. In a study of class sizes, a principal listed the size of 9 classrooms. What is the median class size for the 9 classes?

13, 13, 18, 19, 21, 23, 23, 28, 30

(a) 21   (b) 22   (c) 23   (d) 10

225. Which statement best describes the following inequality?

$$4 + 2x < \frac{2}{3}$$

(a) Two-thirds of a number is greater than four plus two.
(b) Twice a number when added to four is less than two-thirds.
(c) The difference of four and twice a number is two-thirds.
(d) The sum of four plus two is less than two-thirds.

GO TO THE NEXT PAGE ➡

226. What is another way to write 6^4?

    (a) $6 + 6 + 6 + 6$

    (b) $6 \times 6 \times 6 \times 6$

    (c) 6×4

    (d) 64

227. A restaurant recorded their profit for one 5-day workweek. The profits are listed below. Find the mean sales for the week.

    $275, $300, $250, $365, $410

    (a) $320   (c) $300

    (b) $252   (d) $324

228. Gregory rents a hotel room that costs $125 per night. In addition he must pay $10 per night for each of his children. If Gregory and his 4 children stay for 2 nights, what will be his total cost to rent the room?

    (a) $330   (c) $625

    (b) $205   (d) $1,425

229. Which of the following represents a proportion?

    (a) $4 : 7 = 12 : 21$ (c) $4 : 21 = 7 : 12$

    (b) $4 : 12 = 21 : 7$ (d) $7 : 4 = 12 : 21$

230. Which line segment shows the diameter of the circle?

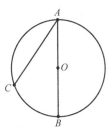

    (a) $\overline{AC}$ (b) $\overline{AB}$ (c) $\overline{AO}$ (d) $\overline{OB}$

231. Charles is 6 feet and 2 inches. How tall is he in inches?

    (a) 76 in.   (c) 62 in.

    (b) 72 in.   (d) 74 in.

232. Which equation represents the following graph ?

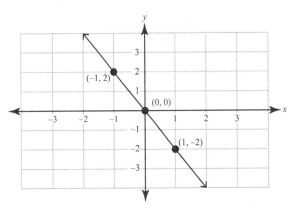

    (a) $y = -\dfrac{1}{2}x - 2$ (c) $y = -2x$

    (b) $y = 2x$ (d) $y = \dfrac{1}{2}x$

233. Which triangle shows angles A and B to be complementary?

    (a)

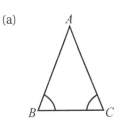

    (b)

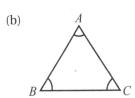

    (c)

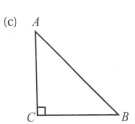

    (d)

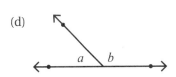

GO TO THE NEXT PAGE ➡

234. Which of the following would best be displayed on a pie chart?

    (a) birth weight of babies
    (b) the types of businesses in a town
    (c) temperature changes during the year
    (d) price of homes in the Midwest

235. What number is equal to $\sqrt[3]{64}$?

    (a) 3   (b) 8   (c) 4   (d) 16

236. A bottle of water is equal to 16 ounces. If a person should drink 64 ounces of water each day, how many bottles of water should a person drink each day?

    (a) 4   (b) 8   (c) 6   (d) 9

237. Using the number line, what is the distance between a and c?

    (a) 2   (b) 3.75   (c) 2.5   (d) 2.75

238. Solve when $a = 1$, $b = 2$, and $c = 4$.

$$6b(c^2 - 6a) + a^{10} =$$

    (a) −23   (b) 130   (c) 27   (d) 121

STOP

ANSWERS EXPLAINED FOR PRACTICE MATHEMATICS SUBTEST

NOTE

Answer explanations in this section are labeled with their corresponding question types. You will need this for the scoring chart on page 252.

175. **(b)** When adding, remember to carry the tens value to the hundreds column on the left if the sum is greater than 9. Always estimate first to see if you can rule out any answer choices. (Basics)

176. **(b)** The 83 does not repeat, just the 3, so put a bar over the 3 to indicate a repeating value. (Decimals)

177. **(b)** (Basics)

$$
\begin{array}{r}
1073 \\
\times\, 128 \\
\hline
8584 \\
21460 \\
+\, 107300 \\
\hline
137344
\end{array}
$$

178. **(d)** Move the decimals to the right so that the divisor is an integer, prior to completing the division. (Decimals)

$$
8.2\overline{)25.502} \Rightarrow 82\overline{)255.02} = 82\overline{)255.02}
$$

$$
\begin{array}{r}
3.11 \\
82\overline{)255.02} \\
-246\downarrow\ \ \, \\
\hline
90\ \ \ \, \\
-82\downarrow \\
\hline
82 \\
-82 \\
\hline
0
\end{array}
$$

179. **(c)** $\dfrac{3}{5} \div \dfrac{2}{15} = \dfrac{3}{5} \times \dfrac{15}{2}$ which reduces to $\dfrac{3}{\cancel{5}_1} \times \dfrac{\cancel{15}^{\,3}}{2} = \dfrac{3}{1} \times \dfrac{3}{2} = \dfrac{9}{2} = 4\dfrac{1}{2}$. (Fractions)

180. **(a)** There are four quarts in one gallon. If you have six gallons, then $4 \times 6 = 24$ quarts.
$\dfrac{4 \text{ quarts}}{1 \text{ gallon}} = \dfrac{x \text{ quarts}}{6 \text{ gallons}}$. Because $1 \times 6 = 6$ then $4 \times 6 = x$, and $x = 24$. (Conversions)

181. **(c)** Remember to line up the decimal points when adding or subtracting decimals. (Decimals)

$$
\begin{array}{r}
1.67 \\
-\, 0.96 \\
\hline
0.71
\end{array}
$$

182. **(d)** This is a 3–4–5 triangle. If you don't recognize that, you can apply the Pythagorean theorem ($a^2 + b^2 = c^2$) where c is the longest side. $4^2 + x^2 = 5^2$, so $x^2 = 9$ and x must be equal to 3. (Geometry)

183. **(b)** The square root of 121 is 11 because $11^2 = 11 \times 11 = 121$. (Radicals)

184. **(c)** 17 hundredths is equal to 0.17. The second place to the right of the decimal is the hundredths place. (Decimals)

185. **(a)** $2^5 = 2 \times 2 \times 2 \times 2 \times 2$, and $2^2 = 2 \times 2$. There are a total of seven 2's each multiplied together, which is expressed in exponential form as 2^7. (Exponents)

186. **(a)** There are 60 minutes in an hour, so the fraction of an hour that represents 36 minutes is $\frac{36}{60}$ which can be reduced to $\frac{36 \div 12}{60 \div 12} = \frac{3}{5}$. (Basics)

187. **(b)** The probability of an event is expressed as the number of ways to obtain a favorable outcome (in this case, choosing a pencil) over the total number of possible outcomes (a total of 30 different things in the drawer). The probability is $\frac{10}{30}$ which can be reduced to $\frac{1}{3}$. (Probability)

188. **(c)** To solve this you may cross multiply; however, it is easier to recognize that 3 is multiplied by 20 to make 60; therefore, 2 should be multiplied by 20 to find x, $2 \times 20 = 40$. If you cross multiply, you will have $\frac{2}{3} = \frac{x}{60} \rightarrow 3x = 120$. Divide both sides by 3 to obtain $x = 40$. (Algebra)

189. **(d)** There are 16 ounces in a pound. If you have 2.5 pounds, you must multiply 16 by 2.5. Do this in steps, first multiply 16 by 2 to obtain 32 then add half of 16 (which is 8) to get a total of 40 ounces. (Conversions)

190. **(a)** 40% of what number is 80? This can be written as an algebraic expression but the easier way is to look at the answer choices. Remember that *of* means to multiply. What must you multiply 4 by to get 8 (ignore the zeros for now). The answer is 2. There is only one answer choice that has 2 for its nonzero digit. You could also figure out 10% of each answer then multiply that by 4 to see which answer choice gives you 80. The algebraic equation would be $0.40x = 80$. Divide both sides by 0.40 to get $x = 80 \div 0.40 = 200$. (Percents)

191. **(d)** Exponents represent the number of times the base is multiplied by itself. The base 3 is multiplied by itself twice and then 6 more times for a total of 8 times or in exponential form, $3^2 \times 3^6 = 3^8$. (Exponents)

192. **(c)** If you set up the ratio $\frac{20}{32} = \frac{60}{x}$, you can cross multiply or solve the easier way by recognizing that 60 is three times 20. Therefore, x must be three times 32; $32 \times 3 = 96$ kilometers per hour. (Conversions)

193. **(b)** This is a ratio problem complicated by the fraction, so instead of setting up a ratio, you should plug in the answer choices starting with the easy values such as 50. $\frac{2}{5}$ of 50 is 20, so the correct answer is 50. (Ratios)

194. **(a)** If *one* gallon will cover $30\frac{1}{3}$ then *three* gallons will cover *three* times that area. $30\frac{1}{3} \times 3 = 91$. You can do this using mental math. $3 \times 30 = 90$ and $3 \times \frac{1}{3} = 1$, so $90 + 1 = 91$. (Fractions)

195. **(c)** You don't have to know the conversion equation for °F to °C. You just have to know that 32°F is freezing, so you can rule out answers (a) and (b). 100°C is boiling (212°F), so half of that, 50°C, is still very hot. Find the correct answer by process of elimination. (Conversions)

196. **(b)** Look at the answer choices starting with the *largest* one and work your way down to see which is the greatest number that is a factor of both 72 and 60. (Basics)

197. **(d)** There are six sides to a cube and each side has an area of 4×4 or 16 in.^{2} Add the area each of the six sides to get the surface area. $16 \times 6 = 96$ in.^{2} (remember to use mental math, 10 times 6 is 60 plus 6 times 6 or 36. $60 + 36 = 96$). (Geometry)

198. **(b)** When multiplying and dividing negative numbers, an even number of negative signs will make a positive answer. Because there are two negatives, this answer will be positive. $-2 \times -3 \times 8 = 6 \times 8 = 48$. (Basics)

199. **(b)** A circle is a two-dimensional object. A basketball is a three-dimensional object, which is a sphere. (Geometry)

200. **(a)** The leftover, when carrying out long division, will be the remainder. (Basics)

$$
\begin{array}{r}
202 \text{ R3} \\
34\overline{)6871} \\
-68 \downarrow\downarrow \\
\hline
071 \\
-68 \\
\hline
3
\end{array}
$$

201. **(d)** When calculating 15%, first figure out 10%. Then cut that in half to get 5% and add the two values together. 10% of 24.20 is $2.42 and half of that is $1.21. The total is $2.42 + $1.21 = $3.63. (Percents)

202. **(c)** Set up a fraction and remember percent means *per* 100. To change a decimal to a percent, move the decimal two places to the right and add the percent symbol. (Percents)

$$\frac{3}{10} = 0.30 = 30\%$$

203. **(d)** One pound is 16 ounces, so 6 pounds is $6 \times 16 = 96$. Then add ten more ounces. (Conversions)

$$\left(6 \text{ pounds} \times \frac{16 \text{ ounces}}{1 \text{ pound}} \right) + 10 \text{ ounces} = 106 \text{ ounces}$$

204. **(c)** The least common multiple is the smallest number that is divisible by both 25 and 5. Don't forget to check if one of these is a multiple of the other. Use your answer choices, starting with the *smallest* one that is at least 25. (Basics)

205. **(b)** When multiplying, remember to check your answer choices to save time. Once you have numbers that match only one of the answers, you can select that answer choice. (Basics)

$$
\begin{array}{r}
37 \\
\times 92 \\
\hline
74 \\
+ 3330 \\
\hline
3404
\end{array}
$$

206. **(c)** Probability is represented by the number of ways to obtain a favorable outcome divided by the number of possible outcomes. (Probability)

$$\frac{40}{40+60+10+40} = \frac{40}{150} = \frac{4}{15}$$

207. **(a)** Area = length × width. 12 ft. × 8 ft. = 96 ft.^{2} (Geometry)

208. **(c)** Look at the answer choices to find one that matches the criteria given. The dimensions that when multiplied give 48 and when added give 28 is answer choice (c). (Geometry)

209. **(d)** Product indicates multiplication, $6x$. Sum is addition, $4 + 36$, $6x = 4 + 36$. (Algebra)

210. **(b)** If Sarah is older than Will and Chris (because Liz is the same age as Chris and younger than Sarah) then Sarah is the oldest. (Word Problems)

211. **(b)** There are 16 ounces in a pound. $68 \div 16 = 4\frac{1}{4}$. (Conversions)

$$16\overline{)68} \quad 4\,R4 = 4\frac{4}{16} = 4\frac{1}{4}$$
$$\underline{-64}$$
$$4$$

212. **(b)** Seven nickels is equal to 35 cents and a quarter is 25 cents. (Basics)

$$\frac{35}{25} = \frac{7}{5}$$

213. **(a)** To change a decimal to a percent, move the decimal point two places to the right and add the percent symbol: 0.465 = 46.5%. (Percents)

214. **(b)** Divide both sides by 9. $x < \frac{-3}{9} \Rightarrow x < -\frac{1}{3}$. (Algebra)

215. **(d)** $(6 \times 10^3) + (7 \times 10^3) + (4 \times 10^2) + (5 + 10^1) = 6000 + 7000 + 400 + 15 = 13{,}415$. Notice that the last term is $5 + 10^1$ resulting in a value that must end in 15. This narrows your answer choices to just one. (Exponents)

216. **(c)** Probability is expressed as the ratio of the number of favorable outcomes over the number of possible outcomes. This probability can be expressed as $\frac{3}{18} = \frac{1}{6}$. (Probability)

217. **(a)** Add the number of towns that had *more* than 10 snow days. $15 + 3 = 18$. (Statistics)

218. **(c)** You can solve this by plugging in answer choices to see which one makes the equation true. Algebraically, you can also solve for x. (Algebra)

$$48 - 6x = 0$$
$$\underline{+6x \quad +6x}$$
$$\frac{48}{6} = \frac{6x}{6}$$
$$8 = x$$

219. **(b)** If $w = 4$ and area = length × width, then $2w \times w = 8 \times 4 = 32$ cm^2. (Geometry)

220. **(a)** Find the area of the roof in square yards by first converting the units.

$$24 \text{ ft.} \times 15 \text{ ft.} = 8 \text{ yd.} \times 5 \text{ yd.} = 40 \text{ yd.}^2$$

At \$80 per yard, the total cost will be 40 yd.^{2} × \$80/yd.^{2} = \$3,200. (Geometry)

221. **(c)** $23 - 4 = 19$. If you subtract an additional $\frac{2}{9}$ the answer will be less than 19 by $\frac{2}{9}$, so the answer is $18\frac{7}{9}$. (Basics)

222. **(b)** Volume = length × width × height = 8 × 8 × 10 = 640 ft.^{3} (Geometry)

223. **(c)** The expression $a < b$, $b < c$, $c < d$ can be rewritten as $a < b < c < d$. (Logic)

224. **(a)** The median is the middle number when the values are arranged in increasing order. There are 9 numbers in order so the middle value, the 5th one, is the median. (Statistics)

225. **(b)** $4 + 2x < \frac{2}{3}$. Twice a number, $2x$, when added, +, to four is less than, <, two thirds. (Algebra)

226. **(b)** $6^4 = 6 \times 6 \times 6 \times 6$. (Exponents)

227. **(a)** To find the mean, add all 5 values and divide by the number of terms. (Statistics)

$$275 + 300 + 250 + 365 + 410 = 1600, 1600 \div 5 = 320$$

228. **(a)** Greg will pay $125 for each night for himself, totaling $250 for both nights. For his 4 children, he will pay an additional $40 per night for a total of $80 for both nights. $250 + $80 = $330. (Word Problems)

229. **(a)** In a proportion, both fractions must be equal as in answer choice (a). $\frac{4}{7} = \frac{12}{21}$ is the answer choice that makes a true equation. (Ratios)

230. **(b)** The diameter of a circle is a line segment passing from side to side and through the center of a circle. (Geometry)

231. **(d)** There are 12 inches in a foot, so $6 \, \text{ft.} \times \frac{12 \text{ in.}}{1 \text{ ft.}} = 72$ inches. Add the additional 2 inches for a total of 74 inches. (Conversions)

232. **(c)** Because the y is decreasing as x increases, the slope of the equation is negative. Look at two points, (0, 0) and (1, –2), and calculate the slope, *rise over run*. The *rise* is –2 and the *run* is 1 for a slope of –2. The y-intercept is zero. (Algebra)

233. **(c)** Complementary angles add up to 90°. If, in answer choice (a), the two angles shown were 45° each, they would be complementary; however, the third angle would have to be a right angle to make the triangle complete, as in answer choice (c). (Geometry)

234. **(b)** Birth weight, temperature, and prices are all things that have an infinite number of values and would not be best represented by a pie chart. Types of businesses are categories and can be clearly shown in a pie chart. (Statistics)

235. **(c)** The cubed root of 64 is 4 because $4 \times 4 \times 4 = 4^3 = 64$. (Radicals)

236. **(a)** $64 \, \text{ounces} \times \frac{1 \text{ bottle}}{16 \text{ ounces}} = 4$ bottles. (Conversions)

237. **(c)** Four spaces on the number line represent a unit of 1. Count the spaces between a and c. There are 10 spaces ÷ 4 = 2.5. (Basics)

238. **(d)** In the given equation, replace each a with 1, b with 2, and c with 4. (Algebra)

$$6b(c^2 - 6a) + a^{10} \rightarrow (6 \times 2)(4^2 - 6 \times 1) + 1^{10} = 12(10) + 1 = 121$$

SCORING YOUR PRACTICE MATHEMATICS SUBTEST

Now that you have reviewed the answers and explanations, let's see how well you are doing. Go through the explanations again and count up the number of each question type you answered correctly. Then fill in the chart below.

	Basics and Conversions	Geometry, Logic, Word Problems	Fractions, Decimals, Percents, Ratios	Exponents, Radicals, Algebra	Statistics and Probability	Total
Number of each question type you answered correctly						
Total of each question type	19	13	12	13	7	64

First, add up the total number of questions you answered correctly. Then divide that number by 64 and multiply by 100 to determine your raw score for the Mathematics subtest:

$$\text{Raw Score} = \frac{\text{Total Number Correct}}{64 \text{ Total Questions}} = \frac{}{64} \times 100 = \underline{}\%$$

Next, to determine your raw score, for each question type, take the number of questions you answered correctly in each category and divide that number by the total number of questions in each question type. Multiply your answer by 100 to convert to a percent.

$$\text{Basics and Conversions} = \frac{\text{Total Number Correct}}{19 \text{ Total Questions}} = \frac{}{19} \times 100 = \underline{}\%$$

$$\text{Geometry, Logic, and Word Problems} = \frac{\text{Total Number Correct}}{13 \text{ Total Questions}} = \frac{}{13} \times 100 = \underline{}\%$$

$$\text{Fractions, Decimals, Percents, and Ratios} = \frac{\text{Total Number Correct}}{12 \text{ Total Questions}} = \frac{}{12} \times 100 = \underline{}\%$$

$$\text{Exponents, Radicals, and Algebra} = \frac{\text{Total Number Correct}}{13 \text{ Total Questions}} = \frac{}{13} \times 100 = \underline{}\%$$

$$\text{Statistics and Probability} = \frac{\text{Total Number Correct}}{7 \text{ Total Questions}} = \frac{}{7} \times 100 = \underline{}\%$$

How well did you do? Make sure to go back and review any areas that you can improve upon.

Language

8

THE LAYOUT

Language is the last subtest of the HSPT. This subtest will assess your knowledge of the English language through questions involving punctuation, capitalization, spelling, usage, sentence structure, and composition. You are most likely learning many of these lessons in your classes at school, but this chapter will consolidate the rules into the essentials that you need to earn a high score on the HSPT.

There are three different sections that make up the Language subtest. The first section will consist of 40 questions that assess your ability to find mistakes in capitalization, punctuation, and usage. The second section is made up of 10 questions where you are asked to find errors in *spelling only*. The last 10 questions of the subtest will focus on paragraph composition and sentence structure.

Language Subtest—25 Minutes and 60 Questions

Question Type	Example	Number of Questions
Capitalization, Punctuation, and Usage	(a) Jackson and Siri are good dogs. (b) Emma and Ryan are my friends. (c) Mr Smith lives next door (d) No mistakes.	40*
Spelling	(a) Maine is north of Virginia. (b) May I have a peice of pie? (c) It's a long drive to Boston. (d) No mistakes.	10
Composition	Which sentence does not belong in this paragraph? Which of these sentences expresses the idea most clearly?	10*

*Note: Some administrations of the HSPT have had only 30 Capitalization, Punctuation, and Usage questions and then 20 Composition questions.

Read this entire chapter but do not try to memorize all of it; just familiarize yourself with the rules and read each example. The more often you see correct capitalization, punctuation, spelling, and word usage, the more likely you are to spot an error on the HSPT.

GENERAL STRATEGIES FOR LANGUAGE

In this chapter you will learn strategies specific to each question type. First let's review some overall strategies that will help you throughout the Language subtest.

Move Along

You have only 25 minutes to answer 60 questions, so you'll have to move quickly. You should answer two to three questions each minute. The good news is many of these, if you spot an error immediately, can be completed in under 10 seconds. Questions where there are no mistakes will take longer. If you find yourself taking more than 30 seconds, make a guess, circle the question number, and move on.

Budget Your Time

Because there are three sections, you should make a point of budgeting your time. It is a good idea to make a note on your test booklet or scrap paper that you should begin the spelling section no later than 15 minutes after the start of the subtest, then spend only 5 minutes on spelling, and the remaining 5 minutes on the composition section.

KNOW IT? SKIP IT!

If you feel that you are already an expert in a particular topic, skip it! Go right to the practice that follows. If you need to review, come back and read the section in detail.

Don't Be Afraid of "No Mistakes"

Since you are looking for errors, you may make a common mistake and assume there is one and waste precious time looking for errors that may not actually be there. In the 50 questions where you are looking for errors, there will be as many as 10 questions where there are none. You will likely find 5–8 no-error questions in capitalization, punctuation, and usage, and then another couple in the spelling section.

Touch Each Word

Because proofreading, reading to find errors, is different from reading for enjoyment, you must focus on each individual word. To stay focused, you should touch your pencil to each word as you read. This can be helpful in spotting a spelling or capitalization mistake.

All Mixed Up

It is important to remember in the first section that you are looking for three different types of errors: capitalization, punctuation, or usage. Be careful, as you may see a sentence where the punctuation is correct and forget to look for usage and capitalization errors. Make sure to look for all three types of error.

Look for Clues in Other Questions

If you are uncertain if a sentence is correct, make a guess. Circle this question and then continue to watch for something similar in future questions. If you see it again, and based on the other answer choices you now know it to be correct, you can come back and fix your previous answer.

When You Know the Answer, Move On

When looking for mistakes, if you spot a glaring error (one where an *I* by itself is not capitalized, or a sentence with no ending punctuation), select that as your answer and do not read the other choices. There is only one correct answer. If you are not sure, then read each of the answer choices.

Eliminate Answer Choices as You Go

When looking for errors, eliminate answer choices that you know have no errors. When looking for the best sentence, make sure to eliminate answers that have grammatical errors. If you have to guess, you will have a better chance of selecting the correct answer if you are able to narrow down your choices.

Extra Time

As in the other subtests, if you have extra time, go back and review the questions that you circled. These should be questions you either didn't answer or questions where you were uncertain of your answer choice. If you still have extra time, go back and look at the questions where you chose *No mistake* as your answer. You may find a mistake the second time around. However, never change your original guess, unless you are absolutely certain that it was the wrong choice.

TYPES OF LANGUAGE QUESTIONS

Capitalization, Punctuation, and Usage

Three types of errors are all mixed up in the first section of the Language subtest. Of the 40 questions, you can expect to see a few with errors in capitalization and the remaining portion split with about half with errors in punctuation and half with errors in usage. Let's first look at how to find errors in capitalization.

CAPITALIZATION

You should become familiar with the basic rules of capitalization for the Language section of the exam. This list focuses on the exact type of capitalization errors that you are likely to find on the HSPT. Read each rule and, in particular, the examples that follow. This will reinforce what you may already know or shed clarity on rules that are less familiar to you.

First Words and Quotes

The first word of a sentence is always capitalized. The first word of a quote is also capitalized, unless it does not begin a full sentence. Do not capitalize a single word that is in quotes.

> I yelled, "Hurry up, or we'll be late."
> Ms. Forbes told us, "Please take your seats."
> "Take your seats," said Ms. Forbes, "and take out your books."
> Some of my classmates like to give themselves the title of "genius."

The Letter I

The letter *I*, when alone, is always capitalized.

> She and I love to take long walks.
> I'll forever love you.

Proper Names

Proper names of people, places, and addresses are always capitalized. Words that reference a sole God are proper nouns and are capitalized, whereas a reference to two or more gods is lowercase.

> My brother, Douglas, has a drone.
> Charles Edward Jr. will graduate in the spring.
> The address, 26 Nelson Avenue, is about 20 minutes away.
> I believe in God and others believe in Allah.
> The ancient Egyptians worshipped many gods.
> Massachusetts Institute of Technology is very competitive.

Titles

Titles that refer to a specific individual, such as Captain Kirk, are capitalized. When using a title to refer to a specific person, both the title and the name should be capitalized. When making a general reference, do not capitalize the titles.

> Coach O'Leary is the head football coach.
> James O'Leary was a coach for 42 years.
> Headmaster Hardiman is very fair.
> Our new headmaster is Dr. Hardiman.
> I heard that Uncle Lewis drives a convertible.
> Will you join us, Uncle?
> Lewis is my uncle.
> The first person to live in the White House was President John Adams.
> I want to be the president of a company one day.

Subjects, Classes, and Languages

Names of languages are always capitalized. Names of subjects, except English, are not capitalized. Specific names of classes are capitalized such as *Physics 202* but not the subject *physics*.

> I learned to speak French this summer.
> My favorite subject is chemistry.
> This fall I will take Math 101A at Salem State University.
> I can speak Spanish fluently.

Dates, Holidays, and Seasons

Dates, days of the week, months, and names of holidays are capitalized. Seasons should not be capitalized.

> I like to give out candy on Halloween.
> My student celebrates Hanukkah.
> New Year's Day there will be no school.
> On Wednesday, there is a team practice.
> Sunday, May 14, is Emmett's big day.
> Of all of the seasons, spring is my favorite.

Names of Geographical Landmarks and Regions and State Abbreviations

Capitalize directions of the compass (north, south, east, west) when referring to a specific region such as the Southwest section of the United States. When referring to direction only, do not capitalize compass points. Both letters in state abbreviations are capitalized (ex. New Hampshire is abbreviated NH). Capitalize each important word of geographical landmarks.

> My family will go hiking in Yosemite National Park.
> The Eiffel Tower is in Paris.
> I love to hike with my dog up Mount Chocorua.
> I live in the Northeast.
> I climbed the highest mountain.
> My house faces southeast.
> We spend our summers in Burlington, VT.

First, Last, and Important

Capitalize the first, last, and important words in book, movie, song, or other titles.

> *A Tale of Two Cities* is a classic.
> *The Curious Incident of the Dog in the Night-Time* is on my summer reading list.
> "How to Build a Better Greenhouse" is an article in the *Boston Sunday Globe*.

Letters and Emails

Capitalize first words in addresses and closings of letters. Other words, unless they are proper nouns, are not capitalized.

> Dear Mom,
> Regards,
> Sincerely yours,
> Director of Human Resources

Now that you've reviewed the rules for capitalization, it's time to see how well you can identify mistakes in capitalization.

Capitalization Practice

In the following questions look for errors in capitalization only. If there are no errors, select choice (d) *No mistakes.*

1. (a) Our family Doctor is very thorough.
   (b) "Please leave me alone," she said.
   (c) I look forward to summer.
   (d) No mistakes.

2. (a) I live in the Northeast.
   (b) Georgetown is west of Boxford.
   (c) At our school, principal Crowley is in charge.
   (d) No mistakes.

3. (a) I live on Nelson street, which is near downtown.
   (b) Have you seen the play *Our Town*?
   (c) Newbury, MA is a nice town.
   (d) No mistakes.

4. (a) This winter I visited the Museum of Fine Arts.
   (b) She lives Southwest of Georgia.
   (c) Coach McHenry is intimidating.
   (d) No mistakes.

5. (a) Will you have lunch with us Auntie?
   (b) Santa Claus is a generous man.
   (c) Dear madam, I accept your offer.
   (d) No mistakes.

6. (a) Aunt Kathryn is having a baby!
   (b) My favorite subject is English.
   (c) French is a romantic language.
   (d) No mistakes.

7. (a) The Pentagon is a very secure building.
   (b) I hiked mount Greylock last month.
   (c) The Queen of England is Elizabeth.
   (d) No mistakes.

8. (a) The fourth of July is my favorite holiday.
   (b) School will not begin until after Labor Day.
   (c) "Never, Ever, and Forever" is a beautiful song.
   (d) No mistakes.

9. (a) The man described himself as wonderful.
   (b) "Mother," she said, "Join us for dinner."
   (c) James Murphy sits in the back of class.
   (d) No mistakes.

10. (a) Director Smith is on duty.
    (b) Larry asked, "will you be moving soon?"
    (c) "Hello," she replied, "I missed you."
    (d) No mistakes.

(Answers are on page 287.)

PUNCTUATION

In the first part of the Language subtest, the majority of the questions will have errors in punctuation. It is very important that you learn the basic rules so you can quickly find these errors.

End Punctuation: Periods, Exclamation Points, and Question Marks

Every sentence must have an ending punctuation mark. Ending punctuations include periods, exclamation points, and questions marks.

PERIODS

Sentences that are not questions or exclamations must end with a period. Periods are also used for abbreviations, often in names, but never after postal abbreviations of states.

> Charles Edward Jr.
> St. Louis, Kentucky
> St. John's Preparatory School
> Boston, MA 02115

EXCLAMATION POINTS

Sentences that are emphatic may end with an exclamation point.

> My team made it to the Super Bowl!
> Wow!
> Look at her dance!

QUESTION MARKS

A question mark belongs at the end of direct questions whether it is at the end of a sentence or inside a quote in the middle of the sentence. A question mark is not used after an indirect question.

> How can I make you believe?
> He asked me if it was going to rain today.
> "Are you kidding me?" he asked his friend.

Commas

The most common punctuation mistakes you will find on the HSPT will be in the use of commas. You will find about 7 or 8 of these. Let's see when and how to use commas.

SALUTATIONS AND CLOSINGS

Salutations and closings in letters, speech, or emails are always followed with a comma.

> Mary, may I speak with you?
> Dear Arthur,
> She asked, "Mary, will you come with me?"
> Sincerely,

INTRODUCTORY PHRASES

Commas are used after an introductory phrase of more than four words. If an introductory phrase has fewer than four words, a comma is optional.

Having stayed up all night, I was very tired.
Being a woman, I was offended.
Because I am a woman, I was offended.
No, I will never tell a lie.
Of course, I was just as surprised as you.
Wow, that show was incredible!

DIRECT QUOTES

A comma is used to separate direct quotes from the speaker. Commas before the quotes are outside the quotation marks, but the comma or end punctuation after the quote should be inside the quotation marks.

Mother said, "Please come in for dinner."
"Come in for dinner," said mother, "or you will go hungry."

APPOSITIVE PHRASES

An appositive is a noun or phrase that renames another noun that comes before it. For example, "My friend, the tall one, is coming over." The appositive phrase is *the tall one* and is not necessary in the sentence. Commas are used to set off an appositive phrase. If the phrase is necessary for the sentence, then it is not set apart by commas.

Larry, my oldest brother, is late for dinner.
He saw the child who was lost and called the police.
My brother Dan is the only one who has a child.
Robert, the dance teacher, is my good friend.

PARENTHETICAL PHRASES

A parenthetical phrase is one that interrupts the sentence and, when removed, does not change the overall meaning of the statement. Commas are used to set off parenthetical phrases.

Rodney, even though he is usually late, was on time for dinner.
I think, however, that I have changed my mind.

CLARIFICATION

Commas are used to clarify sentences that would otherwise be confusing. Generally speaking, if a comma takes the place of a pause, then it is a good idea to insert the comma.

Unclear: Outside the roads were icy.
Clear: Outside, the roads were icy.

LOCATIONS AND DATES

Commas are placed between the name of a city and the state. Do not use a comma between the state abbreviation and the zip code. They are also used in a date, between the day of the month and the year. If a date is used in a sentence, there should be an additional comma after the date.

> Boston, Massachusetts
> January 28, 1936, is the day my mother was born.
> The dance-a-thon will be Saturday, March 4th, at the Claddagh Pub.
> My address is 72 Main Street, Boston, MA 02115.

MULTIPLE ADJECTIVES

When two or more adjectives precede a noun, all but the last are followed by a comma. When they follow a noun, a comma should be placed after each adjective.

> The big, old, red house.
> The dog, big, brown, and playful, is my best friend.

ITEMS IN A LIST

Commas must be placed between more than two items in a list, sometimes including the item before the *and*. It is also considered correct if you omit the comma before the *and*.

> Dinner included roast beef, carrots, peas, and corn.
> Dinner included roast beef, carrots, peas and corn.

> On the HSPT, if you see a missing comma in a list, it will be in the beginning and not after the last item. For example: The menu offered salads entrees, and dessert. The error is that the comma after the word *salads* is missing.

COMBINING TWO OR MORE INDEPENDENT CLAUSES

When combining two or more independent clauses, use a comma before the conjunction (and, but, or, so, yet, etc.). This is not necessary if the phrase after the conjunction cannot stand alone as a sentence.

> Greg ran in the marathon, but he did not win.
> I ran the race, and I won.

WHEN NOT TO USE A COMMA

- Between a subject and its verb.

  Not Correct: Kathryn, is a wonderful mother.

- To join two independent clauses without a conjunction.

  Not correct: My favorite class is algebra, my sister's favorite class is history.
  Correct: My favorite class is algebra, but my sister's favorite class is history.
  Correct: My favorite class is algebra. My sister's favorite class is history.

- Between two verbs joined by *and*.

  Not correct: I like to run, and jump.
  Correct: I like to run, jump, and swim.

Quotations

Quotation marks come in pairs and are used to identify a direct quote. Quotation marks are always outside of commas and periods when used in a direct quote. Quotations are also used to set off titles of short works like poems and songs. Names of longer works like books and movies are italicized or underlined and not in quotation marks.

> "I'll never let go of your hand," said the firefighter.
> The man said, "A promise is a promise."
> One of my favorite poems is "Do Not Go Gentle into That Good Night" by
>   Dylan Thomas.
> *Night* is a powerful book.

Apostrophes

Apostrophes are used in contractions to indicate that one or more of the letters is omitted.

> He's = he is
> Can't = cannot
> It's = it is
>
> Irregular Form: Won't = will not

Apostrophes are also used to show the possessive form of a noun. The apostrophe comes *before* the *s* for a singular noun and *after* the *s* for plural nouns. For singular nouns that end in *s*, the apostrophe is placed after the *s*.

> The *company's profit statement* showed a promising future.
> This *week's high temperature* broke records.
> *Will's favorite book* is *The Jungle Book*.
> *Charles' favorite book* is out of print.
> The *students' school* was renovated over the summer.
>
> Irregular Form: *Its* is the possessive form of *it*. For example: Although the car's exterior is shiny, *its interior* is faded and worn.

Colons and Semicolons

TIP

You will probably not see any semicolons on the HSPT. If you do, they will most likely be used correctly and not represent an error.

At most, you will see one of these errors in the Language subtest.

A colon is used when introducing a list. The phrase before the colon must be an independent clause. A colon should never be used after a preposition or a verb.

> Not Correct: The recipe called for: eggs, butter, and flour.
> Correct: The recipe called for the following: eggs, butter, and flour.

A colon is also used to separate hours from minutes when referring to time.

> I usually wake up at 6:30 A.M. each morning.

A semicolon is used to join two related clauses but only if each phrase is short. It is also acceptable, and more common, to write two separate sentences.

> Correct: The snow is falling; Christmas will be here soon.
> Correct: The snow if falling. Christmas will be here soon.

Punctuation Practice

In the following questions, look for errors in punctuation only. If there are no errors, select choice (d) *No mistakes.*

1. (a) He won't help me shovel the driveway.
   (b) Tom Fier Sr is the newest math teacher.
   (c) At this rate, I will lose the race.
   (d) No mistakes.

2. (a) Kathryn, may we talk please?
   (b) A months time will go by quickly.
   (c) I pray to God that my wish comes true.
   (d) No mistakes.

3. (a) Nelly are you older than Muriel?
   (b) The Greek gods are intriguing.
   (c) Because he was an old dog, he slept a lot.
   (d) No mistakes.

4. (a) The Hastings' house is green.
   (b) No, I don't believe that is mine.
   (c) He asked me to marry him?
   (d) No mistakes.

5. (a) The cute, yellow, playful, dog is named Jackson.
   (b) The recipe calls for the following: flour, sugar, and eggs.
   (c) Finally, a shoe that is comfortable!
   (d) No mistakes.

6. (a) Please pick me up at 11:30 A.M. tomorrow.
   (b) Our anniversary is on Monday, May 28.
   (c) I love to run, swim, and jump.
   (d) No mistakes.

7. (a) He also voted for President Kennedy.
   (b) The herb garden has oregano, sage, and thyme.
   (c) Meg studied for the test, but she did not do well.
   (d) No mistakes.

8. (a) "When," asked Beth, "is dinner?"
   (b) Will you buy me dinner?
   (c) My new position high school history teacher is rewarding.
   (d) No mistakes.

9. (a) K. L. Smith is the newest member.
   (b) Stacy please pass me the salt.
   (c) The long, slow drive is boring.
   (d) No mistakes.

10. (a) We were married on March 28 1987.
    (b) They're always complaining.
    (c) It's a long drive to Maine.
    (d) No mistakes.

(Answers are on page 287.)

USAGE

The first section of the Language subtest includes questions on word usage. Usage is a broad topic and includes a variety of concepts of how words are used correctly. If you have words spelled correctly and capitalized the right way but use the word in a manner that is not correct, then you have made an error in *usage*. You can expect to see approximately 15 or so questions with errors in usage on the Language subtest. Of these, some will contain errors in subject-verb agreement, noun-pronoun agreement, verbs/adverbs/adjectives usage, and parallelism, among others. Let's look at each of these topics in more detail.

Subject-Verb Agreement

The *subject* in a sentence is the person or thing that is doing something or being described. The *verb* is the action that is being done by the subject. It is important to be able to identify the subject and the verb, because you must make sure they agree with each other. Look at the table below to see some examples of subjects and verbs in a sentence.

Sentence	Subject	Verb
Sandra cooked all day.	Sandra	cooked
James coaches football.	James	coaches
The balloon floated away.	balloon	floated

When examining sentences for subject-verb agreement, you should ignore most of the words and simply look at the subject and the verb. In the examples above, you are only concerned with the following: Sandra cooked, James coaches, and balloon floated; all of the other words are unimportant.

THE SUBJECT AND VERB MUST EITHER BOTH BE SINGLE OR BOTH BE PLURAL

If you have a subject that is singular, such as *dog,* the verb that follows must also be in the singular form. The singular form of run is *runs. The dog runs after the cat.* If you used the plural form of run, the sentence would sound odd. *The dog run after the cat.*

Singular: The dog runs after the cat.
Plural: The cats chase the mice.

The subject is not altered by any phrase that may follow it. In the following example, you will see that *mother* is singular and the verb *eats* is singular even though the middle phrase includes the plural noun, *children.*

The mother, with all of her children, eats dessert.

Mother is singular and *eats* is the singular tense of the verb to eat; therefore, the subject and verb are in agreement. Here are some other correct subject-verb statements. (In each example the subject is underlined and the verb is italicized.)

She *dances* each Monday night.
They always *run* to school.
All of the players *are* over six feet tall.
There is always one who *fails* the test.
The teacher, along with her students, *attends* the lecture.

SINGULAR WORDS CAN BE MISTAKEN FOR PLURAL

Some words may appear to be plural when in fact they are singular. *Each, every, anyone, everyone, no one, someone, either,* and *neither* are all singular words, and therefore the corresponding verbs must also be singular. If you are not sure, replace the pronoun with a singular noun such as *I, he,* or *she.* Each of the examples below is followed by a sentence replacing the confusing word with a simpler pronoun.

> *Neither* Stephanie nor Charles *talks* a lot.
> He *talks* a lot.

> *Each* of the seven team members *plays* in the game.
> She *plays* in the game.

PLURAL WORDS CAN BE MISTAKEN FOR SINGULAR

Some words may appear to be singular when in fact they are plural. *Both, few, any, others,* and *several* are all plural pronouns. As in the examples above, here you can replace the confusing pronoun with a simple one such as *we* or *they.*

> *Both of us* are going to Mexico next week.
> *We* are going to Mexico next week.

> *The others* play nicely together.
> *They* play nicely together.

> *Several* ingredients are needed to make a cake.
> *They* are needed to make a cake.

SINGULAR NOUNS OR PRONOUNS JOINED WITH A PLURAL NOUN OR PRONOUN

In this case, the verb must be in the plural form.

> Either you or your friends *are going* to have to clean this up.
> Neither Jerry nor the other players *are willing* to forfeit the game.
> Sandy and her class *feel* confident about the test.

DO NOT AND DOES NOT

The verb *do* is both singular and plural. The first and second person verb is *do,* while the third person is *does.* I *do,* you *do,* he *does* (first person, second person, and third person). Therefore, the negative contractions are I *don't,* you *don't,* and he *doesn't* (again, first person, second person, and third person).

> He *doesn't* make any sense.
> They *do* sound wonderful.
> We *don't* know how to solve the mystery.

Subject-Verb Agreement Practice

Can you find the subject-verb agreement errors in the sentences below?

1. The children has an allergy to cats.

2. The cat love the children.

3. They doesn't know how to unlock the door.

4. The snakes hisses to warn its prey.

5. Bill and his family is very nice neighbors.

6. Susan and her three children eats at the diner.

7. Each of the pets are for sale.

8. The ideas, which are good, is to work together.

9. Many believes there will be a storm on Tuesday.

10. Much are still not known about the universe.

(Answers are on page 288.)

Pronoun-Noun Agreement

A noun is a person, place, or thing. Pronouns are words that take the place of a noun. For an example, look at the following sentence: Riley picked up the ball, and she threw it far away. *Riley* and the *ball* are nouns. *She* is the pronoun referring to *Riley*, and *it* is the pronoun referring to the *ball*.

PRONOUNS MUST AGREE WITH THE NOUN THEY REPRESENT

A singular noun must be represented by a singular pronoun just as a plural noun must be represented by a plural pronoun. Likewise, if a pronoun is in the first, second, or third person, the noun must be in the same person.

> The *children* walked to school, but *they* ran home.
> Kathryn is a travel agent. *She* is very efficient.
> The *piano* is an instrument, *which* has a beautiful sound.
> The *company* is very large, and *it* earns a lot of money.

SUBJECTIVE VERSUS OBJECTIVE CASE

To find errors in usage, you must know when to use a subjective and an objective pronoun. Very often you can tell by the sound. If used incorrectly, the pronoun will simply sound wrong to you. For example, consider "Me is a tall man," and "I am a tall man." Can you hear which one is correct? The second is the correct answer. Here are some examples to remind you of subjective and objective pronouns.

Subjective Pronouns (doing the action): I, you, he, she, it, we, they, who

Objective Pronouns (receiving the action): Me, you, him, her, it, us, them, whom

He is a tall man.
They walk to school each day.

The ball was thrown to *him*.
The meal was eaten by *them*.

To *whom* should I deliver this?
Who is running the show?

TIP

Pronouns that have an *m*, such as *me* and hi*m*, are objective as well as their partners. Hi*m* and her are both objective. The*m* is another objective pronoun.

IF A PRONOUN COMES AFTER A PREPOSITION OR A VERB

If a pronoun follows a preposition (in, between, of, at, into, from, with, etc.) or a verb, the pronoun will be in the objective case (me, you, him, her, it, them, us).

Give the tickets to *me*.
The rain soaked *her*.
The cold weather froze *them*.

If there is more than one noun or pronoun following the preposition or verb, you may not always be able to rely on the sound of the sentence to help you. Consider the following sentence:

Peter gave the tickets to Kaylee and I.

To many people this may sound correct, but it is not. Remember, the noun following a preposition must be in the objective case, and the word *I* is the subjective case. The correct sentence should be:

Peter gave the tickets to Kaylee and me.

This sentence is correct because *me* is the objective case. Here's a helpful hint: each word that follows the preposition must be able to stand alone.

<u>Incorrect</u>: Peter gave the tickets to I.
<u>Correct</u>: Peter gave the tickets to Kaylee.
<u>Correct</u>: Peter gave the tickets to me.

Here is another example.

<u>Incorrect</u>: Please come to the game with James and I. (*I* is the subjective case)
<u>Correct</u>: Please come to the game with James and *me*. (*me* is the objective case)

Review the correct examples listed below.

The mother kissed her son and me.
Respond to Mark and him after you read their email.
I took the books from Laura and her.

TIP

When a noun and pronoun follow a preposition, try swapping them to see if it still sounds okay. *Peter gave the tickets to I and Kaylee* sounds wrong, and it is.

IF A PRONOUN FOLLOWS A LINKING VERB

When a pronoun follows a linking verb (am, is, are, was, were, etc.), the pronoun will be in the same form as it would be if it were the subject (I, you, he, we, they, etc.). Don't worry if the phrase doesn't sound right. You have probably heard some of these phrases spoken incorrectly more often than correctly.

> The winner of the game *was* I.
> The loser of the game *was* he.
> Who *is* she?

VERB TENSE

Verbs have many different tenses, the most common being past, present, and future. There will be an indication in the sentence to let you know what tense of the verb should be used. In the following examples, the indicator words are italicized and the correct verb tenses are underlined.

> *Today* I am studying for a test.
> I studied all of *last week* for my math test.
> *Tomorrow* I plan to study for my history test.

Words That Indicate Verb Tense

Past	Present	Future
yesterday	now	tomorrow
last week, month, year	currently	later
in 1997 (past date)	at present	in 2050 (future date)
once	as we speak	
during (ex: during the ice age)	today	
ago (ex: a while ago)	this week, month, year	
recently		

If English is your first language, mistakes in verb tense will just sound wrong. Read the following examples aloud and see if you can hear the incorrect verb tenses.

> Yesterday, I will go swimming.
> During the 16th century, Henry will be the king.
> Once upon a time, I am learning to ride a bike.
> Tomorrow, I ran home from school.

Here are the corrections:

> Yesterday, I *went* swimming.
> During the 16th century, Henry *was* the king.
> Once upon a time, I *learned* to ride a bike.
> Tomorrow, I *will run* home from school.

Adjectives and Adverbs

You most likely have heard this expression before, but it's worth repeating. *Adjectives modify nouns and adverbs modify everything else.* Adverbs can describe clauses, adjectives, verbs, and other adverbs.

Can you identify the italicized words below as either an adjective or an adverb? Next to each sentence, write what is being described, and then decide if the italicized word is an adjective or an adverb.

Sentence	Describing What?	Adjective or Adverb
The boy is *quick*.		
The boy runs *quickly*.		
The boy runs very *slowly*.		
Unfortunately, we will be late.		

(Answers are on page 288.)

It is important to know the difference between an adjective and an adverb because they are often spelled differently. Adverbs usually have an –*ly* ending. However, this is not a hard and fast rule. Below is a list of adverbs that never end in –*ly* and a list of adjectives that end in –*ly*. You should be familiar with each of the words in these lists.

Adverbs Not Ending in –*ly*

Almost—I *almost* fell down the stairs.

Even—I'm so excited that I'm not *even* tired.

Fast—That sports car drives *fast*.

Low—He limbos *low*.

Never—He *never* runs that fast.

Not—I am *not* dancing tonight.

Often—I *often* eat Good & Plenty candies.

Rather—He is *rather* smart.

Too—I'm not *too* tall for the ride.

Very—The student was *very* bored in her math class.

Well—She is not feeling *well*.

Adjectives Always Ending in –*ly*

Costly—It was a *costly* mistake.

Deadly—The snake's bite is *deadly*.

Easterly—Darren drove in an *easterly* direction.

Elderly—The *elderly* woman is nice.

Holy—The *holy* man blessed the animals.

Lively—The music is *lively*.

Lonely—I am *lonely* when I'm waiting.

Manly—Wayne is very *manly*.

Orderly—The students stood in *orderly* rows.

Silly—What a *silly* girl she is.

Timely—Please complete your work in a *timely* manner.

Ugly—The *ugly* duckling became a swan.

ADVERBS MODIFYING ACTION VERBS

Adverbs that modify *action* verbs end in –*ly*.

> The dancer dances *quickly* across the stage.
> She *silently* hid behind the door.
> The clerk yelled *angrily* at the customer.

CONJUNCTION ADVERBS

Conjunction adverbs make transitions in sentences, but they do not connect two sentences as a regular conjunction does. Conjunction adverbs include: *additionally, furthermore, however, moreover, otherwise,* and *thus,* to name a few. When a conjunction is used as a transitional adverb in the middle of a sentence, it must have punctuation on either side. Typically, there is either a semicolon or a comma before a transitional conjunction, and then it is always followed by a comma. These indicate a shift in tone. Here is an example:

He is a good player; *however,* he does not score a lot.

Notice how the word *however* is used as a transition, and changes the overall direction of the sentence. It begins as a positive comment and ends with a negative thought.

When a conjunction adverb is used as an interruption in a sentence, it must have a comma on either side. Here is an example:

She is, *otherwise,* a very nice person.

In this case, the word *otherwise* is an interruption in the sentence and, if it were removed, the overall sentence still makes sense. For this reason, there is a comma on either side of the conjunction adverb.

Comparison Words

In the first part of the Language subtest, there will be a few questions that have mistakes in comparison words. Comparison words are used to make comparisons such as *greater, smartest, least,* etc.

Here are some rules that will help you to find the errors in this type of question. Each rule is followed by examples demonstrating the correct usage.

1. Do not use superlatives, such as *best* or *most,* unless it is true. While one athlete may be better than another, she is only the best if she is better than ALL others.

   She is the best cook in all of Boston.
   He is the better of the two singers.
   He is the most intelligent of the three.

2. A one-syllable word can be adapted to be a comparison word simply by adding *–er* or *–est* to the end of the word.

   Great, greater, greatest
   Fast, faster, fastest
   Tall, taller, tallest

3. Words with more than one syllable are usually made into comparison words by preceding the word with *more* or *most.*

   Curious, more curious, most curious
   Deceptive, more deceptive, most deceptive
   Intelligent, more intelligent, most intelligent

4. For words that end in *–y,* the *–y* is changed to *–ier* or *–iest.*

   Funny, funnier, funniest
   Happy, happier, happiest
   Silly, sillier, silliest

5. As with most rules in the English language, there are some exceptions.

   Bad, worse, worst
   Good, better, best

DOUBLE NEGATIVES

The incorrect use of two negatives in the same sentence is known as a double negative. Two negatives turn the sentence into a positive one and can be confusing. You can expect to see a couple of these errors on the HSPT. You will have an easy time identifying them if you become familiar with the following list of incorrect uses of negatives.

Don't hardly	Hasn't had none	Can't hardly
Can't never	Don't know nothing	Hardly none
Barely none		

Commonly Misused Words

The English language has many words that are often misused. Below are some examples that you may see on the HSPT. There may only be one or two of these on the test, but if you familiarize yourself with the words below, you will answer them quickly and correctly.

ACCEPT/EXCEPT

Accept is a verb meaning to take something that is given, while *except* is a preposition meaning to exclude something.

> I *accept* your apology.
> I love all vegetables *except* lima beans.

ALLOT/A LOT

Allot is a verb meaning to give out or apportion. *A lot*, on the other hand, is an expression used to refer to many.

> I have *a lot* of friends.
> I will *allot* each child two doughnuts.

ALREADY/ALL READY

Already is an adverb meaning that something was done previously, while *all ready* means that someone or something is completely ready to go.

> I am *all ready* to go.
> I *already* told you I'll be there.

AMONG/BETWEEN

Between is used to refer to an object or person being somewhere in the middle of two other people or things. You cannot be *between* three or more things. *Among* is used when referring to more than two.

> *Between* the two brothers there is a sister.
> *Among* the four children, the boy is the tallest.

BESIDE/BESIDES

Beside is a preposition meaning next to someone or something. *Besides* is an adverb meaning in addition to.

> I am right here *beside* you.
> *Besides* being smart, she is also beautiful.

DESSERT/DESERT/DESERT

Dessert is a noun referring to sweets. *Desert* is a noun referring to a very dry region. *Desert* is also a verb meaning to leave someone or something behind.

> I love having pudding for *dessert.*
> Living in the *desert* can be difficult because it is so dry.
> She was *deserted* by her friends.

FEWER/LESS

Fewer is an adjective used to refer to items that can be counted, while *less* is an adjective that refers to things that are not counted.

> This lane is for customers with ten or *fewer* items.
> I weigh *less* than my daughter.

GOOD/WELL

Feel *good*, and do *well*. That's all you need to know.

> How do you *feel* today? I *feel good*; how do you feel?
> How did you *do* on the math test? I did *well*, thank you.

IT'S/ITS

It's is the contraction for *it is*, while *its* is the possessive form of the pronoun *it*. You can always replace *it's* with *it is* and the sentence will have the same meaning.

> *It's* not clear who is in charge. (*It is* not clear who is in charge.)
> The car was in good shape, but *its* tire was flat. (The car's tire was flat.)

LOSE/LOOSE

Lose is a verb meaning to misplace or to become unable to find or have. *Loose* is an adjective referring to something that is not tight or secure.

> I always *lose* my keys.
> My jeans are very *loose* in the waist.
> The doorknob is *loose* and wiggles when turned.

THEIR/THERE/THEY'RE

Their is the possessive pronoun for *they*; *there* is an adverb referring to location; and *they're* is a contraction for *they are*.

> The blue one is *their* car.
> I will be over *there* when you are ready.
> *They're* less likely to make that mistake again.

THAN/THEN

Than is a preposition used in comparisons, while *then* is an adverb referring to a point in time.

> I am taller *than* my brother.
> I will pack up and *then* leave.

TO/TOO/TWO

To is a preposition expressing motion or direction; *too* is an adverb meaning to an excessive degree; and *two* is the number 2.

> She came *to* the house to pick me up.
> She is much *too* tall.
> I have *two* classes this semester.

WHETHER/WEATHER

Whether is a conjunction indicating that something applies to one or the other. *Weather* refers to the climate.

> I'm going skiing *whether* you come or not.
> Do you know what the *weather* is for Wednesday?

WHO'S/WHOSE

Who's is the contraction for *who is*, while *whose* is the possessive case of *who*.

> *Who's* coming with us on the field trip? (*Who is* coming with us on the field trip?)
> *Whose* pen is this?

YOUR/YOU'RE

Your is the possessive form of *you*. *You're* is the contraction for *you are*.

> Is this *your* book?
> *You're* always complaining about work. (*You are* always complaining about work.)

WHICH/WHO/THAT

Which is a pronoun that refers only to objects, while *who* is a pronoun used to refer only to people. *That* is used to refer to either objects or people but is only used in a phrase that is necessary to the meaning of the sentence.

> This piano, *which* was just tuned, will be used at the recital.
> That woman, *who* is my friend, will join us today.
> This is the woman *that* I told you about.

WHO/WHOM

Who is used when referring to the subject in a sentence. If you can replace the word *who* with *he* or *she*, then you are using it correctly. *Whom* is used when referring to the object of a verb or a preposition in a sentence. If you can replace the word *whom* with *him* or *her*, then you are using it correctly.

> *Who* is the man that I am supposed to meet?
> *He* is the man I am supposed to meet.
> *Whom* should I report to when I get to work?
> I should report to *him* when I get to work.

Commonly Misused Words Practice

In each of the sentences below, you are given a choice of words in parentheses. Circle the word that best completes the sentence. Check the answers at the end of this chapter to see you how well you did.

1. I wish I were smarter (then/than) my teacher.

2. If you weigh (fewer/less) than 80 pounds you cannot go on the ride.

3. I have (a lot/allot) of confidence in your abilities.

4. Arizona has many (desserts/deserts).

5. (Accept/Except) for me, there will only be one other girl there.

6. (There/Their/They're) are way (to/too/two) many people in this elevator.

7. He is the only one (beside/besides) me who will take the class.

8. The parking valet cannot (lose/loose) the keys or he'll be fired.

9. (Who's/Whose) shirt is this?

10. I think that (between/among) all of the players, Jim is the best.

11. (It's/Its) a shame that vacation is almost over.

12. I hope (their/they're/there) ready when we get (their/they're/there).

13. I wish the (weather/whether) would change so we can play our game.

14. Stand (beside/besides) me if you want to see.

15. The teacher, (who/which) is new this year, is my favorite.

16. My favorite (dessert/desert) is apple pie.

17. This is the friend (which/that) I have known the longest.

18. (Who's/Whose) ever going to know if we don't tell?

19. To (who/whom) does this sneaker belong?

20. (Between/among) the two of us, I can keep a secret.

(Answers are on page 288.)

Sentence Structure

The last type of error you will find in the first section of the Language subtest is an error in sentence structure. There are always questions that have errors in parallelism and less often a question that involves a sentence fragment error.

PARALLELISM

It's not important that you understand what this word means but that you are able to recognize when parallelism is not maintained throughout a sentence. It will be easier to explain after you see an example.

Correct: She got out of the car, shut the door, and walked away.
Incorrect: She opened her trumpet case, took the instrument out, and will begin to play.

The first sentence is correct, and the second sentence is incorrect because it lacks parallelism. Parallelism is the use of successive phrases written in the same grammatical tense or structure. The second sentence should read as, "She opened her trumpet case, took the instrument out, and *began* to play." Because the first two actions are in the past tense, the third should be in the past tense as well. Sentences must also maintain the same format in lists. The following example has an error. Can you find it?

She wanted to read a book, to knit a sweater, and eat ice cream.

This should read instead as, "She wanted to read a book, to knit a sweater, and *to* eat ice cream."

SENTENCE FRAGMENTS

Every sentence must complete a thought. *At 7:30 this morning, I went to the gym.* This is a complete sentence. A complete sentence contains both a subject and a verb. A sentence ends with a punctuation mark and has to convey a thought on its own. Here are some examples of sentence fragments.

Because I ate my vegetables. (Begins with a conjunction)
At 7:30 this morning. (No verb)
Began to play the song. (No subject)
I learned that everyone besides me. (No verb for *everyone*)

Usage Practice

Take a few minutes to answer the following questions. Look for errors in usage only. If there are no errors, choose (d) *No mistakes.*

1. (a) I don't know weather or not he is coming.
   (b) She doesn't know how to cook.
   (c) He is the greatest of all the chefs.
   (d) No mistakes.

2. (a) The scarf is the warmest of all of them.
   (b) Once, I wear a dress that was too long.
   (c) My shoes are lovely.
   (d) No mistakes.

3. (a) My father's business are very successful.
   (b) Won't you join us?
   (c) They're always on time.
   (d) No mistakes.

4. (a) There is no reason to expect foul play.
   (b) When you are done, please return the book to Charles or me.
   (c) Was Danny hungry tomorrow?
   (d) No mistakes.

5. (a) She hardly has any jewelry.
   (b) The dark, red house is the larger of the two.
   (c) Randy bake pies for Thanksgiving dinner.
   (d) I love reading, writing, and bird watching.

6. (a) I hardly never skip my homework.
   (b) Lee and her children love to garden.
   (c) The boy and his father went fishing.
   (d) No mistakes.

7. (a) He ran fast around the track.
   (b) There are scarcely any people at the train station.
   (c) She rode the bus, walked a mile, then climbing the stairs.
   (d) No mistakes.

8. (a) She and I love to watch movies.
   (b) The kittens run away from the dog.
   (c) The brownies smell sweet.
   (d) No mistakes.

9. (a) There are fewer plays each season.
   (b) The cyclist rode slow down the hill.
   (c) Sarah and her family are all tall.
   (d) No mistakes.

10. (a) You're the best friend I have.
    (b) He is the fastest of the two runners.
    (c) She chose Pam and me as the winners.
    (d) No mistakes.

(Answers are on page 289.)

SPELLING

Spelling is an important skill and one that is critical to both reading and writing. In your future, you will write essays, reports, and eventually resumes. Spelling and vocabulary play a very important role in all communications, and both are tools that you should improve on throughout your academic, professional, and personal life.

Since you have no idea which misspelled words will be on the test, you'll have to be comfortable with all of the basic spelling rules as well as familiar with common word lists. When you review and expand your vocabulary, you should also pay careful attention to spelling. This will ensure that you find the mistakes in these questions. Of the 10 questions, there will be one or two that have no mistakes. So, you only have to find about 8 incorrectly spelled words.

Spelling can be challenging for many students. The English language has many spelling rules and for every rule there are many exceptions. Here are some rules that you should become familiar with. Don't feel like you have to memorize each rule. But if you understand most of them AND continue to review your vocabulary in regard to the correct spelling, you will do well in the spelling section of the HSPT. Organizing spelling rules in a simple format is challenging because there is a fair amount of overlap as well as exceptions for each rule. If the list of rules is too overwhelming, then feel free to go right to the word list and try to learn correct spelling by sight.

TIP

While spelling has not been linked to intelligence, it has been shown to make connections between sound and letters and plays a significant role in one's reading ability. Knowing the basic rules will help in both reading and writing.

Spelling Rules and Exceptions

A FEW EASY RULES

The letter *Q* is *always* followed by *U*.
The letter *V never* ends a word and is *never* doubled.
The letters *K, J, W,* and *X* are *never* doubled.

I BEFORE E EXCEPT AFTER C

This rule is often but not always true. The poem that you may remember from grammar school is "I before E except after C or when sounded as A as in neighbor and weigh, but weird is just weird." The following are some examples of this rule as well as some exceptions.

The Rule: I before E except after C or when sounded as A		Exception: I before E even after C	Exception: E before I when not after C	
Believe	Perceive	Ancient	Caffeine	Leisure
Die	Piece	Conscientious	Counterfeit	Neither
Fierce	Receipt	Science	Either	Protein
Friend	Receive	Society	Foreign	Seizure
Neighbor			Height	Their
			Heir	Weird

MAKING A WORD PLURAL

Words are usually made plural by adding –es or –s to the root word.

- If a word ends in a consonant, you can *usually* make the root word plural simply by adding –s.

    Bug, bugs
    Cat, cats
    Hand, hands
    Magnet, magnets

- If the word ends with –ch, –sh, –ss, –x, or –z, make the root plural by adding –es rather than –s.

    Church, churches
    Dish, dishes
    Toss, tosses
    Tax, taxes
    Buzz, buzzes

- If the root word ends in the vowel –o, make the root plural by adding –es rather than –s.

    Do, does
    Echo, echoes
    Tomato, tomatoes

    Exceptions:

    Piano, pianos
    Radio, radios
    Solo, solos

- If the word ends in –y preceded by a vowel, simply add an –s to the root word.

    Boys
    Keys
    Plays

- If the word ends in –y preceded by a consonant, change the y to an i and add an –es to the root.

    Cry, Cries
    Lady, Ladies
    Pry, Pries

PREFIXES

A prefix is a word part, such as *anti–, dis–, extra–,* that is added to the beginning of a word to change its meaning. When adding a prefix to a word, you can simply add the prefix to the beginning. There is never a need to drop letters or otherwise change the root word.

Dis + advantage = Disadvantage
Extra + ordinary = Extraordinary
Mis + speak = Misspeak
Un + nerving = Unnerving

SUFFIXES

Suffixes are a bit more complicated than prefixes. Suffixes are word parts, such as *–ly, –ness, –less,* that when added to the end of a root word changes its meaning. Different rules exist for adding suffixes, depending upon the root word and whether or not the suffix begins with a vowel or a consonant.

There are only 10 spelling questions on the HSPT, and of those, there may be only one that involves suffixes; so we won't spend much time here on the many rules that you will learn in your English class. Instead, let's look at some examples of properly used suffixes.

Consonant Suffixes (ex: *–ful, –less, –ly, –ment, –ness*)

Advertise, advertise*ment*
Flaw, flaw*less*
Soft, Soft*ly*
Ultimate, ultimate*ly*

Hope, hope*ful*
Doubt, doubt*ful*
Happy, happ*iness*

Vowel Suffixes (ex: *–able, –ed, –er, –ing*)

Agree, agree*able*
Begin, begi*nner*
Cry, Cry*ing*
Fry, fr*ies*, fry*ing*
Manage, manage*able*
Marry, marr*ied*
Move, mov*ed*
Offense, offens*ive*

Parent, parent*ing*
Plan, plan*ning*
Phone, phon*ing*
Sway, sway*ing*
Swim, swim*mer*

HSPT Spelling Word List

Below is a list of words that you may see on the HSPT in the spelling section of the Language subtest. You may either read this list and become familiar with them or have someone read the words to you to see if you know the correct spelling. If there are words on the list that you find challenging, add them to your journal and practice spelling them.

addition	dilemma	perjury
admiral	disastrous	personality
access	echo	performed
accommodate	especially	perturbed
accuracy	essential	piece
accumulate	exhausted	politician
acquiring	explanation	possessive
acquit	expire	precocious
across	feisty	prescription
adjective	forehead	primarily
aerobic	forty	protein
ambiguous	gorgeous	radioactive
annoyance	hatched	receipt
antivirus	horrifying	receive
anxious	hospital	recite
apparently	hundredth	refreshments
arctic	insatiable	rehearse
assignment	jeopardize	reliably
authority	jewelry	responsible
awkward	knowledge	revolution
basically	library	scholarly
beginning	license	serviceable
biannually	literature	sieve
brilliant	malicious	skating
burglary	meant	sleepiness
capably	melody	souvenir
celebrity	miniature	studious
colonel	minimizing	tedious
columns	miracle	testimony
compatible	mischievous	tyranny
compliment	mysteriously	unanimous
concerned	naturally	unavoidable
contagious	necessary	unconscious
contentment	necessity	unique
correlation	noticeable	universally
council	novelist	unnatural
counselor	occasion	usually
critique	ominous	vaccinate
cylinder	opponent	vigilant
deficit	optimistic	
depress	pacifier	

Spelling Practice

Now it's time to find some spelling errors. In the following questions look for errors in spelling only. If there are no errors, choose (d) *No mistakes.*

1. (a) I am not responsable for the mistake.
   (b) The baby does not need a pacifier.
   (c) The scholarly article is very long.
   (d) No mistakes.

2. (a) I would like to be a novelist when I graduate.
   (b) The birds hatched on time.
   (c) The plant is most unnatural.
   (d) No mistakes.

3. (a) The vote was unanimous.
   (b) Protein is a big part of my diet.
   (c) I like to watch figure skateing.
   (d) No mistakes.

4. (a) He can aquire the knowledge over time.
   (b) I remain optimistic.
   (c) There is no malicious intent.
   (d) No mistakes.

5. (a) Literature is my favorite class.
   (b) That is not necesary.
   (c) Flour is an essential ingredient.
   (d) No mistakes.

6. (a) I should live in the libary.
   (b) The explanation is satisfactory.
   (c) There is a small deficit.
   (d) No mistakes.

7. (a) Finaly, I won the game.
   (b) That is a real dilemma.
   (c) He is truly a miracle.
   (d) No mistakes.

8. (a) She is very mischievous.
   (b) The conversation was awkward.
   (c) I am slightly disapointed.
   (d) No mistakes.

9. (a) I hope they acquit the innocent woman.
   (b) Just walk accross the bridge.
   (c) I am paid biannually.
   (d) No mistakes.

10. (a) I'm basically a superhero.
    (b) Burglary is a terrible thing.
    (c) She is no longer contagious.
    (d) No mistakes.

(Answers are on page 289.)

COMPOSITION

The last part of the language subtest is the composition section. This section will begin with question 289 and end with the very last question of the HSPT, number 298! The composition section has a few different question types, each designed to test your knowledge of sentence or paragraph structure. There are also questions that ask you to either label a paragraph with a title or to choose a sentence that best fits under a given title. Let's take a look at each type of composition question, and the various formats, that you will see on your HSPT.

Sentence Completion

You will see a couple of different types of sentence completion questions. One will ask you to choose a missing word or two and the other will ask you to finish the sentence.

CHOOSE THE MISSING WORD OR WORDS

The sentence you are given will be missing a word needed to join two parts of the sentence. The two parts will either be similar or different in meaning. You must choose the correct word or words to join the two parts of the sentence together. Once you identify the two phrases as being similar or different, you can then look at the answer choices to find the correct transition word. Look at the following example.

➡ **Example 1** _____

Choose the correct word or words to join the thoughts together.

I really like her _____ she can be selfish.

(a) because
(b) in addition
(c) even though
(d) None of these

Notice the two phrases above. The first is positive, *I really like her*, and the second is negative, *she can be selfish*. Because the complete sentence begins with a positive tone and ends with a negative phrase, the word that joins them must be a reversal word or words. The correct answer is the only answer choice that changes the direction of the sentence, which is choice (c) *even though*.

In the sentence completion questions, you will be choosing answers that either continue the first thought, *continuing words*, or answers that link the phrases in a manner that explains the differences, *reversal words*. The following are some examples of answer choices you may see, listed as either *continuing* or *reversal* words.

Continuing Words Practice

See how many different words from the below list of *continuing* words can be used to complete the sentences that follow.

and	furthermore	since
because	in fact	so
consequently	likewise	therefore
for example	meanwhile	thus
for instance	moreover	

1. I really love eating healthy food, _____ it makes me feel so good.

2. My mother is my favorite person, _____ she always makes me laugh.

3. She is always volunteering; _____ she worked at the food pantry just this week.

4. He never studies; _____ he failed the English test.

5. I enjoy skiing; _____ I live near a ski resort.

(Answers are on page 290.)

Reversal Words Practice

Use *reversal* words to complete sentences such as those listed below. See how many different words from the list of reversal words could be used to complete each of the following sentences.

although	in contrast	otherwise
but	in spite of	rather
conversely	instead	though
despite	nevertheless	while
even though	nonetheless	yet
however	not withstanding	

1. She is very patient, _____ yesterday she really threw a fit.

2. Bob cannot play the trumpet, _____ he took lessons for years.

3. I love the beach, _____ I hate when sand gets between my toes.

4. My feet are so sore,_____ I'm going to dance all night.

5. Cats and dogs are usually enemies, _____ my dog and cat are great friends.

(Answers are on page 290.)

COMPLETE THE SENTENCE

You will see another type of sentence completion question in which you will be asked to finish a sentence rather than find the missing word. Look at the following example.

➡ Example 2_____

Choose the group of words that *best* completes the sentence.

My boss said I would receive a raise if _____.

(a) the project assigned I was working on I do well
(b) the project is a good job that I work on
(c) I did well on the project I was assigned
(d) the project I was assigned is done good

The key to answering this question correctly is to eliminate answer choices that you know to be grammatically incorrect or wordy. You should also look for answer choices where the subject is *doing* the action rather than the subject being *acted upon*. Let's look at each of the answer choices for Example 2. Are there any that are grammatically incorrect? The answer is yes, answer choice (b). The word *work* should be *worked*. Answer choice (d) is also incorrect. The word *good* should be *well* (feel good, do well). Next, rule out answers that do not make sense, like answer choice (a). Now you've narrowed it down to just one answer choice, which is concise, grammatically correct, and has all of the information in a format that makes sense.

Here is a set of steps for answering questions that involve completing a sentence or choosing the best sentence.

1. Read the sentence prompt, then all four answer choices.
2. As you read, eliminate any sentences that have errors or poor grammar.
3. If you have more than one choice remaining, eliminate sentences that sound awkward or confusing.
4. If you've narrowed it down to two sentences, choose a sentence that uses action verbs rather than passive verbs, where subjects act rather than being acted upon.
5. If you still have more than one choice left, choose the shortest answer choice but one that is not missing any information.

Some things to watch for when choosing the best sentence include run-on sentences, repeated information, and dangling modifiers. Let's take a brief look at each.

RUN-ON SENTENCES

These have more than one complete sentence that is joined to another by a comma, or worse, no comma.

> Mary purchased all of the yarn that she needed to make the sweater, she made a beautiful sweater.

To correct the above sentence, use a conjunction to join two parts or rewrite it as two separate sentences.

> Mary purchased all of the yarn and used it to make a beautiful sweater.
> Mary purchased all of the yarn. She knitted a beautiful sweater.

DON'T REPEAT

The shortest sentence that contains all of the pertinent information is most likely the correct one. Avoid sentences that are repetitive.

> Mary purchased yarn and made a sweater with the yarn she purchased.

This sentence would read better if it was either:

> Mary purchased yarn and made a sweater.
> Mary made a sweater with yarn she purchased.

AVOID DANGLING MODIFIERS

A dangling modifier is a word or phrase that describes something that is missing.

> While eating, the food tasted bad.

In the example above, the person that is actually eating is not in the sentence. The sentence reads as if the *food* is doing the eating. If a statement is unclear, then it is not the *best* sentence. Look at the example below.

> When boating across the ocean, a shark attacked the bottom of the boat.

It appears as though the shark is the one operating the boat. A better sentence would be clearer.

> As the man sailed across the ocean, a shark attacked the bottom of his boat.

EXPRESSING THE IDEA MOST CLEARLY

This type of question is very similar to the *Complete the Sentence* type of question, with one exception: you are not completing a sentence but choosing a complete sentence as your answer. You will be given four sentences and asked which one expresses the idea most clearly.

➡️ **Example 3**_____

Which of these expresses the idea most clearly?

(a) The author writes very long books and he is also elderly.
(b) The elderly author's books are very long.
(c) The author is elderly and his long books are written.
(d) All of the long books are written by the old author.

Use the same strategies for sentence completions for this type of question. Remember to look for the shortest answer that has no errors and contains all of the information. The answer to Example 3 is choice (b). It is the clearest and most concise of the answer choices.

WHICH OF THESE FITS UNDER THE TOPIC/BEST TOPIC TITLE

In this type of question, you'll be given a topic and asked to read four sentences to find which *one* will best fit under that topic. It is important that you read all of the answer choices then find the *best* one. Cross out wrong answers as you go, and once you have it narrowed down to two, or better yet just one, make your choice.

➡️ **Example 4**_____

Which of these best fits in under the topic "Adjusting to College Life?"

(a) Students should try to resolve roommate conflicts quickly.
(b) College graduates tend to have high starting salaries.
(c) Ask your favorite high school teacher for a recommendation for your application.
(d) Good study habits are essential to getting into college.

The correct answer is choice (a). All of the answer choices have something to do with college; however, only answer choice (a) is specifically related to adjusting to college life.

A similar form of this question is one in which you are given a paragraph and asked to find the best title.

➡️ **Example 5**_____

Which of these would be the best title for the following paragraph?

Composting is a form of recycling. When composting, save all non-meat food scraps and throw them in a pile in your yard. Mix in leaves and grass clippings. Mix up your compost pile often. In just six months, the compost is ready to use as fertilizer in your garden.

(a) Composting Saves Money
(b) The Many Uses for Compost
(c) How to Compost
(d) None of these

Each of the answer choices is about composting, so you must be careful. Notice that the paragraph never mentions money. It does mention recycling, so you may think the passage implies that you are saving money; however, you should base your answer *only* on what is written. The paragraph mentions only one use for compost—fertilizer—so answer choice (b) is incorrect. The correct answer is choice (c) How to Compost.

BEST THEME FOR ONE PARAGRAPH

If you think carefully, this question type can be easy. However, since these are usually the last couple of questions on the test, you may by now feel tired and rushed. All you have to do is skim through each answer and ask yourself if this is a small topic or a big topic. For a theme to be meaningful in just one paragraph, it cannot be too broad a topic.

➡ Example 6

Which of these would be best for a theme for one paragraph?

(a) The Effects of Recycling on Global Warming
(b) Easy Ways to Recycle in Your Own Home
(c) What Are the Impacts of Global Warming?
(d) This History of Climate Changes

Global warming is a very broad topic and, chances are, any piece of it will also be a broad topic. The only topic here small enough to discuss meaningfully in one paragraph is answer choice (b) Easy Ways to Recycle in Your Own Home. While it is true that one could write a book on this topic, it is by far the simplest topic of the four choices and therefore the *best* answer.

Best Theme for One Paragraph Practice

Can you find the <u>three</u> topics of the ten listed below that would be best suited for a one-paragraph essay?

1. Understanding the Global Economy

2. Why Yeast Is an Important Ingredient for Bread Making

3. The History of Australia

4. Four Ways to Reduce Your Food Budget

5. Should College Tuition Be Free for All Americans? Include Pros and Cons

6. The Evolution of Humans

7. How to Dance to the Cupid Shuffle

8. Gun Control in America

9. The Biography of Steve Jobs

10. The Evolution of Speech

(Answers are on page 290.)

PARAGRAPH STRUCTURE

There are two types of questions that come under this heading. The first is a question that will ask you to find one sentence that does not belong in the paragraph. The second is a question that asks you to identify the best place in a paragraph to insert a given sentence. Here you must make sure that the ideas in each sentence have a logical progression or flow to the next sentence. Let's look at each type in the following examples.

➡ Example 7

Which sentence does not belong in this paragraph?

(1) To apply to high school, you must fill out an online application. (2) Only 30% of those who apply are accepted. (3) Next, you must submit a recommendation by your math teacher. (4) Finally, ask your school's guidance department to mail your official transcripts to the high school.

(a) Sentence 1
(b) Sentence 2
(c) Sentence 3
(d) Sentence 4

While each of the four sentences has something to do with the high school application process, only sentence (2) is not specifically about the process itself. Knowing how many students are accepted is not part of the application process. The correct answer is therefore choice (b).

➡ Example 8

Where should the sentence, "Bring the eggs to room temperature before adding," be placed in the paragraph below?

(1) To make a cheesecake, you must mix together the butter and the cheese. (2) Add the eggs. (3) Add the sugar and mix well. (4) Pour the batter in a pan and bake.

(a) Between sentences 1 and 2
(b) Between sentences 2 and 3
(c) Between sentences 3 and 4
(d) After sentence 4

Because the sentence is about the eggs being at room temperature, this sentence must come before sentence (2) where you are told to add the eggs. It wouldn't make sense to add it after that point, and it is not an option for it to come before the first sentence. You may sometimes see choice (d) as "the sentence does not fit." When this choice is offered, it is *not likely* the correct answer. If you feel that the sentence doesn't fit, reread the passage before selecting this for your answer.

ANSWERS EXPLAINED FOR CHAPTER 8

Capitalization Practice (page 258)

1. **(a)** *Doctor* should only be capitalized when referring to a specific person. Remember, as soon as you find the answer with a mistake (and you are certain), don't waste time reading the rest of the answer choices.

2. **(c)** *Principal* Crowley is a specific person, so his title should be capitalized.

3. **(a)** *Street* is part of the proper noun in an address and should be capitalized. Nelson *Street*.

4. **(b)** *Southwest*, as used in this sentence, is a compass point, not a place, and should not be capitalized.

5. **(c)** In an address, all words are capitalized. Dear *Madam*.

6. **(d)** No mistakes.

7. **(b)** *Mount* is part of the landmark and should be capitalized. *Mount* Greylock.

8. **(a)** *Fourth* is part of the holiday name and should be capitalized. The *Fourth* of July.

9. **(b)** *Join* is a continuation of the initial sentence and is not the first word of a quote; therefore, it should not be capitalized. "Mother," she said, "*join* us for dinner."

10. **(b)** *Will* is the first word of a quote and the beginning of Larry's sentence, so it should be capitalized. Larry asked, "*Will* you be moving soon?"

Punctuation Practice (page 263)

1. **(b)** *Sr.* is an abbreviation for Senior and must have a period. Tom Fier *Sr.*

2. **(b)** *Month*, in this case, is possessive, and should include an apostrophe *s*. A *month's* time will go by quickly.

3. **(a)** *Nelly* is an address and should be followed by a comma. *Nelly*, are you older than Muriel?

4. **(c)** This is an indirect question and should not be followed by a question mark.

5. **(a)** The last adjective to precede a noun should not be followed by a comma. The cute, yellow, *playful* dog is named Jackson.

6. **(d)** No mistakes.

7. **(d)** No mistakes.

8. **(c)** The parenthetical phrase should be set off by commas. My new position, *high school history teacher*, is rewarding.

9. **(b)** The introductory name should be followed by a comma. *Stacy*, please pass me the salt.

10. **(a)** The day, in a date, is always followed by a comma. We were married on March *28*, 1987.

Subject-Verb Agreement Practice (page 266)

1. The children *have* an allergy to cats.
   The *child* has an allergy to cats.

2. The *cats* love the children.
   The cat *loves* the children.

3. They *don't* know how to unlock the door.
   He doesn't know how to unlock the door.

4. The *snake* hisses to warn its prey.

5. Bill and his family *are* very nice neighbors.

6. Susan and her three children *eat* at the diner.

7. Each of the pets *is* for sale.
   All of the pets are for sale.

8. The *idea, which is a good one*, is to work together.

9. Many *believe* there will be a storm on Tuesday.

10. Much *is* still not known about global warming.

Adjectives and Adverbs Practice (page 269)

Sentence	Describing What?	Adjective or Adverb
The boy is *quick*.	the boy—a noun	Adjective
The boy runs *quickly*.	runs—a verb	Adverb
The boy runs very *slowly*.	slowly—an adverb	Adverb
Unfortunately, we will be late.	we will be late—the entire clause	Adverb

Commonly Misused Words Practice (page 274)

1. I wish I were smarter *than* my teacher.

2. If you weigh *less* than 80 pounds you cannot go on the ride.

3. I have *a lot* of confidence in your abilities.

4. Arizona has many *deserts*.

5. *Except* for me, there will only be one other girl there.

6. *There* are way *too* many people in this elevator.

7. He is the only one, *besides* me, who will take the class.

8. The parking valet cannot *lose* the keys or he'll be fired.

9. *Whose* shirt is this?

10. I think that *among* all of the players, Jim is the best.

11. **It's** a shame that vacation is almost over.

12. I hope **they're** ready when we get **there**.

13. I wish that the **weather** would change so we can play our game.

14. Stand **beside** me if you want to see.

15. The teacher, **who** is new this year, is my favorite.

16. My favorite **dessert** is apple pie.

17. This is the friend **that** I have known the longest.

18. **Who's** ever going to know if we don't tell?

19. To **whom** does this sneaker belong?

20. **Between** the two of us, I can keep a secret.

Usage Practice (pages 275–276)

1. **(a)** *Weather* refers to the climate and should be replaced with *whether*. I don't know *whether* or not he is coming.

2. **(b)** *Once* is past tense and must be paired with a past tense verb. Once, I *wore* a dress that was too long.

3. **(a)** *Business* is singular, so the verb should be *is* and not *are*. My father's business *is* very successful.

4. **(c)** The subject does not agree with the verb tense. Was Danny hungry *yesterday*?

5. **(c)** *Randy* is singular but *bake* is the plural tense. Randy *bakes* pies for Thanksgiving dinner.

6. **(a)** This sentence has a double negative, *hardly never*. I hardly *ever* skip my homework.

7. **(c)** This sentence does not maintain parallelism. The last verb should be the same tense as the first two. She rode the bus, walked a mile, then *climbed* the stairs.

8. **(d)** No mistakes.

9. **(b)** Because *slow* is modifying the action verb, it should end in *–ly*. The cyclist rode *slowly* down the hill.

10. **(b)** Because there are only two, the word *faster* should be used to compare. He is the *faster* of the two runners.

Spelling Practice (page 280)

1. **(a)** *Responsable* is correctly spelled *responsible*.

2. **(d)** No mistakes.

3. **(c)** *Skateing* is correctly spelled *skating*.

4. **(a)** *Aquire* is correctly spelled *acquire*.

5. **(b)** *Necesary* is correctly spelled *necessary*.

6. **(a)** *Libary* is correctly spelled *library*.

7. **(a)** *Finaly* is correctly spelled *finally*.

8. **(c)** *Disapointed* is correctly spelled *disappointed*.

9. **(b)** *Accross* is correctly spelled *across*.

10. **(d)** No mistakes.

Continuing Words Practice (page 281)

1. **Because** and **since** are possible answers.

2. **And, because, moreover,** and **furthermore** are possible answers.

3. **For example, in fact,** and **for instance** are possible answers.

4. **Consequently, therefore,** and **furthermore** are possible answers.

5. **Furthermore** and **moreover** are possible answers.

Reversal Words Practice (page 282)

1. **But, even though,** and **although** are possible answers.

2. **But, however, nevertheless,** and **though** are possible answers.

3. **Although, but,** and **yet** are possible answers.

4. **Nonetheless, but,** and **yet** are possible answers.

5. **However, though,** and **although** are possible answers.

Best Theme for One Paragraph Practice (page 285)

The correct answer is **2**, **4**, and **7**. All of the other answer choices would take considerably longer than one paragraph to explain.

WRAP IT UP WITH PRACTICE

The difficulty with the Language subtest, as you most likely figured out by now, is that there is a lot to know! Not only are there 60 questions, but there are many different types of questions, all attempting to assess a wide array of skills from spelling and punctuation to sentence structure and paragraph form. Let's take a look at the important strategies to remember as we wrap things up.

General Language Strategies

- Remember the timing, and answer 2–3 questions per minute.
- It's okay to choose choice (d) *No mistakes*, but selecting it more than 4 or 5 times would be unusual. Circle these, and if you have extra time, you can come back and double check them.
- Use your instinct, common sense, and sound of words/phrases to guide you.

Capitalization, Punctuation, and Usage

- Read each sentence until you find one with a mistake.
- If you are CERTAIN that you have found a mistake, choose that as your answer and move on.
- Review the list of commonly misused words such as *they're, their, there*.
- You may find 4–5 with *No mistakes*. More than that would be unusual.

Spelling

- If you see a word that you are CERTAIN is misspelled, choose that as your answer and move on.
- As you read the answer choices, cross out any that you KNOW have no mistakes.
- You may find 1–2 with *No mistakes*. More than that would be unusual.

Composition

- For sentence completions, identify if the two phrases are similar or different, then look for the correct transition word.
- Read the sentence in your head to see if it sounds correct.
- When finishing sentences, always avoid run-on sentences and dangling modifiers.
- Rule out any answer choices that have errors in grammar or usage.
- When unsure, choose the shortest sentence that contains all of the information.

Now that you've reviewed the Language subtest, you are ready to try it on your own, putting all of your knowledge and strategies to the test.

25 MINUTES

Samples:

A. (a) Jackson and Siri are good dogs.
   (b) Emma and Ryan are my friends.
   (c) Mr Smith lives next door.
   (d) No mistakes.

B. (a) Maine is north of Virginia.
   (b) May I have a peice of pie?
   (c) It's a long drive to Boston.
   (d) No mistakes.

Correct marking of samples:

A. Ⓐ Ⓑ ● Ⓓ

B. Ⓐ ● Ⓒ Ⓓ

In questions 239–278 try to find errors in punctuation, capitalization, or word usage. If you find a mistake, select the letter in front of that sentence as your answer. Some questions will have *No mistakes* for choice (d). For these questions, if you do not find any errors, mark (d) *No mistakes* as your answer.

239. (a) Jay Grabow sr. owns a golf course.
    (b) You'll need to read the directions first.
    (c) The teachers love their students.
    (d) No mistakes.

240. (a) Sales increased this year by eleven percent.
    (b) My friends are visiting family in Lynn, Massachusetts.
    (c) George spoke to Sarah and he earlier today.
    (d) No mistakes.

241. (a) Why did you say that?
    (b) Jeannie was too tall for the ride.
    (c) Mom asked, "What time is it?"
    (d) Each dot on the map represent a city.

242. (a) How did you make this?
    (b) In a months time I will graduate.
    (c) The movie begins at six o'clock today.
    (d) No mistakes.

243. (a) Will you be at school tomorrow?
    (b) Katrina and Joe play soccer.
    (c) I think his father is very tall.
    (d) No mistakes.

244. (a) I will have a week's worth of homework.
    (b) No, I don't think it will rain today.
    (c) There were hardly no snow days this winter.
    (d) No mistakes.

245. (a) My dog always trying to please me brought me my slippers.
    (b) I played with the boy who lives next door.
    (c) Sally, please help me carry the groceries.
    (d) No mistakes.

246. (a) Usually, I read slowly.
    (b) Colleen held Jada's hand.
    (c) Don't these taste awful?
    (d) Max said, "if you insist, then okay."

247. (a) He also loves to swim.
    (b) Greg said "Wait in line."
    (c) Denise, please teach the class.
    (d) No mistakes.

GO TO THE NEXT PAGE ➡

248. (a) Christina, please behave today.
(b) "Well, I give up," said the woman.
(c) His cousin served in the gulf war.
(d) No mistakes.

249. (a) This is the best soup I ever made.
(b) Bill, will Betty be attending today?
(c) The flu has been spreading at school.
(d) The jewelry belongs to Hannah and I.

250. (a) Add the flour add the milk, and mix the batter.
(b) By the way, I will be late tomorrow.
(c) Monday at noontime, she went away to college.
(d) No mistakes.

251. (a) Waitress, please bring the check.
(b) Debbie ate bread and crackers.
(c) Did school close early today.
(d) Everyone loves ice cream.

252. (a) The clouds arrived suddenly.
(b) Wow, he said, "I'm beat!"
(c) No one will ever know.
(d) No mistakes.

253. (a) You should get your sneakers put them on and go for a run.
(b) Harrison is the taller of the two brothers.
(c) Why, this pie is delicious!
(d) No mistakes.

254. (a) "Jackson, do you want to go for a walk?"
(b) "I see where you are hiding," said Dakota.
(c) He is the funnier of all of them.
(d) The ship's captain will be honored at the ceremony.

255. (a) She will leave at 2:30 P.M.
(b) Where is Elizabeth at?
(c) She and I walk together on Mondays.
(d) Sylvia proudly refused.

256. (a) The mountains of the northeast are beautiful.
(b) Pardon me, may I order now?
(c) Linda, who is very talented, sings in the choir.
(d) No mistakes.

257. (a) My brother loves reading novels.
(b) There are hardly any days left of summer.
(c) I like them kids on the soccer team.
(d) No mistakes.

258. (a) Siri, my new puppy, is so cute.
(b) "It's a lovely day," she replied.
(c) They're a very smart group.
(d) The school has it's own gym.

259. (a) Please respond to Mark or I.
(b) The company is doing well this year.
(c) Their farm has cows, pigs, and chickens.
(d) No mistakes.

260. (a) Will I be able to leave early today?
(b) Between the three of them, Susan is the tallest.
(c) He is the most intelligent student in the class.
(d) No mistakes.

261. (a) All of the snacks, except the oatmeal cookies, have nuts.
(b) Whipped cream and nuts are perfect on ice cream.
(c) Neither Sam or Will is allergic to peanuts.
(d) No mistakes.

262. (a) Please forgive us for being late.
(b) Have you met the dance instructor?
(c) It is too far for me to walk.
(d) "I will see you," said Jennifer, "When I return."

GO TO THE NEXT PAGE ➡

263. (a) She attended a boarding school, which was in New Hampshire.
   (b) My middle name given to me by my grandfather is Lee.
   (c) I can at least hold the door for you.
   (d) I knew they had already left.

264. (a) The magazine story, "Hiking the White Mountains," inspired me.
   (b) How old is Matthew.
   (c) After all, I'm only a sophomore.
   (d) No mistakes.

265. (a) Either Mr. Topel or Ms. Meyer will be there.
   (b) Their always talking in class.
   (c) Her employer pays her biweekly.
   (d) No mistakes.

266. (a) They was here, but I'm not sure on which day.
   (b) I visited Reston, Virginia, Orlando, Florida, and Austin, Texas.
   (c) Some of the dogs ran away from the kennel.
   (d) My sister decided to finish raking the yard on her own.

267. (a) Coach O'Leary may I play now?
   (b) *The Giving Tree*, a children's book, is my favorite.
   (c) Have you ever seen such a giant pumpkin?
   (d) No mistakes.

268. (a) "Santiago scored the highest on the test," said Jacome.
   (b) Pam, Donna, and I love to dance.
   (c) By the way I will not be able to attend the meeting.
   (d) No mistakes.

269. (a) If you are not careful, you'll hurt yourself.
   (b) I like to read and knit, hiking.
   (c) My business is based in Leesburg, Virginia.
   (d) The train was not delayed.

270. (a) A leave fell from the tree.
   (b) S. L. Smith is the author of the novel.
   (c) I'm vacationing in Portland, Maine.
   (d) No mistakes.

271. (a) It's not the right time.
   (b) How often should I floss my teeth?
   (c) I'm not ready!" yelled Rodney.
   (d) No mistakes.

272. (a) Where should I set the statue?
   (b) The recipe calls for the following, flour, sugar, and eggs.
   (c) "Kathy," said Larry, "please put the horse in the barn."
   (d) No mistakes.

273. (a) The turtle crawled slow during the race.
   (b) I have a few vegetables left.
   (c) I studied Spanish in college.
   (d) Would you write me a letter?

274. (a) Some houses, according to the stories, are haunted.
   (b) "I Feel Lucky" is her daughter's favorite song.
   (c) However, I feeling much better today.
   (d) No mistakes.

275. (a) Jim went to the luncheon with Jennifer.
   (b) He's running around the track.
   (c) She had fewer milk than her brother.
   (d) No mistakes.

GO TO THE NEXT PAGE ➡

276. (a) It rained on Monday, but on Tuesday the sun came out.
   (b) She sews and iron her son's shirts.
   (c) Kevin Wu was this year's valedictorian.
   (d) Ryan and Scott both like chocolate.

277. (a) William has ate the last of the pie.
   (b) When I was sad, my friend made me feel better.
   (c) My dog and my cat were lost.
   (d) No mistakes.

278. (a) The whole garden was wet from the rain.
   (b) She was hardly no good at mathematics.
   (c) You're the best friend I've ever known.
   (d) No mistakes.

For questions 279–288, look only for mistakes in spelling.

279. (a) Her grandmother gave her a new carrige.
   (b) Naturally, she loves her child.
   (c) It is unnecessary to lock both doors.
   (d) No mistakes.

280. (a) It can be a nuisance to read every detail.
   (b) The food was included in the cost of lodging.
   (c) In adition to math, I like history.
   (d) No mistakes.

281. (a) I was dissatisfied with the service.
   (b) He was ademant about following rules.
   (c) There is no scientific proof.
   (d) No mistakes.

282. (a) I sprained my wrist while dribbling.
   (b) My ankel is very sore today.
   (c) You are essentially correct.
   (d) No mistakes.

283. (a) He is always running somewhere.
   (b) I served on the zoning committee.
   (c) I cannot accommodate your request.
   (d) No mistakes.

284. (a) You must have an occupancy permit to live there.
   (b) He completed the test successfully.
   (c) The doctor preformed the operation quickly.
   (d) No mistakes.

285. (a) The sauce was bubbling over the pot.
   (b) He was granted amnesty by the board.
   (c) It occured to Sean that he may be wrong.
   (d) No mistakes.

286. (a) By tripleing the ingredients you can make more.
   (b) You have a charming personality.
   (c) Personally, I love sleeping late.
   (d) No mistakes.

287. (a) That's very aggravating.
   (b) The new calender has larger print.
   (c) He has always been my adversary.
   (d) No mistakes.

288. (a) It is unnatural to dislike candy.
   (b) Please disregard that last comment.
   (c) That was very surprising.
   (d) No mistakes.

GO TO THE NEXT PAGE ➡

289. Choose the best word to join the two phrases.

I ate my entire dinner _____ it was delicious.

(a) even though
(b) because
(c) however
(d) None of these

290. Choose the best word to join the two phrases.

He had a low grade, _____ he studied all of the time.

(a) even though
(b) because
(c) moreover
(d) None of these

291. Which of these sentences expresses the idea most clearly?

(a) The basketball team has a tall captain and he is not only tall but thin too.
(b) The captain of the basketball team is tall and thin.
(c) There is a person who is tall and thin and he is the captain of the basketball team.
(d) The tall captain is thin and is on the basketball team.

292. Choose the group of words that best completes the sentence.

The chef instructed us to _____.

(a) grill the meat but not until we put salt on it for 10 minutes
(b) grill the meat only after putting salt on it then grill it for 10 minutes
(c) put salt on the meat and then grill it for 10 minutes
(d) for ten minutes grill the meat after putting salt on it

293. Which of these sentences expresses the idea most clearly?

(a) Sleeping well is part of eating right, exercising and being healthy.
(b) Exercise and healthy people usually eat right and sleep well.
(c) People who exercise are healthy which makes them sleep well and eat right.
(d) People who exercise, eat right, and sleep well are healthy.

294. Which of these would fit best under the topic "Math in Real Life"?

(a) There are many different types of math.
(b) Do girls and boys learn math in the same way?
(c) Four years of math are required in high school.
(d) Shoppers use percentages to figure discounts on sale items.

295. Which topic is the *best* for a one-paragraph essay?

(a) The History of the Presidential Election
(b) A Year in the Life of the President
(c) How to Change a Flat Tire
(d) None of these

296. Which of these would be the best topic for the following paragraph?

Rabbits make great pets for children. They are lovable and playful. Rabbits can live in hutches outdoors year round in most areas.

(a) How to Care for a Rabbit
(b) The Difference between Wild and Domestic Rabbits
(c) Why Rabbits Make Good Pets
(d) None of these

GO TO THE NEXT PAGE ➡

297. Where should the sentence, "Players roll the dice and count the dots they see," be placed in the paragraph below?

(1) Give each player a token. (2) Each player places their token on the starting square of the game board. (3) Players then advance their token one space for each dot on the dice.

(a) Between sentences (1) and (2).
(b) Between sentences (2) and (3).
(c) After sentence (3).
(d) The sentence does not fit in the paragraph.

298. Which sentence does *not* belong in the paragraph?

(1) Carrot seeds should be planted early in the summer. (2) Carrots will begin to sprout plants after 10 days. (3) Rabbits love to eat fresh carrots. (4) Carrots will be ready to harvest after 60 days.

(a) Sentence 1
(b) Sentence 2
(c) Sentence 3
(d) Sentence 4

STOP

NOTE

Answer explanations in this section are labeled with their corresponding question types. You will need this for the scoring chart on page 301.

ANSWERS EXPLAINED FOR PRACTICE LANGUAGE SUBTEST

239. **(a)** *Sr.*, in Jay Grabow sr., should be capitalized. Jay Grabow *Sr.* (Capitalization)

240. **(c)** The sentence should read, "George spoke to Sarah and him earlier today." Remember that each object should be able to stand alone. George spoke to Sarah. "George spoke to he" doesn't sound right but "George spoke to *him*" sounds perfect. (Usage)

241. **(d)** The subject-verb agreement is not correct. *Each* is singular but *represent* is plural. The sentence should read, "Each dot on the map represent*s* a city." (Usage)

242. **(b)** *Month* should be possessive. "In a *month's* time I will graduate." (Punctuation)

243. **(d)** No mistakes. (Capitalization, Punctuation, Usage)

244. **(c)** This has a double negative, *hardly* and *no*. It should read, "There were hardly *any* snow days this winter." (Usage)

245. **(a)** This sentence is missing commas around the parenthetical phase. It should read, "My dog, always trying to please me, brought me my slippers." (Punctuation)

246. **(d)** *If* should be capitalized because it is the beginning of Max's sentence. The first word inside an initial quote should always be capitalized. (Capitalization)

247. **(b)** A comma is missing after *yelled*. Greg yelled, "Wait in line." (Punctuation)

248. **(c)** Because the Gulf War is the name of a war, it should be capitalized. (Capitalization)

249. **(d)** *Hannah and I* should be *Hannah and me*. Each object must be able to make sense in the sentence by itself. "The jewelry belongs to *me*." (Usage)

250. **(a)** There is a missing comma. In a list, there should be a comma after each item and one before the word *and*. "Add the flour, add the milk, and mix the batter." (Punctuation)

251. **(c)** This is a question and therefore should end with a question mark. "Did school close early today?" (Punctuation)

252. **(b)** Because *Wow* is part of the quote, it should be in quotation marks. "Wow," he said, "I'm beat!" (Punctuation)

253. **(a)** Each action in the list should be followed by a comma. "You should get your sneakers, put them on, and go for a run." (Punctuation)

254. **(c)** When comparing two things, it is appropriate to say *funnier*; however, if someone is the *most* funny of a group, the correct description is *funniest*. (Usage)

255. **(b)** Sentences should never end with a preposition. The word *at* is unnecessary and incorrect. "Where is Elizabeth?" (Usage)

256. **(a)** Because the *Northeast* is describing a region and not a direction, it should be capitalized. "The mountains of the Northeast are beautiful." (Capitalization)

257. **(c)** *Them*, *these*, and *those* can all be used as objects in a sentence; however, only *those* and *these* may be used as modifiers. "I like *those* kids on the soccer team." (Usage)

258. **(d)** *It's* in this case is possessive and should not have an apostrophe. *It's* is a contraction for *it is*. The possessive form of *its* does not have an apostrophe. "The school has *its* own gym." (Usage)

259. **(a)** Separating this into "Please respond to Mark" and "Please respond to I" makes it clear that this sentence should read, "Please respond to Mark or *me*." (Usage)

260. **(b)** *Between* can only be used when referring to two things. How can you be between three things? *Among* is used for more than two things. "*Among* the three of them, Susan is the tallest." (Usage)

261. **(c)** Either/or and neither/nor. "Neither Sam *nor* Will is allergic to peanuts." (Usage)

262. **(d)** Because the word *when* is in the middle of the overall sentence, it should not be capitalized. "I will see you," said Jennifer, "when I return." (Capitalization)

263. **(b)** Commas are used to separate parenthetical phrases or additional information. "My middle name, given to me by my grandfather, is Lee." (Punctuation)

264. **(b)** This is a question and should end with a question mark. "How old is Matthew?" (Punctuation)

265. **(b)** *Their* is possessive; however, in this case the contraction should be used. *They're* is a contraction for they are. "*They're* always talking in class." (Usage)

266. **(a)** *They* is plural but *was* is singular. *Was* should be replaced with *were*. "They *were* here, but I'm not sure on which day." (Usage)

267. **(a)** There should be a comma before the question. "Coach O'Leary, may I play now?" (Punctuation)

268. **(c)** Introductory comments should be separated by a comma. "By the way, I will not be able to attend the meeting." (Punctuation)

269. **(b)** There are two problems with this sentence. Because there is a list of three things, the word *and* should be between the second and third items. The form of the three verbs should be the same: read, knit, and hike (not hiking). "I like to read, knit, and hike." (Usage)

270. **(a)** The article *A* is used to refer to a single item. The singular word for *leaves* is *leaf*. "A *leaf* fell from the tree." (Usage)

271. **(c)** Quotation marks are always in pairs; the first one here is missing. "I'm not ready!" yelled Rodney. (Punctuation)

272. **(b)** Colons should be used when introducing a list. "The recipe calls for the following: flour, sugar, and eggs." (Punctuation)

273. **(a)** The adverb, *slow*, should be *slowly* because crawled is an action and not a linking verb. "The turtle crawled *slowly* during the race." (Usage)

274. **(c)** A sentence can read "I am feeling" or "I feel" but not "I feeling." "However, I *am* feeling much better today." (Usage)

275. **(c)** *Fewer* is a word used when referring to things that can be counted. *Less* is used for things that are measured and not counted. "She had *less* milk than her brother." (Usage)

276. **(b)** Each verb should have the same tense. "She sews and *irons* her son's shirts." (Usage)

277. **(a)** Perfect tense should be *has eaten* and not *had ate*. "William has *eaten* the last of the pie." (Usage)

278. **(b)** This has a double negative *hardly/no*. A double negative is considered poor grammar. "She was hardly *any* good at mathematics." (Usage)

279. **(a)** *Carrige* is correctly spelled *carriage*. (Spelling)

280. **(c)** *Adition* is correctly spelled *addition*. (Spelling)

281. **(b)** *Ademant* is correctly spelled *adamant*. (Spelling)

282. **(b)** *Ankel* is correctly spelled *ankle*. (Spelling)

283. **(d)** No mistakes. (Spelling)

284. **(c)** *Preformed* is correctly spelled *performed*. (Spelling)

285. **(c)** *Occured* is correctly spelled *occurred*. When adding *–ed* to a word that is two syllables, if the emphasis is on the second syllable, you must double the ending consonant. (Spelling)

286. **(a)** When adding *–ing* to a word that ends in *–e*, first drop the *–e* before adding *–ing*. *Tripling*. (Spelling)

287. **(b)** *Calender* is correctly spelled *calendar*. (Spelling)

288. **(d)** No mistakes. (Spelling)

289. **(b)** The correct word must continue the sentence and not reverse it. "I ate my entire dinner *because* it was delicious." (Composition)

290. **(a)** The correct word here must connect the two contradictory parts, so it is a reversal word. "He had one low quiz score, *even though* he studied all of the time." (Composition)

291. **(b)** Always look for the shortest sentence that has no grammatical errors and is not missing any information. (Composition)

292. **(c)** This is the shortest and most clearly expressed sentence. The others are confusing. (Composition)

293. **(d)** This is the only choice that makes sense. The others make unreasonable claims or have grammatical errors. (Composition)

294. **(d)** While math is required in high school, this sentence does not involve using math in "real life." This expression usually means outside of school. (Composition)

295. **(c)** Changing a tire involves only a few steps that can easily be described in one paragraph. The other choices would require more than one paragraph. (Composition)

296. **(c)** The paragraph mentions that rabbits can stay outdoors but does not specifically discuss how to care for rabbits or anything about wild rabbits. (Composition)

297. **(b)** Players must roll the dice before they can move their token. (Composition)

298. **(c)** The other sentences have to do with growing carrots and not about which animals may enjoy them. (Composition)

SCORING YOUR PRACTICE LANGUAGE SUBTEST

Now that you have reviewed the answers and explanations, let's see how well you are doing. Go through the explanations again and count up the number of each question type you answered correctly. Then fill in the chart below.

	Capitalization, Punctuation, Usage	Spelling	Composition	Total
Number of each question type you answered correctly				
Total of each question type	40	10	10	60

First, add up the total number of questions you answered correctly. Then divide that number by 60 and multiply by 100 to determine your raw score for the Language subtest:

$$\text{Raw Score} = \frac{\text{Total Number Correct}}{60 \text{ Total Questions}} = \frac{}{60} \times 100 = \underline{\qquad}\%$$

Next, to determine your raw score for each question type, take the number of questions you answered correctly in each category and divide that number by the total number of questions in each question type. Multiply each answer by 100 to convert to a percent.

$$\text{Capitalization, Punctuation, and Usage} = \frac{\text{Total Number Correct}}{40 \text{ Total Questions}} = \frac{}{40} \times 100 = \underline{\qquad}\%$$

$$\text{Spelling} = \frac{\text{Total Number Correct}}{10 \text{ Total Questions}} = \frac{}{10} \times 100 = \underline{\qquad}\%$$

$$\text{Composition} = \frac{\text{Total Number Correct}}{10 \text{ Total Questions}} = \frac{}{10} \times 100 = \underline{\qquad}\%$$

How well did you do? Make sure to go back and review any areas that you can improve upon.

HSPT Practice Test 1

HOW TO GET THE MOST FROM PRACTICE TEST 1

This test will take two and a half hours to complete and about another half an hour to grade. This is time well spent and will help to lay the groundwork for improving your HSPT score. Here are some of the benefits of taking a practice test. You will:

- familiarize yourself with the test format and subtest instructions.
- get comfortable with the timing and the pace for each subtest.
- get a sense of the level of difficulty of the vocabulary and mathematics.
- determine which topics you have not yet learned and those that need review.
- see how well you do when guessing.

Directions

Tear out the bubble sheets on the following pages and use them to mark your answers. Because this is practice and not the real test, your goal is to learn about yourself. How good are you at guessing on questions you don't know? Did you spend too long on a certain type of question? These are questions you should be able to answer after you complete HSPT Practice Test 1. Remember to note the following:

- Circle question numbers that you had trouble with, skipped, or guessed on, so you can come back to them later if you have extra time. Also review these topics after you score the practice test.
- Circle your answers on the test before you bubble them on your answer sheet.
- There is no penalty for guessing. NEVER LEAVE A QUESTION UNANSWERED.
- Put a check ✔ next to the questions that you feel confident about. It is important that you are getting these correct, and this will build your confidence level.
- Try to do the work in the book if you can. The less time you spend hopping back and forth from test to scratch paper, the more time you will have to answer questions.

Take the practice test in a quiet place where you will not be disturbed. Make sure to time yourself for each subtest. When you are finished, review your score using the scoring tables that follow the test. This will allow you to see which questions you had the most difficulty with, so you can continue working on them. You'll want to pay extra attention to these questions to improve your score.

ANSWER SHEET
HSPT Practice Test 1

HSPT PRACTICE TEST 1

VERBAL SKILLS SUBTEST

1. Ⓐ Ⓑ Ⓒ Ⓓ   16. Ⓐ Ⓑ Ⓒ Ⓓ   31. Ⓐ Ⓑ Ⓒ Ⓓ   46. Ⓐ Ⓑ Ⓒ Ⓓ
2. Ⓐ Ⓑ Ⓒ Ⓓ   17. Ⓐ Ⓑ Ⓒ Ⓓ   32. Ⓐ Ⓑ Ⓒ Ⓓ   47. Ⓐ Ⓑ Ⓒ Ⓓ
3. Ⓐ Ⓑ Ⓒ Ⓓ   18. Ⓐ Ⓑ Ⓒ Ⓓ   33. Ⓐ Ⓑ Ⓒ Ⓓ   48. Ⓐ Ⓑ Ⓒ Ⓓ
4. Ⓐ Ⓑ Ⓒ Ⓓ   19. Ⓐ Ⓑ Ⓒ Ⓓ   34. Ⓐ Ⓑ Ⓒ Ⓓ   49. Ⓐ Ⓑ Ⓒ Ⓓ
5. Ⓐ Ⓑ Ⓒ Ⓓ   20. Ⓐ Ⓑ Ⓒ Ⓓ   35. Ⓐ Ⓑ Ⓒ Ⓓ   50. Ⓐ Ⓑ Ⓒ Ⓓ
6. Ⓐ Ⓑ Ⓒ Ⓓ   21. Ⓐ Ⓑ Ⓒ Ⓓ   36. Ⓐ Ⓑ Ⓒ Ⓓ   51. Ⓐ Ⓑ Ⓒ Ⓓ
7. Ⓐ Ⓑ Ⓒ Ⓓ   22. Ⓐ Ⓑ Ⓒ Ⓓ   37. Ⓐ Ⓑ Ⓒ Ⓓ   52. Ⓐ Ⓑ Ⓒ Ⓓ
8. Ⓐ Ⓑ Ⓒ Ⓓ   23. Ⓐ Ⓑ Ⓒ Ⓓ   38. Ⓐ Ⓑ Ⓒ Ⓓ   53. Ⓐ Ⓑ Ⓒ Ⓓ
9. Ⓐ Ⓑ Ⓒ Ⓓ   24. Ⓐ Ⓑ Ⓒ Ⓓ   39. Ⓐ Ⓑ Ⓒ Ⓓ   54. Ⓐ Ⓑ Ⓒ Ⓓ
10. Ⓐ Ⓑ Ⓒ Ⓓ   25. Ⓐ Ⓑ Ⓒ Ⓓ   40. Ⓐ Ⓑ Ⓒ Ⓓ   55. Ⓐ Ⓑ Ⓒ Ⓓ
11. Ⓐ Ⓑ Ⓒ Ⓓ   26. Ⓐ Ⓑ Ⓒ Ⓓ   41. Ⓐ Ⓑ Ⓒ Ⓓ   56. Ⓐ Ⓑ Ⓒ Ⓓ
12. Ⓐ Ⓑ Ⓒ Ⓓ   27. Ⓐ Ⓑ Ⓒ Ⓓ   42. Ⓐ Ⓑ Ⓒ Ⓓ   57. Ⓐ Ⓑ Ⓒ Ⓓ
13. Ⓐ Ⓑ Ⓒ Ⓓ   28. Ⓐ Ⓑ Ⓒ Ⓓ   43. Ⓐ Ⓑ Ⓒ Ⓓ   58. Ⓐ Ⓑ Ⓒ Ⓓ
14. Ⓐ Ⓑ Ⓒ Ⓓ   29. Ⓐ Ⓑ Ⓒ Ⓓ   44. Ⓐ Ⓑ Ⓒ Ⓓ   59. Ⓐ Ⓑ Ⓒ Ⓓ
15. Ⓐ Ⓑ Ⓒ Ⓓ   30. Ⓐ Ⓑ Ⓒ Ⓓ   45. Ⓐ Ⓑ Ⓒ Ⓓ   60. Ⓐ Ⓑ Ⓒ Ⓓ

QUANTITATIVE SKILLS SUBTEST

61. Ⓐ Ⓑ Ⓒ Ⓓ   74. Ⓐ Ⓑ Ⓒ Ⓓ   87. Ⓐ Ⓑ Ⓒ Ⓓ   100. Ⓐ Ⓑ Ⓒ Ⓓ
62. Ⓐ Ⓑ Ⓒ Ⓓ   75. Ⓐ Ⓑ Ⓒ Ⓓ   88. Ⓐ Ⓑ Ⓒ Ⓓ   101. Ⓐ Ⓑ Ⓒ Ⓓ
63. Ⓐ Ⓑ Ⓒ Ⓓ   76. Ⓐ Ⓑ Ⓒ Ⓓ   89. Ⓐ Ⓑ Ⓒ Ⓓ   102. Ⓐ Ⓑ Ⓒ Ⓓ
64. Ⓐ Ⓑ Ⓒ Ⓓ   77. Ⓐ Ⓑ Ⓒ Ⓓ   90. Ⓐ Ⓑ Ⓒ Ⓓ   103. Ⓐ Ⓑ Ⓒ Ⓓ
65. Ⓐ Ⓑ Ⓒ Ⓓ   78. Ⓐ Ⓑ Ⓒ Ⓓ   91. Ⓐ Ⓑ Ⓒ Ⓓ   104. Ⓐ Ⓑ Ⓒ Ⓓ
66. Ⓐ Ⓑ Ⓒ Ⓓ   79. Ⓐ Ⓑ Ⓒ Ⓓ   92. Ⓐ Ⓑ Ⓒ Ⓓ   105. Ⓐ Ⓑ Ⓒ Ⓓ
67. Ⓐ Ⓑ Ⓒ Ⓓ   80. Ⓐ Ⓑ Ⓒ Ⓓ   93. Ⓐ Ⓑ Ⓒ Ⓓ   106. Ⓐ Ⓑ Ⓒ Ⓓ
68. Ⓐ Ⓑ Ⓒ Ⓓ   81. Ⓐ Ⓑ Ⓒ Ⓓ   94. Ⓐ Ⓑ Ⓒ Ⓓ   107. Ⓐ Ⓑ Ⓒ Ⓓ
69. Ⓐ Ⓑ Ⓒ Ⓓ   82. Ⓐ Ⓑ Ⓒ Ⓓ   95. Ⓐ Ⓑ Ⓒ Ⓓ   108. Ⓐ Ⓑ Ⓒ Ⓓ
70. Ⓐ Ⓑ Ⓒ Ⓓ   83. Ⓐ Ⓑ Ⓒ Ⓓ   96. Ⓐ Ⓑ Ⓒ Ⓓ   109. Ⓐ Ⓑ Ⓒ Ⓓ
71. Ⓐ Ⓑ Ⓒ Ⓓ   84. Ⓐ Ⓑ Ⓒ Ⓓ   97. Ⓐ Ⓑ Ⓒ Ⓓ   110. Ⓐ Ⓑ Ⓒ Ⓓ
72. Ⓐ Ⓑ Ⓒ Ⓓ   85. Ⓐ Ⓑ Ⓒ Ⓓ   98. Ⓐ Ⓑ Ⓒ Ⓓ   111. Ⓐ Ⓑ Ⓒ Ⓓ
73. Ⓐ Ⓑ Ⓒ Ⓓ   86. Ⓐ Ⓑ Ⓒ Ⓓ   99. Ⓐ Ⓑ Ⓒ Ⓓ   112. Ⓐ Ⓑ Ⓒ Ⓓ

ANSWER SHEET
HSPT Practice Test 1

READING SUBTEST

113. Ⓐ Ⓑ Ⓒ Ⓓ	129. Ⓐ Ⓑ Ⓒ Ⓓ	145. Ⓐ Ⓑ Ⓒ Ⓓ	161. Ⓐ Ⓑ Ⓒ Ⓓ
114. Ⓐ Ⓑ Ⓒ Ⓓ	130. Ⓐ Ⓑ Ⓒ Ⓓ	146. Ⓐ Ⓑ Ⓒ Ⓓ	162. Ⓐ Ⓑ Ⓒ Ⓓ
115. Ⓐ Ⓑ Ⓒ Ⓓ	131. Ⓐ Ⓑ Ⓒ Ⓓ	147. Ⓐ Ⓑ Ⓒ Ⓓ	163. Ⓐ Ⓑ Ⓒ Ⓓ
116. Ⓐ Ⓑ Ⓒ Ⓓ	132. Ⓐ Ⓑ Ⓒ Ⓓ	148. Ⓐ Ⓑ Ⓒ Ⓓ	164. Ⓐ Ⓑ Ⓒ Ⓓ
117. Ⓐ Ⓑ Ⓒ Ⓓ	133. Ⓐ Ⓑ Ⓒ Ⓓ	149. Ⓐ Ⓑ Ⓒ Ⓓ	165. Ⓐ Ⓑ Ⓒ Ⓓ
118. Ⓐ Ⓑ Ⓒ Ⓓ	134. Ⓐ Ⓑ Ⓒ Ⓓ	150. Ⓐ Ⓑ Ⓒ Ⓓ	166. Ⓐ Ⓑ Ⓒ Ⓓ
119. Ⓐ Ⓑ Ⓒ Ⓓ	135. Ⓐ Ⓑ Ⓒ Ⓓ	151. Ⓐ Ⓑ Ⓒ Ⓓ	167. Ⓐ Ⓑ Ⓒ Ⓓ
120. Ⓐ Ⓑ Ⓒ Ⓓ	136. Ⓐ Ⓑ Ⓒ Ⓓ	152. Ⓐ Ⓑ Ⓒ Ⓓ	168. Ⓐ Ⓑ Ⓒ Ⓓ
121. Ⓐ Ⓑ Ⓒ Ⓓ	137. Ⓐ Ⓑ Ⓒ Ⓓ	153. Ⓐ Ⓑ Ⓒ Ⓓ	169. Ⓐ Ⓑ Ⓒ Ⓓ
122. Ⓐ Ⓑ Ⓒ Ⓓ	138. Ⓐ Ⓑ Ⓒ Ⓓ	154. Ⓐ Ⓑ Ⓒ Ⓓ	170. Ⓐ Ⓑ Ⓒ Ⓓ
123. Ⓐ Ⓑ Ⓒ Ⓓ	139. Ⓐ Ⓑ Ⓒ Ⓓ	155. Ⓐ Ⓑ Ⓒ Ⓓ	171. Ⓐ Ⓑ Ⓒ Ⓓ
124. Ⓐ Ⓑ Ⓒ Ⓓ	140. Ⓐ Ⓑ Ⓒ Ⓓ	156. Ⓐ Ⓑ Ⓒ Ⓓ	172. Ⓐ Ⓑ Ⓒ Ⓓ
125. Ⓐ Ⓑ Ⓒ Ⓓ	141. Ⓐ Ⓑ Ⓒ Ⓓ	157. Ⓐ Ⓑ Ⓒ Ⓓ	173. Ⓐ Ⓑ Ⓒ Ⓓ
126. Ⓐ Ⓑ Ⓒ Ⓓ	142. Ⓐ Ⓑ Ⓒ Ⓓ	158. Ⓐ Ⓑ Ⓒ Ⓓ	174. Ⓐ Ⓑ Ⓒ Ⓓ
127. Ⓐ Ⓑ Ⓒ Ⓓ	143. Ⓐ Ⓑ Ⓒ Ⓓ	159. Ⓐ Ⓑ Ⓒ Ⓓ	
128. Ⓐ Ⓑ Ⓒ Ⓓ	144. Ⓐ Ⓑ Ⓒ Ⓓ	160. Ⓐ Ⓑ Ⓒ Ⓓ	

ANSWER SHEET
HSPT Practice Test 1

MATHEMATICS SUBTEST

175. Ⓐ Ⓑ Ⓒ Ⓓ   191. Ⓐ Ⓑ Ⓒ Ⓓ   207. Ⓐ Ⓑ Ⓒ Ⓓ   223. Ⓐ Ⓑ Ⓒ Ⓓ
176. Ⓐ Ⓑ Ⓒ Ⓓ   192. Ⓐ Ⓑ Ⓒ Ⓓ   208. Ⓐ Ⓑ Ⓒ Ⓓ   224. Ⓐ Ⓑ Ⓒ Ⓓ
177. Ⓐ Ⓑ Ⓒ Ⓓ   193. Ⓐ Ⓑ Ⓒ Ⓓ   209. Ⓐ Ⓑ Ⓒ Ⓓ   225. Ⓐ Ⓑ Ⓒ Ⓓ
178. Ⓐ Ⓑ Ⓒ Ⓓ   194. Ⓐ Ⓑ Ⓒ Ⓓ   210. Ⓐ Ⓑ Ⓒ Ⓓ   226. Ⓐ Ⓑ Ⓒ Ⓓ
179. Ⓐ Ⓑ Ⓒ Ⓓ   195. Ⓐ Ⓑ Ⓒ Ⓓ   211. Ⓐ Ⓑ Ⓒ Ⓓ   227. Ⓐ Ⓑ Ⓒ Ⓓ
180. Ⓐ Ⓑ Ⓒ Ⓓ   196. Ⓐ Ⓑ Ⓒ Ⓓ   212. Ⓐ Ⓑ Ⓒ Ⓓ   228. Ⓐ Ⓑ Ⓒ Ⓓ
181. Ⓐ Ⓑ Ⓒ Ⓓ   197. Ⓐ Ⓑ Ⓒ Ⓓ   213. Ⓐ Ⓑ Ⓒ Ⓓ   229. Ⓐ Ⓑ Ⓒ Ⓓ
182. Ⓐ Ⓑ Ⓒ Ⓓ   198. Ⓐ Ⓑ Ⓒ Ⓓ   214. Ⓐ Ⓑ Ⓒ Ⓓ   230. Ⓐ Ⓑ Ⓒ Ⓓ
183. Ⓐ Ⓑ Ⓒ Ⓓ   199. Ⓐ Ⓑ Ⓒ Ⓓ   215. Ⓐ Ⓑ Ⓒ Ⓓ   231. Ⓐ Ⓑ Ⓒ Ⓓ
184. Ⓐ Ⓑ Ⓒ Ⓓ   200. Ⓐ Ⓑ Ⓒ Ⓓ   216. Ⓐ Ⓑ Ⓒ Ⓓ   232. Ⓐ Ⓑ Ⓒ Ⓓ
185. Ⓐ Ⓑ Ⓒ Ⓓ   201. Ⓐ Ⓑ Ⓒ Ⓓ   217. Ⓐ Ⓑ Ⓒ Ⓓ   233. Ⓐ Ⓑ Ⓒ Ⓓ
186. Ⓐ Ⓑ Ⓒ Ⓓ   202. Ⓐ Ⓑ Ⓒ Ⓓ   218. Ⓐ Ⓑ Ⓒ Ⓓ   234. Ⓐ Ⓑ Ⓒ Ⓓ
187. Ⓐ Ⓑ Ⓒ Ⓓ   203. Ⓐ Ⓑ Ⓒ Ⓓ   219. Ⓐ Ⓑ Ⓒ Ⓓ   235. Ⓐ Ⓑ Ⓒ Ⓓ
188. Ⓐ Ⓑ Ⓒ Ⓓ   204. Ⓐ Ⓑ Ⓒ Ⓓ   220. Ⓐ Ⓑ Ⓒ Ⓓ   236. Ⓐ Ⓑ Ⓒ Ⓓ
189. Ⓐ Ⓑ Ⓒ Ⓓ   205. Ⓐ Ⓑ Ⓒ Ⓓ   221. Ⓐ Ⓑ Ⓒ Ⓓ   237. Ⓐ Ⓑ Ⓒ Ⓓ
190. Ⓐ Ⓑ Ⓒ Ⓓ   206. Ⓐ Ⓑ Ⓒ Ⓓ   222. Ⓐ Ⓑ Ⓒ Ⓓ   238. Ⓐ Ⓑ Ⓒ Ⓓ

ANSWER SHEET
HSPT Practice Test 1

LANGUAGE SUBTEST

239. Ⓐ Ⓑ Ⓒ Ⓓ
240. Ⓐ Ⓑ Ⓒ Ⓓ
241. Ⓐ Ⓑ Ⓒ Ⓓ
242. Ⓐ Ⓑ Ⓒ Ⓓ
243. Ⓐ Ⓑ Ⓒ Ⓓ
244. Ⓐ Ⓑ Ⓒ Ⓓ
245. Ⓐ Ⓑ Ⓒ Ⓓ
246. Ⓐ Ⓑ Ⓒ Ⓓ
247. Ⓐ Ⓑ Ⓒ Ⓓ
248. Ⓐ Ⓑ Ⓒ Ⓓ
249. Ⓐ Ⓑ Ⓒ Ⓓ
250. Ⓐ Ⓑ Ⓒ Ⓓ
251. Ⓐ Ⓑ Ⓒ Ⓓ
252. Ⓐ Ⓑ Ⓒ Ⓓ
253. Ⓐ Ⓑ Ⓒ Ⓓ

254. Ⓐ Ⓑ Ⓒ Ⓓ
255. Ⓐ Ⓑ Ⓒ Ⓓ
256. Ⓐ Ⓑ Ⓒ Ⓓ
257. Ⓐ Ⓑ Ⓒ Ⓓ
258. Ⓐ Ⓑ Ⓒ Ⓓ
259. Ⓐ Ⓑ Ⓒ Ⓓ
260. Ⓐ Ⓑ Ⓒ Ⓓ
261. Ⓐ Ⓑ Ⓒ Ⓓ
262. Ⓐ Ⓑ Ⓒ Ⓓ
263. Ⓐ Ⓑ Ⓒ Ⓓ
264. Ⓐ Ⓑ Ⓒ Ⓓ
265. Ⓐ Ⓑ Ⓒ Ⓓ
266. Ⓐ Ⓑ Ⓒ Ⓓ
267. Ⓐ Ⓑ Ⓒ Ⓓ
268. Ⓐ Ⓑ Ⓒ Ⓓ

269. Ⓐ Ⓑ Ⓒ Ⓓ
270. Ⓐ Ⓑ Ⓒ Ⓓ
271. Ⓐ Ⓑ Ⓒ Ⓓ
272. Ⓐ Ⓑ Ⓒ Ⓓ
273. Ⓐ Ⓑ Ⓒ Ⓓ
274. Ⓐ Ⓑ Ⓒ Ⓓ
275. Ⓐ Ⓑ Ⓒ Ⓓ
276. Ⓐ Ⓑ Ⓒ Ⓓ
277. Ⓐ Ⓑ Ⓒ Ⓓ
278. Ⓐ Ⓑ Ⓒ Ⓓ
279. Ⓐ Ⓑ Ⓒ Ⓓ
280. Ⓐ Ⓑ Ⓒ Ⓓ
281. Ⓐ Ⓑ Ⓒ Ⓓ
282. Ⓐ Ⓑ Ⓒ Ⓓ
283. Ⓐ Ⓑ Ⓒ Ⓓ

284. Ⓐ Ⓑ Ⓒ Ⓓ
285. Ⓐ Ⓑ Ⓒ Ⓓ
286. Ⓐ Ⓑ Ⓒ Ⓓ
287. Ⓐ Ⓑ Ⓒ Ⓓ
288. Ⓐ Ⓑ Ⓒ Ⓓ
289. Ⓐ Ⓑ Ⓒ Ⓓ
290. Ⓐ Ⓑ Ⓒ Ⓓ
291. Ⓐ Ⓑ Ⓒ Ⓓ
292. Ⓐ Ⓑ Ⓒ Ⓓ
293. Ⓐ Ⓑ Ⓒ Ⓓ
294. Ⓐ Ⓑ Ⓒ Ⓓ
295. Ⓐ Ⓑ Ⓒ Ⓓ
296. Ⓐ Ⓑ Ⓒ Ⓓ
297. Ⓐ Ⓑ Ⓒ Ⓓ
298. Ⓐ Ⓑ Ⓒ Ⓓ

18 MINUTES

Samples:

A. Hurl most nearly means

  (a) run.
  (b) fall.
  (c) throw.
  (d) drop.

B. Baby is to adult as cub is to

  (a) mother.
  (b) bear.
  (c) dog.
  (d) infant.

Correct marking of samples:

A. Ⓐ Ⓑ ● Ⓓ

B. Ⓐ ● Ⓒ Ⓓ

---

1. Confiscate most nearly means

  (a) arrest.
  (b) take.
  (c) supply.
  (d) confuse.

2. Which word does *not* belong with the others?

  (a) incorporate
  (b) unite
  (c) disperse
  (d) merge

3. Which word does *not* belong with the others?

  (a) Boston
  (b) Chicago
  (c) Los Angeles
  (d) Arizona

4. All snakes are cold-blooded. Verdi is not cold-blooded. Verdi is a snake. If the first two statements are true, the third is

  (a) true.
  (b) false.
  (c) uncertain.

5. Aloof means the *opposite* of

  (a) detached.
  (b) distant.
  (c) concerned.
  (d) casual.

6. Diner is to eating as school is to

  (a) teaching.
  (b) learning.
  (c) education.
  (d) building.

7. Deter most nearly means

  (a) prod.
  (b) hinder.
  (c) facilitate.
  (d) force.

8. Which word does *not* belong with the others?

  (a) impede
  (b) slow
  (c) accelerate
  (d) delay

9. Decipher means the *opposite* of

  (a) encode.
  (b) solve.
  (c) reveal.
  (d) analyze.

10. Drape most nearly means

  (a) cover.
  (b) decorate.
  (c) close.
  (d) plan.

GO TO THE NEXT PAGE ➡

11. Flagrant most nearly means

(a) subtle.
(b) quiet.
(c) pungent.
(d) bold.

12. Mitten is to hand as hat is to

(a) cap.
(b) head.
(c) face.
(d) snow.

13. Which word does *not* belong with the others?

(a) contagious
(b) infectious
(c) harmless
(d) spreading

14. Distraught most nearly means

(a) untrusting.
(b) troubled.
(c) thirsty.
(d) heavy.

15. Swelter means the *opposite* of

(a) sweat.
(b) freeze.
(c) broil.
(d) perspire.

16. Button is to coat as lock is to

(a) key.
(b) secure.
(c) door.
(d) fasten.

17. All of the boys at Georgetown Middle School wear ties to school. Charles does not wear a tie to school. Charles does not attend Georgetown Middle School. If the first two statements are true, the third is

(a) true.
(b) false.
(c) uncertain.

18. Which word does *not* belong with the others?

(a) lament
(b) cry
(c) moan
(d) praise

19. Act is to play as chapter is to

(a) novel.
(b) opera.
(c) actor.
(d) movie.

20. Which word does *not* belong with the others?

(a) treaty
(b) agreement
(c) contract
(d) debate

21. Allot most nearly means

(a) abundant.
(b) allocate.
(c) keep.
(d) reject.

22. Knoll is to mountain as lake is to

(a) ocean.
(b) pond.
(c) river.
(d) puddle.

23. Piano is to keys as guitar is to

(a) instrument.
(b) frets.
(c) strings.
(d) music.

24. Which word does *not* belong with the others?

(a) felon
(b) prisoner
(c) policeman
(d) inmate

GO TO THE NEXT PAGE ➡

25. Matthew has the highest grade in Mr. Smith's class. His brother Nick is in Mr. Smith's class. Nick's grade is lower than Matthew's grade. If the first two statements are true, the third is

    (a) true.
    (b) false.
    (c) uncertain.

26. Corrupt most nearly means

    (a) ethical.
    (b) good.
    (c) clean.
    (d) unethical.

27. Weight is to gram as temperature is to

    (a) degree.
    (b) cold.
    (c) pound.
    (d) heat.

28. Bellow means the *opposite* of

    (a) yell.
    (b) shout.
    (c) whisper.
    (d) talk.

29. Cascade does *not* mean

    (a) fall.
    (b) down rush.
    (c) climb.
    (d) collapse.

30. Which word does *not* belong with the others?

    (a) snap
    (b) shirt
    (c) zipper
    (d) button

31. Viscous most nearly means

    (a) smart.
    (b) thick.
    (c) wicked.
    (d) kind.

32. Which word does *not* belong with the others?

    (a) conceal
    (b) declare
    (c) tell
    (d) claim

33. Which word does *not* belong with the others?

    (a) cautious
    (b) wary
    (c) calm
    (d) nervous

34. Malicious is to kind as spiteful is to

    (a) mean.
    (b) evil.
    (c) sad.
    (d) helpful.

35. Sandra's hair is longer than Kaylee's hair. Elizabeth's hair is longer than Kaylee's hair. Elizabeth's hair is shorter than Sandra's hair. If the first two statements are true, the third is

    (a) true.
    (b) false.
    (c) uncertain.

36. Gaunt does *not* mean

    (a) scary.
    (b) thin.
    (c) spare.
    (d) skinny.

37. Kathleen collected more crystals than Karla. Karla collected fewer crystals than Colleen. Kathleen collected more crystals than Colleen. If the first two statements are true, the third is

    (a) true.
    (b) false.
    (c) uncertain.

GO TO THE NEXT PAGE ➡

38. Black is to gray as red is to

    (a) solid.
    (b) pink.
    (c) purple.
    (d) apple.

39. To demolish is to

    (a) hide.
    (b) twist.
    (c) destroy.
    (d) construct.

40. Integrate is the *opposite* of

    (a) incorporate.
    (b) accommodate.
    (c) separate.
    (d) consolidate.

41. Seed is to plant as nut is to

    (a) cashew.
    (b) tree.
    (c) shell.
    (d) acorn.

42. Sporadic is *not*

    (a) inconsistent.
    (b) regular.
    (c) spastic.
    (d) unpredictable.

43. Shovel is to snow as rake is to

    (a) collect.
    (b) tarp.
    (c) leaves.
    (d) tree.

44. Which word does *not* belong with the others?

    (a) accelerate
    (b) propel
    (c) impede
    (d) hasten

45. Which word does *not* belong with the others?

    (a) confident
    (b) poised
    (c) agitated
    (d) assured

46. Lee hiked more miles than Joseph. Dorothy hiked fewer miles than Joseph. Lee hiked fewer miles than Dorothy. If the first two statements are true, the third is

    (a) true.
    (b) false.
    (c) uncertain.

47. Dakota has more cats than Jada. Jada has fewer cats than Jordan. Dakota has fewer cats than Jordan. If the first two statements are true, the third is

    (a) true.
    (b) false.
    (c) uncertain.

48. Conor lives further away than Braden. Chandler lives further away than Braden. Chandler lives further away than Conor. If the first two statements are true, the third is

    (a) true.
    (b) false.
    (c) uncertain.

49. Which word does *not* belong with the others?

    (a) hood
    (b) hat
    (c) scarf
    (d) boots

50. Culminate most nearly means

    (a) finish.
    (b) commence.
    (c) open.
    (d) bottom.

GO TO THE NEXT PAGE ➡

51. Most students at the University of Hartford live in Connecticut. Aidan attends the University of Hartford. Aidan lives in Connecticut. If the first two statements are true, the third is

    (a) true.
    (b) false.
    (c) uncertain.

52. Which word does *not* belong with the others?

    (a) dismantle
    (b) build
    (c) assemble
    (d) construct

53. Formidable does *not* mean

    (a) intimidating.
    (b) large.
    (c) mediocre.
    (d) frightful.

54. Which word does *not* belong with the others?

    (a) skeptical
    (b) untrusting
    (c) concerned
    (d) gullible

55. Radiant most nearly means

    (a) beaming.
    (b) heating.
    (c) dull.
    (d) gloomy.

56. Which word does *not* belong with the others?

    (a) bank
    (b) penny
    (c) nickel
    (d) quarter

57. Which word does *not* belong with the others?

    (a) add
    (b) calculator
    (c) subtract
    (d) divide

58. Mt. Washington is the highest mountain in New Hampshire. Mt. Chocorua is in New Hampshire. Mt. Chocorua is lower than Mt. Washington. If the first two statements are true, the third is

    (a) true.
    (b) false.
    (c) uncertain.

59. To shriek is to

    (a) whimper.
    (b) bellow.
    (c) gossip.
    (d) smile.

60. Charles' video game score was lower than Aidan's. Austin's video game score was higher than Charles'. Austin's video game score was higher than Aidan's. If the first two statements are true, the third is

    (a) true.
    (b) false.
    (c) uncertain.

STOP

30 MINUTES

Samples:

A. What number added to 3 makes 2 plus 5?

   (a) 3   (b) 4   (c) 5   (d) 7

B. In the sequence: 1, 2, 3, 4, 5, . . . , what number should come next?

   (a) 3   (b) 6   (c) 5   (d) 4

C. Examine (A), (B), and (C) and find the *best* answer.

   (A) (3 − 2) − 1
   (B) (3 − 1) − 2
   (C) 3 − (2 − 1)

   (a) (A) is greater than (B).
   (b) (A), (B), and (C) are equal.
   (c) (C) is greater than (A) and (B).
   (d) (B) is greater than (A).

D. Examine the hourglasses (A), (B), and (C) and find the *best* answer.

     (A)   (B)   (C)

   (a) (A) shows the most time passed.
   (b) (B) shows the most time passed.
   (c) (C) shows the most time passed.
   (d) (A) and (B) show the same time has passed.

Correct marking of samples:

A. Ⓐ ● Ⓒ Ⓓ

B. Ⓐ ● Ⓒ Ⓓ

C. Ⓐ Ⓑ ● Ⓓ

D. Ⓐ Ⓑ ● Ⓓ

---

61. In the sequence: −0.4, −1.6, −4.8, −9.6, . . . , what number should come next?

   (a) 19.2 (b) −9.8 (c) −9.6 (d) −19.2

62. Examine (A), (B), and (C) and find the *best* answer.

    (A)   (B)   (C)

   (a) (A) + (C) < (B)
   (b) (B) − (C) = (A)
   (c) (B) + (A) < (C)
   (d) (A) + (B) = (C)

63. In the sequence: 4, 16, 5, 25, 6, 36, . . . , what number should come next?

   (a) 49   (b) 7   (c) 40   (d) 16

64. What number subtracted from 18 makes 5 more than 11?

   (a) 8   (b) 13   (c) 2   (d) 29

65. In the sequence: 87, 76, 65, . . . , what number should come next?

   (a) 78   (b) 54   (c) 66   (d) 56

GO TO THE NEXT PAGE ➡

66. Examine (A), (B), and (C) and find the *best* answer.

    (A) $\frac{5}{6}$ of 36

    (B) $\frac{1}{3}$ of 60

    (C) $\frac{4}{7}$ of 49

    (a) (A) < (B) < (C)
    (b) (A) = (B)
    (c) (A) > (C) > (B)
    (d) (B) = (C)

67. In the sequence: B8, F10, J30, N32, . . . , what comes next?

    (a) O22   (b) R64   (c) P9   (d) R96

68. What number subtracted from 7^2 makes 20% of 50?

    (a) 10   (b) 39   (c) 20   (d) 25

69. Examine the angles A, B, and C and find the *best* answer.

    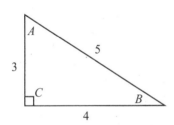

    (a) $A > C$
    (b) $C > A > B$
    (c) $B = C$
    (d) $B > A = C$

70. In the sequence: 61, 68, 75, 82, . . . , what number should come next?

    (a) 85   (b) 89   (c) 92   (d) 95

71. In the sequence: 54, 18, 6, 2, . . . , what number should come next?

    (a) 0.2   (b) $\frac{2}{3}$ (c) 2   (d) 0.6

72. Examine (A), (B), and (C) and find the *best* answer.

    (A) $\frac{5}{11}$

    (B) $\frac{5}{18}$

    (C) $\frac{1}{3}$

    (a) (C) > (A) > (B)
    (b) (A) = (B)
    (c) (A) > (C) > (B)
    (d) (B) = (C)

73. In the sequence: 875, 175, 35, 7, . . . , what number should come next?

    (a) 1   (b) –7   (c) $1\frac{2}{5}$ (d) 0

74. In the sequence: 400, 200, 150, 75, 25, . . . , what number should come next?

    (a) 75   (b) –25   (c) $12\frac{1}{2}$ (d) 22

75. In the sequence: I, II, VI, XII, XVI, . . . , what numeral should come next?

    (a) XXXII
    (b) XII
    (c) XX
    (d) XXII

76. Examine (A), (B), and (C) and find the *best* answer when x and y are both positive.

    (A) $3x + 5y$
    (B) $3(x + y)$
    (C) $3x + y$

    (a) (B) and (C) are equal.
    (b) (A) is less than (C).
    (c) (B) is greater than (C).
    (d) (C) is greater than (A).

77. In the sequence: 46M, 40P, 44S, . . , what comes next?

    (a) 40C   (b) 31B   (c) 38V   (d) 41U

GO TO THE NEXT PAGE ➡

78. In the sequence: 64DW, 67EX, 70FY, . . . , what comes next?

   (a) 67IZ
   (b) 73GM
   (c) 71KM
   (d) 73GZ

79. What number when subtracted from 87 makes $\frac{1}{4}$ of 80?

   (a) 7   (b) 84   (c) 67   (d) 23

80. In the sequence: 90, 30, 36, 12, 18, . . . , what two numbers should come next?

   (a) 6, 12   (c) 6, 18
   (b) 24, 25   (d) 18, 24

81. What number is 11 less than $\frac{4}{5}$ of 50?

   (a) 40   (b) 29   (c) 39   (d) 16

82. Examine (A), (B), and (C) and find the *best* answer.

   (A) $(4 \times 9) + 5$
   (B) $5 + (4 \times 9)$
   (C) $4 \times (9 + 5)$

   (a) (B) is equal to (A) and less than (C).
   (b) (B) is equal to (C) which is greater than (A).
   (c) (B) is greater than (A) which is greater than (C).
   (d) (B) is greater than (C) which is greater than (A).

83. Examine (A), (B), and (C) and find the *best* answer.

   (A)

   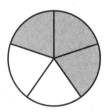

   (B)

   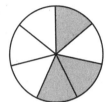

   (C)

   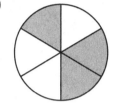

   (a) (A), (B), and (C) are equally shaded.
   (b) (C) is shaded less than (B) and more than (A).
   (c) (B) and (C) are shaded equally.
   (d) (C) is shaded more than (B) and less than (A).

84. What number subtracted from 68 leaves 7 more than 3 times 8?

   (a) 61   (b) 24   (c) 59   (d) 37

85. In the sequence: 33, 30, 32, 28, 31, 26, . . . , what two numbers should come next?

   (a) 29, 34   (c) 31, 30
   (b) 31, 29   (d) 30, 24

86. In the sequence: −92, −85, −78, −71, . . . , what number should come next?

   (a) −64   (b) −70   (c) −63   (d) −58

GO TO THE NEXT PAGE ➡

87. Examine (A), (B), and (C) and find the *best* answer.

    (A) 10% of 60

    (B) $\frac{1}{6}$ of 36

    (C) 60 % of 10

    (a) (A) > (C)
    (b) (A) < (B) < (C)
    (c) (B) > (C)
    (d) (A) = (B) = (C)

88. In the sequence: 18, 31, 45, 60, . . . , what number should come next?

    (a) 76   (b) 71   (c) 68   (d) 72

89. Examine (A), (B), and (C) and find the *best* answer.

    (A) 420%

    (B) 0.42

    (C) $\frac{2}{5}$

    (a) (B) is greater than (A).
    (b) (B) is equal to (C).
    (c) (C) is less than (B) and (A).
    (d) (A) is equal to (B).

90. What number is twice as much as $\frac{2}{3}$ of 66?

    (a) 88   (b) 25   (c) 44   (d) 22

91. In the sequence: 42, 51, 63, 72, 84, . . . , what comes next?

    (a) 92   (b) 82   (c) 89   (d) 93

92. What number subtracted from 54 makes 26 more than 3?

    (a) 25   (b) 28   (c) 29   (d) 53

93. In the sequence: J12, I24, H36, . . . , what should come next?

    (a) I40   (c) G48
    (b) F50   (d) G38

94. Examine (A), (B), and (C) and find the *best* answer.

    (A) $\frac{1}{4}$

    (B) 24%

    (C) 0.24

    (a) (A), (B), and (C) are equal.
    (b) (B) is less than (A) and equal to (C).
    (c) (C) is less than (A) or (B).
    (d) (A) and (C) are greater than (B).

95. In the sequence: 56, 3, 52, 6, . . . , what number should come next?

    (a) 9   (b) 48   (c) 50   (d) 12

96. What number is 6 more than 15% of 80?

    (a) 10   (b) 18   (c) 21   (d) 46

97. In the sequence: 3, 27, 5, 45, 7, . . . , what number should come next?

    (a) 9   (c) 720
    (b) 555   (d) 63

98. Examine the bar graph and find the *best* answer.

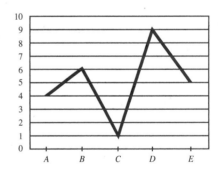

    (a) A plus E equals D.
    (b) B plus C equals D.
    (c) A plus B equals D.
    (d) A, C, and D are equal.

99. In the sequence: 24, 28, 36, 42, 48, . . . , one number is *wrong*. That number should be

    (a) 30   (b) 32   (c) 44   (d) 54

GO TO THE NEXT PAGE ➡

100. In the sequence: 13CZ, 26DY, 39EX, 52FW, . . . , what should come next?

(a) 65GV   (c) 55HO

(b) 60GP   (d) 65OV

101. Examine the area in the polygons below and find the *best* answer.

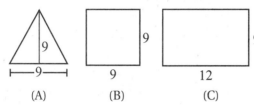

(A)   (B)   (C)

(a) (A) = (B) = (C)

(b) (A) < (B) < (C)

(c) (A) = (B) = (C)

(d) (A) = (C) > (B)

102. What number multiplied by 13 is equal to 15 more than 24?

(a) 4   (b) 11   (c) 2   (d) 3

103. Examine (A), (B), and (C) and find the *best* answer.

(A) 4 feet

(B) 37 inches

(C) 1 yard

(a) (A) > (B) > (C)

(b) (A) < (B) < (C)

(c) (C) < (A) < (B)

(d) (A) < (C) < (B)

104. In the sequence: 40, 32, 25, 19, 14, . . . , what number should come next?

(a) 10   (b) 12   (c) 8   (d) 6

105. Examine (A), (B), and (C) and find the *best* answer.

(A) $(12 \times 6) \div 3$

(B) $(12 \times 3) \div 6$

(C) $12 \times (6 \div 3)$

(a) (A) is equal to (B).

(b) (C) is equal to (A).

(c) (B) is greater than (A).

(d) (C) is equal to (B).

106. Examine (A), (B), and (C) and find the *best* answer.

(A) $\dfrac{9}{40}$

(B) $\dfrac{21}{80}$

(C) $\dfrac{1}{4}$

(a) (C) > (A) > (B)

(b) (A) > (B) > (C)

(c) (A) > (B) = (C)

(d) (B) > (C) > (A)

107. What number multiplied by 12 makes 8 less than 44?

(a) 3   (b) 4   (c) 7   (d) 5

108. Examine the angles *A*, *B*, *C*, and *D* and find the *best* answer.

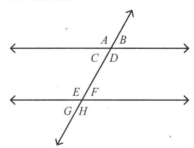

(a) $A = B$

(b) $A = D$

(c) $B = D$

(d) $C = A$

GO TO THE NEXT PAGE ➡

109. Examine (A), (B), and (C) and find the *best* answer.

  (A) 30% of 40
  (B) 40% of 30
  (C) 12

  (a) (A) is equal to (B) and greater than (C).
  (b) (A), (B), and (C) are equal.
  (c) (C) is greater than (A) or (B).
  (d) (B) is greater than (A).

110. $\frac{1}{3}$ of what number is 9 times 5?

  (a) 135   (b) 15   (c) 20   (d) 45

111. Examine (A), (B), and (C) and find the *best* answer.

  (A) $(-11 + 6) \times 2$
  (B) $(-3 \times 11) \times 3$
  (C) $(-11 \times 6) \times 2$

  (a) (A) and (C) are equal.
  (b) (A) and (B) are equal.
  (c) (B) is less than (A).
  (d) (A) is less than (B).

112. Examine (A), (B), and (C) and find the *best* answer.

  (A)   (B)   (C)

  (a) (A) shows the most time passed.
  (b) (B) shows the most time passed.
  (c) (C) shows the most time passed.
  (d) (A) and (C) show the same time has passed.

STOP

25 MINUTES

Sample:

A. The passage below is followed by a series of questions.

The passages in this section of the test will be

(a) very easy to understand.
(b) very boring.
(c) followed by a series of questions.
(d) in very large font.

Correct marking of sample:

A. Ⓐ Ⓑ ● Ⓓ

READING—Comprehension

Questions 113–122 refer to the following passage.

Tyrants are known to be leaders who ruled without law and often used cruel methods to control their subjects. They often took their power by force. Many of the Greek states in the seventh century were filled with civil <u>strife</u> but the tyrants, by banishing the disorderly and by compelling those who remained at home to submit to the laws, reduced their countries to peace and harmony. They made promises to the people to put an end to the oppressive rule of the great nobles and to enforce the existing laws. In spite of their promises, they were also known for having robbed the people of the vitality of freedom.

The tyrants encouraged religion, literature, and art. They educated the common people by fostering the forms of religion and poetry adapted to them. By training all classes alike to obey authority, they prepared the way for self-government. Their treaties with foreign states, secured their countries the advantages of commerce and helped to establish <u>concord</u> throughout. They were the first organizers of peace, the founders of the first standing armies after that of Sparta, and the first able protectors of their states against civil and foreign foes.

Tyrants utilized a variety of methods to rule. These methods included controlling all public information, rigging political elections, oppressing the people, and monopolizing the government. Through these methods, tyrants restored order in times of chaos, and in spite of these methods, they were often looked upon with favor by the people they ruled.

GO TO THE NEXT PAGE ➡

113. Tyrants were the first organizers of what?

  (a) religion
  (b) peace
  (c) architecture
  (d) poetry

114. The *best* title for this passage is

  (a) "The Armies of Sparta."
  (b) "A Complete History of Greece."
  (c) "Tyrants: Good, Bad, or Both?"
  (d) "A Complete History of Tyrants."

115. The word strife, as underlined and used in the passage, most nearly means

  (a) strength.
  (b) disagreement.
  (c) happiness.
  (d) power.

116. Tyrants encouraged peace and harmony by which of the following?

  (a) punishment
  (b) promoting art and poetry
  (c) banishing the disorderly
  (d) forming armies

117. The word concord, as underlined and used in the passage, most nearly means

  (a) prosperity.
  (b) darkness.
  (c) dictatorship.
  (d) harmony.

118. Tyrants secured a strong commerce by

  (a) ending oppressive rule.
  (b) making promises to the people.
  (c) establishing treaties with foreign states.
  (d) taking away freedom.

119. Tyrants promoted self-government by which of the following means?

  (a) by training people to obey authority
  (b) by banishing the disorderly
  (c) by promoting the arts
  (d) by robbing people of freedom

120. Tyrants became rulers by

  (a) popular vote.
  (b) inheritance.
  (c) force.
  (d) election.

121. Which methods were *not* used by tyrants?

  (a) monopolizing the government
  (b) holding fair elections
  (c) controlling public information
  (d) oppressing people

122. What is the main idea of the passage?

  (a) to provide an overall image of tyrants
  (b) to let the reader know that tyrants were good people
  (c) to show that tyrants were truly evil rulers
  (d) to describe how tyrants were known mostly for their love of art

GO TO THE NEXT PAGE ➡

Questions 123–132 refer to the following passage.

Perennials are the mainstay of most gardens. The top part of a perennial will die each year, but the root system remains alive and will grow a new plant the following year. Unlike annuals, which must be replanted every year, perennials bloom year after year with little or no effort. Most gardeners choose to grow perennials because of the ease of care and because they offer a <u>plethora</u> of shapes and colors.

If cared for properly, perennials will continue to beautify gardens for many years. Some species are short-lived and will bloom for four to five years, while others will bring life to a garden for fifteen years or more. Some common examples of perennials are purple coneflowers, daisies, and bleeding hearts.

Some perennials thrive in the sun, while others require full shade. The black-eyed Susan is a perennial that has bright orange flowers with black centers. They bloom in late summer and <u>thrive</u> when in full sun. Hosta is a perennial that includes a wide variety of plants with large leafy greens. They have vibrant colors when planted in a shady spot.

Gardeners cultivate a variety of perennials in their gardens but also supplement with annuals. Even though annuals must be reseeded each year, they are considered invaluable in most gardens. Annuals, such as zinnias, offer a vibrant array of colors and often bloom in the heat of the summer when perennials have long since lost their flowers. A mix of perennials and annuals is the key to a successful garden.

123. The benefit of planting perennials is that

    (a) they live only one year.
    (b) they do not require sun to bloom.
    (c) they are inexpensive to purchase.
    (d) they bloom every year without replanting.

124. What is the main idea of the passage?

    (a) Gardeners should only plant perennials.
    (b) Annuals are the only flowers with vibrant color.
    (c) A well planned garden is comprised of annuals and perennials.
    (d) The life cycle of a perennial is one year.

125. The word <u>plethora</u>, as underlined and used in the passage, most nearly means

    (a) vibrant.
    (b) rarity.
    (c) abundance.
    (d) annually.

126. This passage is an example of

    (a) a dramatic novel.
    (b) a research article.
    (c) a magazine article.
    (d) biography.

127. Annuals can be desirable because

    (a) they are short-lived.
    (b) they bloom when perennials may not.
    (c) they are expensive.
    (d) they come back each year without replanting.

GO TO THE NEXT PAGE ➡

128. Perennials include all of the following *except*

    (a) hosta.

    (b) black-eyed Susan.

    (c) zinnia.

    (d) daisy.

129. Thrive, as underlined and used in the passage, most nearly means to

    (a) grow

    (b) wilt

    (c) die

    (d) dig

130. According to the passage, what is *not* true of hosta?

    (a) They have many varieties.

    (b) They have large leafy greens.

    (c) They grow in the shade.

    (d) They are annuals.

131. What is *not* true of perennial flowers?

    (a) Some prefer sun and others shade.

    (b) They bloom each year.

    (c) The root system dies each year.

    (d) They are the mainstay of a good garden.

132. What is the author's main purpose in writing this passage?

    (a) to convince gardeners to use only perennials

    (b) to provide a map of the perfect garden

    (c) to highlight the benefits of perennial plants

    (d) to talk about the disadvantages of annual flowers

GO TO THE NEXT PAGE ➡

Questions 133–142 refer to the following passage.

Have you ever wondered why or how crickets make that <u>unique</u> chirping sound? Only the male crickets can chirp. This chirping is a means of attracting a female cricket with a loud and constant sound. The same sound also sends a message to other male crickets to stay away. Crickets are <u>nocturnal</u> insects, so their chirping is an important way of letting other potential mates know where to find them during the night.

It has long been known that there is a relationship between the frequency of chirps and the outside temperature. For over one hundred years, people have been counting the number of cricket chirps in a time interval and using this to estimate the temperature. One method instructs listeners to count the number of chirps in a 14-second interval and add 40. This will yield an approximate temperature in degrees Fahrenheit. Some methods suggest adding 38 rather than 40, while other methods suggest using an interval of 15 seconds. The formula for converting to degrees Celsius is a little more complicated. The variety of methods is a reminder that this is not an exact science but rather an estimate of the actual temperature.

So how do crickets manage to create such a unique sound? Male crickets chirp by rubbing an edge of their wing against ridges on the other wing. The exact sound depends on the number of ridges and the distance between them. So the next time you hear that summer sound of chirping crickets, you'll be able to estimate the temperature while appreciating the conversation.

133. Crickets make a chirping sound

    (a) to attract other male crickets.
    (b) to let humans know the temperature.
    (c) so they don't get stepped on by people.
    (d) to attract a mate.

134. From this passage you can infer that

    (a) there is a formula for estimating degrees Celsius from cricket chirps.
    (b) female crickets can also chirp but not as loudly as males.
    (c) determining the temperature from cricket chirps is an exact science.
    (d) there is only one proven method for determining temperature from chirping.

135. The word <u>nocturnal</u>, as underlined and used in the passage, most nearly means

    (a) to be an insect.
    (b) to be awake during the day.
    (c) to be cold-blooded.
    (d) to be occurring at night.

136. The author of this passage is most likely a

    (a) movie critic.
    (b) science teacher.
    (c) lawyer.
    (d) government official.

137. How does a cricket chirp?

    (a) by rubbing its legs together
    (b) by measuring the outside temperature
    (c) by opening and closing its wings
    (d) by rubbing one wing on the other

GO TO THE NEXT PAGE ➡

138. The relationship between temperature and chirping

    (a) was just discovered this decade.
    (b) has been known for over 100 years.
    (c) was discovered in the 13th century.
    (d) is a myth.

139. According to the passage, it is *true* that

    (a) by adding 40 to the number of chirps in a minute one can estimate the temperature.
    (b) only degrees Celsius can be determined from chirping.
    (c) female crickets chirp to ward off males.
    (d) the number of chirps in a 14- or 15-second interval can be used to estimate temperature.

140. The word unique, as underlined and used in the passage, most nearly means

    (a) insect.
    (b) funny.
    (c) one of a kind.
    (d) typical.

141. This passage is an example of

    (a) gossip.
    (b) a biography.
    (c) a saga.
    (d) an article.

142. The *best* title for this passage is

    (a) "The Curious Sounds of Crickets."
    (b) "Global Warming and Crickets."
    (c) "How to Find a Cricket."
    (d) "Research Findings of Grasshoppers."

GO TO THE NEXT PAGE ➡

Tom Brady is a quarterback for the New England Patriots football team. He has become known as the most winning quarterback in the history of the National Football League. He <u>instills</u> fear in his competitors, is beloved by all his fans, and is admired by his rivals.

Tom was recruited to play professional baseball in 1995, upon graduating from high school, but made the choice to attend college instead. He accepted a scholarship to the University of Michigan where he majored in business and psychology. He joined the football team but spent most of his time on the bench. It was not until he was a junior in college that he became the starting quarterback.

Tom Brady's real fame came after he was drafted by the New England Patriots in 2000 and became their starting quarterback in 2001. That year he won his first Super Bowl. The New England Patriots, led by the team's head coach, Bill Belichick, have played in the Super Bowl eight times. Tom Brady was the quarterback for seven of the Super Bowl games and with his team approach and expert skills, Tom led the team to Super Bowl victory five times, more than any other quarterback in the National Football League. He has won over 200 games during his career, beating the previous record held by Peyton Manning, and has averaged over two touchdowns per game.

When asked about his success, he is always quick to give credit to his coaches and teammates. He remains <u>humble</u> in spite of so much fame. Tom Brady will forever be known as one of the greatest quarterbacks in football history.

143. Tom Brady graduated high school in what year?

  (a) 2001
  (b) 1995
  (c) 2000
  (d) 2016

144. The *best* title for this passage is

  (a) "Tom Brady—a Football Legend."
  (b) "The History of NFL Quarterbacks."
  (c) "How to Become a Quarterback."
  (d) "Salaries of NFL Quarterbacks."

145. The word <u>humble</u>, as underlined and used in the passage, most nearly means

  (a) proud.
  (b) nervous.
  (c) modest.
  (d) impressed.

146. Bill Belichick was the New England Patriots'

  (a) starting quarterback.
  (b) team captain.
  (c) head coach.
  (d) team owner.

GO TO THE NEXT PAGE ➡

147. Tom Brady did all of the following *except*

    (a) played in the Super Bowl eight times.
    (b) won five Super Bowl titles.
    (c) averaged over two touchdowns per game.
    (d) won over 200 games.

148. Who else is credited for the success of the New England Patriots?

    (a) Peyton Manning
    (b) Bill Belichick
    (c) University of Michigan's coach
    (d) Tom Brady's opponents

149. When Tom Brady played for the University of Michigan

    (a) he was an overnight superstar.
    (b) he was team captain as a freshman.
    (c) he first spent a lot of time on the bench.
    (d) he had his first injury.

150. The word instills, as underlined and used in the passage, most nearly means

    (a) reduces.
    (b) confuses.
    (c) takes away.
    (d) establishes.

151. What is the main idea of the passage?

    (a) to show how rich quarterbacks can be
    (b) to chronicle the successes of Tom Brady
    (c) to remind students to stay in school
    (d) to explain how Super Bowls are won

152. The author is most likely a

    (a) sports writer.
    (b) novelist.
    (c) opponent.
    (d) critic.

GO TO THE NEXT PAGE ➡

Directions: Choose the word that means the same or about the same as the underlined word or words.

153. a timid child

    (a) tall
    (b) confident
    (c) shy
    (d) bold

154. to resume a discussion

    (a) argue
    (b) end
    (c) begin
    (d) continue

155. a blatant lie

    (a) secret
    (b) subtle
    (c) bold
    (d) small

156. the ultimate goal

    (a) final
    (b) first
    (c) personal
    (d) middle

157. a vague question

    (a) funny
    (b) difficult
    (c) direct
    (d) unclear

158. to loathe someone

    (a) admire
    (b) dislike
    (c) envy
    (d) miss

159. to resolve a problem

    (a) challenge
    (b) fix
    (c) understand
    (d) question

160. a compassionate person

    (a) caring
    (b) large
    (c) smart
    (d) sad

161. an envious friend

    (a) jealous
    (b) close
    (c) angry
    (d) temporary

162. critical supplies

    (a) extra
    (b) necessary
    (c) artistic
    (d) medical

163. a lucrative offer

    (a) bad
    (b) beneficial
    (c) liquid
    (d) secret

164. an intriguing idea

    (a) financial
    (b) routing
    (c) dangerous
    (d) curious

GO TO THE NEXT PAGE ➡

165. to embark on a trip

   (a) walk
   (b) leave
   (c) pack
   (d) return

166. an amassed fortune

   (a) extra
   (b) necessary
   (c) collected
   (d) small

167. a lucid description

   (a) confusing
   (b) serious
   (c) angry
   (d) easy to understand

168. an unkempt room

   (a) messy
   (b) small
   (c) dark
   (d) locked

169. a throbbing headache

   (a) lasting
   (b) small
   (c) pounding
   (d) quiet

170. a temporary home

   (a) permanent
   (b) large
   (c) not lasting
   (d) tiny

171. to forfeit the game

   (a) challenge
   (b) give up
   (c) make up
   (d) win

172. An agitated student is

   (a) confident.
   (b) intelligent.
   (c) organized.
   (d) nervous.

173. The epitome of good manners

   (a) opposite
   (b) perfect example
   (c) story
   (d) lack

174. a placid lake

   (a) rough
   (b) calm
   (c) clean
   (d) populated

STOP

45 MINUTES

Sample:

A. The number thirty-seven is also written as

  (a) 27 (b) 33 (c) 37 (d) 63

Correct marking of sample:

A. Ⓐ Ⓑ ● Ⓓ

175. What is the name of this polygon?

  (a) hexagon
  (b) octagon
  (c) pentagon
  (d) heptagon

176. Solve: $21\overline{)4264}$

  (a) 204 R1
  (b) 203 R1
  (c) 203 R21
  (d) 203

177. Two hundredths can be written as

  (a) 0.2   (c) 0.0002
  (b) 0.02   (d) 200

178. Express $\frac{5}{12}$ as a decimal.

  (a) $0.4\overline{1}$
  (b) $0.41\overline{6}$
  (c) $0.\overline{416}$
  (d) $0.41\overline{61}$

179. The greatest common factor of 108 and 72 is

  (a) 6
  (b) 18
  (c) 36
  (d) 9

180. How many pints of milk will fit in a 2-gallon container?

  (a) 4 pints
  (b) 32 pints
  (c) 16 pints
  (d) 8 pints

181. Solve: $\frac{3}{7} \div \frac{1}{5}$

  (a) $2\frac{1}{7}$ (c) $\frac{3}{35}$
  (b) $2\frac{1}{2}$ (d) $\frac{5}{7}$

182. Solve:

$$\begin{array}{r} 24.6 \\ \times\, 0.31 \\ \hline \end{array}$$

  (a) 63.25   (c) 76.26
  (b) 0.7626   (d) 7.626

183. Solve: $\sqrt{81}$

  (a) 6   (b) 5   (c) 9   (d) 18

GO TO THE NEXT PAGE ➡

184. What is equivalent to $7^6 \times 7^2$?

    (a) 7^{12} (b) 7^8 (c) 7^4 (d) 49^8

185. 0.18 kilometers equals

    (a) 18 meters

    (b) 180 meters

    (c) 1,800 meters

    (d) 1.8 meters

186. What number is in the tens place after simplifying $(4 \times 10^2) + (3 \times 10^3) + (21 + 10^1)$?

    (a) 3   (b) 4   (c) 7   (d) 0

187. Solve: $(-4) \times (-2) \times (-9) =$

    (a) 54   (b) –54   (c) 72   (d) –72

188. The pie chart shows the favorite colors of a school of 1,200 students. How many students have blue as their favorite color?

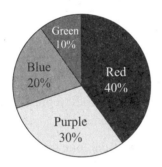

    (a) 20   (b) 480   (c) 120   (d) 240

189. Which information is best displayed on a bar graph?

    (a) daily temperatures

    (b) family income

    (c) types of pets owned by families

    (d) finish times for a race

190. In Massachusetts, sales tax is 5% of the purchase. If Emmett buys a toy for $28.80, how much will he pay in sales tax?

    (a) $14.40   (c) $28.00

    (b) $0.44   (d) $1.44

191. Larry read 3 more books than Kathy. Kathy read twice as many books as Matthew. Matthew read 2 fewer books than Nick. Together they read 23 books. How many books did Nick read?

    (a) 5   (b) 18   (c) 8   (d) 12

192. What is the area of a square that has a perimeter of 32 inches?

    (a) 64 in.²   (c) 1,024 in.²

    (b) 16 in.²   (d) 320 in.²

193. Which diagram shows complementary angles?

(a)

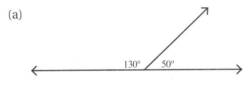

(b)

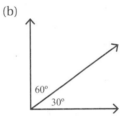

(c)

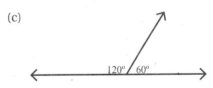

(d)

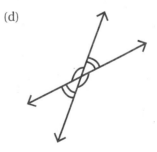

GO TO THE NEXT PAGE ➡

194. What is the measure of angle *x*?

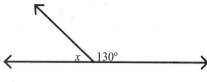

(a) 50° (b) 60° (c) 180° (d) 45°

195. Three quarters are equivalent to what fraction of $2.00?

(a) $\frac{1}{4}$ (b) $\frac{3}{4}$ (c) $\frac{3}{8}$ (d) $\frac{6}{7}$

196. The perimeter of a rectangle is 28 cm and the sides are made up of even integers. The longest that one side can be is

(a) 6 cm   (c) 12 cm
(b) 14 cm   (d) 8 cm

197. Which of the following is true of a trapezoid?

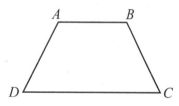

(a) $\overline{AD}$ is parallel to $\overline{BC}$
(b) $\angle A$ is equal to $\angle B$
(c) $\overline{AB}$ is equal to $\overline{CD}$
(d) $\overline{AB}$ is parallel to $\overline{CD}$

198. During a basketball game Charles scored 9 points, Kyle scored 12 points, Ben scored 11 points, and Joe did not score any points. How many points did the boys score on average during the game?

(a) 10 (b) $8\frac{2}{3}$ (c) $10\frac{2}{3}$ (d) 8

199. A jar holds 3 red candies, 3 yellow candies, and 1 blue candy. If you choose a piece of candy at random, what is the probability of choosing a red candy?

(a) $\frac{1}{7}$ (b) $\frac{3}{4}$ (c) $\frac{3}{10}$ (d) $\frac{3}{7}$

200. The time plot below shows the number of school absences per month for a local elementary school. What is the average number of absences for the time period shown?

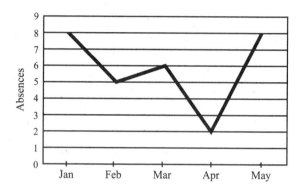

(a) 5 (b) $5\frac{2}{5}$ (c) $5\frac{4}{5}$ (d) 4

201. Which expression best represents the following problem?

The sum of 2 times one number and 18 is 72. What is the number?

(a) $2 + x = 18$
(b) $2 + 18x = 72$
(c) $2x + 18 = 72$
(d) $2 = 72 + 18x$

GO TO THE NEXT PAGE ➡

202. If △ABC ≅ △DEF, which statement is *not* true?

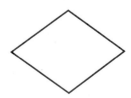

(a) $\angle C = \angle F$
(b) $\overline{AB} \cong \overline{DF}$
(c) $\overline{BC} \cong \overline{EF}$
(d) $\angle B = \angle E$

203. 2 lb. 8 oz. equals

(a) 28 oz. (c) 40 oz.
(b) 24 oz. (d) 32 oz.

204. Solve: $8.2\overline{)4.592}$

(a) 0.55 (b) 0.66 (c) 5.6 (d) 0.56

205. Solve: $\dfrac{2}{3} \div \dfrac{9}{4} =$

(a) $\dfrac{3}{2}$ (b) $\dfrac{8}{27}$ (c) $\dfrac{4}{9}$ (d) $\dfrac{18}{12}$

206. Five students reported the following scores from a standardized test. What is the mean score among the 5 students?

780, 520, 400, 650, 600

(a) 710 (b) 590 (c) 600 (d) 550

207. How many sides are there in a hexagon?

(a) 6 (b) 5 (c) 4 (d) 7

208. This shape is an example of a

(a) square (c) rectangle
(b) rhombus (d) trapezoid

209. If the highest value in a set of numbers is doubled what will happen to the median of the set of numbers?

(a) It will double.
(b) It will remain the same.
(c) It will increase by 4.
(d) It will be reduced by half.

210. What is the diameter of a circle with a radius of 32?

(a) 64 (b) 16 (c) 8 (d) 32^2

211. What number is $\sqrt[3]{8}$

(a) 64 (b) 3 (c) 2 (d) –2

212. Which statement best describes the following inequality?

$$2x - 4 < \frac{2}{3}$$

(a) The difference of two times a number and 4 is greater than two-thirds.
(b) The sum of 2 and a number is less than two-thirds.
(c) The difference of two times a number and 4 is less than two-thirds .
(d) The product of 2 and a number is greater than two-thirds.

213. If Betty earns $20,000 and was given a raise of $6,000, what percent increase does her raise represent?

(a) 30 (b) 60 (c) 6 (d) 20

214. Solve for *m*: $\dfrac{2}{3} \times 7 = 12m$

(a) $\dfrac{15}{36}$ (b) $\dfrac{10}{3}$ (c) 19 (d) $\dfrac{7}{18}$

GO TO THE NEXT PAGE ➡

215. If the length of a side of a square is doubled, what will happen to the area?

   (a) It doubles.
   (b) It is multiplied by 4.
   (c) It remains the same.
   (d) It increases by 2.

216. Kathleen has 17 grandchildren. Five are girls and the rest are boys. If she randomly selects one grandchild, what is the probability that it will be a girl?

   (a) $\frac{5}{12}$ (b) $\frac{7}{12}$ (c) $\frac{7}{17}$ (d) $\frac{5}{17}$

217. Kathryn gets paid for babysitting at a rate of $11 per hour. Last week she babysat for 6 hours on Monday, 3 hours on Thursday, and 7 hours on Friday. How much money, in dollars, did she earn last week?

   (a) $176   (b) $170   (c) $16   (d) $181

218. What is the surface area of this figure?

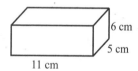

6 cm
5 cm
11 cm

   (a) 324 cm^2 (c) 41 cm^2
   (b) 66 cm^2 (d) 302 cm^2

219. Solve:

$$2,685$$
$$1,372$$
$$+\ 9,201$$

   (a) 13,354   (c) 12,368
   (b) 12,356   (d) 13,258

220. Sandra has $50 for holiday shopping. She buys some quantity of the same gifts for $5 each and receives $7 in change. Which expression best represents this?

   (a) $50 - x = 7 \times 5$
   (b) $50 - 7x = 5$
   (c) $50 - 5x = 7$
   (d) $5x - 7 = 50$

221. If a drawing is created using a scale where 3 inches is equal to 2 feet, how wide would a drawing be of a room that is 12 feet wide?

   (a) 1 foot   (c) 6 inches
   (b) 18 inches   (d) 12 inches

222. Solve:

$$1,285$$
$$\times\ 372$$

   (a) 186,320   (c) 478,020
   (b) 378,022   (d) 488,030

223. Solve: $-12x > 36$

   (a) $x > -3$ (c) $x < -3$
   (b) $x > 3$ (d) $x < 3$

224. A meteorologist measured the temperature for the first week of November and recorded the following.

   18, 18, 23, 24, 34, 41, 52

   What is the median temperature for the week?

   (a) 24   (c) 18
   (b) 30.1   (d) 34

225. Emmett is taller than Sarah. Christina is taller than William. Sarah is the same height as Christina so

   (a) Emmett is the same height as William.
   (b) Emmett is taller than Christina.
   (c) William is taller than Sarah.
   (d) Sarah is the same height as William.

GO TO THE NEXT PAGE ➡

226. Mary travels 5 hours at 50 miles per hour. What equation represents the distance she traveled?

(a) $D = 5 \times 50$

(b) $D = \frac{50}{5}$

(c) $5 = 50 \times D$

(d) $D \times 5 = 50$

227. The following are rankings that students gave their math teacher at St. John's High School. Find the mode of the set of scores.

7, 2, 4, 6, 7, 8, 3, 4, 7, 2, 3, 6, 4, 7, 8, 3, 7, 5, 8

(a) 4   (b) 3   (c) 7   (d) 8

228. Karyn can shovel $\frac{2}{5}$ of the snow from her driveway each hour. How long will it take her to shovel snow from her entire driveway?

(a) 2.5 hours

(b) 1.25 hours

(c) 2 hours

(d) 1.5 hours

229. Sarah is making a curtain that is 12 feet by 9 feet. Fabric for the curtain costs $28.00 per square yard. How much will Sarah spend on fabric?

(a) $336.00

(b) $ 72.00

(c) $2,016.00

(d) $280.00

230. Three Girl Scouts sold cookies for $4.25 per box. The first Girl Scout sold 5 boxes, the second sold 12 boxes, and the third sold 8 boxes. How much money did the three Girl Scouts earn in cookie sales?

(a) $80.50

(b) $104.50

(c) $106.25

(d) $25.00

231. Solve: $-6 - 12 =$

(a) -18 (b) 6   (c) -6 (d) 18

232. What is the volume of this object?

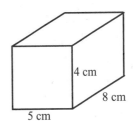

(a) 160 cm³

(b) 64 cm³

(c) 34 cm³

(d) 320 cm³

233. Mrs. Pickering purchased a plant for 60% of the original price. If she paid $54.60, what was the original price of the plant?

(a) $136.50

(b) $91.00

(c) $327.60

(d) $21.84

234. What is the slope of the line shown in the graph below?

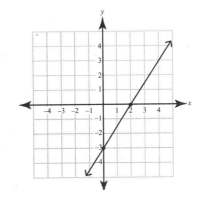

(a) $-\frac{2}{3}$ (b) $\frac{2}{3}$ (c) $\frac{3}{2}$ (d) $-\frac{3}{2}$

235. Driving home, Lawrence drove for 30 minutes at 50 miles per hour and then drove another 20 minutes at 60 miles per hour. What distance did Lawrence travel home?

(a) 110 miles

(b) 25 miles

(c) 55 miles

(d) 45 miles

GO TO THE NEXT PAGE ➡

236. A cup of milk is equal to 8 ounces. If a recipe calls for 400 ounces of milk, how many cups of milk are needed?

    (a) 25 cups   (c) 32 cups

    (b) 50 cups   (d) $5\frac{1}{2}$ cups

237. Solve: $\dfrac{\frac{2}{7}}{\frac{1}{3}} =$

    (a) $\dfrac{7}{6}$ (b) $\dfrac{6}{7}$ (c) $\dfrac{2}{21}$ (d) 2

238. The ratio of girls to boys is 5 to 13. If there are 25 girls, how many boys are there?

    (a) 18   (b) 60   (c) 65   (d) 5

STOP

25 MINUTES

Samples:

A. (a) Lee was reading a book.
   (b) We will run fast.
   (c) larry and I were late.
   (d) No mistakes.

B. (a) Who was at the door?
   (b) We all sat at the tabel.
   (c) The rose is yellow.
   (d) No mistakes.

Correct marking of samples:

A. Ⓐ Ⓑ ● Ⓓ
B. Ⓐ ● Ⓒ Ⓓ

In questions 239–278 try to find errors in punctuation, capitalization, or word usage. If you find a mistake, select the letter in front of that sentence as your answer. Some questions will have *No mistakes* for choice (d). For these questions, if you do not find any errors, mark (d) *No mistakes* as your answer.

239. (a) Here is the dish you wanted.
   (b) Whose book is this?
   (c) The picnic is on the last day of Summer.
   (d) I counted all five hundred marbles.

240. (a) My mother's company are very successful.
   (b) The principal is well-liked.
   (c) Charles, please feed the dogs.
   (d) Kaylee is the very best tennis player.

241. (a) Among the three of us there will be a winner.
   (b) There are fewer than three.
   (c) It's because of the weather that there is no school today.
   (d) No mistakes.

242. (a) Her father and I will discuss this.
   (b) There were hardly no relatives at the reunion.
   (c) Neither Peter nor Paul borrowed any money.
   (d) No mistakes.

243. (a) Football is the least favorite sport.
   (b) Susan and me are always on time.
   (c) Peter is the tallest basketball player.
   (d) No mistakes.

244. (a) Jody goes to work at seven o'clock each morning.
   (b) Jackson is an older dog than Siri.
   (c) Gregory and me went to the movies on Wednesday.
   (d) No mistakes.

245. (a) I love reading, singing, and dancing.
   (b) "Stop the car!" she shouted.
   (c) Please respond to Elizabeth and I.
   (d) No mistakes.

246. (a) Kaylee went to school tomorrow.
   (b) Charles' room is always messy.
   (c) Kimmy is a dear friend.
   (d) Sparky lived longer than the other dogs.

GO TO THE NEXT PAGE ➡

247. (a) Have you ever seen a full moon?
    (b) My house is the oldest on Nelson Avenue.
    (c) I'm already late.
    (d) No mistakes.

248. (a) Lawrence Sr was born in Lynn, Massachusetts.
    (b) Debbie yelled, "Why are you late?"
    (c) No, I don't think I like the dessert.
    (d) No mistakes.

249. (a) My favorite colors are blue red and green.
    (b) I ran as fast as I could.
    (c) Never will I admit to anything.
    (d) No mistakes

250. (a) Randy, please tell me a story.
    (b) Enter the room take a seat and wait until you are called.
    (c) I love having novels read to me.
    (d) No mistakes.

251. (a) My father is a veteran of the korean war.
    (b) I visited Boston, MA last week.
    (c) I took an algebra class this semester.
    (d) He and I went to lunch today.

252. (a) I live in Bridgton, Maine.
    (b) Teacher, I have a question.
    (c) Is it possible to jump twelve feet.
    (d) No mistakes.

253. (a) Glen and Ray are friends of mine.
    (b) I play darts tennis, pool, and cards.
    (c) My sister is an accomplished pianist.
    (d) I love watching the snow slowly falling.

254. (a) Each of the cats are soft.
    (b) She could never resist a good dessert.
    (c) Fifty people attended the party.
    (d) No mistakes.

255. (a) Who's that outside the door?
    (b) The boy who ran away was found.
    (c) The runner ran quick at the end of the race.
    (d) He did not know everything.

256. (a) We couldn't scarcely climb the steep hill.
    (b) Neither Steve nor Aidan is organized.
    (c) Put the boxes over there.
    (d) I will be all ready by tomorrow.

257. (a) He is not only nice but smart too.
    (b) Beside me, he is the smartest in the class.
    (c) My mother will drive Jody and me to school.
    (d) No mistakes.

258. (a) Kathleen could never pass up a good bargain.
    (b) He is the epitome of lazy.
    (c) Jim, Jameson, and I attended the meeting.
    (d) No mistakes.

259. (a) "I can't believe this." Said Kaylee.
    (b) She always stays too late.
    (c) I go to school too often.
    (d) Doug lives in Leesburg, Virginia.

260. (a) The dog, named after the town was a retriever.
    (b) The baby was the largest in the hospital.
    (c) I love carrots, peas, and turnips.
    (d) No mistakes.

261. (a) Gregory and i went to Merrimack College.
    (b) She was the valedictorian.
    (c) Meghan was too tired to sleep.
    (d) No mistakes.

GO TO THE NEXT PAGE ➡

262. (a) The city's population is growing.
    (b) A tablecloth is an essential part of a dinner party.
    (c) Easter is always on a sunday.
    (d) No mistakes.

263. (a) He told me to leave him alone.
    (b) The recipe uses flour sugar, and eggs.
    (c) I talked to the principal about my grade.
    (d) I am never tired.

264. (a) The kitten is so cute.
    (b) The mothers child is five years old.
    (c) At 9 o'clock my favorite show begins.
    (d) No mistakes.

265. (a) Elizabeth, please call me tonight.
    (b) Charles' mother is so nice.
    (c) Please pick up vegetables milk, and butter.
    (d) No mistakes.

266. (a) We are always together during holidays.
    (b) There are too teachers for every fifteen students.
    (c) I wish the weather would improve.
    (d) No mistakes.

267. (a) Douglas was too kind to speak up.
    (b) Colleen and I went hiking.
    (c) Dakota and Jada are twins.
    (d) No mistakes.

268. (a) The name on his passport is Mr William Hastings.
    (b) Betty reads the most of all of the neighbors.
    (c) Linda wants to learn to make cheese.
    (d) No mistakes.

269. (a) Rod, Doug, and Darren are all brothers.
    (b) This is the woman which I admire the most.
    (c) Ms. Lutz is very young.
    (d) No mistakes.

270. (a) Santiago is the taller of the two brothers.
    (b) Nicholas is the most intelligent applicant.
    (c) She flew out of Logan international Airport in Boston, MA.
    (d) No mistakes.

271. (a) There was a parade on Labor Day.
    (b) The mountains of the West are breathtaking.
    (c) Kaylee was born on April 28 1993.
    (d) She is either one or two years old.

272. (a) A package was delivered but I don't know where.
    (b) He is the smartest in his group.
    (c) A week's gone by and we still don't know.
    (d) No mistakes.

273. (a) because there is no class today I slept late.
    (b) Iava's brother is in the fourth grade.
    (c) Memorizing vocabulary words can be difficult.
    (d) No mistakes.

274. (a) Lemonade is delicious in the summer.
    (b) Sparky is the name of there dog.
    (c) Susan's aunt is her mother's sister.
    (d) No mistakes.

275. (a) The Boston Public Library is a great resource.
    (b) My sibling is very young.
    (c) Line dancing is a great form of exercise.
    (d) No mistakes.

276. (a) There are always more questions than answers.
    (b) Between the three of us there will be a winner.
    (c) Rather than wait, we should begin now.
    (d) No mistakes.

GO TO THE NEXT PAGE ➡

277. (a) I prefer an essay over a test.
(b) Regis College is in Weston, Massachusetts.
(c) Julie get paid biweekly.
(d) No mistakes.

278. (a) Among the three, one will be chosen.
(b) There are no less than eight.
(c) Due to the weather, schools will be closed.
(d) No mistakes.

For questions 279–288, look only for mistakes in spelling.

279. (a) Sometimes mistakes are unavoidible.
(b) Depress the button to unlock the door.
(c) There was a dispute over an invoice.
(d) No mistakes.

280. (a) A good book can nourish the soul.
(b) As a collector, he can be very possesive.
(c) He will resign his position at the end of the day.
(d) No mistakes.

281. (a) School discipline has changed over time.
(b) He committed perjury during the trial.
(c) What kind of refreshements will there be?
(d) No mistakes.

282. (a) Poor weather may intervene with our plans.
(b) Detectives thoroughly review all evidence.
(c) The doctor performed the surgery perfectly.
(d) No mistakes.

283. (a) When I am morose I feel sad.
(b) The hurricane was disasterous.
(c) The British will secede from Europe.
(d) No mistakes.

284. (a) He chose a peice of chocolate pie.
(b) The comment is not relevant.
(c) The occurrence of the flu is on the rise.
(d) No mistakes.

285. (a) Many titles can be abbreviated.
(b) They eventually won the game.
(c) After falling, the man was unconscious.
(d) No mistakes.

286. (a) Some math questions can be tedious.
(b) Please acknowlege my question.
(c) Transplanted organs must be compatible.
(d) No mistakes.

287. (a) I allready finished the assignment.
(b) Some cats can be ferocious.
(c) He is a real estate tycoon.
(d) No mistakes.

288. (a) Sound can echo loudly in the mountains.
(b) People should do aerobics daily.
(c) She bought a postcard for a souvenire.
(d) No mistakes.

For Questions 289–298, follow the directions for each question.

289. Choose the correct word or words to join the thoughts together.

I really like her _____ she is very selfish.

(a) because
(b) in addition,
(c) even though
(d) None of these

GO TO THE NEXT PAGE ➡

290. Choose the correct word or words to join the thoughts together.

I cheated on my test; _____ I received a zero for a score.

(a) although
(b) consequently
(c) but
(d) because

291. Choose the group of words that *best* completes the sentence.

My boss said I would receive a raise if _____

(a) the project assigned I was working on I do well.
(b) the project is a good job that I work on.
(c) I do well on the project I was assigned.
(d) the project I was assigned is done good.

292. Which of these expresses the idea most clearly?

(a) The author writes very long books and he is also elderly.
(b) The elderly author's books are very long.
(c) The author is elderly and his long books are written.
(d) All of the long books are written by the old author.

293. Which of the following falls under the topic "First Year of College?"

(a) Students should try to resolve roommate conflicts quickly.
(b) College graduates tend to have high starting salaries.
(c) Ask your favorite high school teacher for a recommendation for your application.
(d) Good study habits are essential to get into college.

294. Which of these expresses the idea most clearly?

(a) I like the gloves that you purchased from Cressy's.
(b) The gloves at Cressy's that you purchased are nice.
(c) I like the gloves, the ones that you bought at Cressy's.
(d) The gloves at Cressy's are the ones that I like.

295. Which of these would be best for a theme for one paragraph?

(a) The Effects of Renewable Energy on Global Warming
(b) Easy Ways to Recycle in Your Own Home
(c) The Impacts of Global Warming
(d) The History of Climate Change

296. Which sentence does not belong in this paragraph?

(1) Homes in New England require heating systems to keep interiors warm in the winter. (2) Most heating systems use either natural gas or oil for fuel. (3) The cost of oil this year is very low. (4) The type of heating system often determines what type of fuel is needed.

(a) Sentence 1
(b) Sentence 2
(c) Sentence 3
(d) Sentence 4

GO TO THE NEXT PAGE ➡

297. Where should the sentence, "Sift the flour and the salt together," be placed in the below paragraph?

(1) To make cookies, you must first mix together the sugar and the butter. (2) Next, add the eggs. (3) Add the mixture of dry ingredients and mix well. (4) Place spoonfuls of the batter on a cookie sheet and bake.

(a) Between sentences 1 and 2
(b) Between sentences 2 and 3
(c) Between sentences 3 and 4
(d) After sentence 4

298. Where should the sentence, "Interest rates today are 5%," be placed in the below paragraph?

(1) At Georgetown Bank, customers receive interest based on current interest rates. (2) Total interest is calculated by multiplying a customer's balance by 5%. (3) The interest is then added to the customer's account.

(a) Between sentences 1 and 2
(b) Between sentences 2 and 3
(c) After sentence 3
(d) The sentence does not fit in this paragraph.

STOP

ANSWER KEY
HSPT Practice Test 1

VERBAL SKILLS SUBTEST

1. **b**	16. **c**	31. **b**	46. **b**
2. **c**	17. **a**	32. **a**	47. **c**
3. **d**	18. **d**	33. **c**	48. **c**
4. **b**	19. **a**	34. **d**	49. **d**
5. **c**	20. **d**	35. **c**	50. **a**
6. **b**	21. **b**	36. **a**	51. **c**
7. **b**	22. **a**	37. **c**	52. **a**
8. **c**	23. **c**	38. **b**	53. **c**
9. **a**	24. **c**	39. **c**	54. **d**
10. **a**	25. **a**	40. **c**	55. **a**
11. **d**	26. **d**	41. **b**	56. **a**
12. **b**	27. **a**	42. **b**	57. **b**
13. **c**	28. **c**	43. **c**	58. **a**
14. **b**	29. **c**	44. **c**	59. **b**
15. **b**	30. **b**	45. **c**	60. **c**

QUANTITATIVE SKILLS SUBTEST

61. **c**	74. **c**	87. **d**	100. **a**
62. **c**	75. **a**	88. **a**	101. **b**
63. **b**	76. **c**	89. **c**	102. **d**
64. **c**	77. **c**	90. **a**	103. **a**
65. **b**	78. **d**	91. **d**	104. **a**
66. **c**	79. **c**	92. **a**	105. **b**
67. **d**	80. **a**	93. **c**	106. **d**
68. **b**	81. **b**	94. **b**	107. **a**
69. **b**	82. **a**	95. **b**	108. **b**
70. **b**	83. **d**	96. **b**	109. **b**
71. **b**	84. **d**	97. **d**	110. **a**
72. **c**	85. **d**	98. **a**	111. **c**
73. **c**	86. **a**	99. **a**	112. **c**

ANSWER KEY
HSPT Practice Test 1

READING SUBTEST

113. **b**	129. **a**	145. **c**	161. **a**
114. **c**	130. **d**	146. **c**	162. **b**
115. **b**	131. **c**	147. **a**	163. **b**
116. **c**	132. **c**	148. **b**	164. **d**
117. **d**	133. **d**	149. **c**	165. **b**
118. **c**	134. **a**	150. **d**	166. **c**
119. **a**	135. **d**	151. **b**	167. **d**
120. **c**	136. **b**	152. **a**	168. **a**
121. **b**	137. **d**	153. **c**	169. **c**
122. **a**	138. **b**	154. **d**	170. **c**
123. **d**	139. **d**	155. **c**	171. **b**
124. **c**	140. **c**	156. **a**	172. **d**
125. **c**	141. **d**	157. **d**	173. **b**
126. **c**	142. **a**	158. **b**	174. **b**
127. **b**	143. **b**	159. **b**	
128. **c**	144. **a**	160. **a**	

MATHEMATICS SUBTEST

175. **c**	191. **a**	207. **a**	223. **c**
176. **b**	192. **a**	208. **b**	224. **a**
177. **b**	193. **b**	209. **b**	225. **b**
178. **b**	194. **a**	210. **a**	226. **a**
179. **c**	195. **c**	211. **c**	227. **c**
180. **c**	196. **c**	212. **c**	228. **a**
181. **a**	197. **d**	213. **a**	229. **a**
182. **d**	198. **d**	214. **d**	230. **c**
183. **c**	199. **d**	215. **b**	231. **a**
184. **b**	200. **c**	216. **d**	232. **a**
185. **b**	201. **c**	217. **a**	233. **b**
186. **a**	202. **b**	218. **d**	234. **c**
187. **d**	203. **c**	219. **d**	235. **d**
188. **d**	204. **d**	220. **c**	236. **b**
189. **c**	205. **b**	221. **b**	237. **b**
190. **d**	206. **b**	222. **c**	238. **c**

LANGUAGE SUBTEST

239. **c**	254. **a**	269. **b**	284. **a**
240. **a**	255. **c**	270. **c**	285. **b**
241. **d**	256. **a**	271. **c**	286. **b**
242. **b**	257. **b**	272. **d**	287. **a**
243. **b**	258. **d**	273. **a**	288. **c**
244. **c**	259. **a**	274. **b**	289. **c**
245. **c**	260. **a**	275. **d**	290. **b**
246. **a**	261. **a**	276. **b**	291. **c**
247. **d**	262. **c**	277. **c**	292. **b**
248. **a**	263. **b**	278. **b**	293. **a**
249. **a**	264. **b**	279. **a**	294. **a**
250. **b**	265. **c**	280. **b**	295. **b**
251. **a**	266. **b**	281. **c**	296. **c**
252. **c**	267. **d**	282. **d**	297. **b**
253. **b**	268. **a**	283. **b**	298. **a**

SCORING YOUR PRACTICE TEST

Now that you have finished HSPT Practice Test 1, let's see how well you did. The following charts are scoring rubrics, which will not only help you calculate your raw score but also show your results for the different question types within each subtest.

1. Copy the answers from your bubble sheet next to each corresponding number in the second column of the chart for each of the five subtests.
2. For each question, there is an empty space in one of the columns to the right. These columns represent the different question-type categories. If you answered a question correctly, put a check in the open space under the question type category. If you answered the question incorrectly, leave the space blank.
3. When you have finished checking off the question types for each of your correct answers, add up the total number of check marks you have in each column to determine how well you did.
4. See the example below to better understand the scoring rubric.

Example:

Question	Your Answer	Correct Answer	Logic	Analogy	Classification	Antonym	Synonym
1	a	a		✔			

Verbal Skills Subtest Scoring Rubric

Question	Your Answer	Correct Answer	Logic	Analogy	Classification	Antonym	Synonym
1		b					
2		c					
3		d					
4		b					
5		c					
6		b					
7		b					
8		c					
9		a					
10		a					
11		d					
12		b					
13		c					
14		b					
15		b					
16		c					
17		a					
18		d					

Question	Your Answer	Correct Answer	Logic	Analogy	Classification	Antonym	Synonym
19		a					
20		d					
21		b					
22		a					
23		c					
24		c					
25		a					
26		d					
27		a					
28		c					
29		c					
30		b					
31		b					
32		a					
33		c					
34		d					
35		c					
36		a					
37		c					
38		b					
39		c					
40		c					
41		b					
42		b					
43		c					
44		c					
45		c					
46		b					
47		c					
48		c					
49		d					
50		a					
51		c					
52		a					
53		c					
54		d					
55		a					
56		a					
57		b					
58		a					

Question	Your Answer	Correct Answer	Logic	Analogy	Classification	Antonym	Synonym
59		b					
60		c					
Add up the number of check marks in each of the five columns to the right							
Total of each question type	11	11	17	9	12		

First, add up the total number of questions you answered correctly. Then divide that number by 60 and multiply by 100 to determine your raw score for the Verbal Skills subtest:

$$\text{Raw Score} = \frac{\text{Total Number Correct}}{60 \text{ Total Questions}} = \frac{}{60} \times 100 = \underline{}\%$$

Next, to determine your raw score for each question type, take the number of questions you answered correctly in each category and divide that number by the total number of questions in each question type. Multiply each answer by 100 to convert to a percent.

$$\text{Logic} = \frac{\text{Total Number Correct}}{11 \text{ Total Questions}} = \frac{}{11} \times 100 = \underline{}\%$$

$$\text{Analogy} = \frac{\text{Total Number Correct}}{11 \text{ Total Questions}} = \frac{}{11} \times 100 = \underline{}\%$$

$$\text{Classification} = \frac{\text{Total Number Correct}}{17 \text{ Total Questions}} = \frac{}{17} \times 100 = \underline{}\%$$

$$\text{Antonym} = \frac{\text{Total Number Correct}}{9 \text{ Total Questions}} = \frac{}{9} \times 100 = \underline{}\%$$

$$\text{Synonym} = \frac{\text{Total Number Correct}}{12 \text{ Total Questions}} = \frac{}{12} \times 100 = \underline{}\%$$

Quantitative Skills Subtest Scoring Rubric

Question	Your Answer	Correct Answer	Sequence	Geometric Comparison	Non-geometric Comparison	Computation
61		c				
62		c				
63		b				
64		c				
65		b				
66		c				
67		d				
68		b				
69		b				
70		b				
71		b				
72		c				
73		c				
74		c				
75		a				
76		c				
77		c				
78		d				
79		c				
80		a				
81		b				
82		a				
83		d				
84		d				
85		d				
86		a				
87		d				
88		a				
89		c				
90		a				
91		d				
92		a				
93		c				
94		b				
95		b				
96		b				
97		d				
98		a				
99		a				
100		a				

Question	Your Answer	Correct Answer	Sequence	Geometric Comparison	Non-geometric Comparison	Computation
101		b				
102		d				
103		a				
104		a				
105		b				
106		d				
107		a				
108		b				
109		b				
110		a				
111		c				
112		c				
Add up the total number of check marks in each of the four columns to the right						
Total of each question type			22	6	13	11

First, add up the total number of questions you answered correctly. Then divide that number by 52 and multiply by 100 to determine your raw score for the Quantitative Skills subtest:

$$\text{Raw Score} = \frac{\text{Total Number Correct}}{52 \text{ Total Questions}} = \frac{\quad}{52} \times 100 = \underline{\quad}\%$$

Next, to determine your raw score for each question type, take the number of questions you answered correctly in each category and divide that number by the total number of questions in each question type. Multiply each answer by 100 to convert to a percent.

$$\text{Sequence} = \frac{\text{Total Number Correct}}{22 \text{ Total Questions}} = \frac{\quad}{22} \times 100 = \underline{\quad}\%$$

$$\text{Geometric Comparison} = \frac{\text{Total Number Correct}}{6 \text{ Total Questions}} = \frac{\quad}{6} \times 100 = \underline{\quad}\%$$

$$\text{Non-geometric Comparison} = \frac{\text{Total Number Correct}}{13 \text{ Total Questions}} = \frac{\quad}{13} \times 100 = \underline{\quad}\%$$

$$\text{Computation} = \frac{\text{Total Number Correct}}{11 \text{ Total Questions}} = \frac{\quad}{11} \times 100 = \underline{\quad}\%$$

Reading Subtest Scoring Rubric

Question	Your Answer	Correct Answer	Vocabulary	Specific	General
113		b			
114		c			
115		b			
116		c			
117		d			
118		c			
119		a			
120		c			
121		b			
122		a			
123		d			
124		c			
125		c			
126		c			
127		b			
128		c			
129		a			
130		d			
131		c			
132		c			
133		d			
134		a			
135		d			
136		b			
137		d			
138		b			
139		d			
140		c			
141		d			
142		a			
143		b			
144		a			
145		c			
146		c			
147		a			
148		b			
149		c			
150		d			
151		b			

Question	Your Answer	Correct Answer	Vocabulary	Specific	General
152		a			
153		c			
154		d			
155		c			
156		a			
157		d			
158		b			
159		b			
160		a			
161		a			
162		b			
163		b			
164		d			
165		b			
166		c			
167		d			
168		a			
169		c			
170		c			
171		b			
172		d			
173		b			
174		b			
Add up the total number of check marks in each of the three columns to the right					
Total of each question type			30	21	11

First, add up the total number of questions you answered correctly. Then divide that number by 62 and multiply by 100 to determine your raw score for the Reading subtest:

$$\text{Raw Score} = \frac{\text{Total Number Correct}}{62 \text{ Total Questions}} = \frac{}{62} \times 100 = \underline{\qquad}\%$$

Next, to determine your raw score for each question type, take the number of questions you answered correctly in each category and divide that number by the total number of questions in each question type. Multiply each answer by 100 to convert to a percent.

$$\text{Vocabulary} = \frac{\text{Total Number Correct}}{30 \text{ Total Questions}} = \frac{}{30} \times 100 = \underline{\qquad}\%$$

$$\text{Specific} = \frac{\text{Total Number Correct}}{21 \text{ Total Questions}} = \frac{}{21} \times 100 = \underline{\qquad}\%$$

$$\text{General} = \frac{\text{Total Number Correct}}{11 \text{ Total Questions}} = \frac{}{11} \times 100 = \underline{\qquad}\%$$

Mathematics Subtest Scoring Rubric

Question	Your Answer	Correct Answer	Basics and Conversions	Geometry, Logic, Word Problems	Fractions, Decimals, Percents, Ratios	Exponents, Radicals, Algebra	Statistics and Probability
175		c					
176		b					
177		b					
178		b					
179		c					
180		c					
181		a					
182		d					
183		c					
184		b					
185		b					
186		a					
187		d					
188		d					
189		c					
190		d					
191		a					
192		a					
193		b					
194		a					
195		c					
196		c					
197		d					

Question	Your Answer	Correct Answer	Basics and Conversions	Geometry, Logic, Word Problems	Fractions, Decimals, Percents, Ratios	Exponents, Radicals, Algebra	Statistics and Probability
198		d					X
199		d					X
200		c					X
201		c				X	
202		b		X			
203		c	X				
204		d	X				
205		b	X				
206		b					X
207		a		X			
208		b					X
209		b					X
210		a		X			
211		c				X	
212		c				X	
213		a			X		
214		d				X	
215		b		X			
216		d					X
217		a		X			
218		d		X			
219		d	X				
220		c				X	
221		b		X			
222		c	X				
223		c				X	
224		a					X
225		b	X				
226		a		X			
227		c					X
228		a		X			
229		a		X			
230		c		X			
231		a	X				
232		a		X			
233		b		X			
234		c				X	
235		d		X			
236		b	X				

Question	Your Answer	Correct Answer	Basics and Conversions	Geometry, Logic, Word Problems	Fractions, Decimals, Percents, Ratios	Exponents, Radicals, Algebra	Statistics and Probability
237		b					
238		c					
Add up the number of check marks in each of the five columns to the right							
Total of each question type			18	22	4	10	10

First, add up the total number of questions you answered correctly. Then divide that number by 64 and multiply by 100 to determine your raw score for the Mathematics subtest:

$$\text{Raw Score} = \frac{\text{Total Number Correct}}{64 \text{ Total Questions}} = \frac{\quad}{64} \times 100 = \underline{\quad}\%$$

Next, to determine your raw score for each question type, take the number of questions you answered correctly in each category and divide that number by the total number of questions in each question type. Multiply each answer by 100 to convert to a percent.

$$\text{Basics and Conversions} = \frac{\text{Total Number Correct}}{18 \text{ Total Questions}} = \frac{\quad}{18} \times 100 = \underline{\quad}\%$$

$$\text{Geometry, Logic, and Word Problems} = \frac{\text{Total Number Correct}}{22 \text{ Total Questions}} = \frac{\quad}{22} \times 100 = \underline{\quad}\%$$

$$\text{Fractions, Decimals, Percents, and Ratios} = \frac{\text{Total Number Correct}}{4 \text{ Total Questions}} = \frac{\quad}{4} \times 100 = \underline{\quad}\%$$

$$\text{Exponents, Radicals, and Algebra} = \frac{\text{Total Number Correct}}{10 \text{ Total Questions}} = \frac{\quad}{10} \times 100 = \underline{\quad}\%$$

$$\text{Statistics and Probability} = \frac{\text{Total Number Correct}}{10 \text{ Total Questions}} = \frac{\quad}{10} \times 100 = \underline{\quad}\%$$

Language Subtest Scoring Rubric

Question	Your Answer	Correct Answer	Capitalization, Punctuation, Usage	Spelling	Composition
239		c			
240		a			
241		d			
242		b			
243		b			
244		c			
245		c			
246		a			
247		d			
248		a			
249		a			
250		b			
251		a			
252		c			
253		b			
254		a			
255		c			
256		a			
257		b			
258		d			
259		a			
260		a			
261		a			
262		c			
263		b			
264		b			
265		c			
266		b			
267		d			
268		a			
269		b			
270		c			
271		c			
272		d			
273		a			
274		b			
275		d			
276		b			
277		c			

Question	Your Answer	Correct Answer	Capitalization, Punctuation, Usage	Spelling	Composition
278		b			
279		a			
280		b			
282		c			
282		d			
283		b			
284		a			
285		b			
286		b			
287		a			
288		c			
289		c			
290		b			
291		c			
292		b			
293		a			
294		a			
295		b			
296		c			
297		b			
298		a			
Add up the total number of check marks in each of the three columns to the right					
Total of each question type			40	10	10

First, add up the total number of questions you answered correctly. Then divide that number by 60 and multiply by 100 to determine your raw score for the Language subtest:

$$\text{Raw Score} = \frac{\text{Total Number Correct}}{60 \text{ Total Questions}} = \frac{\rule{2cm}{0.4pt}}{60} \times 100 = \underline{\hspace{1cm}}\%$$

Next, to determine your raw score for each question type, take the number of questions you answered correctly in each category and divide that number by the total number of questions in each question type. Multiply each answer by 100 to convert to a percent.

$$\text{Capitalization, Punctuation, and Usage} = \frac{\text{Total Number Correct}}{40 \text{ Total Questions}} = \frac{}{40} \times 100 = \underline{\quad}\%$$

$$\text{Spelling} = \frac{\text{Total Number Correct}}{10 \text{ Total Questions}} = \frac{}{10} \times 100 = \underline{\quad}\%$$

$$\text{Composition} = \frac{\text{Total Number Correct}}{10 \text{ Total Questions}} = \frac{}{10} \times 100 = \underline{\quad}\%$$

Overall Practice Test Score

To get an idea of your overall score on the practice test, you can find the raw score. First, add up the number of questions you answered correctly on the entire practice test. This can be easily calculated by adding the number of questions correct from each subtest. Then divide your total number of questions that were correct by a total of 298 questions on the test. Multiply this number by 100 to calculate your score out of 100%.

$$\text{Raw Score} = \frac{\text{Total Number Correct}}{298 \text{ Total Questions}} = \frac{}{298} \times 100 = \underline{\quad}\%$$

ANSWERS EXPLAINED FOR HSPT PRACTICE TEST 1

Verbal Skills Subtest

1. **(b)** *Confiscate* means to take something.

2. **(c)** *Incorporate, unite,* and *merge* are all words having to do with putting things closer together. *Disperse* means to spread out.

3. **(d)** *Boston, Chicago,* and *Los Angeles* are all cities while *Arizona* is a state.

4. **(b)** False. If Verdi were a snake, he would have to be cold-blooded.

5. **(c)** *Aloof* means to be *detached* and uninterested. *Concerned* is the opposite of uninterested. *Distant* and *casual* are synonyms of *aloof.*

6. **(b)** A *diner* is a place where people go to *eat* and a *school* is a place where people go to *learn.*

7. **(b)** *Deter* means to put off or slow the progress of something, to *hinder. Prod, facilitate,* and *force* all have to do with making something happen.

8. **(c)** *Accelerate* means to speed something along, whereas *impede, slow,* and *delay* all mean the opposite of *accelerate.*

9. **(a)** *Decipher* means to figure something out. *Encode* is to make something difficult to figure out.

10. **(a)** *Drape,* while it can be used to *decorate* something, is a verb that means to *cover* something such as a window.

11. **(d)** *Flagrant* means to be *bold,* upfront, or obvious. *Pungent* has to do with odors and both *subtle* and *quiet* are antonyms of *flagrant.*

12. **(b)** A *mitten* is worn on a *hand* and a *hat* is worn on a *head.*

13. **(c)** *Contagious* is to be both *infectious* and *spreading. Harmless* is the word that does not belong.

14. **(b)** *Distraught* is to be *troubled. Untrusting* may be a component or a cause of being *distraught* but is not a synonym.

15. **(b)** *Swelter* means to be very hot. The opposite of *swelter* is *freeze.*

16. **(c)** A *button* is used to close or fasten a *coat* and a *lock* is used to close or fasten a *door* shut.

17. **(a)** If all of the boys at the school wear a tie and Charles does not have a tie, then he must not attend that school. Don't overthink it and wonder if he just forgot his tie!

18. **(d)** *Lament, cry,* and *moan* are all things that a sad person does. *Praise* does not belong.

19. **(a)** *Act* is part of a *play* and *chapter* is part of a *novel.* You may also consider that a *play* is divided into *acts* and a *novel* is divided into *chapters.*

20. **(d)** A *treaty,* an *agreement,* and a *contract* are all means of working together, and a *debate* occurs when people disagree.

21. **(b)** *Allot* means to give out, distribute, or *allocate.*

22. **(a)** A *knoll* is a small hill compared to a *mountain* which is a large hill. A *lake* is a small body of water compared to an *ocean* which is a large body of water.

23. **(c)** A *piano* is played by striking *keys* and a *guitar* is played by plucking *strings*. The other answer choices are related but cannot form a similar sentence.

24. **(c)** *Felon*, *prisoner*, and *inmate* are all references to a person in jail, whereas a *policeman* is not in jail.

25. **(a)** If Matthew has the highest grade and his brother is in the same class, then Nick must have a lower grade than Matthew.

26. **(d)** *Corrupt* means to be *unethical*. The other answer choices are all positive in meaning while *corrupt* is the only negative choice.

27. **(a)** *Weight* is measured in *grams* and *temperature* is measured in *degrees*. *Temperature* refers to *heat* but degrees represent the unit of measure just as *grams* are a unit of measure for *weight*.

28. **(c)** *Bellow* means to *yell* or *shout*. *Talk* is in between *bellow* and *whisper* in volume. *Whisper* is the opposite of *bellow*.

29. **(c)** *Cascade* means to *fall* or *collapse*. *Climb* is the opposite of *fall*.

30. **(b)** *Snap, zipper,* and *button* are all items used in clothing as fasteners. A *shirt* is a type of clothing and not a fastener.

31. **(b)** *Viscous* means *thick* and sticky. Do not confuse this with vicious, which means *wicked*.

32. **(a)** To *tell, declare,* or *claim* are all acts of revealing something. *Conceal* is the opposite, meaning to hide.

33. **(c)** *Cautious, wary,* and *nervous* are all adjectives having to do with being suspicious. *Calm* means to be at ease and does not belong.

34. **(d)** *Malicious* is the opposite of *kind* while *spiteful* is the opposite of *helpful*.

35. **(c)** Uncertain. Sandra's hair is longer than Kaylee's. S > K. If Elizabeth's hair is longer than Kaylee's it may or may not be longer than Sandra's $_ES_E$ > K. If you are making a diagram, you can see that even though E is to the left of K, it is on either side of S.

36. **(a)** *Gaunt* means to be *thin* in an unhealthy way. While a person who is *gaunt* may be *scary*, scary is not part of the definition of *gaunt*. *Spare* means to be lean or have no excess.

37. **(c)** Uncertain. Kathleen, T, collected more crystals than Karla, K, so T > K. Karla collected fewer than Colleen, C. In a diagram, C would be on either side of T and to the left of K. So while C is more than K, it may be more or less than T. $_CT_C$ > K.

38. **(b)** *Black* is a darker shade of *gray* and *red* is a darker shade of *pink*.

39. **(c)** *Demolish* means to *destroy* or deconstruct. *Construct* is the opposite of deconstruct. *Twist* and *hide* are unrelated.

40. **(c)** *Integrate* means to *incorporate* or put together. This is similar in meaning to *consolidate*. *Accommodate* is unrelated. *Separate* is an antonym of *integrate*.

41. **(b)** A *plant* grows from a *seed* and a *tree* <u>grows from a</u> *nut*. A *cashew* and an *acorn* are types of nuts.

42. **(b)** *Sporadic* means to be all over the place. Words with similar meanings are *spastic*, *inconsistent*, and *unpredictable*. *Regular* is the opposite of *sporadic*.

43. **(c)** A *shovel* <u>is used to</u> remove *snow* and a *rake* <u>is used to</u> remove *leaves*.

44. **(c)** *Accelerate*, *propel*, and *hasten* are all verbs that have to do with making something happen, whereas *impede* is the act of slowing down progress.

45. **(c)** *Confident*, *poised*, and *assured* are all related to a feeling of certainty, whereas *agitated* is related to being uncertain or nervous.

46. **(b)** False. Lee hiked more miles than Joseph, $L > J$. If Dorothy hiked fewer miles than Joseph that one statement can be constructed as $L > J > D$. It can be seen that Lee hiked more miles than Dorothy and not fewer.

47. **(c)** Uncertain. If Dakota has more cats than Jada, Ja, $(D > Ja)$ and Jada has fewer cats than Jordan, Jo, $(Jo > Ja)$ it is unclear if Dakota has more or fewer cats than Jordan. $_{Jo}D_{Jo} > Ja$.

48. **(c)** Uncertain. If Conor, Co, lives further away than Braden, and Chandler, Ch, lives further away than Braden, then it is unclear who (Conor or Chandler) lives the furthest away, $_{Ch}Co_{Ch} > Br$.

49. **(d)** A *hood*, *hat*, and *scarf* are all items of clothing that are worn on the neck or head. *Boots* are worn on the feet. Don't overthink this and decide that that a scarf is the only one you don't put something into. Choose the obvious relationship.

50. **(a)** *Culminate* means to *finish* or to complete. *Commence* means to begin, so it is the opposite of *culminate*. *Open* and *bottom* are unrelated to *culminate*.

51. **(c)** Uncertain. Because the first sentence states *most* students and not *all* students, we cannot know for certain if Aidan lives in Connecticut just because he attends the University of Hartford.

52. **(a)** *Build*, *assemble*, and *construct* are all verbs that mean to put something together. *Dismantle* means to take apart and does not belong.

53. **(c)** *Formidable* means to be large in size or personality (as *intimidating* or *frightful*). *Mediocre* means average or in the middle and does not belong.

54. **(d)** *Skeptical* means to be *untrusting*. *Concerned* is not an exact synonym of *skeptical* but is similar. To be *gullible* is to be overly trusting and therefore does not belong.

55. **(a)** *Radiant* means shining or *beaming*. Opposites would be *dull* or *gloomy*. *Heat* can radiate but it is not *radiant*.

56. **(a)** A *penny*, a *nickel*, and a *quarter* are all coins that can be kept in a bank. This is a question where three things are a part of the fourth.

57. **(b)** A *calculator* can *add*, *subtract*, and *divide*. This is another question where three things are a part of the fourth.

58. **(a)** True. If Mt. Washington is the highest mountain in New Hampshire, then it must be higher than every other mountain in that state, including Mt. Chocorua.

59. **(b)** To *shriek* is to scream or *bellow*. *Whimper* is the opposite. *Smile* and *gossip* are unrelated.

60. **(c)** Uncertain. If Austin's (S) score is higher than Charles' (C), it can be either higher or lower than Aidan's (A) score. $_SA_S > C$.

Quantitative Skills Subtest

61. **(c)** This is a difficult one. Each term is being multiplied, first by 4, then by 3, then by 2, and lastly by 1. So $-.4 \times 4 = -1.6, \times 3 = -4.8, \times 2 = -9.6, \times 1 = -9.6$.

62. **(c)** Beneath each coin write its value. The first is a penny (1¢), then next is a nickel (5¢), and the last is a dime (10¢). Plug the values into each answer choice to find the correct comparison.

63. **(b)** If you look at every other term you'll see 4, 5, 6, . . . so the next will be 7. The pattern (which you do not have to decipher here) is 4, 4^2, 5, 5^2, 6, 6^2, etc.

64. **(c)** Working from right to left, add 11 and 5 to get 16. Then the question remains, *what number subtracted from 18 is 16*, and the answer is 2. The question is represented by $18 - x = 5 + 11$.

65. **(b)** The pattern here is –11, –11, –11, etc. So, $65 - 11 = 54$.

66. **(c)** For each product write a value next to it, then read the answer choices. (A) $\frac{5}{6}$ of 36 is 30, (B) $\frac{1}{3}$ of 60 is 20, and (C) $\frac{4}{7}$ of 49 is 28. You can see that (A) > (C) > (B).

67. **(d)** In a letter/number sequence like this, start with the first item—in this case it is a letter—B, and determine how many letters are missing. B, missing C, D, E, next F then missing G, H, I, etc., so after N, the missing letters are O, P, Q and the next letter will be R. Look at your answer choices to see that there are two possible answers so next look at the numbers. Beginning with 8, $+ 2, \times 3, + 2, \times 3$ gives 96.

68. **(b)** Working from the right, 20% of 50 is 10 (remember to use the 10% rule—10% of 50 is 5, then double it to get 20% or 10). Then, what number subtracted from 49 is 10? The answer is 39. The equation representing this is $7^2 - x = .20 \times 50$.

69. **(b)** This is a right triangle. Angle *C* is 90 degrees as shown by the right angle symbol in the corner. In a triangle, the angle opposite a longer side is always larger than the angle opposite a shorter side, so angle *B* is smaller than angle *A* (because 3 is smaller than 4). In a right triangle, the 90-degree angle is always the largest angle.

70. **(b)** This is a simple addition sequence. Each term is 7 higher than the previous.

71. **(b)** The sequence is decreasing by a factor one third (dividing by 3) with each term. $54 \div 3 = 18, \div$ by $3 = 6$, etc. $2 \div 3 = \frac{2}{3}$.

72. **(c)** $\frac{1}{3}$ is more than $\frac{5}{18}$ because the numerator is less than $\frac{1}{3}$ of 18 (i.e., 6). Next, use the cross-up method to compare $\frac{1}{3}$ to $\frac{5}{11}$, $\left(\overset{15}{\frac{5}{11}} \times \overset{11}{\frac{1}{3}}\right)$. This shows that $\frac{5}{11}$ is larger than $\frac{1}{3}$ because the value above it (15), is larger than the value above one third (11). Therefore $\frac{5}{11} > \frac{1}{3} > \frac{5}{18}$.

73. **(c)** This is a division sequence. $875 \div 5$ is 175, etc. $7 \div 5$ is 1 remainder 2 or $1\frac{2}{5}$. Remember to look at the easier numbers first ($35 \div 5 = 7$) to find the pattern.

74. **(c)** The pattern here is $\div 2, - 50, \div 2, - 50$, etc. The last term should be $25 \div 2$, which is equal to $12\frac{1}{2}$.

75. **(a)** Converting Roman numerals to Arabic numbers gives 1, 2, 6, 12, 16. So the pattern is $\times 2, + 4, \times 2, + 4$, etc. The next term will be 32 or XXXII.

76. **(c)** Using the distributive property, rewrite (B): $3(x + y) = 3x + 3y$. Since each expression has a $3x$, you only have to compare the y terms to see that (A) is the largest expression for positive numbers x and y, and that (B) > (C).

77. **(c)** The number sequence is $- 6, + 4, - 6, + 4$, etc. The next number should be 38, so the answer is choice (c). The letter sequence skips two letters each time.

78. **(d)** The numbers in this sequence are increasing by 3 each time, but there is more than one answer choice beginning with 73. The first letter in each term is increasing by one letter, so the next letter will be G. The last letter in each term is also increasing by one letter so W, X, Y and the next letter will be Z.

79. **(c)** One fourth of 80 is 20. 20 subtracted from 87 is 67. The equation is $87 - x = \frac{1}{4}(80)$.

80. **(a)** This sequence is $\div 3$, then $+ 6$. The next two terms will be $18 \div 3 = 6$, then $6 + 6 = 12$.

81. **(b)** Working from the right, $\frac{4}{5}$ of 50 is 40 (first take one fifth of $50 = 10$, then multiply it by 4 to get 40). Subtract 11 to get 29. The equation is $x = \frac{4}{5}(50) - 11$.

82. **(a)** Simplify each expression. (A) $36 + 5 = 41$, (B) $5 + 36 = 41$, (C) $4 \times 14 = 56$. Then compare your values.

83. **(d)** Convert each drawing to a fraction. The denominator is the total number of pieces and the numerator is the number of shaded pieces. (A) is $\frac{3}{5}$, (B) is $\frac{3}{7}$, (C) is $\frac{3}{6}$. Remember that when the numerators are the same, the larger the denominator, the smaller the fraction, so (B) < (C) < (A).

84. **(d)** Working from the right, 3 times 8 is 24. Then 24 plus 7 is 31. What number subtracted from 68 is 31? $68 - 31 = 37$. The equation is $68 - x = 7 + (3 \times 8)$.

85. **(d)** In this sequence there is a pattern in the differences. Here is a list of the differences between each term: $- 3, + 2, - 4, + 3, - 5$. Now look at every other difference starting with 2, then 3, so the next term will be $26 + 4$ for 30. Looking at the first difference, $- 3$, then every other difference, $- 4, - 5$, means the last term will be $30 - 6 = 24$.

86. **(a)** The pattern here is $+ 7, + 7, + 7$, etc. so the last term will be $-71 + 7 = -64$.

87. **(d)** Convert each of these expressions to a number. (A) 10% of $60 = 6$, (B) $\frac{1}{6}$ of $36 = 6$, (C) 60% of $10 = 6$. Now you can see they are all equal.

88. **(a)** The sequence is increasing by $+ 13, + 14, + 15$. Then $60 + 16 = 76$.

89. **(c)** Compare each as a percent. (A) is 420%, (B) is 42%, and (C) is 40%. Now you can see that (C) is the least of the three percents.

90. **(a)** $\left(\frac{2}{3}\right)$ of 66 is 44 (one third is 22 and doubled is 44). Next double 44 to get 88. The equation that represents this is $x = 2 \times \left(\frac{2}{3}\right) \times 66$

91. **(d)** This sequence is + 9, + 12, + 9, + 12, etc. The last term will be 84 + 9 = 93.

92. **(a)** Working from the right, add 26 and 3 to get 29. Then subtract 29 from 54 (or better yet subtract 30 from 54 then add one back) to get 25. The equation is 54 – x = 26 + 3.

93. **(c)** The first letter of each term is going backwards, so the next letter will be G. The numbers are increasing by 12, meaning the next number will be 48 for an answer of G48.

94. **(b)** One fourth is 25%. (C) 0.24 = 24% so (A) > (B) = (C).

95. **(b)** This is a sequence in a sequence. Looking at the sequence beginning with 56 is simply 56 – 4, then 52 – 4 gives 48. Ignore the 3, 6, . . . sequence.

96. **(b)** Remember to use 10%. Ten percent of 80 is 8. Half of that (5%) is 4. Add 8 and 4 to get 12 (which is 15%). Next, add 6 to get the correct answer of 18. This can be represented by: $x = 6 + .15 \, (80)$.

97. **(d)** Every other term, beginning with 3, increases by 2. Each other term is 9 times the term in front of it, so the last term will be 9 × 7 = 63.

98. **(a)** A is 4 and E is 5, so A plus E is 9.

99. **(a)** The sequence, near the end, seems to be + 6. If 28 were changed to 30 this would confirm a + 6 sequence.

100. **(a)** Each number in the sequence is increasing by 13, so the next number will be 65. The second letter of each term is increasing by one letter each time, so the next letter in the will be G. This narrows the answer choices to only one, so stop figuring out the rest of the sequence.

101. **(b)** The area of the triangle (A) is $\frac{1}{2}$ (9 × 9) = 40.5. The area of the square (B) is 9 × 9 = 81. The area of the rectangle (C) is 12 × 9 = 108.

102. **(d)** Adding 15 and 24 gives a sum of 39. 13 × 3 = 39. The equation representing this is $13x = 15 + 24$.

103. **(a)** There are 36 inches in a yard (12 inches in a foot and three feet in a yard). So (B) is just one inch over a yard, 37 in., whereas (A) is one foot more than a yard, or 48 in.

104. **(a)** The differences in the sequence are – 8, – 7, – 6, – 5, so the next term will be 14 – 4 = 10.

105. **(b)** Simplify each expression. (A) 72 ÷ 3 = 24, (B) 36 ÷ 6 = 6, (C) 12 × 2 = 24.

106. **(d)** Compare each value to one fourth. (A) $\frac{9}{40}$ is just under one fourth and (B) $\frac{21}{80}$ is just over one fourth. (C) $\frac{1}{4}$ is in the middle and none are equivalent, so the answer must be choice (d).

107. **(a)** Subtract 8 from 44 to get 36. Then divide 36 by 12 to get the answer of 3. The equation can be written $12x = 44 - 8$.

108. **(b)** In the diagram, angles A and D are equal just as C and B are equal because they are vertical angles.

109. **(b)** Each of these are equal. Notice the numbers in (A) and (B) are the same just rearranged. 30% of 40 = 40% of 30 and each is equal to 12.

110. **(a)** Starting at the right of the statement, 9 times 5 is 45. *One third of what number is 45?* To find this you must multiply 45 times 3. However, there is only one answer that is over 45, so you don't have to do all of the math. This can be represented by $\frac{1}{3}x = 9 \times 5$.

111. **(c)** Simplify each expression: (A) $-5 \times 2 = -10$, (B) $-33 \times 3 = -99$, (C) $-66 \times 2 = -132$.

112. **(c)** The hourglass that has the most sand at the bottom shows the most time that has passed. (C) > (B) > (A).

Reading Subtest

113. **(b)** In second paragraph, the passage reads, "They were the first organizers of peace."

114. **(c)** Process of elimination is the strategy for this question. Choices (a), (b), and (d) are all inaccurate or are too extreme.

115. **(b)** *Strife*, in this context, most nearly means a hardship or *disagreement*.

116. **(c)** In the first paragraph, it can be found "by banishing the disorderly . . . reduced their countries to peace and harmony."

117. **(d)** In the passage, *concord* means *harmony*.

118. **(c)** In paragraph three, the passage reads "Their treaties with foreign states secured their countries the advantages of commerce . . . ."

119. **(a)** In paragraph two, it says, "training all classes alike to obey authority, they prepared the way for self-government."

120. **(c)** In the first paragraph, the passage reads, "They often took their power by force."

121. **(b)** All of the answer choices can be found in the passage except for choice (b) holding fair elections. It states in paragraph three that elections were often rigged meaning *not* fair.

122. **(a)** The main idea of the passage is to provide an overall picture of tyrants.

123. **(d)** One benefit of perennials is they do not have to be replanted each year.

124. **(c)** While some of the other choices are true, the main idea of the passage is that both types of plants, perennials and annuals, are useful in a well-planned garden.

125. **(c)** *Plethora* means a large amount or *abundant*.

126. **(c)** The passage is not detailed enough to be a research article and is most likely a magazine article.

127. **(b)** Annuals do not regrow each year but are beneficial as they bloom in the heat when some perennials do not.

128. **(c)** Zinnias are annual flowers as stated in the last paragraph.

129. **(a)** *Thrive* means to succeed or in the case of flowers and plants, to *grow*.

130. **(d)** Hosta are not annuals—they are perennials. All other statements can found in the passage.

131. **(c)** Perennial plants lose their tops each year but the root system lives.

132. **(c)** Perennial plants are the highlight of the article, but the author is not trying to convince the reader to use only perennials.

133. **(d)** Chirping serves to attract a female mate, not a male.

134. **(a)** The passage states that there are multiple methods and that none are an exact science.

135. **(d)** *Nocturnal* means to occur during the nighttime.

136. **(b)** The other three choices can be eliminated. The author is most likely a science teacher.

137. **(d)** As stated in the last paragraph, the sound is made by crickets rubbing their wings together.

138. **(b)** The relationship, as stated in the second paragraph, has been known for over a hundred years.

139. **(d)** The number of chirps in a 14 or 15 second interval is used to determine the temperature. The other statements are inaccurate.

140. **(c)** *Unique* means to be *one of a kind*.

141. **(d)** This is most likely a short article and is not a saga (a story over a long period of time) or a biography.

142. **(a)** This is the only answer choice that is addressed in the passage.

143. **(b)** In the second paragraph, it can be found that Tom graduated in 1995.

144. **(a)** The passage is discussing only Tom Brady and his successes.

145. **(c)** *Humble* means to be *modest* and not bragging.

146. **(c)** The third paragraph describes Bill Belichick as the team's head coach.

147. **(a)** The passage states that the Patriots played in 8 Super Bowls; however, Tom Brady played in only 7.

148. **(b)** Bill Belichick, as head coach, is also credited with the team's success. Peyton Manning and the opponents are on other teams, and the college coach is not affiliated with the Patriots.

149. **(c)** In the second paragraph, the passage states that Tom spent a lot of time on the bench before becoming the starting quarterback.

150. **(d)** *Instill* means to firmly *establish* something.

151. **(b)** The passage is about the successes, over time, of Tom Brady.

152. **(a)** The author is most likely a fan or a sports writer.

153. **(c)** *Timid* means to be *shy*.

154. **(d)** *Resume*, the verb, means to *continue* something.

155. **(c)** *Blatant* means *bold* or obvious.

156. **(a)** *Ultimate* means *final.*

157. **(d)** *Vague* means to be *unclear.*

158. **(b)** *Loathe* means to strongly *dislike.*

159. **(b)** *Resolve* means to *fix* something.

160. **(a)** To be *compassionate* is to be *caring* or concerned.

161. **(a)** *Envious* most nearly means *jealous.*

162. **(b)** *Critical* means important, vital, or *necessary.*

163. **(b)** *Lucrative* means to produce profit and most nearly means *beneficial.*

164. **(d)** *Intriguing* means to be interesting or *curious.*

165. **(b)** *Embark* means to begin a trip or to *leave.*

166. **(c)** *Amassed* means *collected.*

167. **(d)** *Lucid* means to be clear or *easy to understand.*

168. **(a)** *Unkempt* is to be *messy.*

169. **(c)** *Throbbing* means to be *pounding.*

170. **(c)** *Temporary* means short term or *not lasting.*

171. **(b)** To *forfeit* is to *give up.*

172. **(d)** To be *agitated* means to be confused or *nervous.*

173. **(b)** *Epitome* means to be the best or the *perfect example* of something.

174. **(b)** *Placid* is *calm.*

Mathematics Subtest

175. **(c)** A five-sided polygon is a pentagon. (The root *pent* means five).

176. **(b)** Long division gives a quotient of 203 with 1 left over as a remainder. You can also solve this by plugging in answer choices, ex: 203 times 21 is 4263 and one more (remainder 1) makes 4264.

177. **(b)** Careful not to confuse "hundred" with "hundredths" place. Hundredths is the second decimal place, 0.02 and not 200.

178. **(b)** Treat this as a long division problem $5\overline{)12}$. Keep checking your answer choices to see where the quotient repeats. You can tell from the answer choices that your quotient

will be 0.416; you only have to find the repeat. The quotient will be 0.416666 . . . which is written $0.41\overline{6}$.

179. **(c)** The largest factor that 108 and 72 have in common is 36. Plug in each answer choice beginning with the largest to quickly find the answer.

180. **(c)** There are 2 pints in a quart and 4 quarts in a gallon. Therefore there are 8 pints in one gallon and 16 in two gallons.

181. **(a)** Dividing by one fraction is the same as multiplying by the reciprocal of the fraction. $\frac{3}{7} \times \frac{5}{1} = \frac{15}{7}$. Since this is not an answer choice, you must change the improper fraction to a mixed number by dividing 15 by 7. 7 goes into 15 twice with a remainder of 1. The remainder goes over the divisor of 7 for $2\frac{1}{7}$.

182. **(d)** Remember when multiplying decimal numbers, you can ignore the decimals until you are done multiplying. You must then count the number of decimal places from the right in the problem. The number 24.6 has one decimal place and the number 0.31 has two, so you would move the decimal in your product three places to the left, for an answer of 7.626.

183. **(c)** The square root of 81 is 9 because 9 × 9 = 81.

184. **(b)** The rule for multiplying exponential expressions with the same base is $a^m \times a^n = a^{m+n}$. So the answer is $7^{(6+2)} = 7^8$.

185. **(b)** There are 1,000 meters in a kilometer. To convert kilometers to meters you must multiply by 1,000; 0.18 kilometers × 1,000 meters/kilometer = 180 meters.

186. **(a)** When converting a number from scientific notation, move the decimal point to the right for each value in the positive exponent. $4 \times 10^2 = 400$, $3 \times 10^3 = 3,000$, and $21 + 10^1 = 31$. Add the three terms: 400 + 3,000 + 31 = 3,431. The number in the tens place is 3.

187. **(d)** When multiplying or dividing negative numbers, your answer will be positive if you have an even number of negative signs and negative if you have an odd number. The product of 4, 2, and 9 is 72 with an odd number of negative signs, so the answer is –72.

188. **(d)** 20% of the students prefer blue, so you must find 20% of 1,200. Ten percent of 1,200 is 120, then double it to get 20% or 240.

189. **(c)** Categorical data, such as type of pet, is best displayed on a bar graph or a circle graph. The other data is best shown on a line graph or time plot.

190. **(d)** To determine 5% of $28.80, you can first figure out 10% then cut it in half to get 5%. 10% of $28.80 is $2.88 and half of that is $1.44.

191. **(a)** For this type of question, plug in answer choices to find the correct answer. Begin with a value that is in the middle of the answer choices; in this case, you can try 8 or 12. If we start with 8, we assume that Nick read 8 books. Matthew read 2 fewer, so he read 6 books. Kathy read twice as many as Matthew, which would be 12. Larry read 3 more than Kathy, making 15. Then add them all up for a total of 41. Since the total should only be 23, a guess of 8 is too high. Therefore the answer must be 5. You can double check this to verify and will find the new sum is 23.

192. **(a)** If the perimeter is 32 inches, the length of one side (all sides are equal in a square) is one fourth of that, or 8. The area is the square of the length of a side, making an area of 64 square inches.

193. **(b)** Complementary angles are angles that add up to 90 degrees. The diagram showing 60 degrees plus 30 degrees is correct.

194. **(a)** Supplementary angles are those that make up a line and add up to 180 degrees. Since x and 130 degrees make up a line, the total must be 180 degrees.

195. **(c)** There are 8 quarters in 2 dollars. Three divided by eight is $\frac{3}{8}$.

196. **(c)** If the perimeter is 28 cm, it is not possible for the length of any side to be half of that, 14. Rectangles are made up of two sets of identical length sides. So if two sides are 14, the other two sides must be 0, which is impossible. The next even integer less than 14 is 12. If two sides are 12 cm, then each of the other two sides will be 2, for a total perimeter of 28 cm.

197. **(d)** In a trapezoid, two sides are parallel while the other two sides are not. In this case, the top and bottom sides are parallel. While it is possible that some angles in a trapezoid may be the same, it is not a requirement.

198. **(d)** The average is $(9 + 12 + 11 + 0) \div 4$. Remember you must still divide by 4 even though one student scored 0.

199. **(d)** There are a total of 7 candies in the jar (denominator) and 3 are red (numerator), so there is a $\frac{3}{7}$ chance of selecting a red candy.

200. **(c)** The average is $(8 + 5 + 6 + 2 + 8) \div 5 = \frac{29}{5} = 5$ R4 or $5\frac{4}{5}$.

201. **(c)** When a number is multiplied by a variable, there is no need for a multiplication sign between them. $2x$ means "two times a number" so the answer is $2x + 18 = 72$.

202. **(b)** In similar triangles, corresponding angles are the same measure and the lengths of corresponding sides are proportional. $\overline{AB}$ and $\overline{DF}$ are not corresponding and therefore are not similar or proportional to each other.

203. **(c)** There are 16 ounces in a pound, so 2 pounds is 32 ounces. Adding another 8 ounces makes a total of 40 ounces.

204. **(d)** When performing long division with decimals, remember to move the decimal point in the divisor all the way to the right and move the decimal in the dividend the same number of places to the right.

205. **(b)** Dividing by one fraction is the same as multiplying by the reciprocal of the second fraction. So $\frac{2}{3} \div \frac{9}{4} = \frac{2}{3} \times \frac{4}{9} = \frac{8}{27}$.

206. **(b)** To determine the mean, you must add all of the values and divide the sum by the total number of values. $(780 + 520 + 400 + 650 + 600) \div 5 = 590$.

207. **(a)** A hexagon has 6 sides.

208. **(b)** A rhombus is a parallelogram with opposite equal acute angles and opposite equal obtuse angles. All sides are equal length.

209. **(b)** The median is the middle number when the numbers are in increasing order. Doubling the highest number will not change the median—it will still be in the middle.

210. **(a)** The diameter of a circle is twice the circle's radius. $32 \times 2 = 64$.

211. **(c)** The cube root of 8 is 2 because $2 \times 2 \times 2$ is equal to 8.

212. **(c)** The left side of the inequality is the difference of two terms. The symbol is the less-than symbol, so the correct answer is choice (c).

213. **(a)** Use the 10% rule for this problem. 10% of 20,000 is 2,000. Three times that (6,000) is then three times 10%, or 30%.

214. **(d)** Simplify the left side of the equation first. $\frac{2}{3} \times 7 = \frac{14}{3}$. To isolate m, multiply both sides of the equation by $\frac{1}{12}$. $m = \frac{14}{36}$, which reduces to $\frac{7}{18}$.

215. **(b)** The area of a square is the square of the length of a side. If the side is doubled, the area will increase 4 times. You can answer this by making up a value for a side. The area of a square with a side of 3 is 9, and the area of a square with a side of 6 (twice 3) is 36. 36 is four times 9.

216. **(d)** The denominator is the total number of grandchildren, 17, and the numerator is the number of girls, 5.

217. **(a)** Kathryn babysat a total of 16 hours at a rate of $11/hour. 16 hours $\times$ $11/hour = $176.

218. **(d)** Surface area is the sum of the areas of each of the sides. There are six sides to a rectangular prism. The side in the front of the diagram is 6×11, or 66 cm^2 and there are 2 of these sides. The other two sides each have an area of 11×55, or 55 cm^2. The area of each of the last two sides is 30 cm^2, (5×6). Add each of these areas for a total of 324 cm^2.

$$(66 \times 2) + (55 \times 2) + (30 \times 2) = 132 + 110 + 60 = 302 \text{ cm}^2$$

219. **(d)** Remember to check your answer choices as you go so you can do as little math as possible. If only one answer had an 8 in the ones column, you would have very little work to do.

220. **(c)** Sandra has a total of $50 and from that she must subtract $5 for each item ($5x$). The remainder, the right side of the equation, represents the leftover or the change of $7.

221. **(b)** This is a direct variation problem. $\frac{3 \text{ in.}}{2 \text{ ft.}} = \frac{x}{12 \text{ ft.}}$. Look at the relationship between 2 and 12 (times 6), then do the same to 3 inches ($3 \times 6 = 18$ inches). You can also solve by cross multiplying $\frac{3 \text{ in.}}{2 \text{ ft.}} = \frac{x}{12 \text{ ft.}}$. Cross multiply to get $3 \times 12 = 2x$. Then $36 = 2x$, so $x = \frac{36}{2} = 18$.

222. **(c)** Remember to check your answer choices as you go. The product must end with a 0 ($5 \times 2 = 10$). Check to see if you can eliminate any answer choices before you continue.

223. **(c)** To isolate x, you must divide both sides by –12. Remember, when you divide or multiply by a negative value, switch the greater-than sign to a less-than sign to get $x < -3$.

224. **(a)** The median is the number in the middle of a group of ascending values.

225. **(b)** If Emmett is taller than Sarah, who is the same height as Christina, then Emmett must also be taller than Christina.

226. **(a)** Distance equals rate times time. D = 5 hours × 50 mph.

227. **(c)** The mode is the value that occurs most often, which here is 7.

228. **(a)** This can be reasoned through if you don't want to set up an equation. If Karyn works for one hour, she will complete two fifths, and if she works another hour, she will complete four fifths. This means she must work *more* than two hours so the answer must be 2.5 hours (there is only one answer that is larger than 2). The equation would be $.4x = 1$ where x represents the number of hours worked.

229. **(a)** When solving a problem with mixed units of measure (feet and yards), convert the higher values to small values (in this case convert feet to yards). Since there are three feet in a yard, the fabric is 4 yards by 3 yards for a total of 12 square yards (4 × 3). 12 square yards at $28 per yard is 12 × 18 or $336.

230. **(c)** The Girl Scouts sold a total of 25 boxes (5 + 12 + 8) at $4.25 per box.

$$25 \times \$4.25 = \$106.25$$

231. **(a)** Remember the song "... *same sign add 'em up opposites subtract.*" Here you have addition of the same signs. –6 – 12 = (–6) + (–12) so you simply add them together and keep the same sign. –6 + (–12) = –18.

232. **(a)** Volume of a rectangular prism is length × width × height, or 8 cm × 5 cm × 4 cm = 160 cm^3.

233. **(b)** Process of elimination is your best approach for this problem. Since Mrs. Pickering paid 60%, she paid a little more than half of the original price. If she paid $54.60 then the original cost must have been a little less than double that, so no more than $109.20. To solve algebraically (the long and time-consuming way) you would solve this: 54.60 = 0.60x. Divide both sides by 0.6 to solve for x. You can plug in your answer to check: 0.60 ($91.00) = $54.60.

234. **(c)** The slope of a line is rise over run (change in y over change in x). Between the two points shown, there is a rise of 3 and a run of 2 for a slope of $\frac{3}{2}$. Also notice that the line is increasing as the x gets larger, which indicates that the slope is positive.

235. **(d)** Lawrence traveled the first part of the trip at 50 miles per hour. Therefore, in a half hour he traveled only 25 miles. For the next part of the trip, he traveled at 60 miles per hour for a third of an hour (20 minutes) so 20 miles was traveled for a total of 45 miles. 25 miles + 20 miles = 45 miles.

236. **(b)** 400 ounces of milk divided by 8 ounces per cup is 50 cups of milk.

237. **(b)** Remember to *Keep–Change–Change* here. Change the division question into a multiplication one.

$$\frac{\frac{2}{7}}{\frac{1}{3}} = \frac{2}{7} \div \frac{1}{3} = \frac{2}{7} \times \frac{3}{1} = \frac{6}{7}$$

238. **(c)** This is a direct proportion problem. There are 5 girls to 13 boys, so if there are 25 girls (5 × 5) then there must be 65 boys (13 × 5). The equation to show the ratio is $\frac{5}{13} = \frac{25}{x}$. Cross multiplication will give you 13 × 25 = 5x. Simplify to 325 = 5x and divide both sides by 5 to get an answer of 65.

Language Skills Subtest

239. **(c)** Summer should not be capitalized. Seasons are only capitalized when used as part of a title, such as the Summer Olympics.

240. **(a)** Company is singular, not plural. The statement should read *My mother's company is very successful.*

241. **(d)** No mistakes.

242. **(b)** This is an example of a double negative; *hardly no* should be *hardly any.*

243. **(b)** The statement should read *Susan and I.* Remember to try each pronoun separately. *Me is always on time* is not correct. *I am always on time* is correct.

244. **(c)** *Gregory and I went to the movies* is correct.

245. **(c)** *Please respond to Elizabeth and me* is correct. Remember to try each pronoun separately.

246. **(a)** *Kaylee went* is past tense and *tomorrow* is future tense. The sentence should read *Kaylee went to school yesterday* or *Kaylee will go to school tomorrow.*

247. **(d)** No mistakes.

248. **(a)** There should be a period after Sr in *Lawrence Sr.*

249. **(a)** There should be a comma after each item in a list and before the word *and.* My favorite colors are blue, red, and green.

250. **(b)** *Enter the room, take a seat, and wait until you are called.*

251. **(a)** *Korean War* should be capitalized.

252. **(c)** There should be a question mark at the end of the question.

253. **(b)** There should be a comma after *darts.*

254. **(a)** *Each* is singular and *are* is used for plural. The sentence should read *Each of the cats is soft.*

255. **(c)** *Quick* is used as an adverb and describes the action verb and therefore should have an *–ly* at the end. The runner ran *quickly* at the end of the race.

256. **(a)** This is a double negative; *couldn't scarcely* should read *could scarcely.*

257. **(b)** The word *beside* should be *besides. Besides* means in addition to, and *beside* means next to.

258. **(d)** No mistakes.

259. **(a)** The word *Said* should not be capitalized.

260. **(a)** There should be a comma after the word *town.*

261. **(a)** The pronoun, *I,* should always be capitalized.

262. **(c)** Days of the week are always capitalized. *Sunday* should be capitalized.

263. **(b)** There should be a comma after the word *flour.*

264. **(b)** *Mothers* is possessive and should have an apostrophe, *mother's.*

265. **(c)** In a list there should be a comma after each item. This statement is missing the comma after the word *vegetables.*

266. **(b)** *Too* should be *two* since it is referring to a quantity, the number 2.

267. **(d)** No mistakes.

268. **(a)** There should be a period after *Mr.* The name should read *Mr. William Hastings.*

269. **(b)** When referencing a person, the pronoun *who* should be used, not *which.*

270. **(c)** The word *international* is part of the name of the airport and should be capitalized, *Logan International Airport.*

271. **(c)** A date should always have a comma between the day and the year. *April 28, 1993.*

272. **(d)** No mistakes.

273. **(a)** The first letter of a sentence must always be capitalized.

274. **(b)** *There* should be *their* since it is possessive.

275. **(d)** No mistakes.

276. **(b)** When there are more than two, the word *between* cannot be used. *Between* should be *among.*

277. **(c)** *Julie* is singular but *get* is plural. It should read *Julie gets paid biweekly.*

278. **(b)** When referring to a specific number of things, the word *fewer* should be used rather than *less. There are no fewer than eight.*

279. **(a)** *Unavoidible* is correctly spelled *unavoidable.*

280. **(b)** *Possesive* is correctly spelled *possessive.*

281. **(c)** *Refreshements* is correctly spelled *refreshments.*

282. **(d)** No mistakes.

283. **(b)** *Disasterous* is correctly spelled *disastrous.*

284. **(a)** *Peice* is correctly spelled *piece.*

285. **(b)** *Eventully* is correctly spelled *eventually.*

286. **(b)** *Acknowlege* is correctly spelled *acknowledge.*

287. **(a)** *Allready* is correctly spelled *already.*

288. **(c)** *Souvenire* is correctly spelled *souvenir.*

289. **(c)** The missing word should be a reversal word. To the left of the blank is a positive and to the right is a negative.

290. **(b)** The missing word must continue the thought. Cheating caused the poor grade; it was not caused by it (which is why *because* is not correct).

291. **(c)** Remember to choose the shortest answer that has no grammatical errors.

292. **(b)** *The elderly author's books are very long.* The other sentences are grammatically incorrect or longer than the correct answer choice.

293. **(a)** While the other sentences may be true, they are not specific to a college student's first year experience.

294. **(a)** This is the most concise sentence with no errors.

295. **(b)** The other answer choices involve topics that are too lengthy for a one-paragraph essay.

296. **(c)** While the cost of oil is related to heating systems, sentence 3 is the only statement solely about fuel and not the heating system.

297. **(b)** Sentence 3 indicates that the dry ingredients have already been mixed so the sentence, *Sift the flour and the salt together,* should come before sentence 3.

298. **(a)** To fully understand the calculation in statement 2, one must know that the 5% refers to the current interest rate.

HSPT Practice Test 2

HOW TO GET THE MOST FROM PRACTICE TEST 2

This test will take two and a half hours to complete and about another half an hour to grade. This is time well spent and will help you recognize your progress. Here are some of the benefits of taking a second practice test. You will be able to:

- skip reading directions and examples to save valuable time.
- apply the strategies that you have learned while reading this book.
- see if your timing has improved, allowing you to finish each subtest in the time allowed.
- gauge your improvement in vocabulary (hopefully you've been expanding it).
- determine which topics may still be giving you some trouble.
- see if your ability to guess or narrow down answer choices is improving.

Directions

Tear out the bubble sheets on the following pages and use them to mark your answers. Because this is practice and not the real test, your goal is to continue learning about yourself. Are you using the correct strategies? Are there concepts that you do not understand? These are questions you should be able to answer after you complete the practice test. Remember to note the following, as you did in HSPT Practice Test 1:

- Circle question numbers that you had trouble with, skipped, or guessed on, so you can come back to answer them later if you have extra time. Also review these topics after you score the practice test.
- Circle your answers on the test before you bubble them on your answer sheet.
- There is no penalty for guessing. NEVER LEAVE A QUESTION UNANSWERED.
- Put a check ✔ next to the questions that you feel confident about. It is important that you are getting these correct, and this will build your confidence level.
- Try to do the work in the book if you can. The less time you spend hopping back and forth from test to scratch paper, the more time you will have to answer questions.

Take the practice test in a quiet place where you will not be disturbed. Make sure to time yourself for each subtest. When you are finished, review your score using the scoring tables that follow the test. You will be able to see which questions you had the most difficulty with and continue to work on them.

ANSWER SHEET
HSPT Practice Test 2

VERBAL SKILLS SUBTEST

1. Ⓐ Ⓑ Ⓒ Ⓓ	16. Ⓐ Ⓑ Ⓒ Ⓓ	31. Ⓐ Ⓑ Ⓒ Ⓓ	46. Ⓐ Ⓑ Ⓒ Ⓓ
2. Ⓐ Ⓑ Ⓒ Ⓓ	17. Ⓐ Ⓑ Ⓒ Ⓓ	32. Ⓐ Ⓑ Ⓒ Ⓓ	47. Ⓐ Ⓑ Ⓒ Ⓓ
3. Ⓐ Ⓑ Ⓒ Ⓓ	18. Ⓐ Ⓑ Ⓒ Ⓓ	33. Ⓐ Ⓑ Ⓒ Ⓓ	48. Ⓐ Ⓑ Ⓒ Ⓓ
4. Ⓐ Ⓑ Ⓒ Ⓓ	19. Ⓐ Ⓑ Ⓒ Ⓓ	34. Ⓐ Ⓑ Ⓒ Ⓓ	49. Ⓐ Ⓑ Ⓒ Ⓓ
5. Ⓐ Ⓑ Ⓒ Ⓓ	20. Ⓐ Ⓑ Ⓒ Ⓓ	35. Ⓐ Ⓑ Ⓒ Ⓓ	50. Ⓐ Ⓑ Ⓒ Ⓓ
6. Ⓐ Ⓑ Ⓒ Ⓓ	21. Ⓐ Ⓑ Ⓒ Ⓓ	36. Ⓐ Ⓑ Ⓒ Ⓓ	51. Ⓐ Ⓑ Ⓒ Ⓓ
7. Ⓐ Ⓑ Ⓒ Ⓓ	22. Ⓐ Ⓑ Ⓒ Ⓓ	37. Ⓐ Ⓑ Ⓒ Ⓓ	52. Ⓐ Ⓑ Ⓒ Ⓓ
8. Ⓐ Ⓑ Ⓒ Ⓓ	23. Ⓐ Ⓑ Ⓒ Ⓓ	38. Ⓐ Ⓑ Ⓒ Ⓓ	53. Ⓐ Ⓑ Ⓒ Ⓓ
9. Ⓐ Ⓑ Ⓒ Ⓓ	24. Ⓐ Ⓑ Ⓒ Ⓓ	39. Ⓐ Ⓑ Ⓒ Ⓓ	54. Ⓐ Ⓑ Ⓒ Ⓓ
10. Ⓐ Ⓑ Ⓒ Ⓓ	25. Ⓐ Ⓑ Ⓒ Ⓓ	40. Ⓐ Ⓑ Ⓒ Ⓓ	55. Ⓐ Ⓑ Ⓒ Ⓓ
11. Ⓐ Ⓑ Ⓒ Ⓓ	26. Ⓐ Ⓑ Ⓒ Ⓓ	41. Ⓐ Ⓑ Ⓒ Ⓓ	56. Ⓐ Ⓑ Ⓒ Ⓓ
12. Ⓐ Ⓑ Ⓒ Ⓓ	27. Ⓐ Ⓑ Ⓒ Ⓓ	42. Ⓐ Ⓑ Ⓒ Ⓓ	57. Ⓐ Ⓑ Ⓒ Ⓓ
13. Ⓐ Ⓑ Ⓒ Ⓓ	28. Ⓐ Ⓑ Ⓒ Ⓓ	43. Ⓐ Ⓑ Ⓒ Ⓓ	58. Ⓐ Ⓑ Ⓒ Ⓓ
14. Ⓐ Ⓑ Ⓒ Ⓓ	29. Ⓐ Ⓑ Ⓒ Ⓓ	44. Ⓐ Ⓑ Ⓒ Ⓓ	59. Ⓐ Ⓑ Ⓒ Ⓓ
15. Ⓐ Ⓑ Ⓒ Ⓓ	30. Ⓐ Ⓑ Ⓒ Ⓓ	45. Ⓐ Ⓑ Ⓒ Ⓓ	60. Ⓐ Ⓑ Ⓒ Ⓓ

QUANTITATIVE SKILLS SUBTEST

61. Ⓐ Ⓑ Ⓒ Ⓓ	74. Ⓐ Ⓑ Ⓒ Ⓓ	87. Ⓐ Ⓑ Ⓒ Ⓓ	100. Ⓐ Ⓑ Ⓒ Ⓓ
62. Ⓐ Ⓑ Ⓒ Ⓓ	75. Ⓐ Ⓑ Ⓒ Ⓓ	88. Ⓐ Ⓑ Ⓒ Ⓓ	101. Ⓐ Ⓑ Ⓒ Ⓓ
63. Ⓐ Ⓑ Ⓒ Ⓓ	76. Ⓐ Ⓑ Ⓒ Ⓓ	89. Ⓐ Ⓑ Ⓒ Ⓓ	102. Ⓐ Ⓑ Ⓒ Ⓓ
64. Ⓐ Ⓑ Ⓒ Ⓓ	77. Ⓐ Ⓑ Ⓒ Ⓓ	90. Ⓐ Ⓑ Ⓒ Ⓓ	103. Ⓐ Ⓑ Ⓒ Ⓓ
65. Ⓐ Ⓑ Ⓒ Ⓓ	78. Ⓐ Ⓑ Ⓒ Ⓓ	91. Ⓐ Ⓑ Ⓒ Ⓓ	104. Ⓐ Ⓑ Ⓒ Ⓓ
66. Ⓐ Ⓑ Ⓒ Ⓓ	79. Ⓐ Ⓑ Ⓒ Ⓓ	92. Ⓐ Ⓑ Ⓒ Ⓓ	105. Ⓐ Ⓑ Ⓒ Ⓓ
67. Ⓐ Ⓑ Ⓒ Ⓓ	80. Ⓐ Ⓑ Ⓒ Ⓓ	93. Ⓐ Ⓑ Ⓒ Ⓓ	106. Ⓐ Ⓑ Ⓒ Ⓓ
68. Ⓐ Ⓑ Ⓒ Ⓓ	81. Ⓐ Ⓑ Ⓒ Ⓓ	94. Ⓐ Ⓑ Ⓒ Ⓓ	107. Ⓐ Ⓑ Ⓒ Ⓓ
69. Ⓐ Ⓑ Ⓒ Ⓓ	82. Ⓐ Ⓑ Ⓒ Ⓓ	95. Ⓐ Ⓑ Ⓒ Ⓓ	108. Ⓐ Ⓑ Ⓒ Ⓓ
70. Ⓐ Ⓑ Ⓒ Ⓓ	83. Ⓐ Ⓑ Ⓒ Ⓓ	96. Ⓐ Ⓑ Ⓒ Ⓓ	109. Ⓐ Ⓑ Ⓒ Ⓓ
71. Ⓐ Ⓑ Ⓒ Ⓓ	84. Ⓐ Ⓑ Ⓒ Ⓓ	97. Ⓐ Ⓑ Ⓒ Ⓓ	110. Ⓐ Ⓑ Ⓒ Ⓓ
72. Ⓐ Ⓑ Ⓒ Ⓓ	85. Ⓐ Ⓑ Ⓒ Ⓓ	98. Ⓐ Ⓑ Ⓒ Ⓓ	111. Ⓐ Ⓑ Ⓒ Ⓓ
73. Ⓐ Ⓑ Ⓒ Ⓓ	86. Ⓐ Ⓑ Ⓒ Ⓓ	99. Ⓐ Ⓑ Ⓒ Ⓓ	112. Ⓐ Ⓑ Ⓒ Ⓓ

ANSWER SHEET
HSPT Practice Test 2

READING SUBTEST

113. Ⓐ Ⓑ Ⓒ Ⓓ	129. Ⓐ Ⓑ Ⓒ Ⓓ	145. Ⓐ Ⓑ Ⓒ Ⓓ	161. Ⓐ Ⓑ Ⓒ Ⓓ
114. Ⓐ Ⓑ Ⓒ Ⓓ	130. Ⓐ Ⓑ Ⓒ Ⓓ	146. Ⓐ Ⓑ Ⓒ Ⓓ	162. Ⓐ Ⓑ Ⓒ Ⓓ
115. Ⓐ Ⓑ Ⓒ Ⓓ	131. Ⓐ Ⓑ Ⓒ Ⓓ	147. Ⓐ Ⓑ Ⓒ Ⓓ	163. Ⓐ Ⓑ Ⓒ Ⓓ
116. Ⓐ Ⓑ Ⓒ Ⓓ	132. Ⓐ Ⓑ Ⓒ Ⓓ	148. Ⓐ Ⓑ Ⓒ Ⓓ	164. Ⓐ Ⓑ Ⓒ Ⓓ
117. Ⓐ Ⓑ Ⓒ Ⓓ	133. Ⓐ Ⓑ Ⓒ Ⓓ	149. Ⓐ Ⓑ Ⓒ Ⓓ	165. Ⓐ Ⓑ Ⓒ Ⓓ
118. Ⓐ Ⓑ Ⓒ Ⓓ	134. Ⓐ Ⓑ Ⓒ Ⓓ	150. Ⓐ Ⓑ Ⓒ Ⓓ	166. Ⓐ Ⓑ Ⓒ Ⓓ
119. Ⓐ Ⓑ Ⓒ Ⓓ	135. Ⓐ Ⓑ Ⓒ Ⓓ	151. Ⓐ Ⓑ Ⓒ Ⓓ	167. Ⓐ Ⓑ Ⓒ Ⓓ
120. Ⓐ Ⓑ Ⓒ Ⓓ	136. Ⓐ Ⓑ Ⓒ Ⓓ	152. Ⓐ Ⓑ Ⓒ Ⓓ	168. Ⓐ Ⓑ Ⓒ Ⓓ
121. Ⓐ Ⓑ Ⓒ Ⓓ	137. Ⓐ Ⓑ Ⓒ Ⓓ	153. Ⓐ Ⓑ Ⓒ Ⓓ	169. Ⓐ Ⓑ Ⓒ Ⓓ
122. Ⓐ Ⓑ Ⓒ Ⓓ	138. Ⓐ Ⓑ Ⓒ Ⓓ	154. Ⓐ Ⓑ Ⓒ Ⓓ	170. Ⓐ Ⓑ Ⓒ Ⓓ
123. Ⓐ Ⓑ Ⓒ Ⓓ	139. Ⓐ Ⓑ Ⓒ Ⓓ	155. Ⓐ Ⓑ Ⓒ Ⓓ	171. Ⓐ Ⓑ Ⓒ Ⓓ
124. Ⓐ Ⓑ Ⓒ Ⓓ	140. Ⓐ Ⓑ Ⓒ Ⓓ	156. Ⓐ Ⓑ Ⓒ Ⓓ	172. Ⓐ Ⓑ Ⓒ Ⓓ
125. Ⓐ Ⓑ Ⓒ Ⓓ	141. Ⓐ Ⓑ Ⓒ Ⓓ	157. Ⓐ Ⓑ Ⓒ Ⓓ	173. Ⓐ Ⓑ Ⓒ Ⓓ
126. Ⓐ Ⓑ Ⓒ Ⓓ	142. Ⓐ Ⓑ Ⓒ Ⓓ	158. Ⓐ Ⓑ Ⓒ Ⓓ	174. Ⓐ Ⓑ Ⓒ Ⓓ
127. Ⓐ Ⓑ Ⓒ Ⓓ	143. Ⓐ Ⓑ Ⓒ Ⓓ	159. Ⓐ Ⓑ Ⓒ Ⓓ	
128. Ⓐ Ⓑ Ⓒ Ⓓ	144. Ⓐ Ⓑ Ⓒ Ⓓ	160. Ⓐ Ⓑ Ⓒ Ⓓ	

ANSWER SHEET
HSPT Practice Test 2

MATHEMATICS SUBTEST

175. Ⓐ Ⓑ Ⓒ Ⓓ
176. Ⓐ Ⓑ Ⓒ Ⓓ
177. Ⓐ Ⓑ Ⓒ Ⓓ
178. Ⓐ Ⓑ Ⓒ Ⓓ
179. Ⓐ Ⓑ Ⓒ Ⓓ
180. Ⓐ Ⓑ Ⓒ Ⓓ
181. Ⓐ Ⓑ Ⓒ Ⓓ
182. Ⓐ Ⓑ Ⓒ Ⓓ
183. Ⓐ Ⓑ Ⓒ Ⓓ
184. Ⓐ Ⓑ Ⓒ Ⓓ
185. Ⓐ Ⓑ Ⓒ Ⓓ
186. Ⓐ Ⓑ Ⓒ Ⓓ
187. Ⓐ Ⓑ Ⓒ Ⓓ
188. Ⓐ Ⓑ Ⓒ Ⓓ
189. Ⓐ Ⓑ Ⓒ Ⓓ
190. Ⓐ Ⓑ Ⓒ Ⓓ

191. Ⓐ Ⓑ Ⓒ Ⓓ
192. Ⓐ Ⓑ Ⓒ Ⓓ
193. Ⓐ Ⓑ Ⓒ Ⓓ
194. Ⓐ Ⓑ Ⓒ Ⓓ
195. Ⓐ Ⓑ Ⓒ Ⓓ
196. Ⓐ Ⓑ Ⓒ Ⓓ
197. Ⓐ Ⓑ Ⓒ Ⓓ
198. Ⓐ Ⓑ Ⓒ Ⓓ
199. Ⓐ Ⓑ Ⓒ Ⓓ
200. Ⓐ Ⓑ Ⓒ Ⓓ
201. Ⓐ Ⓑ Ⓒ Ⓓ
202. Ⓐ Ⓑ Ⓒ Ⓓ
203. Ⓐ Ⓑ Ⓒ Ⓓ
204. Ⓐ Ⓑ Ⓒ Ⓓ
205. Ⓐ Ⓑ Ⓒ Ⓓ
206. Ⓐ Ⓑ Ⓒ Ⓓ

207. Ⓐ Ⓑ Ⓒ Ⓓ
208. Ⓐ Ⓑ Ⓒ Ⓓ
209. Ⓐ Ⓑ Ⓒ Ⓓ
210. Ⓐ Ⓑ Ⓒ Ⓓ
211. Ⓐ Ⓑ Ⓒ Ⓓ
212. Ⓐ Ⓑ Ⓒ Ⓓ
213. Ⓐ Ⓑ Ⓒ Ⓓ
214. Ⓐ Ⓑ Ⓒ Ⓓ
215. Ⓐ Ⓑ Ⓒ Ⓓ
216. Ⓐ Ⓑ Ⓒ Ⓓ
217. Ⓐ Ⓑ Ⓒ Ⓓ
218. Ⓐ Ⓑ Ⓒ Ⓓ
219. Ⓐ Ⓑ Ⓒ Ⓓ
220. Ⓐ Ⓑ Ⓒ Ⓓ
221. Ⓐ Ⓑ Ⓒ Ⓓ
222. Ⓐ Ⓑ Ⓒ Ⓓ

223. Ⓐ Ⓑ Ⓒ Ⓓ
224. Ⓐ Ⓑ Ⓒ Ⓓ
225. Ⓐ Ⓑ Ⓒ Ⓓ
226. Ⓐ Ⓑ Ⓒ Ⓓ
227. Ⓐ Ⓑ Ⓒ Ⓓ
228. Ⓐ Ⓑ Ⓒ Ⓓ
229. Ⓐ Ⓑ Ⓒ Ⓓ
230. Ⓐ Ⓑ Ⓒ Ⓓ
231. Ⓐ Ⓑ Ⓒ Ⓓ
232. Ⓐ Ⓑ Ⓒ Ⓓ
233. Ⓐ Ⓑ Ⓒ Ⓓ
234. Ⓐ Ⓑ Ⓒ Ⓓ
235. Ⓐ Ⓑ Ⓒ Ⓓ
236. Ⓐ Ⓑ Ⓒ Ⓓ
237. Ⓐ Ⓑ Ⓒ Ⓓ
238. Ⓐ Ⓑ Ⓒ Ⓓ

LANGUAGE SUBTEST

239. Ⓐ Ⓑ Ⓒ Ⓓ
240. Ⓐ Ⓑ Ⓒ Ⓓ
241. Ⓐ Ⓑ Ⓒ Ⓓ
242. Ⓐ Ⓑ Ⓒ Ⓓ
243. Ⓐ Ⓑ Ⓒ Ⓓ
244. Ⓐ Ⓑ Ⓒ Ⓓ
245. Ⓐ Ⓑ Ⓒ Ⓓ
246. Ⓐ Ⓑ Ⓒ Ⓓ
247. Ⓐ Ⓑ Ⓒ Ⓓ
248. Ⓐ Ⓑ Ⓒ Ⓓ
249. Ⓐ Ⓑ Ⓒ Ⓓ
250. Ⓐ Ⓑ Ⓒ Ⓓ
251. Ⓐ Ⓑ Ⓒ Ⓓ
252. Ⓐ Ⓑ Ⓒ Ⓓ
253. Ⓐ Ⓑ Ⓒ Ⓓ

254. Ⓐ Ⓑ Ⓒ Ⓓ
255. Ⓐ Ⓑ Ⓒ Ⓓ
256. Ⓐ Ⓑ Ⓒ Ⓓ
257. Ⓐ Ⓑ Ⓒ Ⓓ
258. Ⓐ Ⓑ Ⓒ Ⓓ
259. Ⓐ Ⓑ Ⓒ Ⓓ
260. Ⓐ Ⓑ Ⓒ Ⓓ
261. Ⓐ Ⓑ Ⓒ Ⓓ
262. Ⓐ Ⓑ Ⓒ Ⓓ
263. Ⓐ Ⓑ Ⓒ Ⓓ
264. Ⓐ Ⓑ Ⓒ Ⓓ
265. Ⓐ Ⓑ Ⓒ Ⓓ
266. Ⓐ Ⓑ Ⓒ Ⓓ
267. Ⓐ Ⓑ Ⓒ Ⓓ
268. Ⓐ Ⓑ Ⓒ Ⓓ

269. Ⓐ Ⓑ Ⓒ Ⓓ
270. Ⓐ Ⓑ Ⓒ Ⓓ
271. Ⓐ Ⓑ Ⓒ Ⓓ
272. Ⓐ Ⓑ Ⓒ Ⓓ
273. Ⓐ Ⓑ Ⓒ Ⓓ
274. Ⓐ Ⓑ Ⓒ Ⓓ
275. Ⓐ Ⓑ Ⓒ Ⓓ
276. Ⓐ Ⓑ Ⓒ Ⓓ
277. Ⓐ Ⓑ Ⓒ Ⓓ
278. Ⓐ Ⓑ Ⓒ Ⓓ
279. Ⓐ Ⓑ Ⓒ Ⓓ
280. Ⓐ Ⓑ Ⓒ Ⓓ
281. Ⓐ Ⓑ Ⓒ Ⓓ
282. Ⓐ Ⓑ Ⓒ Ⓓ
283. Ⓐ Ⓑ Ⓒ Ⓓ

284. Ⓐ Ⓑ Ⓒ Ⓓ
285. Ⓐ Ⓑ Ⓒ Ⓓ
286. Ⓐ Ⓑ Ⓒ Ⓓ
287. Ⓐ Ⓑ Ⓒ Ⓓ
288. Ⓐ Ⓑ Ⓒ Ⓓ
289. Ⓐ Ⓑ Ⓒ Ⓓ
290. Ⓐ Ⓑ Ⓒ Ⓓ
291. Ⓐ Ⓑ Ⓒ Ⓓ
292. Ⓐ Ⓑ Ⓒ Ⓓ
293. Ⓐ Ⓑ Ⓒ Ⓓ
294. Ⓐ Ⓑ Ⓒ Ⓓ
295. Ⓐ Ⓑ Ⓒ Ⓓ
296. Ⓐ Ⓑ Ⓒ Ⓓ
297. Ⓐ Ⓑ Ⓒ Ⓓ
298. Ⓐ Ⓑ Ⓒ Ⓓ

18 MINUTES

Samples:

A. Hurl most nearly means

   (a) run.
   (b) fall.
   (c) throw.
   (d) drop.

B. Baby is to adult as cub is to

   (a) mother.
   (b) bear.
   (c) dog.
   (d) infant.

Correct marking of samples:

A. Ⓐ Ⓑ ● Ⓓ

B. Ⓐ ● Ⓒ Ⓓ

---

1. Endanger most nearly means

   (a) isolate.
   (b) threaten.
   (c) warn.
   (d) jail.

2. Which word does *not* belong with the others?

   (a) distort.
   (b) deform.
   (c) preserve.
   (d) mangle.

3. Which word does *not* belong with the others?

   (a) futile
   (b) critical
   (c) ineffective
   (d) pointless

4. All of the books at Bridgton Bookstore are hardcovers. There is a dictionary for sale at the Bridgton Bookstore. The dictionary may be a paperback book. If the first two statements are true, the third is

   (a) true.
   (b) false.
   (c) uncertain.

5. Vigorous means the *opposite* of

   (a) strong.
   (b) energetic.
   (c) sedentary.
   (d) victorious.

6. Recipe is to cooking as blueprint is to

   (a) tree.
   (b) designer.
   (c) building.
   (d) paper.

7. Boisterous most nearly means

   (a) noisy.
   (b) clumsy.
   (c) angry.
   (d) wealthy.

8. Which word does *not* belong with the others?

   (a) arrogant
   (b) polite
   (c) proud
   (d) confident

GO TO THE NEXT PAGE ➡

9. Delinquent means the *opposite* of

   (a) derelict.
   (b) irresponsible.
   (c) tardy.
   (d) early.

10. Squander most nearly means

    (a) meander.
    (b) call.
    (c) replace.
    (d) waste.

11. Intimidate most nearly means

    (a) bribe.
    (b) scare.
    (c) copy.
    (d) alleviate.

12. Bird is to wing as fish is to

    (a) fin.
    (b) gill.
    (c) scales.
    (d) water.

13. Which word does *not* belong with the others?

    (a) furious
    (b) irate
    (c) grateful
    (d) angry

14. Sever most nearly means

    (a) sustain.
    (b) cut off.
    (c) add.
    (d) throb.

15. Bizarre means the *opposite* of

    (a) unique.
    (b) unusual.
    (c) odd.
    (d) conventional.

16. Grave is to serious as authentic is to

    (a) old.
    (b) real.
    (c) antique.
    (d) reading.

17. All of the campers at Pondicherry Park are able to swim. Jordan cannot swim. Jordan is a camper at Pondicherry Park. If the first two statements are true, the third is

    (a) true.
    (b) false.
    (c) uncertain.

18. Which word does *not* belong with the others?

    (a) procrastinate
    (b) delay
    (c) rush
    (d) stall

19. Pilot is to plane as captain is to

    (a) ship.
    (b) train.
    (c) car.
    (d) bus.

20. Which word does *not* belong with the others?

    (a) oration
    (b) postcard
    (c) eulogy
    (d) speech

21. Rejuvenate most nearly means

    (a) refresh.
    (b) create.
    (c) play.
    (d) reimburse.

22. Lion is to pride as wolf is to

    (a) dog.
    (b) pack.
    (c) wild.
    (d) smart.

GO TO THE NEXT PAGE ➡

23. Paternal is to maternal as uncle is to

    (a) brother.
    (b) relative.
    (c) aunt.
    (d) father.

24. Which word does *not* belong with the others?

    (a) prolific
    (b) abundant
    (c) productive
    (d) reclusive

25. Kimmy baked more cookies than Alex. Alex baked more cookies than Jonny. Jonny baked fewer cookies than Kimmy. If the first two statements are true, the third is

    (a) true.
    (b) false.
    (c) uncertain.

26. Arduous most nearly means

    (a) effortless.
    (b) rigorous.
    (c) evergreen.
    (d) kind.

27. Mailbox is to letter as bank is to

    (a) money.
    (b) vault.
    (c) invest.
    (d) safe.

28. Omnipotent means the *opposite* of

    (a) weak.
    (b) almighty.
    (c) unlimited.
    (d) all powerful.

29. Prohibit does *not* mean

    (a) forbid.
    (b) hinder.
    (c) permit.
    (d) interfere.

30. Which word does *not* belong with the others?

    (a) jeer
    (b) taunt
    (c) revere
    (d) insult

31. Gingerly most nearly means

    (a) rough.
    (b) careless.
    (c) tasty.
    (d) cautious.

32. Which word does *not* belong with the others?

    (a) stove
    (b) sink
    (c) refrigerator
    (d) dishwasher

33. Which word does *not* belong with the others?

    (a) paper
    (b) envelope
    (c) folder
    (d) binder

34. Machine is to invent as book is to

    (a) author.
    (b) novel.
    (c) publish.
    (d) write.

35. Karla's diamond is bigger than Kim's diamond. Colleen's diamond is bigger than Kim's. Colleen's diamond is bigger than Karla's diamond. If the first two statements are true, the third is

    (a) true.
    (b) false.
    (c) uncertain.

36. Reticent does *not* mean

    (a) garrulous.
    (b) timid.
    (c) quiet.
    (d) taciturn.

GO TO THE NEXT PAGE ➡

37. Frank can mow his lawn in less time than Bill. It takes Craig less time to mow his lawn than Frank. Bill can mow his lawn faster than Craig can. If the first two statements are true, the third is

(a) true.
(b) false.
(c) uncertain.

38. Touch is to finger as hear is to

(a) listen.
(b) ear.
(c) sound.
(d) head.

39. To admonish is to

(a) warn.
(b) confess.
(c) modify.
(d) decorate.

40. Belligerent is the *opposite* of

(a) consolidate.
(b) contort.
(c) humble.
(d) congenial.

41. Month is to week as year is to

(a) day.
(b) decade.
(c) month.
(d) holidays.

42. Obsolete is *not*

(a) current.
(b) antique.
(c) archaic.
(d) dated.

43. Vote is to election as run is to

(a) walk.
(b) fast.
(c) race.
(d) crawl.

44. Which word does *not* belong with the others?

(a) lucid
(b) awake
(c) fatigued
(d) alert

45. Which word does *not* belong with the others?

(a) medicine
(b) antibiotic
(c) vaccine
(d) virus

46. Jay climbed more mountains than Joe. Sue climbed fewer mountains than Joe. Jay climbed fewer mountains than Sue. If the first two statements are true, the third is

(a) true.
(b) false.
(c) uncertain.

47. The Franklin Zoo has four more giraffes than the Stone Zoo. The York Zoo has three fewer giraffes than the Stone Zoo. The Franklin Zoo has seven more giraffes than the York Zoo. If the first two statements are true, the third is

(a) true.
(b) false.
(c) uncertain.

48. Ashley has more siblings than Meredith. Steve has more siblings than Ashley. Meredith has more siblings than Steve. If the first two statements are true, the third is

(a) true.
(b) false.
(c) uncertain.

49. Which word does *not* belong with the others?

(a) mar
(b) restore
(c) maintain
(d) rejuvenate

GO TO THE NEXT PAGE ➡

50. Morose most nearly means

    (a) prevalent.
    (b) content.
    (c) gloomy.
    (d) amiable.

51. All students who take the HSPT are applying to high schools. Gregory is not taking the HSPT. Gregory is not going to high school. If the first two statements are true, the third is

    (a) true.
    (b) false.
    (c) uncertain.

52. Which word does *not* belong with the others?

    (a) sparrow
    (b) blue jay
    (c) robin
    (d) ostrich

53. Stagnant does *not* mean

    (a) still.
    (b) delicate.
    (c) stationary.
    (d) dormant.

54. Which word does *not* belong with the others?

    (a) corrupt
    (b) diverse
    (c) unethical
    (d) shady

55. Flagrant most nearly means

    (a) inconspicuous.
    (b) conceal.
    (c) dull.
    (d) blatant.

56. Which word does *not* belong with the others?

    (a) crucial
    (b) imperative
    (c) frivolous
    (d) important

57. Which word does *not* belong with the others?

    (a) flexible
    (b) staunch
    (c) loyal
    (d) devoted

58. Mr. Shelly has the fastest boat on Highland Lake. Mr. Bing has a boat on Highland Lake. Mr. Bing's boat is slower than Mr. Shelly's boat. If the first two statements are true, the third is

    (a) true.
    (b) false.
    (c) uncertain.

59. To endure is to

    (a) run from.
    (b) sustain.
    (c) surrender.
    (d) release.

60. Joanne's essay had more words than Tom's essay. Aidan's essay had fewer words than Joanne's. Aidan's essay had more words than Tom's essay. If the first two statements are true, the third is

    (a) true.
    (b) false.
    (c) uncertain.

STOP

30 MINUTES

Samples:

A. What number added to 3 makes 2 plus 5?

   (a) 3   (b) 4   (c) 5   (d) 7

B. In the sequence: 1, 2, 3, 4, 5, . . . , what number should come next?

   (a) 3   (b) 6   (c) 5   (d) 4

C. Examine (A), (B), and (C) and find the *best* answer.

   (A) (3 − 2) − 1
   (B) (3 − 1) − 2
   (C) 3 − (2 − 1)

   (a) (A) is greater than (B).
   (b) (A), (B), and (C) are equal.
   (c) (C) is greater than (A) and (B).
   (d) (B) is greater than (A).

D. Examine the hourglasses (A), (B), and (C) and find the *best* answer.

    (A)   (B)   (C)

   (a) (A) shows the most time passed.
   (b) (B) shows the most time passed.
   (c) (C) shows the most time passed.
   (d) (A) and (B) show the same time has passed.

Correct marking of samples:

A. Ⓐ ● Ⓒ Ⓓ
B. Ⓐ ● Ⓒ Ⓓ
C. Ⓐ Ⓑ ● Ⓓ
D. Ⓐ Ⓑ ● Ⓓ

---

61. In the sequence: −0.2, −0.8, −0.24, −0.96 , . . . , what number should come next?

   (a) 1.44   (c) −1.44
   (b) −2.6   (d) −2.88

62. In the sequence: 92, 78, 73, 59, 54, . . . , what number should come next?

   (a) 39   (b) 49   (c) 40   (d) 30

63. What number subtracted from 36 makes 7 more than 18?

   (a) 8   (b) 11   (c) 2   (d) 25

64. Examine (A), (B), and (C) and find the *best* answer.

    (A)   (B)   (C)

   (a) (A) + (C) < (B)
   (b) (B) > (C) > (A)
   (c) (B) > (A) > (C)
   (d) (A) = (B)

GO TO THE NEXT PAGE ➡

65. In the sequence: 0.25, 1, 4, 16, . . . , what number should come next?

(a) 64   (b) 18   (c) 12   (d) 28

66. Examine (A), (B), and (C) and find the *best* answer.

(A) $\frac{1}{8}$ of 56

(B) $\frac{1}{5}$ of 80

(C) $\frac{1}{4}$ of 60

(a) (A) < (B) < (C)
(b) (A) = (B)
(c) (B) > (C) > (A)
(d) (B) = (C)

67. In the sequence: G4, J7, M14, P17, . . . , what comes next?

(a) R30   (b) S19   (c) R19   (d) S34

68. What number when subtracted from 2^4 makes 20% of 25?

(a) 6   (b) 11   (c) 16   (d) 15

69. Examine the angles in the figure below and find the *best* answer.

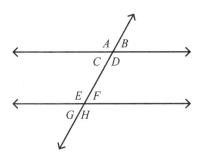

(a) $B > F$
(b) $C > A$
(c) $A = C$
(d) $A = E$

70. In the sequence: 864, 144, 72, 12, 6, . . . , what number should come next?

(a) 1   (b) 18   (c) 0   (d) 3

71. In the sequence: 64, 16, 4, 1, . . . , what number should come next?

(a) −4   (b) $\frac{2}{3}$ (c) $\frac{1}{4}$ (d) 2

72. Examine (A), (B), and (C) and find the *best* answer.

(A) $\frac{5}{21}$

(B) $\frac{3}{20}$

(C) $\frac{1}{4}$

(a) (C) < (A) < (B)
(b) (A) = (B)
(c) (C) > (A) > (B)
(d) (B) = (C)

73. In the sequence: 300, 150, 120, 60, . . . , what number should come next?

(a) 54   (b) 30   (c) 15   (d) 45

74. In the sequence: 14, 18, 26, 38, 54, . . . , what number should come next?

(a) 75   (b) 74   (c) 212   (d) 57

75. In the sequence: III, VI, IX, XII, . . . , what numeral should come next?

(a) XV   (b) VIII   (c) XX   (d) XIII

76. Examine (A), (B), and (C) and find the *best* answer when x and y are both positive.

(A) $2x - 6y$
(B) $2(x - y)$
(C) $-2(y - x)$

(a) (C) is less than (A).
(b) (A) is greater than (B).
(c) (B) and (C) are equal.
(d) (B) is greater than (C).

GO TO THE NEXT PAGE ➡

77. In the sequence: NM, JP, FS, . . . , what comes next?

(a) BU (b) TB (c) BV (d) DU

78. In the sequence: 20×DW, 23×EX, 26×FY, . . . , what comes next?

(a) 23×IZ (c) 29×KM
(b) 23×GM (d) 29×GZ

79. What number when subtracted from 47 leaves 4 less than $\frac{1}{4}$ of 60?

(a) 11 (b) 36 (c) 23 (d) 20

80. In the sequence: 40, 55, 47, 59, 53, 62, 58, . . . , what three numbers should come next?

(a) 60, 58, 62 (c) 65, 63, 68
(b) 55, 60, 57 (d) 64, 62, 65

81. What number is 12 less than $\frac{1}{3}$ of 48?

(a) 4 (b) 16 (c) 18 (d) 24

82. Examine (A), (B), and (C) and find the *best* answer.

(A) (4 – 9) – 5
(B) 9 – (4 – 5)
(C) (9 – 5) – 4

(a) (B) is equal to (A) and less than (C).
(b) (B) is equal to (C) which is greater than (A).
(c) (B) is greater than (A) which is greater than (C).
(d) (B) is greater than (C) which is greater than (A).

83. Examine (A), (B), and (C) and find the *best* answer.

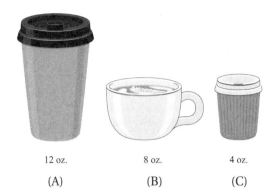

12 oz.   8 oz.   4 oz.
(A)   (B)   (C)

(a) (B) – (C) = (A)
(b) (A) > (B) + (C)
(c) (A) = (B) + (C)
(d) (B) + (A) = (C)

84. What number subtracted from 107 leaves 7 more than 5 times 7?

(a) 65 (b) 114 (c) 35 (d) 56

85. In the sequence: 370, 290, 220, 160, . . . , what number should come next?

(a) 100 (b) 110 (c) 80 (d) 130

86. In the sequence: –108, –100, –92, –84, . . . , what number should come next?

(a) –80 (b) –76 (c) 78 (d) 76

87. Examine (A), (B), and (C) and find the *best* answer.

(A) 40% of $20.00
(B) 60% of $10.00
(C) 15% of $40.00

(a) (A) = (C)
(b) (A) < (B) < (C)
(c) (B) = (C)
(d) (A) > (B) > (C)

GO TO THE NEXT PAGE ➡

88. In the sequence: 14, 32, 51, 71, . . . , what number should come next?

(a) 91　(b) 71　(c) 67　(d) 92

89. Examine (A), (B), and (C) and find the *best* answer.

(A) 1^8

(B) 1×8

(C) 8^1

(a) (B) is greater than (C).

(b) (B) is equal to (C).

(c) (C) is less than (B) and (A).

(d) (A) is greater than (B).

90. What number is twice as much as $\frac{5}{7}$ of 56?

(a) 80　(b) 8　(c) 40　(d) 77

91. In the sequence: 60, 53, 65, 58, 70, . . . , what comes next?

(a) 73　(b) 63　(c) 53　(d) 68

92. What number subtracted from 72 makes 13 more than 3?

(a) 16　(b) 60　(c) 88　(d) 56

93. In the sequence: S + 72, P + 36, M + 18, . . . , what should come next?

(a) N + 9　　(c) K + 19

(b) N + 19　　(d) J + 9

94. Examine (A), (B), and (C) and find the *best* answer.

(A) 0.63

(B) $\frac{5}{8}$

(C) 63%

(a) (A) is less than (B).

(b) (B) is less than (A) and equal to (C).

(c) (C) is less than (A) or (B).

(d) (A) and (C) are greater than (B).

95. In the sequence: 5, 7, 12, ___, ___, 21, 26, 28, . . . , what two numbers are missing?

(a) 13, 18　　(c) 14, 19

(b) 16, 19　　(d) 15, 20

96. What number added to 2^3 is 25% of 80?

(a) 12　(b) 8　(c) 20　(d) 25

97. In the sequence: 37, 32, 28, 25, . . . , what number should come next?

(a) 20　(b) 23　(c) 18　(d) 22

98. Examine the bar graph and find the *best* answer.

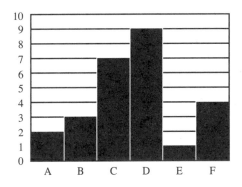

(a) D plus F equals B.

(b) F plus B equals C.

(c) C plus A plus F equals E.

(d) A, C, and D are equal.

99. In the sequence: 4, 8, 10, 18, 22, 44, 46, . . . , one number is *wrong*. That number should be

(a) 16　(b) 32　(c) 20　(d) 12

100. In the sequence: ZA, YC, XE, WG, . . . , what should come next?

(a) IV　　(c) UH

(b) VI　　(d) VH

GO TO THE NEXT PAGE ➡

101. Examine the angles below and find the *best* answer.

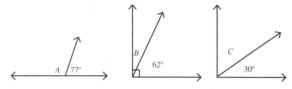

(a) A > C > B
(b) A > B = C
(c) A = B = C
(d) A = C > B

102. What number multiplied by 9 is equal to 16 more than 20?

(a) 3   (b) 36   (c) 29   (d) 4

103. Examine (A), (B), and (C) and find the *best* answer.

(A) 1.5 hours
(B) 125 minutes
(C) 1 hour and 5 minutes

(a) (A) > (B) = (C)
(b) (C) < (A) = (B)
(c) (C) < (A) < (B)
(d) (A) < (B) < (C)

104. In the sequence: 1, 3, 12, 14, 56, . . . , what number should come next?

(a) 58   (b) 124   (c) 112   (d) 28

105. Examine (A), (B), and (C) and find the *best* answer.

(A) $6 \div 0.2$
(B) 6×0.2
(C) $0.2 \div 6$

(a) (A) is equal to (C).
(b) (A) is greater than (B) and (C).
(c) (B) is greater than (A) and (C).
(d) (C) is greater than (A) and (B).

106. Examine (A), (B), and (C) and find the *best* answer.

(A) $5^2 - 8$
(B) $3^3 - 4$
(C) 2×4^2

(a) (C) > (A) > (B)
(b) (A) > (B) > (C)
(c) (A) > (B) = (C)
(d) (C) > (B) > (A)

107. What number subtracted from 68 makes 7 less than 36?

(a) 40   (b) 39   (c) 61   (d) 42

108. Examine (A), (B), and (C) and find the *best* answer.

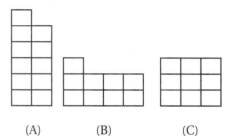

(A)   (B)   (C)

(a) (A) = (B)
(b) (B) > (C)
(c) (B) = (C)
(d) (A) = (B) > (C)

109. Examine (A), (B), and (C) and find the *best* answer.

(A) 8,650
(B) 0.865×10^3
(C) 8.65×10^2

(a) (A) is equal to (B) and greater than (C).
(b) (B) is equal to (C) and less than (A).
(c) (C) is greater than (A) or (B).
(d) (B) is greater than (A).

GO TO THE NEXT PAGE ➡

110. $\frac{1}{2}$ of what number is 11 times 8?

    (a) 88   (b) 44   (c) 176   (d) 19

111. Examine (A), (B), and (C) and find the *best* answer if $x = 4$.

    (A) $4 - x + 7$
    (B) $8 \div x$
    (C) $8 + 2 - x$

    (a) (A) and (B) are equal.
    (b) (A) and (C) are equal.
    (c) (B) is less than (A).
    (d) (A) is less than (C).

112. Examine (A), (B), and (C) and find the *best* answer.

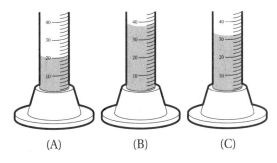

    (A)   (B)   (C)

    (a) (A) is more full than (C).
    (b) (B) contains the most.
    (c) (C) is the least full.
    (d) (B) and (C) are equally full.

STOP

25 MINUTES

Sample:

A. The passage below is followed by a series of questions.

The passages in this section of the test will be

(a) very easy to understand.
(b) very boring.
(c) followed by a series of questions.
(d) in very large font.

Correct marking of sample:

A. Ⓐ Ⓑ ● Ⓓ

READING—Comprehension

Questions 113–122 refer to the following passage.

Ludwig van Beethoven was born in Germany in December of 1770. Birth records have never been found; however, there are records showing that he was baptized on December 17, 1770. Because infants were typically baptized the day after birth, it is believed that Beethoven was born on December 16th. His father, Johann, began to teach Ludwig to play the piano before the boy was four years old. Johann tried to turn his son into a musical genius largely through cruelty and punishment. When Ludwig was only eight years old, his father coerced him into holding a public performance. Later, Ludwig took it upon himself to become the organist for local parishes. Meanwhile, his father tried to profit from his child prodigy by scheduling public performances and eventually Beethoven became a breadwinner for the family.

Ludwig eventually moved to Vienna with the hope of studying under Mozart. When his mother became ill, Ludwig returned to Bonn. After her death, Ludwig, at the age of just 19, became the legal guardian of his siblings. He later returned to Vienna to continue pursuing his passion for music. After the premiere of his first and second symphonies, Beethoven soon became known as the most prolific composer next to Haydn and Mozart.

At the young age of 26, Ludwig van Beethoven suffered significant hearing loss. Eventually, he had to give up performing in public. During his career, Beethoven was credited with being the musical genius that his father always envisioned. Up until his death in 1827, at the age of 57, Beethoven composed over 650 musical pieces and will forever be remembered as one of the most talented composers in all of history.

GO TO THE NEXT PAGE ➡

113. Why is Ludwig's birthday thought to be on December 16th?

    (a) Historians made a good guess.

    (b) It is the same day as his baptism.

    (c) At the time, babies were usually baptized the day after they were born.

    (d) His birth records state December 16 as his birthday.

114. The *best* title for this passage is

    (a) "The Education of Ludwig van Beethoven."

    (b) "Beethoven's Greatest Musical Pieces."

    (c) "A Brief Biography of Beethoven."

    (d) "The Medical History of Beethoven."

115. The word prolific, as underlined and used in the passage, most nearly means

    (a) abundant.

    (b) hard of hearing.

    (c) talented.

    (d) challenged.

116. Ludwig's father encouraged his son to be a great musician by what methods?

    (a) love and encouragement

    (b) promise of fame

    (c) cruelty and punishment

    (d) rewards

117. The word coerced, as underlined and used in the passage, most nearly means

    (a) begged.

    (b) tricked.

    (c) appreciated.

    (d) forced.

118. Ludwig van Beethoven is best known for being

    (a) a good sibling.

    (b) a loving son.

    (c) a talented composer.

    (d) a church organist.

119. It can be implied from the passage that

    (a) excessive music caused Beethoven's hearing loss.

    (b) Beethoven stopped composing when he lost his hearing.

    (c) Ludwig did not have a good relationship with his father.

    (d) to become a composer one must start training as a child.

120. This passage would most likely be found where?

    (a) a local newspaper.

    (b) a high school textbook.

    (c) a medical journal.

    (d) a parenting book.

121. Which event was *not* part of Beethoven's life?

    (a) hearing loss

    (b) living in Vienna

    (c) getting married

    (d) working as an organist

122. What is the main idea of the passage?

    (a) to show how awful Ludwig's father was

    (b) to provide a glimpse of the life of Beethoven

    (c) to show what a good brother Ludwig was to his siblings

    (d) to distinguish Beethoven from other composers

GO TO THE NEXT PAGE ➡

Questions 123–132 refer to the following passage.

Aesop's Fables were written by a Greek slave during the middle of the 16th century. They are well known for their moral messages. There are more than 700 Aesop's Fables originally shared from person to person in the form of storytelling. One of the fables is called *The Fox and the Goat.*

A Fox one day fell into a deep well and could find no means of escape. A Goat, overcome with thirst, came to the same well, and seeing the Fox, inquired if the water was good. Concealing his sad plight under a merry guise, the Fox indulged in a lavish praise of the water, saying it was excellent beyond measure, and encouraged the Goat to descend. The Goat, mindful only of his thirst, thoughtlessly jumped down, but just as he drank, the Fox informed him of the difficulty they were both in and suggested a scheme for their common escape.

"If," said he, "you will place your forefeet upon the wall and bend your head, I will run up your back and escape and help you out afterwards." The Goat readily <u>assented</u>, and the Fox leaped upon his back. Steadying himself with the Goat's horns, he safely reached the mouth of the well and made off as fast as he could. When the Goat <u>upbraided</u> him for breaking his promise, he turned around and cried out, "You foolish old fellow! If you had as many brains in your head as you have hairs in your beard, you would never have gone down before you had inspected the way up, nor have exposed yourself to dangers from which you had no means of escape."

123. Aesop's fables can be described as

    (a) biographies.
    (b) journal entries.
    (c) tales.
    (d) factual accounts.

124. What is the *best* moral of the story?

    (a) Don't drink from a well.
    (b) Always be untrusting.
    (c) Look before you leap.
    (d) Make the most of a bad situation.

125. The word <u>assented</u>, as underlined and used in the passage, most nearly means

    (a) agreed.
    (b) jumped.
    (c) denied.
    (d) disapproved.

126. If the Goat had to choose a title for the passage it would be

    (a) "Never Drink from a Well."
    (b) "Never Trust a Fox."
    (c) "How My Horns Saved My Life."
    (d) "Goats Have More Hair than Brains."

127. The Fox can best be described as

    (a) compassionate.
    (b) wily.
    (c) angry.
    (d) thoughtful.

128. It is implied from the passage that

    (a) the Fox tripped and fell into the well.
    (b) the Goat trusted the Fox.
    (c) the Fox hated the Goat.
    (d) the Goat was very old.

GO TO THE NEXT PAGE ➡

129. <u>Upbraided</u>, as underlined and used in the passage, most nearly means

    (a) brushed.

    (b) scolded.

    (c) praised.

    (d) embarrassed.

130. According to the passage, what did the Fox *not* do?

    (a) encourage the Goat to descend

    (b) praise the wonderful water

    (c) suggest an escape plan

    (d) follow the entire plan

131. The Fox lavishly praised the water

    (a) to share his excitement with the Goat.

    (b) to trick the Goat into coming down the well.

    (c) because he was very thirsty.

    (d) to be polite to the Goat.

132. What is the author's main purpose in writing this passage?

    (a) to encourage children to be afraid of foxes

    (b) to make the reader laugh

    (c) to convey advice to the reader through a story

    (d) to show people how gullible goats are

GO TO THE NEXT PAGE ➡

Questions 133–142 refer to the following passage.

Have you ever wondered how potato chips were invented? The potato chip was first discovered in New York during the 1850s by a chef named George Crum. Folklore has it that a customer complained that his fried potatoes were too thick. Insulted, Chef Crum responded by cutting the potatoes paper thin. The customer loved the thin chips and the rest is history. Because the chips were first made in Saratoga, NY, they were first known as Saratoga Chips.

Wise Potato Chips were first produced in 1915 by a grocer named Earl Wise, who had a large overstock of potatoes. Sales grew so quickly that by 1920 the Wise Potato Chip Company was established in Pennsylvania. Other companies began making chips as well, but it was not until 1925 that potato chips went into mass production. This was made possible by the invention of the automatic potato peeler. Contributing to increased chip sales was the invention of the television. Families enjoyed having a readymade snack that could be eaten while families gathered around the television.

In 1942, the government declared the potato chip an <u>essential</u> food because it was considered a ready-to-eat vegetable. During World War II, when other factories were <u>mandated</u> to close, potato chip companies were allowed to continue production.

Today some farmers dedicate their entire potato crop to growing potatoes for the sole purpose of the manufacture of potato chips. Potato chips represent over 40% of all snack food consumed by Americans with over a billion pounds of potatoes eaten annually. The potato chip even has its own day, March 14, which is National Potato Chip Day. Recently, potato chips have been under scrutiny for being an unhealthy snack; however, they still remain America's number one snack food.

133. This passage would be best titled

    (a) "The Many Ways to Eat Potatoes."
    (b) "The History of the Potato Chip."
    (c) "The Impact of Chips on World War II."
    (d) "The History of Wise Potato Chips"

134. What made mass production of potato chips possible?

    (a) the invention of the television
    (b) World War II
    (c) the invention of the automatic potato peeler
    (d) the creation of a national chip holiday

135. The word <u>essential</u>, as underlined and used in the passage, most nearly means

    (a) needless.
    (b) necessary.
    (c) fattening.
    (d) inexpensive.

136. The invention of the potato chip was made by

    (a) George Crum.
    (b) George Lays.
    (c) an unsatisfied customer.
    (d) Earl Wise.

GO TO THE NEXT PAGE ➡

137. Production of chips was allowed during World War II because

    (a) soldiers enjoyed the snack.
    (b) potato chips are high in calories.
    (c) they were a ready-to-eat vegetable.
    (d) they didn't go bad over time.

138. The tone of the passage can best be described as

    (a) sarcastic.
    (b) elated.
    (c) rational.
    (d) deceptive.

139. This passage would most likely be found in what publication?

    (a) *American Medical Journal*
    (b) *Journal of Engineering*
    (c) *Food Network Magazine*
    (d) *National Geographic*

140. The word <u>mandated</u>, as underlined and used in the passage, most nearly means

    (a) suggested.
    (b) encouraged.
    (c) forbidden.
    (d) forced.

141. This passage is an example of
    (a) scientific research.
    (b) an autobiography.
    (c) an informational article.
    (d) fiction.

142. The television contributed to potato chips because

    (a) of potato chip commercials.
    (b) families ate chips while watching television.
    (c) more chips can fit in a bowl than popcorn.
    (d) television characters were seen eating chips.

GO TO THE NEXT PAGE ➡

Questions 143–152 refer to the following passage.

In February of 1978, New England experienced the worst weather that most residents had seen in their lifetime. It was the storm that all snowstorms are now compared to and has since been hailed as the Blizzard of '78. New Englanders had a large snowstorm in January, which brought 20 inches of snow, so when weathermen predicted another storm, most residents were nonchalant. In the 1970s, meteorologists did not have the tools that exist today. Satellite images, 3D maps, cell phone weather apps, and ten-day forecasts were not household concepts. News stations predicted the storm; however, they greatly underestimated its severity.

The storm was predicted to be relatively weak as it came up from the Carolinas. The storm turned and came across the Appalachian Mountains, where it combined with an arctic cold front and a high pressure system. The storm arrived in the morning while students where leaving for school and commuters were heading to work. By the early afternoon, the snow was falling at an alarming rate of over two inches per hour, prompting schools to issue early releases and commuters to leave work. In addition to crippling snowfall, winds of 70 miles per hour were prevalent, and in some areas wind gusts were over 100 miles an hour. The storm lingered over the Boston area for 36 hours, causing tractors to flip over on highways, sea walls to crumble, houses to get sucked into the ocean, hundreds of commuters to get trapped in their cars, and thousands of residents to be left without heat or electricity for days.

When the blizzard left New England three days later, it left a wake of destruction. Boston received 30 inches of snow, while Rhode Island had 40 inches. There were close to 100 storm-related deaths, over 4,000 injuries, and an estimated $500 million dollars in damage. The Blizzard of '78 was the worst winter storm to hit New England since the storm of 1888 and will be remembered for years to come.

143. The Blizzard of '78 did *not*

    (a) last three days.
    (b) take the lives of 4,000 people.
    (c) cause flooding.
    (d) arrive in the morning.

144. The best title for this passage is

    (a) "The Blizzard of '78."
    (b) "Why Not to Live in New England."
    (c) "How to Predict a Storm."
    (d) "What Causes a Blizzard."

145. The word prevalent, as underlined and used in the passage, most nearly means

    (a) predicted.
    (b) concentrated.
    (c) widespread.
    (d) strange.

146. Which of the following statements is true?

    (a) Meteorologists failed to predict the storm in 1978.
    (b) Weather forecasts predicted a dangerous storm but no one believed them.
    (c) Because people had no cell phones, they were unaware of the coming storm.
    (d) Forecasters predicted the storm but misjudged its severity.

GO TO THE NEXT PAGE ➡

147. According to the passage,

    (a) snowfall, at times, was over 12 inches per hour.
    (b) in some areas winds were 100 miles per hour.
    (c) the storm was never predicted.
    (d) the blizzard came from the Northeast.

148. It is implied by the passage that the reason the storm was more severe than predicted was because

    (a) there were no computers to make predictions.
    (b) the temperature was warmer than expected.
    (c) the storm combined with other weather as it approached.
    (d) the meteorologists made a mistake.

149. This passage is an example of a

    (a) critique.
    (b) autobiography.
    (c) factual account.
    (d) saga.

150. The word lingered, as underlined and used in the passage, most nearly means

    (a) snowed.
    (b) darkened.
    (c) stayed.
    (d) left.

151. What is the main idea of the passage?

    (a) to explain why one should not live in New England
    (b) to provide a brief description of an historic event
    (c) to explain how a winter storm is formed
    (d) to pay tribute to those who died in a storm

152. After 1978, meteorologists were more likely to

    (a) give worst case scenarios in their storm predictions.
    (b) not inform people of a storm unless they were certain.
    (c) remind people all the time of 1978.
    (d) assume that there will never be a blizzard as bad as 1978.

GO TO THE NEXT PAGE ➡

READING—Vocabulary

Directions: Choose the word that means the same or about the same as the underlined word or words.

153. sense of <u>remorse</u>

    (a) guilt
    (b) anticipation
    (c) eagerness
    (d) fear

154. a <u>feasible</u> alternative

    (a) possible
    (b) boring
    (c) harsh
    (d) comical

155. to <u>mitigate</u> fear

    (a) worsen
    (b) create
    (c) reduce
    (d) aggravate

156. a <u>precocious</u> child

    (a) careful
    (b) premature
    (c) tired
    (d) weary

157. <u>noxious</u> fumes

    (a) pleasant
    (b) heavy
    (c) odorless
    (d) deadly

158. to <u>preserve</u> peace

    (a) destroy
    (b) celebrate
    (c) maintain
    (d) draw

159. <u>ponder</u> the question

    (a) consider
    (b) write
    (c) read
    (d) argue

160. a <u>stealthy</u> attack

    (a) dangerous
    (b) quiet
    (c) minimal
    (d) quick

161. a <u>temperate</u> climate

    (a) mild
    (b) hot
    (c) windy
    (d) frozen

162. <u>disclose</u> a secret

    (a) reveal
    (b) hide
    (c) bury
    (d) ignore

163. a <u>conspicuous</u> error

    (a) hidden
    (b) quiet
    (c) obvious
    (d) minor

164. a common <u>misconception</u>

    (a) puzzle
    (b) struggle
    (c) belief
    (d) fallacy

GO TO THE NEXT PAGE ➡

165. a benevolent donor

    (a) healthy
    (b) selfish
    (c) charitable
    (d) unusual

166. an inevitable outcome

    (a) unavoidable
    (b) unlikely
    (c) difficult
    (d) amazing

167. a rickety ladder

    (a) handmade
    (b) flimsy
    (c) original
    (d) antique

168. a negligent act

    (a) trivial
    (b) careless
    (c) thoughtful
    (d) small

169. a mundane speech

    (a) brief
    (b) loud
    (c) boring
    (d) original

170. to stimulate growth

    (a) alter
    (b) stifle
    (c) hinder
    (d) provoke

171. a routine checkup

    (a) lengthy
    (b) regular
    (c) unusual
    (d) grueling

172. a reluctant volunteer

    (a) cheery
    (b) eager
    (c) hesitant
    (d) young

173. a staunch admirer

    (a) heavy
    (b) loyal
    (c) angry
    (d) devious

174. an impartial jury

    (a) biased
    (b) famous
    (c) arrogant
    (d) unprejudiced

STOP

45 MINUTES

Sample:

A. The number thirty-seven is also written as

(a) 27 (b) 33 (c) 37 (d) 63

Correct marking of sample

A. Ⓐ Ⓑ ● Ⓓ

---

175. What is the name of this triangle?

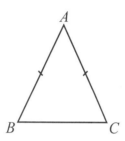

(a) Isosceles triangle
(b) Right triangle
(c) Equilateral triangle
(d) None of these

176. A one-third cup serving of soup has 10 grams of sodium. A can of soup is 2 cups. How much sodium is in one can of soup?

(a) 30 grams (c) 300 grams
(b) 60 grams (d) 90 grams

177. How many cups are in 3 quarts?

(a) 12 cups (c) 6 cups
(b) 24 cups (d) 18 cups

178. Solve 6.4 − (−0.781)

(a) 5.619 (c) 7.181
(b) −7.181 (d) −5.619

179. If $\frac{2}{3}$ of a number is 60, what is half of that number?

(a) 45 (b) 90 (c) 30 (d) 120

180. The volume of a cube is 125 cubic inches. What is the area of one of the sides?

(a) 50 (c) 15
(b) $\sqrt{125}$ (d) 25

181. The ratio of dogs to cats at a local pet store is 4 to 3. If there are 16 dogs, how many dogs and cats are there in total?

(a) 31 (b) 9 (c) 28 (d) 26

182. Solve:

$$\begin{array}{r} 41.2 \\ \times\, 0.96 \\ \hline \end{array}$$

(a) 40.28 (c) 39.552
(b) 39.25 (d) 40.552

183. Solve: −18 ÷ 6

(a) 3 (b) −3 (c) 2 (d) −108

184. The number 7 has the same value as

(a) 7^1 (b) 7^0 (c) 1^7 (d) $-\frac{1}{7}$

185. Solve: $\sqrt{144}$

(a) 7 (b) 12 (c) 11 (d) 14

GO TO THE NEXT PAGE ➡

186. What number is in the thousands place after simplifying

$(4 \times 10^2) + (6 \times 10^3) + (9.2 \times 10^2) + (25 \times 10^1)$?

(a) 7   (b) 3   (c) 4   (d) 5

187. 60 is 30% of what number?

(a) 630   (b) 180   (c) 200   (d) 120

188. What is the best description for line segment *AC*?

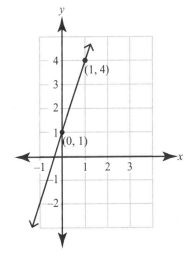

(a) diameter
(b) circumference
(c) radius
(d) secant

189. Express $\frac{7}{15}$ as a decimal.

(a) 0.46   (c) $0.46\overline{7}$
(b) $0.4\overline{6}$ (d) 0.47

190. Which amount is equal to $\frac{3}{5}$ of 4 dollars ?

(a) $2.40   (c) $3.50
(b) $3.00   (d) $0.80

191. Four cubed plus 6 is equal to

(a) 18   (b) 30   (c) 64   (d) 70

192. A model of a building is built with a scale of 1 inch of the model is equal to 6 feet of the building. How tall is the model if the building is 39 feet?

(a) 6.5 in.   (c) 18 in.
(b) 6 in.   (d) 39 in.

193. Solve: $\sqrt{225}$

(a) 15   (b) 25   (c) 14   (d) 16

194. The two figures below are similar triangles. What is the length of side *x*?

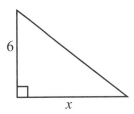

(a) 6   (b) 12   (c) 4   (d) 8

195. If the length of a side of a cube is 4 inches, what is the surface area?

(a) 96 in.²   (c) 16 in.²
(b) 64 in.²   (d) 32 in.²

196. How many meters is 5,432 cm?

(a) 59,320 m   (c) 0.5432 m
(b) 54.32 m   (d) 5.432 m

197. Which of the following equations represents the graph below?

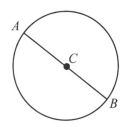

(a) $y = 3x + 4$
(b) $y = x + 1$
(c) $y = 3x + 1$
(d) $y = 3x - 1$

198. If $x = 2$, $y = 5$, and $z = -4$, what is $z^2 - y + x$?

(a) −19   (b) 19   (c) 13   (d) 11

GO TO THE NEXT PAGE ➡

199. If $-6 + x \geq 10$ then which of the following is true?

    (a) $x \leq -4$ (c) $x \geq 4$

    (b) $x \geq 16$ (d) $x \geq 40$

200. Solve:

$$\begin{array}{r} 1,785 \\ \times\ 389 \\ \hline \end{array}$$

    (a) 694,365   (c) 684,365

    (b) 494,265   (d) 498,366

201. A six-sided die is an example of what?

    (a) sphere

    (b) cube

    (c) cylinder

    (d) square

202. How many inches are in 2.5 yards?

    (a) 90 in.   (c) 6.5 in.

    (b) 78 in.   (d) 75 in.

203. Which angle is obtuse?

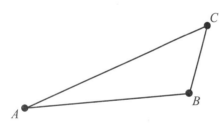

    (a) $\angle A$ (c) $\angle C$

    (b) $\angle B$ (d) none of these

204. Solve: $4.6 - 0.945$

    (a) 5.545   (c) 1.878

    (b) −3.665   (d) 3.655

205. Solve: $16 - 5\frac{7}{8}$

    (a) $10\frac{1}{8}$ (b) $11\frac{1}{8}$ (c) $10\frac{7}{8}$ (d) $\frac{1}{8}$

206. A garden measures 12 feet by 6 feet. Sandy can plant 16 onions per square yard. How many onions can Sandy plant?

    (a) 1,152   (c) 46

    (b) 590   (d) 128

207. Which property is demonstrated below?

$$4 \times (2 + 3) = (2 + 3) \times 4$$

    (a) distributive property

    (b) associative property

    (c) commutative property

    (d) inverse property

208. This shape is an example of a(n)

    (a) pentagon   (c) heptagon

    (b) hexagon   (d) octagon

209. Solve: $\frac{2}{5} \div \frac{10}{3}$

    (a) $\frac{4}{3}$ (b) $\frac{3}{50}$ (c) $\frac{3}{25}$ (d) $\frac{12}{8}$

210. If a car is driving at 32 kilometers per hour, how many miles per hour is the car traveling (1 mile = 1.6 kilometers)?

    (a) 51.2 mph   (c) 16 mph

    (b) 64 mph   (d) 20 mph

211. Kathy is renting a car at a cost of $30 per day and an additional one-time fee of $50 for insurance. If she keeps the car for 7 days, what will be her total cost?

    (a) $280   (c) $260

    (b) $80   (d) $210

GO TO THE NEXT PAGE ➡

212. Which expression best represents the following sentence?

The difference of twice a number and 6 is 400.

(a) $x - (2 \times 6) = 400$

(b) $2x - 6 = 400$

(c) $2x + 6 = 400$

(d) $400 - 2x = 400$

213. If Robert buys shoes at a 20% discounted price, how much will he pay for shoes that originally cost $80.00?

(a) $64.00   (c) $72.00

(b) $62.00   (d) $60.00

214. Solve for m: $\frac{2}{3} \times 21 = 56m$

(a) 4   (b) $\frac{10}{3}$ (c) 19   (d) $\frac{1}{4}$

215. Mr. Grundy's property tax is 3% of the value of his home. If his home is valued at $210,000, how much is his property tax?

(a) $6,300   (c) $63.00

(b) $18,000   (d) $1,620

216. A vegetable pizza weighs 68 ounces and is cut into 8 slices. How much will 3 slices weigh?

(a) 24 oz.   (c) 30.4 oz.

(b) 25.5 oz.   (d) 41.65 oz.

217. If there are 6 red gumdrops, 4 blue gumdrops, and 7 yellow gumdrops in a bowl, what is the chance that you will randomly choose a blue gumdrop?

(a) $\frac{10}{17}$ (b) $\frac{4}{17}$ (c) $\frac{1}{4}$ (d) $\frac{6}{10}$

218. What is the area of this figure?

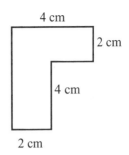

(a) 16 cm^2 (c) 26 cm^2

(b) 24 cm^2 (d) 12 cm^2

219. Simplify: $1\frac{2}{3} + 2\frac{1}{3} + \frac{1}{6} =$

(a) 4   (b) $4\frac{1}{6}$ (c) $5\frac{1}{6}$ (d) $\frac{11}{6}$

220. Mrs. McGillvary makes granola with 2 pounds of nuts and 3.5 pounds of oats. Oats cost $1.50 per pound, and nuts cost $7.25 per pound. How much will Mrs. McGillvary's granola cost to make?

(a) $19.75   (c) $19.63

(b) $28.38   (d) $21.75

221. What is the volume of a rectangular box that is 10 inches long, 5 inches wide, and 2 inches high?

(a) 25 in.^{3} (c) 50 in.^{3}

(b) 100 in.^{3} (d) 225 in.^{3}

222. Solve: $26 - 3.248$

(a) 22.752   (c) 23.752

(b) 23.842   (d) 22.842

223. Solve: $-15x > 75$

(a) $x > -3$ (c) $x < -5$

(b) $x > -5$ (d) $x < 3$

GO TO THE NEXT PAGE ➡

224. What is y in the following expression?

$$6 \times 0.75 \times 3 = 3y \times 6$$

(a) 0.5

(b) $\dfrac{4}{3}$

(c) $\dfrac{3}{4}$

(d) cannot be determined

225. Jackson is 9 years older than Sirius. Sirius is half as old as Maddy. The sum of the ages of all three is 21 years. How old is Maddy?

(a) 6 years old
(c) 2 years old
(b) 12 years old
(d) 8 years old

226. What fraction of a day is 18 hours?

(a) $\dfrac{3}{4}$
(b) $\dfrac{2}{3}$
(c) $\dfrac{4}{5}$
(d) $\dfrac{5}{6}$

227. The chart below represents the number of days that had rain per month in West Newbury.

Which month showed the largest increase from the month before?

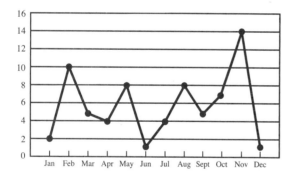

(a) June
(c) October
(b) November
(d) February

228. The dimensions of the trapezoid are given in inches. What is the area?

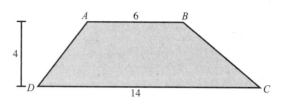

(a) 56 in.^{2}
(c) 80 in.^{2}
(b) 40 in.^{2}
(d) 64 in.^{2}

229. The area of the triangle below is 48 cm^2. If the height of the triangle is 8 cm, what is the length of the base?

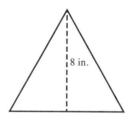

(a) 8 cm
(c) 6 cm
(b) 10 cm
(d) 12 cm

230. How many pints are in 10 gallons of milk?

(a) 20
(b) 40
(c) 80
(d) 1,600

231. How many hours is equal to 28,800 seconds?

(a) 16 hours
(c) 8 hours
(b) 6 hours
(d) 40 hours

232. What is the median of the data set?

18 2 8 5 3 18 24

(a) 6
(b) 22
(c) 18
(d) 8

233. Simplify: $(-7)^8 \div (-7)^2$

(a) $(-7)^6$
(c) 49^{10}
(b) 49^6
(d) $(-7)^{-6}$

GO TO THE NEXT PAGE ➡

234. Linda paid $16 for fruit and twice as much for vegetables. How much did Linda pay for all of her fruit and vegetables?

(a) $48   (b) $40   (c) $42   (d) $52

235. While playing a video game, Kevin scored 20 points, Paul scored 10 points, Tom scored 6 points, and Arioch did not score any points. How many points did the boys average?

(a) 8 points   (c) 12 points
(b) 9 points   (d) 15 points

236. The table below shows the number of pets that 50 different families own. How many families have more than 2 pets?

# of Pets	Families
1	12
2	18
3	10
4	6
5	3
6	1

(a) 9   (b) 10   (c) 20   (d) 12

237. Solve: $4.6 + 0.7 + 0.45$

(a) 4.46   (c) 46.5
(b) 5.75   (d) 9.8

238. Solve for x: $36 - 5x = 11$

(a) $9\frac{2}{5}$ (b) -5 (c) -9 (d) 5

STOP

25 MINUTES

Samples:

A. (a) Lee was reading a book.
   (b) We will run fast.
   (c) larry and I were late.
   (d) No mistakes.

B. (a) Who was at the door?
   (b) We all sat at the tabel.
   (c) The rose is yellow.
   (d) No mistakes.

Correct marking of samples:

A. Ⓐ Ⓑ ● Ⓓ

B. Ⓐ ● Ⓒ Ⓓ

In questions 239–278 try to find errors in punctuation, capitalization, or word usage. If you find a mistake, select the letter in front of that sentence as your answer. Some questions will have *No mistakes* for choice (d). For these questions, if you do not find any errors, mark (d) *No mistakes* as your answer.

239. (a) "Kathleen do you have any brothers?"
     (b) Mayor Menino is loved by all.
     (c) How was your dinner?
     (d) No mistakes.

240. (a) My favorite holiday is independence day.
     (b) There is plenty of room.
     (c) The storm lost its strength after a while.
     (d) No mistakes.

241. (a) Mount Katahdin is the tallest mountain in Maine.
     (b) John's brother is in fourth grade.
     (c) Mom said, "please come in for dinner."
     (d) The brownies are always delicious.

242. (a) Will there be dessert after dinner.
     (b) Her birthday is September 13.
     (c) How you can stand that I'll never know.
     (d) No mistakes.

243. (a) "When you finish your work, John, please leave it here."
     (b) Each of the flowers bloom at a different time.
     (c) Let's begin our walk at noon today.
     (d) No mistakes.

244. (a) "You're impossible!" she yelled.
     (b) No chance, I would never lie.
     (c) Easter is always on a Sunday.
     (d) I grow parsley thyme, and sage.

245. (a) She asked if she could join the club.
     (b) Winter had come and gone.
     (c) He is the famous author which lives in Danvers.
     (d) No mistakes.

246. (a) There was a parade on Labor Day.
     (b) The athlete asked to play third base?
     (c) There is a cat and a dog in the house.
     (d) You can do a better job if you try.

247. (a) He was greeted by the man who lives next door.
     (b) Mr. Monroe is very kind.
     (c) Them people are hungry.
     (d) I already told you I would go.

GO TO THE NEXT PAGE ➡

248. (a) Naturally, I voted for my friend.
     (b) "If you behave, she said, you can have ice cream."
     (c) Take your seats, and be quiet while you wait.
     (d) No mistakes.

249. (a) Karyn bought herself a new dress.
     (b) The lights looked beautifully on the tree.
     (c) We kids should make our own team.
     (d) No mistakes.

250. (a) There are many stately homes in the neighborhood.
     (b) I love my chemistry class.
     (c) The judge spoke with us in her chambers.
     (d) No mistakes.

251. (a) Will you be going to the prom this year?
     (b) Your dancing has made the party exciting.
     (c) I hadnt thought of that.
     (d) No mistakes.

252. (a) My favorite poet is Emily Dickinson.
     (b) The faster of the two runners will win.
     (c) Neither Jim nor Joe was at camp today.
     (d) Us did very well in the relay race.

253. (a) The tree's branches are taller than its trunk.
     (b) Larry, do you have a barn?
     (c) Annette and he make a cute couple.
     (d) No mistakes.

254. (a) Beth's dermatologist, Dr Greenberg, is very nice.
     (b) We have been friends for a long time.
     (c) The children's old toys were donated.
     (d) No mistakes.

255. (a) Are all of the ingredients on the counter?
     (b) Tom's pass was longer than Peyton's.
     (c) He willn't miss the game.
     (d) No mistakes.

256. (a) The new business is very successful.
     (b) Stella brung two contracts for me to sign.
     (c) Last month's low temperature was thirty degrees.
     (d) No mistakes.

257. (a) The McGillvarys' house is the smallest on the street.
     (b) What is good about being so smart?
     (c) I have two favorite hobbies, knitting and gardening.
     (d) There was no one there by midnight.

258. (a) I hardly never win at chess.
     (b) "Don't you love it?" asked Debbie.
     (c) The piano, which has not been used in years, is out of tune.
     (d) No mistakes.

259. (a) The chief engineer will be in charge.
     (b) Among the three of them, Kaylee is the fastest.
     (c) Nelson Avenue is near the center of town.
     (d) No mistakes.

260. (a) You was mistaken when you said it would rain today.
     (b) The race, which was planned for Sunday, was postponed.
     (c) Neither Jim nor Carl can cook.
     (d) No mistakes.

261. (a) I am in favor of the new zoning; however, my husband is against it.
     (b) We will be relieved when this ordeal is over.
     (c) She loves to eat, to play, and running.
     (d) No mistakes.

262. (a) I decided to major in English.
     (b) The car was brand knew.
     (c) Camp Christopher is a day camp for kids ages 5 through 12.
     (d) Jim, please trim my hair.

GO TO THE NEXT PAGE ➡

263. (a) Brady cheered, "Do your job!"
    (b) Have you ever seen Davy Jones locker?
    (c) We won't give up today.
    (d) No mistakes.

264. (a) Did you remember to add the sugar.
    (b) The guest list included the prince, the princess, and the queen.
    (c) Uncle Lewis was my favorite uncle.
    (d) No mistakes.

265. (a) Their father was very angry.
    (b) His is taller than his sister.
    (c) Darren please come for Thanksgiving dinner.
    (d) Her prescription eyeglasses were broken.

266. (a) The sharks swims in the same direction.
    (b) He and I are related by marriage.
    (c) Bob is more talented than Bill.
    (d) If it keeps raining, we will cancel the hike.

267. (a) Noreen said, "we rented a car for the week."
    (b) There are fewer rooms in the cabin than in the house.
    (c) Why are you going to be late?
    (d) No mistakes.

268. (a) The dinner was catered by chef Flay.
    (b) There were 9,000 pieces in the puzzle!
    (c) The home was built in the year 1824.
    (d) Highland Lake is located at the end of Creamery Street.

269. (a) The song was about whom?
    (b) May I please interrupt?
    (c) Her birthday is March 3, 1997.
    (d) No mistakes.

270. (a) Carrye owns three businesses in Bridgton.
    (b) Glen does not own a cell phone or a computer.
    (c) Ray is a magician at the Camp Fire Grill.
    (d) No mistakes.

271. (a) I interviewed the author who wrote *Midwives*.
    (b) Dan and Doug both attended Merrimack College.
    (c) Each one of them feel proud.
    (d) I sometimes sing in the car.

272. (a) The family planned a trip to Yosemite National Park.
    (b) Kathryn is a wonderful aunt.
    (c) Darren went to college in Villanova, Pennsylvania.
    (d) No mistakes.

273. (a) Mrs Pickering moved to New York last spring.
    (b) I honestly don't know how he did it.
    (c) The Houston Astros' World Series win was a miracle.
    (d) No mistakes.

274. (a) The two students were the stars of the play *Our Town*.
    (b) Woman jumped over the large puddle.
    (c) Between Jean and Lisa is a large dog.
    (d) No mistakes.

275. (a) We will harvest the vegetables on August.
    (b) You are right, and I am wrong.
    (c) Kim is the team's soccer coach.
    (d) No mistakes.

276. (a) The officer asked, "Were you speeding?"
    (b) He took his car to the shop on Monday.
    (c) After much saving she bought her dream home.
    (d) Unless you speed things up, we will never finish.

277. (a) Mr. Korol the new math teacher is very funny.
    (b) "I want you home by 10 P.M.," said mother.
    (c) I'm doing well, thank you.
    (d) No mistakes.

GO TO THE NEXT PAGE ➡

278. (a) Did you know she went to Harvard?
     (b) Sadly, the boy did not make the team.
     (c) The concert was amazing!
     (d) No mistakes.

For questions 279–288, look only for mistakes in spelling.

279. (a) Apparantly, she is very wealthy.
     (b) I am very concerned.
     (c) The hundredth customer will win a prize.
     (d) No mistakes.

280. (a) *Pride and Prejudice* is my favorite book.
     (b) She will turn fourty on Wednesday.
     (c) Stop questioning my authority.
     (d) No mistakes.

281. (a) I am thoroughly exhausted.
     (b) You may have an exemption.
     (c) Put the words in five colums.
     (d) No mistakes.

282. (a) I'll have my lisence next week.
     (b) His answer was inaccurate.
     (c) The directions were ambiguous.
     (d) No mistakes.

283. (a) Waiting can be most aggravating.
     (b) His appetite is insatiable.
     (c) I'm looking forward to Febrary vacation.
     (d) No mistakes.

284. (a) Big is an ajective and not an adverb.
     (b) Water always quenches my thirst.
     (c) Do not jeopardize this for me.
     (d) No mistakes.

285. (a) I bumped my forhead during practice.
     (b) The settlement was amicable.
     (c) Nicky often embellishes the truth.
     (d) No mistakes.

286. (a) The guard was vigilant during his watch.
     (b) He is always perturbed.
     (c) Don't forget the reciept.
     (d) No mistakes.

287. (a) He was very courageous.
     (b) She is the heir to the thrown.
     (c) The miniature horse is very small.
     (d) No mistakes.

288. (a) The snitch can be very elusive.
     (b) He is a columnist for the Boston Globe.
     (c) She is usually very relible.
     (d) No mistakes.

For Questions 289–298, follow the directions for each question.

289. Choose the correct word(s) to join the thoughts.

     I enjoyed the book, _____ the fact it was very long.

     (a) because of,
     (b) despite
     (c) moreover,
     (d) None of these

290. Choose the correct word(s) to join the thoughts.

     She was considered to be very short _____ all of the other players on her team were very tall.

     (a) consequently,
     (b) because
     (c) furthermore,
     (d) None of these

291. Which is the best topic for a one-paragraph essay?

     (a) How to Publish Your Own Novel
     (b) Learn to Become a Publisher
     (c) How to Make a Postcard from a Greeting Card
     (d) None of these

GO TO THE NEXT PAGE ➡

292. Which sentence does *not* belong in the paragraph?

(1) Iava finished all of her homework. (2) She had one hour left in her tutoring session. (3) Her math teacher is a young man. (4) Iava studied for her science test for the last hour.

(a) Sentence 1
(b) Sentence 2
(c) Sentence 3
(d) Sentence 4

293. Which sentence best fits under the topic "How to Get a Good Night's Sleep"?

(a) Choose a soft pillow and a good quality mattress.
(b) Sleep is essential to overall health.
(c) Many people do not get the recommended eight hours per night.
(d) Noisy places make sleeping well difficult.

294. Which sentence expresses the idea most clearly?

(a) The roads were very slippery and it was because of the snow.
(b) The snow from the storm was on the slippery roads.
(c) The cause of the roads being slippery was the snowstorm.
(d) The snowstorm caused the roads to be very slippery.

295. Which sentence expresses the idea most clearly?

(a) She performs well but only on the times when she practices.
(b) She is a good performer and takes the time to practice.
(c) Practice can make her perform well if she takes the time.
(d) When she takes the time to practice, she performs very well.

296. Choose the group of words that best completes the statement.

To make a guess on a multiple-choice question, you should

(a) only make a guess from the answers that are left after you eliminate wrong answers.
(b) first eliminate answers you know to be wrong, and then make your guess.
(c) make a guess and eliminate wrong answers.
(d) eliminate answers but only ones that are wrong and then guess at the rest.

297. Which of these would be the best title for the following paragraph?

Elizabeth Quirk was a pianist. Her father taught music to her when she was very young. As a child, she had to stand on a book to reach the piano keys. She had her first recital at the young age of six.

(a) "Learn How to Play the Piano"
(b) "Elizabeth Quirk: The Child Prodigy"
(c) "The Family Life of Elizabeth Quirk"
(d) None of these

298. Where should the sentence, "To hang the puzzle, push tacks through the corners and into the wall," be placed in the selection below?

(1) To frame a puzzle you must first apply a layer of glue to the front of the puzzle. (2) When the glue is dry turn the puzzle over. (3) Glue a large posterboard to the back of the puzzle.

(a) Between sentences 1 and 2
(b) Between sentences 2 and 3
(c) After sentence 3
(d) The sentence does not belong.

STOP

ANSWER KEY
HSPT Practice Test 2

VERBAL SKILLS SUBTEST

1. **b**	16. **b**	31. **d**	46. **b**
2. **c**	17. **b**	32. **b**	47. **a**
3. **b**	18. **c**	33. **a**	48. **b**
4. **b**	19. **a**	34. **d**	49. **a**
5. **c**	20. **b**	35. **c**	50. **c**
6. **c**	21. **a**	36. **a**	51. **c**
7. **a**	22. **b**	37. **b**	52. **d**
8. **b**	23. **c**	38. **b**	53. **b**
9. **d**	24. **d**	39. **a**	54. **b**
10. **d**	25. **a**	40. **d**	55. **d**
11. **b**	26. **b**	41. **c**	56. **c**
12. **a**	27. **a**	42. **a**	57. **a**
13. **c**	28. **a**	43. **c**	58. **a**
14. **b**	29. **c**	44. **c**	59. **b**
15. **d**	30. **c**	45. **d**	60. **c**

QUANTITATIVE SKILLS SUBTEST

61. **d**	74. **b**	87. **c**	100. **b**
62. **c**	75. **a**	88. **d**	101. **a**
63. **b**	76. **c**	89. **b**	102. **d**
64. **c**	77. **c**	90. **a**	103. **c**
65. **a**	78. **d**	91. **b**	104. **a**
66. **c**	79. **b**	92. **d**	105. **b**
67. **d**	80. **d**	93. **d**	106. **d**
68. **b**	81. **a**	94. **d**	107. **b**
69. **d**	82. **d**	95. **c**	108. **c**
70. **a**	83. **c**	96. **a**	109. **b**
71. **c**	84. **a**	97. **b**	110. **c**
72. **c**	85. **b**	98. **b**	111. **c**
73. **b**	86. **b**	99. **c**	112. **b**

ANSWER KEY
HSPT Practice Test 2

READING SUBTEST

113. **c**	129. **b**	145. **c**	161. **a**
114. **c**	130. **d**	146. **d**	162. **a**
115. **a**	131. **b**	147. **b**	163. **c**
116. **c**	132. **c**	148. **c**	164. **d**
117. **d**	133. **b**	149. **c**	165. **c**
118. **c**	134. **c**	150. **c**	166. **a**
119. **c**	135. **b**	151. **b**	167. **b**
120. **b**	136. **a**	152. **a**	168. **b**
121. **c**	137. **c**	153. **a**	169. **c**
122. **b**	138. **c**	154. **a**	170. **d**
123. **c**	139. **c**	155. **c**	171. **b**
124. **c**	140. **d**	156. **b**	172. **c**
125. **a**	141. **c**	157. **d**	173. **b**
126. **b**	142. **b**	158. **c**	174. **d**
127. **b**	143. **b**	159. **a**	
128. **b**	144. **a**	160. **b**	

MATHEMATICS SUBTEST

175. **a**	191. **d**	207. **c**	223. **c**
176. **b**	192. **a**	208. **b**	224. **c**
177. **a**	193. **a**	209. **c**	225. **a**
178. **c**	194. **d**	210. **d**	226. **a**
179. **a**	195. **a**	211. **c**	227. **d**
180. **d**	196. **b**	212. **b**	228. **b**
181. **c**	197. **c**	213. **a**	229. **d**
182. **c**	198. **c**	214. **d**	230. **c**
183. **b**	199. **b**	215. **a**	231. **c**
184. **a**	200. **a**	216. **b**	232. **d**
185. **b**	201. **b**	217. **b**	233. **a**
186. **a**	202. **a**	218. **a**	234. **a**
187. **c**	203. **b**	219. **b**	235. **b**
188. **c**	204. **d**	220. **a**	236. **c**
189. **b**	205. **a**	221. **b**	237. **b**
190. **a**	206. **d**	222. **a**	238. **d**

ANSWER KEY
HSPT Practice Test 2

LANGUAGE SUBTEST

239. **a**	254. **a**	269. **d**	284. **a**
240. **a**	255. **c**	270. **d**	285. **a**
241. **c**	256. **b**	271. **c**	286. **c**
242. **a**	257. **c**	272. **d**	287. **d**
243. **b**	258. **a**	273. **a**	288. **c**
244. **d**	259. **d**	274. **b**	289. **b**
245. **c**	260. **a**	275. **a**	290. **b**
246. **b**	261. **c**	276. **c**	291. **c**
247. **c**	262. **b**	277. **a**	292. **c**
248. **b**	263. **b**	278. **d**	293. **a**
249. **b**	264. **a**	279. **a**	294. **d**
250. **d**	265. **c**	280. **b**	295. **d**
251. **c**	266. **a**	281. **c**	296. **b**
252. **d**	267. **a**	282. **a**	297. **b**
253. **d**	268. **a**	283. **c**	298. **c**

SCORING YOUR PRACTICE TEST

Now that you have finished HSPT Practice Test 2, let's see how well you did. The following charts are scoring rubrics, which will not only help you calculate your raw score but also show your results for the different question types within each subtest.

1. Copy the answers from your bubble sheet next to each corresponding number in the second column of the chart for each of the five subtests.
2. For each question, there is an empty space in one of the columns to the right. These columns represent the different question-type categories. If you answered a question correctly, put a check in the open space under the question type category. If you answered the question incorrectly, leave the space blank.
3. When you have finished checking off the question types for each of your correct answers, add up the total number of check marks you have in each column to determine how well you did.
4. See the example below to better understand the scoring rubric.

Example:

Question	Your Answer	Correct Answer	Logic	Analogy	Classification	Antonym	Synonym
1	a	a		✔			

Verbal Skills Subtest Scoring Rubric

Question	Your Answer	Correct Answer	Logic	Analogy	Classification	Antonym	Synonym
1		b					
2		c					
3		b					
4		b					
5		c					
6		c					
7		a					
8		b					
9		d					
10		d					
11		b					
12		a					
13		c					
14		b					
15		d					
16		b					
17		b					
18		c					

Question	Your Answer	Correct Answer	Logic	Analogy	Classification	Antonym	Synonym
19		a					
20		b					
21		a					
22		b					
23		c					
24		d					
25		a					
26		b					
27		a					
28		a					
29		c					
30		c					
31		d					
32		b					
33		a					
34		d					
35		c					
36		a					
37		b					
38		b					
39		a					
40		d					
41		c					
42		a					
43		c					
44		c					
45		d					
46		b					
47		a					
48		b					
49		a					
50		c					
51		c					
52		d					
53		b					
54		b					
55		d					
56		c					
57		a					
58		a					

Question	Your Answer	Correct Answer	Logic	Analogy	Classification	Antonym	Synonym
59		b					
60		c					
Add up the number of check marks in each of the five columns to the right							
Total of each question type			11	11	17	9	12

First, add up the total number of questions you answered correctly. Then divide that number by 60 and multiply by 100 to determine your raw score for the Verbal Skills subtest:

$$\text{Raw Score} = \frac{\text{Total Number Correct}}{60 \text{ Total Questions}} = \frac{\qquad}{60} \times 100 = \underline{\qquad}\%$$

Next, to determine your raw score for each question type, take the number of questions you answered correctly in each category and divide that number by the total number of questions in each question type. Multiply each answer by 100 to convert to a percent.

$$\text{Logic} = \frac{\text{Total Number Correct}}{11 \text{ Total Questions}} = \frac{\qquad}{11} \times 100 = \underline{\qquad}\%$$

$$\text{Analogy} = \frac{\text{Total Number Correct}}{11 \text{ Total Questions}} = \frac{\qquad}{11} \times 100 = \underline{\qquad}\%$$

$$\text{Classification} = \frac{\text{Total Number Correct}}{17 \text{ Total Questions}} = \frac{\qquad}{17} \times 100 = \underline{\qquad}\%$$

$$\text{Antonym} = \frac{\text{Total Number Correct}}{9 \text{ Total Questions}} = \frac{\qquad}{9} \times 100 = \underline{\qquad}\%$$

$$\text{Synonym} = \frac{\text{Total Number Correct}}{12 \text{ Total Questions}} = \frac{\qquad}{12} \times 100 = \underline{\qquad}\%$$

Quantitative Skills Subtest Scoring Rubric

Question	Your Answer	Correct Answer	Sequence	Geometric Comparison	Non-geometric Comparison	Computation
61		d				
62		c				
63		b				
64		c				
65		a				
66		c				
67		d				
68		b				
69		d				
70		a				
71		c				
72		c				
73		b				
74		b				
75		a				
76		c				
77		c				
78		d				
79		b				
80		d				
81		a				
82		d				
83		c				
84		a				
85		b				
86		b				
87		c				
88		d				
89		b				
90		a				
91		b				
92		d				
93		d				
94		d				
95		c				
96		a				
97		b				
98		b				
99		c				
100		b				

Question	Your Answer	Correct Answer	Sequence	Geometric Comparison	Non-geometric Comparison	Computation
101		a				
102		d				
103		c				
104		a				
105		b				
106		d				
107		b				
108		c				
109		b				
110		c				
111		c				
112		b				
Add up the total number of check marks in each of the four columns to the right						
Total of each question type			22	7	12	11

First, add up the total number of questions you answered correctly. Then divide that number by 52 and multiply by 100 to determine your raw score for the Quantitative Skills subtest:

$$\text{Raw Score} = \frac{\text{Total Number Correct}}{52 \text{ Total Questions}} = \frac{}{52} \times 100 = \underline{\hspace{1cm}}\%$$

Next, to determine your raw score for each question type, take the number of questions you answered correctly in each category and divide that number by the total number of questions in each question type. Multiply each answer by 100 to convert to a percent.

$$\text{Sequence} = \frac{\text{Total Number Correct}}{22 \text{ Total Questions}} = \frac{}{22} \times 100 = \underline{\hspace{1cm}}\%$$

$$\text{Geometric Comparison} = \frac{\text{Total Number Correct}}{7 \text{ Total Questions}} = \frac{}{7} \times 100 = \underline{\hspace{1cm}}\%$$

$$\text{Non-geometric Comparison} = \frac{\text{Total Number Correct}}{12 \text{ Total Questions}} = \frac{}{12} \times 100 = \underline{\hspace{1cm}}\%$$

$$\text{Computation} = \frac{\text{Total Number Correct}}{11 \text{ Total Questions}} = \frac{}{11} \times 100 = \underline{\hspace{1cm}}\%$$

Reading Subtest Scoring Rubric

Question	Your Answer	Correct Answer	Vocabulary	Specific	General
113		c		X	
114		c			X
115		a	X		
116		c			X
117		d	X		
118		c			X
119		c			X
120		b			X
121		c			X
122		b			X
123		c			X
124		c			X
125		a	X		
126		b		X	
127		b		X	
128		b		X	
129		b	X		
130		d		X	
131		b			X
132		c			X
133		b		X	
134		c			X
135		b	X		
136		a			X
137		c			X
138		c			X
139		c			X
140		d	X		
141		c			X
142		b			X
143		b			X
144		a			X
145		c	X		
146		d			X
147		b		X	
148		c			X
149		c			X
150		c	X		
151		b			X
152		a		X	

Question	Your Answer	Correct Answer	Vocabulary	Specific	General
153		a			
154		a			
155		c			
156		b			
157		d			
158		c			
159		a			
160		b			
161		a			
162		a			
163		c			
164		d			
165		c			
166		a			
167		b			
168		b			
169		c			
170		d			
171		b			
172		c			
173		b			
174		d			
Add up the total number of check marks in each of the three columns to the right					
Total of each question type			30	17	15

First, add up the total number of questions answered correctly. Then divide that number by 62 and multiply by 100 to determine your raw score for the Reading subtest:

$$\text{Raw Score} = \frac{\text{Total Number Correct}}{62 \text{ Total Questions}} = \frac{\underline{\quad}}{62} \times 100 = \underline{\quad}\%$$

Next, to determine your raw score for each question type, take the number of questions you answered correctly in each category and divide that number by the total number of questions in each question type. Multiply each answer by 100 to convert to a percent.

$$\text{Vocabulary} = \frac{\text{Total Number Correct}}{30 \text{ Total Questions}} = \frac{\rule{2em}{0.4pt}}{30} \times 100 = \rule{4em}{0.4pt}\%$$

$$\text{Specific} = \frac{\text{Total Number Correct}}{17 \text{ Total Questions}} = \frac{\rule{2em}{0.4pt}}{17} \times 100 = \rule{4em}{0.4pt}\%$$

$$\text{General} = \frac{\text{Total Number Correct}}{15 \text{ Total Questions}} = \frac{\rule{2em}{0.4pt}}{15} \times 100 = \rule{4em}{0.4pt}\%$$

Mathematics Subtest Scoring Rubric

Question	Your Answer	Correct Answer	Basics and Conversions	Geometry, Logic, Word Problems	Fractions, Decimals, Percents, Ratios	Exponents, Radicals, Algebra	Statistics and Probability
175		a					
176		b					
177		a					
178		c					
179		a					
180		d					
181		c					
182		c					
183		b					
184		a					
185		b					
186		a					
187		c					
188		c					
189		b					
190		a					
191		d					
192		a					
193		a					
194		d					
195		a					
196		b					
197		c					
198		c					

Question	Your Answer	Correct Answer	Basics and Conversions	Geometry, Logic, Word Problems	Fractions, Decimals, Percents, Ratios	Exponents, Radicals, Algebra	Statistics and Probability
199		b					
200		a					
201		b					
202		a					
203		b					
204		d					
205		a					
206		d					
207		c					
208		b					
209		c					
210		d					
211		c					
212		b					
213		a					
214		d					
215		a					
216		b					
217		b					
218		a					
219		b					
220		a					
221		b					
222		a					
223		c					
224		c					
225		a					
226		a					
227		d					
228		b					
229		d					
230		c					
231		c					
232		d					
233		a					
234		a					
235		b					
236		c					

Question	Your Answer	Correct Answer	Basics and Conversions	Geometry, Logic, Word Problems	Fractions, Decimals, Percents, Ratios	Exponents, Radicals, Algebra	Statistics and Probability
237		b					
238		d					
Add up the total number of check marks in each of the five columns to the right							
Total of each question type			24	17	6	13	4

First, add up the total number of questions you answered correctly. Then divide that number by 64 and multiply by 100 to determine your raw score for the Mathematics subtest:

$$\text{Raw Score} = \frac{\text{Total Number Correct}}{64 \text{ Total Questions}} = \frac{}{64} \times 100 = \underline{\hspace{1cm}}\%$$

Next, to determine your raw score for each question type, take the number of questions you answered correctly in each category and divide that number by the total number of questions in each question type. Multiply each answer by 100 to convert to a percent.

$$\text{Basics and Conversions} = \frac{\text{Total Number Correct}}{24 \text{ Total Questions}} = \frac{}{24} \times 100 = \underline{\hspace{1cm}}\%$$

$$\text{Geometry, Logic, and Word Problems} = \frac{\text{Total Number Correct}}{17 \text{ Total Questions}} = \frac{}{17} \times 100 = \underline{\hspace{1cm}}\%$$

$$\text{Fractions, Decimals, Percents, and Ratios} = \frac{\text{Total Number Correct}}{6 \text{ Total Questions}} = \frac{}{6} \times 100 = \underline{\hspace{1cm}}\%$$

$$\text{Exponents, Radicals, and Algebra} = \frac{\text{Total Number Correct}}{13 \text{ Total Questions}} = \frac{}{13} \times 100 = \underline{\hspace{1cm}}\%$$

$$\text{Statistics and Probability} = \frac{\text{Total Number Correct}}{4 \text{ Total Questions}} = \frac{}{4} \times 100 = \underline{\hspace{1cm}}\%$$

Language Subtest Scoring Rubric

Question	Your Answer	Correct Answer	Capitalization, Punctuation, Usage	Spelling	Composition
239		a			
240		a			
241		c			
242		a			
243		b			
244		d			
245		c			
246		b			
247		c			
248		b			
249		b			
250		d			
251		c			
252		d			
253		d			
254		a			
255		c			
256		b			
257		c			
258		a			
259		d			
260		a			
261		c			
262		b			
263		b			
264		a			
265		c			
266		a			
267		a			
268		a			
269		d			
270		d			
271		c			
272		d			
273		a			
274		b			
275		a			
276		c			
277		a			

Question	Your Answer	Correct Answer	Capitalization, Punctuation, Usage	Spelling	Composition
278		d			
279		a			
280		b			
281		c			
282		a			
283		c			
284		a			
285		a			
286		c			
287		d			
288		c			
289		b			
290		b			
291		c			
292		c			
293		a			
294		d			
295		d			
296		b			
297		b			
298		c			
Add up the total number of check marks in each of the three columns to the right					
Total of each question type			40	10	10

First, add up the total number of questions you answered correctly. Then divide that number by 60 and multiply by 100 to determine your raw score for the Language subtest:

$$\text{Raw Score} = \frac{\text{Total Number Correct}}{60 \text{ Total Questions}} = \frac{}{60} \times 100 = \underline{\hspace{1cm}}\%$$

Next, to determine your raw score for each question type, take the number of questions you answered correctly in each category and divide that number by the total number of questions in each question type. Multiply each answer by 100 to convert to a percent.

Capitalization, Punctuation, and Usage $= \dfrac{\text{Total Number Correct}}{40 \text{ Total Questions}} = \dfrac{}{40} \times 100 = \underline{}\%$

Spelling $= \dfrac{\text{Total Number Correct}}{10 \text{ Total Questions}} = \dfrac{}{10} \times 100 = \underline{}\%$

Composition $= \dfrac{\text{Total Number Correct}}{10 \text{ Total Questions}} = \dfrac{}{10} \times 100 = \underline{}\%$

Overall Practice Test Score

To get an idea of your overall score on the practice test, you can find the raw score. First, add up the number of questions you answered correctly on the entire practice test. This can be easily calculated by adding the number of questions correct from each subtest. Then divide your total number of questions that were correct by a total of 298 questions on the test. Multiply this number by 100 to calculate your score out of 100%.

$$\text{Raw Score} = \dfrac{\text{Total Number Correct}}{298 \text{ Total Questions}} = \dfrac{}{298} \times 100 = \underline{}\%$$

ANSWERS EXPLAINED FOR HSPT PRACTICE TEST 2

Verbal Skills Subtest

1. **(b)** *Endanger* means to threaten or to put in danger.

2. **(c)** *Distort, deform,* and *mangle* are all means of destroying or altering something. *Preserve* means to maintain or to keep the same.

3. **(b)** *Futile, ineffective,* and *pointless* are all negative words. *Futile* means *ineffective* and are both similar in meaning to *pointless. Critical* means to be necessary or important and therefore does not belong.

4. **(b)** False. If all of the books in the store are hardcovers, then it is not possible for a book in that store to have a cover other than a hardcover. The third statement is then false.

5. **(c)** *Vigorous* means to be *energetic.* The opposite of *energetic* would be *sedentary. Sedentary* means to have the need to sit, which implies a lack of energy.

6. **(c)** A *recipe* gives instructions for *cooking* and a *blueprint* gives instructions for *building.* A *blueprint* or a *recipe* may be printed on paper, and a designer may use a *blueprint* but the only word to make the same relationship as *recipe* and *cooking* would be *building.* In this analogy, *building* is a verb and not a noun.

7. **(a)** To be *boisterous* is to be loud or *noisy.* The other word choices are unrelated.

8. **(b)** *Arrogant,* while having a negative meaning, means to be *proud* in an overly cocky manner. Because of its meaning, it is similar to *proud* and *confident* even thought they are positive words. *Polite* has a very different meaning and therefore does not belong.

9. **(d)** *Delinquent* is an adjective which means to be late or overdue. It is also used to refer to someone who is a wrongdoer. *Early* is the opposite of late and the opposite of being *delinquent.*

10. **(d)** To *squander* is to waste, as in "*squander* your money."

11. **(b)** *Intimidate* means to *scare* someone or to bully.

12. **(a)** A *bird* <u>uses its</u> *wings* to fly and a *fish* <u>uses its</u> *fin* to swim. While a fish has *gills,* they are not used to move the *fish.*

13. **(c)** *Irate* means to be really *angry. Furious* is a synonym of *irate. Grateful* is the only positive word.

14. **(b)** *Sever* is a verb that means to *cut off. Sustain* means to keep something going and *throb* means to pound.

15. **(d)** To be *bizarre* is to be *unusual, unique,* or *odd. Conventional* means to be typical or ordinary and therefore is the opposite of *bizarre.*

16. **(b)** *Grave* <u>is synonymous with</u> *serious* just as *authentic* <u>is synonymous with</u> *real.*

17. **(b)** If all of the campers at Pondicherry Park can swim, then Jordan must not be a camper there because he cannot swim. Therefore the third statement must be false.

18. **(c)** *Procrastinate* is a verb meaning to *delay* or to put off. *Stall* is a synonym of *delay. Rush* is the opposite of these and does not belong.

19. **(a)** A *pilot* is in charge of a *plane* just as a *captain* is in charge of a *ship*.

20. **(b)** *Oration, eulogy,* and *speech* are all forms of speaking. A *postcard* is a written form of communication.

21. **(a)** *Rejuvenate* means to *refresh. Reimburse* means to pay back, so try not to jump to a synonym of the wrong word.

22. **(b)** *Lions* live and travel in a *pride* while *wolves* live and travel in a *pack*.

23. **(c)** *Paternal* is the male equivalent of *maternal* and *uncle* is the male equivalent of *aunt*.

24. **(d)** *Prolific* means to be creative or *productive*, which implies *abundance. Reclusive* means to shut oneself off and is unrelated to the other three words.

25. **(a)** If Kimmy baked more cookies than Alex, K > A, who baked more than Jonny, K > A > J, then Jonny made fewer cookies than both Kimmy and Alex. The third statement is true as shown in the statement: K > A > J.

26. **(b)** *Arduous* means difficult. *Rigorous* means sharp or exact but is the closest in meaning to *arduous*. The other words are unrelated or opposites of *arduous*.

27. **(a)** A *mailbox* is where a person would put a *letter* and a *bank* is where a person would put *money*. There is a *vault* or a *safe* in a bank but money is the more obvious answer. A more specific sentence could be made. A *mailbox* is full of *letters* and a *bank* is full of *money*. People do not deposit vaults in banks.

28. **(a)** *Omnipotent* means to be all powerful. The root *omni* means *all*, which should help you find the correct answer.

29. **(c)** *Prohibit* means to stop or to *forbid. Hinder* and *interfere* have similar meanings but less extreme. *Permit* is the opposite and means to allow.

30. **(c)** *Jeer, taunt,* and *insult* are all verbs that mean to bother someone verbally. *Revere* is to hold someone in high esteem, to admire someone, and therefore does not belong.

31. **(d)** *Gingerly* is an adverb meaning *cautiously. Rough* and *careless* are antonyms of *gingerly*, and *tasty* is unrelated.

32. **(b)** While all four words are things you would find in the kitchen, *sink* is the only word that is not an appliance. A *refrigerator, stove,* and *dishwasher* are all items that do things where a *sink* doesn't do anything.

33. **(a)** This is a verbal classification question where three are part of the fourth. A *folder,* an *envelope,* and a *binder* are all things that hold *paper. Paper* is the thing they all have in common, so *paper* is the word that does not belong.

34. **(d)** A person *invents* a machine and a person *writes* a book. *Novel* and *publish* are related to a book but neither creates the *book*.

35. **(c)** Karla's (K) diamond is bigger than Kim's (Ki), K > Ki. Colleen's is bigger than Kim's, but we don't know if it is bigger or smaller than Karla's, so the third sentence is uncertain. Here is how your note should look: $_C$ K $_C$ > Ki.

36. **(a)** Someone who is *reticent* is *quiet* or shy. *Taciturn* is a synonym for *reticent* and *timid* is similar in that someone who is *timid* is usually quiet. *Garrulous* means chatty, which is the opposite of *reticent*.

37. **(b)** Frank mows his lawn in less time than Bill. Let the left represent less time, F < B. Craig can mow his lawn in less time than Frank, so he should go further to the left, C < F < B. Now you can see that the third statement is false.

38. **(b)** A *finger* is used to *touch* in the same way that an *ear* is used to *hear*.

39. **(a)** To *admonish* is to *warn*. *Confess, modify,* and *decorate* are all unrelated.

40. **(d)** *Belligerent* is to be prone to war or argument. The opposite of that would be polite. The word closest to polite is *congenial*, which means nice or polite. *Humble* is a positive word but not the opposite of *belligerent*.

41. **(c)** A *month* is made up of *weeks* in the way that a *year* is made up of *months*.

42. **(a)** To be *obsolete* is to be outdated like an *antique*. *Archaic* is a synonym. Oddly the word *dated* means the same thing as outdated. It also means old. *Current* is the opposite of *obsolete*.

43. **(c)** *Vote* is what people do at an *election*. *Run* is what people do in a *race*.

44. **(c)** *Lucid, awake,* and *alert* are all very similar in meaning. *Fatigued* is to be tired and does not belong.

45. **(d)** *Medicine, antibiotic,* and *vaccine* are all things that either prevent or cure an illness. A *virus* causes an illness and does not belong.

46. **(b)** Jay climbed more mountains than Joe, Ja > Jo. Sue climbed fewer mountains than Joe, Ja > Jo > S. It is clear that Jay did not climb fewer mountains than Sue. Jay climbed the most, so the third sentence is false.

47. **(a)** For this type of logic problem, you should make up a value as soon as you see the number 4. The Franklin Zoo has 4 more giraffes than the Stone Zoo. Right away make up a number—let's use 10—and put it over the word "Franklin." Next put a 6 over "Stone" because you are told that Franklin has 4 more than the Stone Zoo. Put a 3 over "York" because you are told that the York Zoo has 3 fewer than the Stone Zoo. Now you can see that the third statement is true; the Franklin Zoo has 7 more giraffes than the Stone Zoo.

48. **(b)** Ashley has more siblings than Meredith, A > M. Steve has more siblings than Ashley, so he should be on the left, S > A > M. Meredith cannot have more siblings than Steve, making the third sentence is false.

49. **(a)** *Mar* means to damage. The other answer choices all have to do with repairing or keeping something in the same condition.

50. **(c)** *Morose* means to be *gloomy*. *Content* and *amiable* are positive words that mean happy and friendly, and *prevalent* means widespread.

51. **(c)** All students taking the HSPT are applying to high schools. Gregory is not taking the HSPT, but we don't know whether he is going into high school in the first place.

52. **(d)** A *sparrow*, a *blue jay*, and a *robin* are all small birds that fly and can be seen at bird feeders. An *ostrich* is not likely to be at your bird feeder and does not fly.

53. **(b)** *Stagnant* means to be *still*, in a negative way. The swamp was *stagnant*. *Dormant* is somewhat similar; however, it refers to animals and their physical functions. *Still* is a synonym for *stagnant*.

54. **(b)** *Corrupt, unethical*, and *shady* are all negative words that refer to being amoral. *Diverse* simply means to be different or having variety and therefore does not belong.

55. **(d)** To be *flagrant* is to be bold or *blatant*. *Inconspicuous* means to be unnoticed, and *conceal* means to hide. *Conceal* is also a verb, so it cannot be the correct answer.

56. **(c)** *Frivolous* is an adjective meaning to be silly, trivial, or unnecessary. *Crucial, imperative*, and *important* are all adjectives meaning to be necessary in some way.

57. **(a)** *Staunch* means to be *loyal* or *devoted*. *Flexible* means to be easily changed and therefore does not belong.

58. **(a)** If Mr. Shelly has the fastest boat on the lake, then every boat on the lake has to be slower than his boat. The third sentence must be true.

59. **(b)** *Endure* is a verb that means to last or to *sustain*. The other words are unrelated.

60. **(c)** Joanne's essay has more words than Tom's, J > T. Aidan's essay has fewer words than Joanne's essay, but you don't know if Aidan's essay has more or fewer words than Tom's. $J_A > T_A$. The third sentence is uncertain.

Quantitative Skills Subtest

61. **(d)** Addition does not work for this sequence. This sequence is generated by multiplying, $\times 4, \times 3, \times 4, \times 3$, etc. The next term should be $-0.96 \times 3 = -2.88$.

62. **(c)** The differences are $-14, -5, -14, -5$. To figure out the next number you have to subtract 14 from 54. $54 - 14 = 40$.

63. **(b)** Working from the right, 7 more than 18 is 25. Subtract 25 from 36 to get 11. The equation is $36 - x = 7 + 18$.

64. **(c)** Simply count the shapes and put a number above each. (A) = 7, (B) = 8, and (C) = 6. (B) is the largest.

65. **(a)** This sequence is a simple multiplication by 4. The pattern is easier to see if you ignore the first decimal term. The next term should be $16 \times 4 = 64$.

66. **(c)** Simplify each expression first. (A) $\frac{1}{8} \times 56 = 7$, (B) $\frac{1}{5} \times 80 = 16$, (C) $\frac{1}{4} \times 60 = 15$, (B) > (C) > (A).

67. **(d)** Look first at the letters: G, skip H and I; J, skip K and L; M, skip N and O; P, skip Q and R. The next term must begin with S. The numbers are increasing in the pattern $+3$, $\times 2, +3$, so the next one will double. $17 \times 2 = 34$, which means the next term will be S34.

68. **(b)** Working from the right, first take 20% of 25. Using the 10% rule, 10% of 25 is 2.5, then double that to get 5. Next, $2^4 = 2 \times 2 \times 2 \times 2 = 16$. Now the question remains, what number subtracted from 16 is 5? The answer is 11. The equation for this is $2^4 - x = 0.2 \times 25$.

69. **(d)** When a line intersects two parallel lines as in this question, the following angles are equal: $A = E$, $B = F$, $A = D$, $B = C$, $F = G$, $E = H$, $C = G$, and $D = H$.

70. **(a)** Look at the smaller numbers to figure out the pattern. Begin with $144 \div 2 = 72$, then $72 \div 6 = 12$, $12 \div 2 = 6$; the next term is $6 \div 6 = 1$.

71. **(c)** This is a simple pattern $\div 4$, $\div 4$, $\div 4$. The next term will be $1 \div 4 = \frac{1}{4}$.

72. **(c)** Compare (A) and (B) to $\frac{1}{4}$. Estimate each. $\frac{5}{21}$ is less than $\frac{1}{4}$ because $\frac{5}{20} = \frac{1}{4}$ and when fractions have the same numerators, then the fraction with the larger denominator is the smaller fraction. $\frac{3}{20}$ is approximately $\frac{1}{7}$ and is therefore the smallest fraction of the three.

73. **(b)** The pattern here is $\div 2$, $- 30$, $\div 2$, so the next term is $60 - 30 = 30$.

74. **(b)** The pattern here is $+ 4$, $+ 8$, $+ 12$, $+ 16$. Notice that the differences are increasing by 4 each time. The next term will be $54 + 20 = 74$.

75. **(a)** Convert the Roman numerals to 3, 6, 9, 12. These are increasing by 3 each time, so the next term will be $12 + 3 = 15$, or XV in Roman numerals.

76. **(c)** Use the distributive property to simplify each expression. (B) $2(x - y) = 2x - 2y$. (C) $-2(y - x) = -2y + 2x$. You can see that each expression has a $2x$ in it, so you only have to compare the terms that have y. (B) and (C) are equal and both are greater than (A).

77. **(c)** It is usually easier to say the alphabet forward than backward, so first look at the second letter in each term. M, skip N and O; P, skip Q and R; S, skip T and U. The second letter of the next term must be V. There is only one possible answer choice, so you are done.

78. **(d)** First look at the numbers: 20, 23, 26, etc. The next number would be 29. Next look at the first letter: D, E, F, etc. The next letter would be G. The correct answer must be choice (d).

79. **(b)** Working from the right, $\frac{1}{4}$ of 60 is 15. (A shortcut is to first take half of 60, which is 30, then half again, which is 15). Next subtract 4 to get 11. The remaining question is: *what number must you subtract from 47 to get 11?* The equation is $47 - x = \frac{1}{4} \times 60 - 4$. The answer is 36.

80. **(d)** The differences in the sequence are $+ 15$, $- 8$, $+ 12$, $- 6$, $+ 9$, $- 4$. Another approach is to look at every other number beginning with 55. $55 + 4$ is 59, $+ 3$ is 62, so the next number should be $+ 2 = 64$. This narrows the answer down to choice (d).

81. **(a)** One third of 48 is 16. What number is 12 less than 16? The answer is 4. The equation is $x = \frac{1}{3} \times 48 - 12$.

82. **(d)** Simplify each expression. (A) $(4 - 9) - 5 = -5 - 5 = -10$. (B) $9 - (4 - 5) = 9 - (-1) = 10$. (C) $(9 - 5) - 4 = 4 - 4 = 0$. (B) is greater than (C) which is greater than (A).

83. **(c)** The cups are not really part of the question, just the numbers beneath each. 12 oz. = 8 oz. + 4 oz.

84. **(a)** Working from the right, 5 times 7 is 35. Next, 7 more than 35 is 42. Now the question remains, *what number subtracted from 107 leaves 42?* $107 - 42 = 65$. The equation is $107 - x = 7 + (5 \times 7)$.

85. **(b)** The pattern here is $-80, -70, -60$, so the next difference will be -50. The next term will be $160 - 50 = 110$.

86. **(b)** This sequence is increasing by 8. The next term will be $-84 + 8 = -76$.

87. **(c)** Simplify each expression first. (A) $0.4 \times 20 = 8$. (B) $0.60 \times 10 = 6$. (C) $0.15 \times 40 = 6$. (B) = (C).

88. **(d)** The differences in this sequence are $+18, +19, +20$, so the next term will be $71 + 21 = 92$.

89. **(b)** The number 1 raised to any power is still 1. Any number raised to the power of 1 is itself. (A) $1^8 = 1$, (B) $1 \times 8 = 8$, (C) $8^1 = 8$.

90. **(a)** Working from the right, $\frac{5}{7}$ of 56 is 40 (divide 56 by 7 to get 8, then multiply 8 and 5 to get 40). Twice that will be 80.

91. **(b)** This is a sequence in a sequence. The pattern is $-7, +12, -7, +12$, so the next term will be $70 - 7 = 63$.

92. **(d)** First add $3 + 13 = 16$. Then subtract 13 from 72 to get 56. The equation is $72 - x = 13 + 3$.

93. **(d)** Try the letters first. S, backward skip R and Q; P, backward skip O and N; M, skipping L and K means the next term must begin with J. There is no need to figure out the number part of the sequence.

94. **(d)** One-eighth (a good fraction/decimal to memorize) is equal to 0.125, so $\frac{5}{8}$ must be 5 times larger or 0.625. Now you know that 0.63 is larger than $\frac{5}{8}$. (A) and (C) are equal because $63\% = 0.63$ (percent means "per 100" so just move the decimal two places to the left).

95. **(c)** You can plug in answer choices for this if you don't quickly figure out the sequence at first. The differences are $+2, +5, \_\_\_\_, \_\_\_\_, +2, +5$. It is easy now to see that the missing numbers are 14 and 19.

96. **(a)** One-fourth (25%) of 80 is 20. The next question is *what number when added to 8 ($2^3 = 8$) is 20?* The answer is 12. The equation is $2^3 + x = 0.25 \times 80$.

97. **(b)** The differences are $-5, -4, -3$, so the next difference will be -2. The next term will be $25 - 2 = 23$.

98. **(b)** Write the frequency (the height of each bar) on top of each bar and then read the answer choices. F = 4 and B = 3. Then, $4 + 3 = 7$, which is C.

99. **(c)** The pattern seems to be $\times 2, +2$, except between 10 and 18. Try replacing 18 with 20, and the pattern works throughout the sequence.

100. **(b)** Always choose the easier pattern first. In this case it is easier to say the alphabet forward than backward. Look at A, C, E, G, and you'll see the next letter should be I. There is only one answer choice with I as the second letter.

101. **(a)** Angle *A* is supplemental to 77° (supplemental angles must add up to 180°) so it must be 103°. Angle *B* is complementary to 62° (complementary angles must add up to 90°) so *B* must be 28°. Angle *C* is also a complementary angle and must be 60°.

102. **(d)** Working from the right, 16 more than 20 is 36. *What number multiplied by 9 is 36?* The answer is 4. The equation is $9x = 16 + 20$.

103. **(c)** The smallest unit in this question is minutes, so convert (A) to minutes. 1.5 hours = 90 minutes, $1.5 \, \cancel{hr} \times \dfrac{60 \text{ min.}}{1 \, \cancel{hr}} = 90 \text{ min.}$ (C) is very close to 1 hour and so is the smallest value.

104. **(a)** This sequence is + 2, × 4, + 2, × 4, so the next term will be $56 + 2 = 58$.

105. **(b)** Simplify each expression. (A) $6 \div 0.2 = 6 \div \dfrac{2}{10} = 6 \times \dfrac{10}{2} = 30$. (B) $6 \times 0.2 = 1.2$. Then (C) $0.2 \div 6 = \dfrac{2}{10} \div 6 = \dfrac{2}{10} \times \dfrac{1}{6} = \dfrac{1}{30}$. You can save yourself some work if you realize that in (A) 6 will increase if divided by 0.2 and (B) and (C) will both be small values.

106. **(d)** Simplify each expression. (A) $5^2 - 8 = 25 - 8 = 17$; (B) $3^3 - 4 = 27 - 4 = 23$; (C) $2 \times 4^2 = 2 \times 16 = 32$. (C) is the largest value and (A) is the smallest.

107. **(b)** Subtract 7 from 36 to get 29. *What number subtracted from 68 is 29?* $68 - 29 = 39$.

108. **(c)** Count the squares: (A) = 11, (B) = 9, (C) = 9.

109. **(b)** Simplify each expression. (B) = 865 (move the decimal 3 places to the right) and (C) = 865 (move the decimal two places to the right).

110. **(c)** Multiply $11 \times 8 = 88$. *Half of what number is 88?* The answer is $88 \times 2 = 176$. The equation is $\dfrac{1}{2} x = 11 \times 8$.

111. **(c)** Replace each *x* with the number 4 and evaluate each expression. (A) $4 - x + 7 = 4 - 4 + 7 = 7$. (B) $8 \div x = 8 \div 4 = 2$. (C) $8 + 2 - x = 10 - 4 = 6$.

112. **(b)** This is just a visual question. You should make sure each cylinder has the same scale. Since they do in this question, you can just compare the height of the liquid in each.

Reading Subtest

113. **(c)** In the first paragraph, the passage states that infants were typically baptized the day after birth. It also states that Beethoven was baptized on December 17th.

114. **(c)** While some answers are partially correct, the correct answer is that this is a very short biography of Beethoven's life.

115. **(a)** *Prolific* means to be widespread. In this case, *prolific* refers to the amount of composing that Beethoven did during his life.

116. **(c)** The passage states that Beethoven's father encouraged him to be a musical genius through cruelty and punishment.

117. **(d)** In the passage *coerced* means to have forced.

118. **(c)** The passage mentions Beethoven as a sibling, son, and organist; however, it also mentions that he is *best* known for being a prolific composer.

119. **(c)** The cause of Beethoven's hearing loss was not mentioned nor did the passage say that he did not compose after that. The first paragraph implies that he did not have a good relationship with his father.

120. **(b)** This would not be found in a medical journal or parenting book, and it is unlikely to be in a newspaper as it is not news. A textbook is the most likely place for this brief biography.

121. **(c)** The passage did not make mention of a marriage, while the other three events can all be found in the passage.

122. **(b)** The main idea of the passage is to give a brief history of Beethoven's life.

123. **(c)** Aesop's Fables are stories and not realistic accounts of events. Tale is a synonym for story.

124. **(c)** The moral of the story is "look before you leap," quite literally. The others may be relevant but choice (c) is the most specific to this tale.

125. **(a)** *Assented* means to have *agreed* to something, as the Goat did to the Fox's idea.

126. **(b)** The Goat is most likely very angry at the Fox and would agree to never trust another fox.

127. **(b)** *Wily* means to be tricky or deceptive and best describes the Fox.

128. **(b)** It is implied that the Goat initially trusted the Fox, which is why the Goat jumped into the well.

129. **(b)** *Upbraided* means to *scold* or reprimand.

130. **(d)** The Fox encouraged the Goat to come into the well, praised the water, and suggested an escape plan. He did *not* follow his entire plan and save the Goat.

131. **(b)** The Fox bragged about the water, so the Goat would come into the well and help the Fox to escape.

132. **(c)** The main purpose of Aesop's Fables is to convey a moral or to give advice to readers.

133. **(b)** This passage, according to the introduction, is about the invention of the potato chip.

134. **(c)** It is stated in the second paragraph that mass production was made possible by the invention of the automatic potato peeler.

135. **(b)** *Essential* means to be important and *necessary*.

136. **(a)** As stated in the first paragraph, the potato chip was invented by Chef George Crum in New York.

137. **(c)** While other factories closed down, the chip companies were allowed to remain open because chips were considered a ready-to-eat vegetable.

138. **(c)** *Rational* means to be sane or matter-of-fact. The other answer choices do not apply to this passage. Process of elimination should help you to select choice (c).

139. **(c)** Because this passage is all about a food product, it makes sense that one would find it in a food magazine.

140. **(d)** *Mandated* means dictated or *forced* upon.

141. **(c)** This passage is informational in nature and nonfiction.

142. **(b)** The passages states that families enjoyed eating chips while watching television and also credits the television with increasing chip sales.

143. **(b)** The storm took the lives of only 100, but it injured 4,000 people.

144. **(a)** The passage is all about the Blizzard of '78 making that the best title.

145. **(c)** *Prevalent* means *widespread* or abundant.

146. **(d)** The forecasters did predict the storm but misjudged the severity of it. The other statements are untrue.

147. **(b)** Snowfall was two inches per hour and *not* 12. Winds were up to 100 miles per hour in some areas.

148. **(c)** The passage states in the second paragraph that the storm combined with cold weather and high pressure to increase the severity of the storm.

149. **(c)** This is not a critique or an autobiography and not long enough to be a saga. This is a factual account of an event.

150. **(c)** *Lingered* means to hang around or to *stay*.

151. **(b)** This passage is providing details of a historic event and does not go into detail on the other possible answer choices.

152. **(a)** After 1978, meteorologists were most likely to give viewers the worst case scenario to better prepare them for a storm.

153. **(a)** *Remorse* is regret or sense of *guilt*.

154. **(a)** *Feasible* means to be *possible* or likely.

155. **(c)** To *mitigate* is to lessen or *reduce*.

156. **(b)** *Precocious* is *premature*.

157. **(d)** To be *noxious* is to be poisonous or *deadly*.

158. **(c)** To *preserve* is to *maintain* something in its current or original state.

159. **(a)** To *ponder* is to *consider* or to think about something.

160. **(b)** *Stealthy* means to be *quiet* and sneaky, unnoticed.

161. **(a)** To be *temperate* is to be *mild* or even.

162. **(a)** *Disclose* most nearly means to *reveal* something.

163. **(c)** *Conspicuous* means *obvious* or noticeable.

164. **(d)** A *misconception* is a common belief in something that is not true, a *fallacy*.

165. **(c)** *Benevolent* means to be giving or *charitable*.

166. **(a)** Something that is *inevitable* is *unavoidable*.

167. **(b)** *Rickety* means to be poorly made or *flimsy*.

168. **(b)** *Negligent* means to be *careless*.

169. **(c)** Something that is *mundane* is *boring* or monotonous.

170. **(d)** *Stimulate* means to begin or *provoke* something.

171. **(b)** *Routing* means to be ordinary or *regular*.

172. **(c)** If someone is *reluctant*, he or she is *hesitant* about doing something.

173. **(b)** *Staunch* means to be steadfast, *loyal*, and unchanging.

174. **(d)** *Impartial* means to be unbiased or *unprejudiced*, fair.

Mathematics Subtest

175. **(a)** An isosceles triangle has two equal sides and two equal angles. An equilateral triangle is also isosceles, but an isosceles triangle is not an equilateral.

176. **(b)** There are three thirds in one cup, so two cups must have six thirds. If there are 10 grams of sodium in one third, then you must multiply 6 by 10 for an answer of 60 grams.

177. **(a)** There are 2 cups in a pint and 2 pints in a quart; therefore there are 4 cups in one quart. 4 cups/quart × 3 quarts = 12 cups.

178. **(c)** Subtracting a negative number is the same as adding a positive number (*Keep–Change–Change*). $6.4 + 0.781 = 7.181$.

179. **(a)** If 60 is two-thirds of a number, then 30 must be one-third. Three times 30 is 90 so the number must be 90. Half of 90 is 45.

180. **(d)** The volume of a cube is equal to the length of the side cubed (that's the definition of a cube). 5 cubed is 125, so the length of a side is 5. The area of a square is the length of the side squared. Five squared is 25.

181. **(c)** In a ratio question, set up two fractions: $\frac{4}{3} = \frac{16}{?}$. Now compare the 4 to the 16. Since 16 is 4 times 4, the unknown denominator must be 4 times 3 or 12. You can also cross multiply to find out how many cats there are. $4x = 16 \times 3 \rightarrow 4x = 48 \rightarrow x = 12$. BUT, the question asks how many cats *and* dogs are there in total. $12 + 18 = 28$ cats and dogs.

182. **(c)** Because the last digit is a 2 in the first number and a 6 in the second number (a product of 12), the answer must end in a 2. You can therefore eliminate choices (a) and (b). If you multiply a value by 0.96 the product will be a little less (because if you multiplied it by 1 it would be unchanged and 0.96 is just under 1). The answer has to be choice (c) 39.552. No need to do any math.

183. **(b)** When multiplying or dividing, count the number of negative signs. An odd number of negative signs means the answer will be negative and an even number means your answer will be positive. $-18 \div 6 = -3$.

184. **(a)** Any number raised to the power of 0 is 1. The number 1 raised to any power is still 1. Any number raised to the power of 1 is itself. $7^1 = 7$.

185. **(b)** $\sqrt{144} = 12$ because $12 \times 12 = 144$.

186. **(a)** Simplify each term: $(4 \times 10^2) = 400$; $(6 \times 10^3) = 6,000$; $(9.2 \times 10^2) = 920$; $(25 \times 10^1) = 250$. Then add: $400 + 6,000 + 920 + 250 = 7,570$. The number in the thousands place is 7.

187. **(c)** Ignore the zeros for now. 6 is equal to 3 times what number? The answer must be choice (c) 200 because it is the only number that has only zeros and a 2. To solve using an equation, you must solve for x in the equation $60 = 0.30x$.

188. **(c)** A line from side to side in a circle that passes through the center is the diameter. Half of the diameter of a circle is the radius.

189. **(b)** Because the answers are very close, you will have to use long division to answer this. $15\overline{)7.00} = 0.4\overline{6}$. The bar over the 6 indicates that it is repeating.

190. **(a)** Three-fifths is 60% or 0.60. Next, multiply: $0.6 \times \$4 = \$2.40$.

191. **(d)** Four cubed is equal to $4 \times 4 \times 4 = 64$; add 6 to make 70.

192. **(a)** One inch represents 6 feet, so you must figure out how many times 6 feet goes into 39 feet. $39 \div 6 = 6.5$. The answer is 6.5 inches.

193. **(a)** $\sqrt{225} = 15$ because $15 \times 15 = 225$.

194. **(d)** Similar triangles are triangles that have the same angles. The ratio of the sides of one triangle to the other is constant. Since 6 is 2 times 3, the missing side must be twice the value of the corresponding side. $4 \times 2 = 8$.

195. **(a)** Surface area is the sum of the areas of each side. If the length of a side is 4, then the area of the side is $4 \times 4 = 16$ in.^{2} Since there are 6 sides, 6×16 in.$^2 = 96$ in.^{2}

196. **(b)** There are 100 centimeters in one meter. To convert centimeters to meters, you therefore have to divide by 100. $5,432 \div 100 = 54.32$.

197. **(c)** The slope intercept form of a line is $y = mx + b$, where m is the slope, and b is the y-intercept. The slope of this line is 3, and the y-intercept is 1. $y = 3x + 1$.

198. **(c)** Replace each letter with the given value. $(-4)^2 - (5) + (2) = 13$.

199. **(b)** To solve for x, add 6 to both sides. The inequality sign does not change because you are not multiplying or dividing by a negative value.

$$
\begin{array}{r}
-6 + x \geq 10 \\
+6 \qquad +6 \\
\hline
x \geq 16
\end{array}
$$

200. **(a)** When multiplying, keep checking your answers and stop when reaching a number that is in only one answer choice. $1,785 \times 389 = 694,365$.

201. **(b)** A six-sided die is an example of a cube because each side is the same length.

202. **(a)** A yard is made up of 36 inches; two yards is 72 inches. Another half a yard will be 18 inches (half of 36 inches). $72 + 18 = 90$ inches.

203. **(b)** An obtuse angle is one that is more than 90 degrees and less than 180 degrees and must therefore be angle B.

204. **(d)** When adding or subtracting numbers with decimal points, remember to line up the decimals before solving. Because 0.945 is close to 1, your answer will be near 3.6 but slightly larger. There is only one answer choice near 3.6.

205. **(a)** $16 - 5\frac{7}{8}$. Because $5\frac{7}{8}$ is so close to 6, but just under, the answer will be just a little more than 10 ($\frac{1}{8}$ more to be exact). The answer is $10\frac{1}{8}$.

206. **(d)** Read word problems through before doing any work. While reading, underline units as you go. You'll notice that some are in feet and others in yards. Convert the larger numbers (feet) to the larger unit (yard). 12 feet is 4 yards (cross out the 12 and write a 4), and 6 feet is two yards (cross out the 6 and write a 2). The garden is now 4 by 2 yards or 8 square yards. 8 square yards × 16 onions per square yard = 128 onions.

207. **(c)** The commutative property states $ab = ba$. In $4 \times (2 + 3) = (2 + 3) \times 4$, you can see that the two factors on either side of the equal sign are simply in different places. Don't make the mistake of seeing parentheses and assuming this is the associative property.

208. **(b)** A hexagon is a six-sided polygon.

209. **(c)** Reduce this before multiplying.

$$\frac{2}{5} \div \frac{10}{3} = \frac{2}{5} \times \frac{3}{10} \Rightarrow$$

$$\frac{\overset{1}{\cancel{2}}}{5} \times \frac{3}{\underset{5}{\cancel{10}}} = \frac{1}{5} \times \frac{3}{5} = \frac{3}{25}$$

210. **(d)** To convert to miles, use the conversion given. $\frac{32 \cancel{\text{km}}}{1 \text{ hr.}} \times \frac{1 \text{ mi.}}{1.6 \cancel{\text{km}}} = 20$ mph. Because 32 is 2 times 16, you can quickly see that the only possible answer must be choice (d) 20 mph.

211. **(c)** If Kathy keeps the car for 7 days at $30 per day, the cost will be 7 × $30 = $210. The insurance will be an additional $50. The total cost will be $210 + $50 = $260.

212. **(b)** *Difference* means subtraction, *and* is addition, and *is* means equal: $2x - 6 = 400$.

213. **(a)** If Robert has a discount of 20%, he will be paying 80% of the original cost. 80% of $80 is $64 (simply multiply 8 and 8 and look at your answer choices).

214. **(d)** $\frac{2}{3} \times 21 = 56m$. Two-thirds of 21 is 14, so $14 = 56m$. Divide both sides by 56 to isolate m, then reduce. $m = \frac{14}{56} = \frac{1}{4}$.

215. **(a)** To answer the question you have to find 3% of $210,000. *Of* means multiplication, so ignore the zeros and multiply 3 by 21 to get 63. Now look at the answer choices and use the 10% rule. 10% of $210,000 is $21,000. Your two choices are $6,300 or $63.00. Since you want 3%, your answer should be approximately a third of $21,000 (3% is approximately a third of 10%). The answer must be $6,300.

216. **(b)** 68 ounces divided by 8 slices is 8.5 ounces per slice. Three slices will be 8.5 × 3 = 25.5 ounces.

217. **(b)** There are a total of 17 gumdrops, and 4 of them are blue. The chance of selecting a blue one is $\frac{4}{17}$.

218. **(a)** Look at the object in two pieces. The rectangle on the left is 6 cm tall and 2 cm wide with an area of $6 \times 2 = 12$ cm². The remaining square is $2 \times 2 = 4$ cm². Add the two areas to get a total area of 16 cm².

219. **(b)** Don't take time to add this like you would in math class. Simply look at the integers first and see they add to 3. Next look at the fractions. One-third and two-thirds is three thirds, or 1. Now you are up to 4, with one more fraction of one-sixth. The answer is $4\frac{1}{6}$.

220. **(a)** 2 pounds of nuts × $7.25 per pound = $14.50. Next figure the cost for oats: $1.50 × 3.5 pounds = $5.25. Add the two: $14.50 + $ 5.25 = $19.75 total.

221. **(b)** The volume of a rectangular box is the product of length, width, and height. $V = 10$ in. × 5 in. × 2 in. = 100 in.³

222. **(a)** When subtracting values with decimals, remember to line up the decimals. Estimation will narrow your answer down to a value below 23, leaving you with answer choices (a) and (d). Because 3.248 is close to 3.25, the last two digits of the answer must be close to 0.75 for a correct answer of 22.752.

223. **(c)** $-15x > 75$. To isolate x, you must divide each side by -15. Remember to switch the greater than sign to a less than sign when multiplying or dividing by a negative number. $x < -5$.

224. **(c)** First, divide both sides by 6 to simplify. The remaining equation is $0.75 \times 3 = 3y$. Next, divide both sides by 3. Simply cross out the three on either side (you can do this only because each side is a product and not a sum or difference). $y = 0.75 = \frac{3}{4}$.

225. **(a)** Start by plugging in one of the answer choices that is in the middle. If your answer is too high try a smaller one and if it is too low try a higher one.

226. **(a)** 18 hours divided by 24 hours in a day is three-fourths.

227. **(d)** The largest increase happened between January (2) and February (10) for a difference that represents an increase of 8 days.

228. **(b)** The area of a trapezoid is the product of the average of the top and bottom lengths and the height. $\frac{(6+14)}{2} \times 4 = 40$ in.²

229. **(d)** The area of a triangle is half of the base times the height. $A = 0.5b \times 8 = 48$. Divide both sides by 8 to get $0.5b = 6$. Solve for b to find that the base is 12 cm.

230. **(c)** A gallon is made up of 4 quarts. Each quart has 2 pints, so each gallon has a total of 8 pints. Ten gallons equal 80 pints.

231. **(c)**

$$28{,}800 \text{ seconds} \times \frac{1 \text{ min.}}{60 \text{ sec.}} \times \frac{1 \text{ hour}}{60 \text{ min.}} =$$

$$28{,}800 \ \cancel{\text{seconds}} \times \frac{1 \ \cancel{\text{min.}}}{6\cancel{0} \ \cancel{\text{sec.}}} \times \frac{1 \text{ hour}}{6\cancel{0} \ \cancel{\text{min.}}} =$$

$$\frac{288}{36} = 8 \text{ hours}$$

232. **(d)** The median is the middle number in an ascending list. To save time, you can cross out the highest value, then the lowest, and keep doing this until there is only one left. If there are two left, take the average.

233. **(a)** $(-7)^8$ means that the number (-7) is multiplied by itself 8 times. There are eight (-7)s in the numerator and two in the denominator, which will reduce to $(-7)^6$ (six (-7)s in the numerator). If you know the rules of exponents, you can simply subtract 2 from 8 ($a^m \div a^n = a^{m-n}$).

234. **(a)** If Linda paid $16 for fruit, then she must have spent $32 on vegetables (twice as much). $16 + $32 = $48.

235. **(b)** Remember to include the zero points into the average as a fourth score.

$$\text{Average} = \frac{20+10+6+0}{4} = 9 \text{ points}$$

You can leave the zero out of the numerator, but you cannot divide by 3 rather than 4.

236. **(c)** Do not include the number of families that have 2 pets because the question refers to *more than 2*. Add the number of families that have 3, 4, 5, and 6 pets.

237. **(b)** This is a question to estimate. The answer will be a little more than 5, and there is only one possible answer, choice (b) 5.75.

238. **(d)** $36 - 5x = 11$. First subtract 36 from both sides to get $-5x = -25$. Then divide both sides by -5. Therefore, $x = 5$. You can also solve this by plugging in the answer choices.

Language Skills Subtest

239. **(a)** *Kathleen do you have any brothers?* The sentences is missing a comma. *Kathleen, do you have any brothers?* is correct.

240. **(a)** Holidays should always be capitalized. *My favorite holiday is Independence Day.*

241. **(c)** The first word of a quote is always capitalized. *Mom said, "Please come in for dinner."*

242. **(a)** This is missing a question mark at the end. *Will there be dessert after dinner?*

243. **(b)** *Each* is singular, so the verb *bloom* should be singular, *blooms*. *Each of the flowers blooms at a different time.*

244. **(d)** Items in a list should be followed by a comma. *I grow parsley, thyme, and sage.*

245. **(c)** *Which* or *that* refers to a thing, and *who* refers to a person. *He is the famous author who lives in Danvers.*

246. **(b)** Questions end with a question mark; however, there is no question here. It should read, *The athlete asked to play third base.*

247. **(c)** *Them people are hungry* should instead be *Those people are hungry.*

248. **(b)** Quotations should be around only the speaker's words and not *she said*. *"If you behave," she said, "you can have ice cream."*

249. **(b)** *Beautifully* should be *beautiful*. *The lights looked beautiful on the tree.*

250. **(d)** No mistakes. *Chemistry* is a subject and should not be capitalized.

251. **(c)** An apostrophe is missing in *hadn't. I hadn't thought of that.*

252. **(d)** *We* is used as a subject and not *us. We did very well in the relay race.*

253. **(d)** No mistakes.

254. **(a)** The abbreviation for doctor is Dr. with a period. *Beth's dermatologist, Dr. Greenberg, is very nice.*

255. **(c)** The abbreviation for *will not* is *won't. He won't miss the game.*

256. **(b)** *Brung* should be *brought. Stella brought two contracts for me to sign.*

257. **(c)** A colon should be used to introduce a list. *I have two favorite hobbies: knitting and gardening.*

258. **(a)** This has a double negative *hardly never. I hardly ever win at chess.*

259. **(d)** No mistakes.

260. **(a)** Past tense for *you are* is *you were* and not *you was. You were mistaken when you said it would rain today.*

261. **(c)** *She loves to eat, to play, and running.* This sentence does not maintain parallelism. It should read: *She loves to eat, to play, and to run.*

262. **(b)** *Knew* is past tense of knowing and should be replaced with *new. The car was brand new.* The word *English* is always capitalized.

263. **(b)** The locker belongs to Davy Jones, so Jones should have an apostrophe. *Have you ever seen Davy Jones' locker?*

264. **(a)** A question must end with a question mark. *Did you remember to add the sugar?*

265. **(c)** An address should be followed by a comma. *Darren, please come for Thanksgiving dinner.*

266. **(a)** *Sharks* is a plural noun but the verb *swims* is singular. The sentence should read, *The sharks swim in the same direction.*

267. **(a)** The first word in a quote should always be capitalized. *Noreen said, "We rented a car for the week."*

268. **(a)** The title of a name should be capitalized. *The dinner was catered by Chef Flay.*

269. **(d)** No mistakes.

270. **(d)** No mistakes.

271. **(c)** *Each* is singular but the verb *feel* is used with a plural subject. *Each one of them feels proud.*

272. **(d)** No mistakes.

273. **(a)** *Mrs* should have a period. *Mrs. Pickering moved to New York last spring.*

274. **(b)** The sentence is missing an article at the beginning. *The woman jumped over the large puddle.*

275. **(a)** The preposition *on* should be *in. We will harvest the vegetables in August.*

276. **(c)** The introductory phrase should be followed by a comma. *After much saving, she bought her dream home.*

277. **(a)** A parenthetical phrase should be separated by commas. *Mr. Korol, the new math teacher, is very funny.*

278. **(d)** No mistakes.

279. **(a)** *Apparantly* is correctly spelled *apparently*.

280. **(b)** *Fourty* is correctly spelled *forty*.

281. **(c)** *Colums* is correctly spelled *columns*.

282. **(a)** *Lisence* is correctly spelled *license*.

283. **(c)** *Febrary* is correctly spelled *February*.

284. **(a)** *Ajective* is correctly spelled *adjective*.

285. **(a)** *Forhead* is correctly spelled *forehead*.

286. **(c)** *Reciept* is correctly spelled *receipt*. (I before E, except after C.)

287. **(d)** No mistakes.

288. **(c)** *Relible* is correctly spelled *reliable*.

289. **(b)** *I enjoyed the book, despite the fact it was very long.* Because the first and second phrases are different, the connecting word must be a reversal word.

290. **(b)** *She was considered to be very short because all of the other players on her team were very tall.*

291. **(c)** *How to Make a Postcard from a Greeting Card* is a topic that can be conveyed in one paragraph. The other choices are too lengthy.

292. **(c)** The age of her teacher is the only statement that does not have to do with her tutoring session.

293. **(a)** The other choices are about sleeping or not sleeping, but "Choosing a pillow and mattress" is the only comment that has to do with *how to* get a good night's sleep.

294. **(d)** Remember to choose a short sentence and one with a verb where the subject is *doing* the action rather than having the action done to it. The snowstorm *caused*, rather than the cause of the storm *was*.

295. **(d)** *When she takes the time to practice, she performs very well.* This is the most concise statement that conveys all of the information.

296. **(b)** This is the most concise statement that conveys all of the information.

297. **(b)** *Elizabeth Quirk: The Child Progidy.* The paragraph discusses Elizabeth Quirk, specifically her childhood.

298. **(c)** The last step is to hang the puzzle with the tacks.

Appendix A:
The Layout of the HSPT

Subtest	Timing	Number of Questions
Verbal Skills Synonym Antonym Verbal Analogy Verbal Logic Verbal Classification	18 minutes	60
Quantitative Skills Sequence Geometric Comparison Non-geometric Comparison Computation	30 minutes	52

Reading
Comprehension
  General
  Specific
Vocabulary
	25 minutes	62

Mathematics Basics and Conversions Fractions, Decimals, Percents, and Ratios Geometry, Logic, and Word Problems Exponents, Radicals, and Algebra Statistics and Probability	45 minutes	64
Language Capitalization, Punctuation, and Usage Spelling Composition	25 minutes	60
Total	2 hours 23 minutes	298

Appendix B: Math Concepts and Formulas for the HSPT

AREA AND PERIMETER FOR TWO-DIMENSIONAL OBJECTS

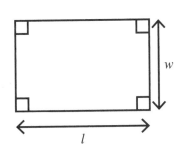

Area = lw

Perimeter = $2l + 2w$

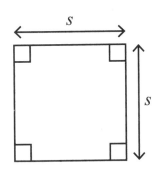

Area = s^2

Perimeter = $4s$

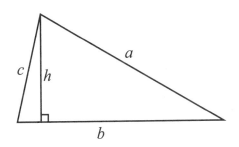

Area = $\frac{1}{2}bh$

Perimeter = $a + b + c$

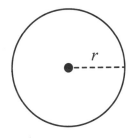

Area = πr^2

Circumference = $2\pi r$

$\pi \approx 3.14$

VOLUME AND SURFACE AREA FOR THREE-DIMENSIONAL OBJECTS

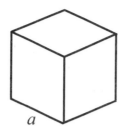

Volume = a^3
Surface area = $6a^2$

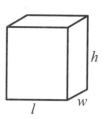

Volume = lwh
Surface area = $2(w \times h) + 2(l \times w) + 2(l \times h)$

NAMES OF POLYGONS

Name of Object	Example	Number of Sides
Triangle		3
Quadrilateral		4
Pentagon		5
Hexagon		6
Heptagon		7
Octagon		8

*Interior angles of a polygon have a combined value of $(n - 2) \times 180°$, where n equals the number of sides.

PYTHAGOREAN THEOREM

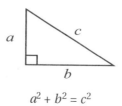

$$a^2 + b^2 = c^2$$

CONVERSIONS

Linear Measure

Inches, Feet, Yards, and Miles
1 yard = 3 feet
1 mile = 5,280 feet
1 foot = 12 inches
1 yard = 36 inches
Meters, Millimeters, Centimeters, and Kilometers
1 meter = 100 centimeters
1 meter = 1,000 millimeters
1 kilometer = 1,000 meters

Time

Seconds, Minutes, Hours, and Days	
1 day = 24 hours	1 hour = 60 minutes
1 minute = 60 seconds	1 hour = 3,600 seconds

Liquid Measure

Ounces, Cups, Pints, Quarts, and Gallons	
1 gallon = 4 quarts	1 quart = 2 pints
1 pint = 2 cups	1 cup = 8 ounces
Liters, Milliliters, and Kiloliters	
1 kiloliter = 1,000 liters	
1 liter = 1,000 milliliters	

Weight Measure

Ounces and Pounds
16 ounces = 1 pound
Milligrams, Grams, and Kilograms
1 kilogram = 1,000 grams
1 gram = 1,000 milligrams

Remember these key conversions:

- Freezing point of water is 32°F = 0°C.
- Boiling point of water is 212°F = 100°C.
- Comfortable indoor temperature is 60°F to 70°F or 16°C to 22°C.

ABBREVIATIONS

Unit	Abbreviation
inch	in.
foot	ft.
yard	yd.
mile	mi.
square inch	sq. in. or in.^{2}
square foot	sq. ft. or ft.^{2}
cubic inch	cu. in. or in.^{3}
cubic foot	cu. ft. or ft.^{3}
ounce	oz.
pound	lb.
quart	qt.
pint	pt.
gallon	gal.

Unit	Abbreviation
centimeter	cm
meter	m
millimeter	mm
kilometer	km
square centimeter	cm^2
cubic centimeter	cm^3
square meter	m^2
cubic meter	m^3
liter	l
milliliter	ml
kilometer	km
gram	g
milligram	mg
kilogram	kg

EXPONENTS

Multiplication Rule: $a^m \times a^n = a^{m+n}$

Division Rule: $a^m \div a^n = a^{m-n}$

Power of Zero: $a^0 = 1$

SCIENTIFIC NOTATION EXAMPLES

Scientific Notation	Decimal Point	Decimal
3.405×10^4	4 places to the right	34,050
1.65×10	1 place to the right	16.5
0.231×10^2	2 places to the right	23.1

SQUARE ROOTS AND PERFECT SQUARES

Exponential	Radical
$2^2 = 4$	$\sqrt{4} = 2$
$3^2 = 9$	$\sqrt{9} = 3$
$4^2 = 16$	$\sqrt{16} = 4$
$5^2 = 25$	$\sqrt{25} = 5$
$6^2 = 36$	$\sqrt{36} = 6$
$7^2 = 49$	$\sqrt{49} = 7$
$8^2 = 64$	$\sqrt{64} = 8$

Exponential	Radical
$9^2 = 81$	$\sqrt{81} = 9$
$10^2 = 100$	$\sqrt{100} = 10$
$11^2 = 121$	$\sqrt{121} = 11$
$12^2 = 144$	$\sqrt{144} = 12$
$13^2 = 169$	$\sqrt{169} = 13$
$14^2 = 196$	$\sqrt{196} = 14$
$15^2 = 225$	$\sqrt{225} = 15$

CUBE ROOTS AND PERFECT CUBES

Exponential	Radical
$2^3 = 8$	$\sqrt[3]{8} = 2$
$3^3 = 27$	$\sqrt[3]{27} = 3$
$4^3 = 64$	$\sqrt[3]{64} = 4$
$5^3 = 125$	$\sqrt[3]{125} = 5$

MATH TERMS AND SYMBOLS

Term	Definition	Symbol
Sum	result of addition	+
Difference	result of subtraction	−
Product, of	result of multiplication	×
Quotient, per	the result of division	÷
A number	a letter or variable	x, y, z, or n
Is, leaves	equal to	=
Is greater than	larger but not equal to	>
Is less than	less but not equal to	<
Greater than or equal to	greater and includes values equal to	≥
Less than or equal to	less than and includes values equal to	≤
Is not equal to	includes values both greater than or less than	≠

DEFINITIONS FOR LINES

Perpendicular lines: Lines that intersect at a 90° angle.

Parallel lines: Lines that have the same slope and never intersect.

Transversal: Any line that crosses at least two parallel lines.

Slope of a line: Slope = $\dfrac{y_2 - y_1}{x_2 - x_1}$

DEFINITIONS FOR ANGLES

Angle: An angle is formed when two lines or line segments intersect.

Acute angle: Any angle that is less than 90°.

Complementary angle: Either of two angles that when added create a sum of 90°.

Obtuse angle: Any angle that is more than 90° and less than 180°.

Right angle: An angle that is 90°.

Congruent angles: Angles that have the same angle measure.

Straight angles: Angles that, when combined, make up a line.

Supplementary angle: Either of two angles that when added create a sum of 180°.

Vertical angles: Opposite and equal angles created by a transversal.

DEFINITIONS FOR TRIANGLES

Acute triangle: A triangle that has only acute, less than 90°, angles.

Congruent triangles: Triangles that have the same measure for corresponding angles and side lengths.

Equilateral triangle: A triangle where all sides are equal in length and all angles are equal in measure.

Isosceles triangle: A triangle that has two angles of equal measure and two sides of the same length.

Obtuse triangle: A triangle that contains an obtuse (greater than 90°) angle.

Right triangle: Any triangle that contains a right, 90°, angle.

Scalene triangle: A triangle that has three unequal sides and three unequal angles.

Similar triangles: Triangles that have the same angles and the same ratio of the sides.

NOTES